Higher National Computing

Core Units for BTEC Higher Nationals in Computing and IT

Second edition

Howard Anderson

Sharon Yull

Bruce Hellingsworth

Edexcel
Success through qualifications

ELSEVIER

AMSTERDAM • BOSTON • HEIDELBERG • LONDON • NEW YORK • OXFORD
PARIS • SAN DIEGO • SAN FRANCISCO • SINGAPORE • SYDNEY • TOKYO

Newnes is an imprint of Elsevier

Newnes

Newnes
An imprint of Elsevier
Linacre House, Jordan Hill, Oxford OX2 8DP
200 Wheeler Road, Burlington, MA 01803

First published 2001
Reprinted 2001, 2002, 2003
Second edition 2004

British Library Cataloguing in Publication Data
A catalogue record for this book is available from the British Library

Library of Congress Cataloguing in Publication Data
A catalogue record for this book is available from the Library of Congress

ISBN 0 7506 6125 9

For information on all Newnes publications
visit our website at http://books.elsevier.com

Typeset by Charon Tec Pvt. Ltd, Chennai, India
Printed and bound in Meppel, The Netherlands by Krips bv.

Contents

Introduction

This book has been written to help you achieve the learning outcomes of the core units of BTEC's new Higher National Computing programme. The three authors have many years' experience of teaching HNC and HND computing students and have worked with BTEC in the team that produced the new HNC/HND computing units. In producing the book, the authors' principal aim has been that of capturing, within a single volume, the core knowledge required of all computing students at HNC/HND level. The seven core units covered in the book are: Computer Platforms, Systems Analysis, Programming Concepts, Concepts of Database Design, Networking concepts, Personal Skills Development, Quality systems.

The book has been organized on a logical basis with each chapter devoted to a single core unit. We have, however, attempted to reduce duplication and some material is appropriate to more than one of the core units. Furthermore, to put supporting concepts into context, we have developed a number of topics within the individual chapters and in sections at the end of the book. You will also find that, where difficult concepts are introduced, we have included notes in the margin. These will provide you with an alternative way of understanding them.

This book has been designed to provide you with a thorough introduction to each of the core units. Despite this, you are advised to make use of other reference books and materials wherever and whenever possible. You should also get into the habit of using all of the resources that are available to you. These include your tutor, your college or university library, computer centre, and other learning resources. Extensive use should be made of the Internet, to help you there are numerous URLs in the text. As this subject is perhaps the most fast changing of all technologies, the most up-to-date information is often only available from the Internet. You should also become familiar with selecting materials that are appropriate to the topics that you are studying. In particular, you may find it useful to refer to materials that will provide you with several different views of a particular topic.

Throughout the book we have provided worked examples that show how the ideas introduced in the text can be put into practice. We have also included problems and questions at various stages in the text. Depending on the nature of the topic, these questions take a variety of forms, from simple problems requiring short numerical answers to those that may require some additional research or that may require the use of an analytical software package in their solution. Your tutor may well ask you to provide answers to these questions as coursework or homework but they can also be used to help you with revision for course assessments.

Finally, we would like to offer a few words of practical advice to students. At the beginning of your HNC or HND course you will undoubtedly find that some topics appear to be more difficult than others. Sometimes you may find the basic concepts difficult to grasp (perhaps you haven't met them before), or you might have difficulty with things that you cannot immediately visualize.

No matter what the cause of your temporary learning block, it is important to remember two things: you won't be the first person to encounter the problem, and there is plenty of material available to you that will help you overcome it. All that you need to do is to recognize that it is a problem and then set about doing something about it. A regular study pattern and a clearly defined set of learning goals will help you get started. In any event, don't give up – computing is a challenging and demanding career and your first challenge along the road is to master the core knowledge, that is what you will find in this book.

May we wish you every success with your Higher National studies!

Howard Anderson
Bruce Hellingsworth
Sharon Yull

1 Computer platforms

Summary

The aim of this chapter of the book is to provide sufficient technical information to enable users to make informed purchasing or specification decisions without becoming over involved with detail. Each heading will present the information from the user's point of view and, where necessary, ignore or gloss over the most technical details. For instance, no real attempt will be made to describe the precise working of a disk drive but the benefits of its performance will be outlined. No attempt has been made to cover other aspects of the use of microprocessors such as embedded systems, mobile communications devices, etc. nor to look at larger machines, mainframe computers or other specialized areas. The focus will be on how to buy a PC but with sufficient content to be at Higher National level.

Introduction

The Edexcel unit says '*This unit is aimed at IT practitioners who need sufficient knowledge of computer architecture to make rational and commercial decisions on the selection and specification of systems. Learners will learn how to evaluate operating systems in order to create their own operating environment. Many IT practitioners communicate with specialist technical support staff during the specification and planning of systems implementation. This unit aims to give learners the confidence to communicate with technical and non-technical specialists to justify their recommendations.*

It is expected that centres will use current personal computer and networking resources. Learners should be encouraged to read current journals to investigate and evaluate new hardware and software developments.'

It is recognized that centres use a diverse range of hardware and software. For this reason, this chapter avoids specific software dependent items as far as possible.

1.1 The basic components of a PC

This part of the book is intended to describe the basic parts of a computer ready to fulfil the requirements of Unit 1, i.e. how to buy a PC.

Students who have embarked on an HNC in Computing will not need to be told that there is a monitor, a system box, etc.; all will have used these items, but they will need the knowledge of how to specify each one or to communicate effectively with experienced technicians.

The system box

This contains the motherboard with the CPU or *Central Processing Unit*, storage devices such as hard drives or CD-ROM drive, the memory, a power supply and any add-on components such as a video card, modem, etc.

Motherboard

So called because older computers were made from a large number of components organized onto several circuit boards. These were plugged into one 'main' or motherboard that contained the CPU and the circuits that communicated with the add-on boards. Modern machines have most of the principal components on one board but the name has stuck. The motherboard will house the CPU, the *chipset*, the memory connectors or expansion buses for the circuits that are still separate and often the I/O (input/output) ports. The chipset controls DMA or *Direct Memory Access*, the *bus interface*, memory, disks, keyboard, I/O ports and timing.

CPU

The CPU is the circuit that is able to execute the instructions stored in the memory. Modern CPUs in the Intel Pentium series and others are able to execute these instructions at high speed and provide considerable computing power in a small component.

Storage

All the instructions and data that form *software* must at one point be stored. This data is all in the form of logical 1s or 0s and any physical property of any substance or device that will remain in one state or another can be used to store this software. Most hard disks are magnetic devices that store 1s and 0s as changes in the patterns of magnetic particles held on a surface. CD-ROMs hold 1s and 0s by optical patterns on the surface of a simple material. The only real reason why magnetic hard drives are common is that they are cheap, fast and reliable. When newer, faster devices with higher capacity are manufactured, magnetic hard drives may become a thing of the past; purely optical devices hold this promise. The point is, there is nothing special about a *hard drive*, it is simply a device that can store a large number of 1s and 0s and deliver them to another circuits at an acceptable speed.

Memory

The memory stores software, i.e. program instructions and data. There are two broad kinds with the rather confusing names RAM for *Random Access Memory* and ROM for *Read Only Memory*. The problem is that both may be randomly accessed and some kinds of ROM can be written too! The key point is that RAM is *volatile*, i.e. it loses its data when the power is turned off, ROM does not, it is *non-volatile*.

Power supply

The power supply is another misleading name as the power to run the computer usually comes from the mains or from batteries. The job of the power supply is to provide 12 volts to run disk drive motors, etc. and lower (usually 5 or 3.3) volts to run the digital circuits. It must be able to provide enough current to run everything in the machine without overheating and to ensure the voltage is constant with defined limits.

Display

The most commonly used desktop display device is the CRT or *Cathode Ray Tube*, a device first widely used in the sciences and defence in the 1940s and extremely expensive at that time; they were also very unreliable. Now CRTs are made cheaply by the million and are amongst the most reliable devices in common use. With the rise in use of laptop computers and the need to save desk space, etc., newer screen types have also become available and the marketplace has become extremely competitive with LCD or *Liquid Crystal Display* screens currently being the most common. The common name for a CRT is a VDU or *Visual Display Unit*.

Key fact

If you need to buy a PC or just one of the components, you need to know more about its *performance* than how it works. A knowledge of how it works will help with your understanding of the performance and some of the difficulties overcome by the maker but this knowledge does not need to be in great detail. The remaining sections in this chapter are intended to provide the required knowledge.

The hierarchy of design

You know that computers are binary devices often made with silicon circuits and they work with logical 1s and 0s. It is hard to imagine the connection between this statement and seeing a wordprocessor in action with all the screen colours, text and clickable buttons, i.e. a program in action. To illustrate this, imagine you are given the task of explaining the idea of a 'city' to someone who has only ever lived on a desert island and never had need of permanent housing. If you started by describing 'what is a brick' and then immediately described the construction of a whole town using bricks, the connection between the small hard brick and the warm and comfortable rows of houses would be very difficult to follow. If you then took the view of a town planner and spoke of where the hospital should be in your town or how to route a road around a village, any connections with bricks would be entirely lost. The trouble is, towns are made of bricks!

The connection between 1s and 0s and tasks such as installing Windows is of a similar nature. The way to overcome this is to think of 'layers' of knowledge. Using the brick and the town example, consider these layers:

of bricks and towns	of computer hardware	of computer software
Bricks. Study what a brick is made of, how it is made, how strong it is, what will it cost.	1s and 0s, simple digital circuits and how logical arithmetic can be performed with a circuit.	Boolean logic.

of bricks and towns	of computer hardware	of computer software
Walls. Study how to mix cement, how *of bricks and towns*	How a sequence of logical operations can be *of computer hardware*	How to perform arithmetic with *of computer software*
to lay bricks to make a wall, how strong is a wall.	achieved with a circuit, how to add, subtract, perform logical AND and OR operations, etc.	simple numbers.
How to make several walls into a building with spaces for windows and doors, etc. How to build a roof.	How to store many logical instructions and feed them in sequence to a circuit that can execute them.	How to perform arithmetic with multiple digit numbers.
How to install all the services a building needs, water, electricity, gas, heating, etc. and to move in the carpets, furniture, etc.	How to accept human inputs by devices such as a keyboard and to display outputs using devices like a colour monitor.	How to handle data such as text and to edit it, i.e. move a sentence within a paragraph.
How to build a row of houses, provide street lighting, public access, etc.	How to provide a complete set of devices such as a mouse, keyboard, printer, CPU etc. and to make them all connect correctly.	How to present a complete set of facilities in a word processor.
How to plan a town, provide libraries, shops, hospital, bus station, etc.	A complete PC.	How to control the entire machine – the operating system.

In normal life, we expect different people to be expert at these different layers, a brick layer is not a town planner. When studying for the HNC in Computing we do not expect you become expert in any one of the layers, rather to understand all the layers in the same way that you can imagine all the tasks required to build a town; specialization will come later in your studies.

What I am asking you to do here is to take on trust that descriptions of the 'bricks' will lead to an understanding of the 'town council'. It just takes some time.

1.2 Elements in the history of microprocessors

It is said that history is written by the victors. Although this really refers to political history and especially the result of political failure, war, it also applies to vast business areas like computing. Much of the history of computers has been written by the commercial 'victors', the Americans, but you should read it with care; often the rest of the world is left out. As an example, is it often quoted that the world's first computer was an American machine called Electronic Numerical Integrator and Computer (ENIAC) which came out in 1946. The problem is, this machine and others built around the 1940s were not like modern machines so we get into a discussion about what exactly *is* a computer. Amongst other computer projects around the world, in Britain, Germany and other countries, was a highly secret project that pre-dates ENIAC. The design and use of this project was carried out with brilliant success in Britain during the Second World War, it was called the *Colossus* computer; it was used at Bletchley Park in the deciphering of the German Lorenz cypher (not Enigma). It was so secret that its very existence was not officially published until 1974, long after some of the history books were written.

Here is the real problem, some people only use other history books as their source so some 'facts' are propagated with time. If you research the history of microprocessors, you will find that different sources quote 'facts' that vary greatly one from another. As you advance in your studies, you must develop the ability to look critically at these facts and to decide what is the most accurate. The world is a complex place, so simple claims are unlikely to be true. As an example, most people will consider it a fact that Isaac Newton discovered gravity when an apple hit him on his head whilst seated under an apple tree. The trouble is, this is a complete fiction but it is propagated as a fact. Beware!

The first Colossus computer, the Mark 1, was operational in January 1944. It was designed and built by the Post Office at Dollis Hill in London. Like ENIAC, Colossus is not a stored program machine, the 'program' was hard-wired and stored as switch settings. During the decryption process for which it was built, messages to be worked on were stored as a Baudot code (a 5 digit binary code) on a paper tape and these messages were read at 5000 characters a second. In the 200 microseconds it took between each character, Colossus could perform 100 Boolean calculations on each of the 5 binary digits of a character. It is difficult to compare exactly the speed difference between this kind of computer and a modern computer because Colossus did some of its work in parallel but if you take 100 Boolean calculations, one for each of the 5 digits and do this 5000 times a second you get $100 \times 5 \times 5000 = 2\,500\,000$ Boolean calculations per second. It would *not* be right to compare this directly with a speed of 2.5 MIPS (Million Instructions Per Second) but for the world's first computer it is a very respectable performance; this machine was not slow. See www.codesandciphers.org.uk/ for more information.

There is little doubt that the first commercial microprocessor was the Intel 4004 and that Intel has gone on to become a dominant force in the world of microcomputers but other brilliant designs remain less well known. The ubiquitous PC uses Intel microprocessors but Apple machines use the Motorola MC680x0 series and most mobile phones and many small devices use a British designed RISC (Reduced Instruction Set) chip called the ARM.

It is not the purpose of this book to describe in detail each of several hundred different microprocessors, but details can be seen directly from the makers web pages:

Intel	www.intel.com/products/index.htm
Intel past types	www.intel.com/intel/intelis/museum/Exhibits/hist_micro/hof/hof_main.htm
	(this link seems to change all the time. If it fails, start up www.intel.com and search for '80286', one of the resulting hit list should point to the Hall of Fame)

Motorola	The old link was to www.mot.com/SPS/MMTG/mp.html but this no longer works. Motorola seem to have removed microprocessor history links from their website. See www.motorola.com
ARM	www.arm.com (follow links to CPUs)
Cyrix	www.cyrix.com
AMD	www.amd.com and follow links to 'products'
IBM	www.chips.ibm.com/products/powerpc/
Sun	www.sun.com
Zilog	http://www.zilog.com/products/

In the preparation of this second edition, most of the links printed in the first edition were found to fail. If this happens with any of these links, use the main URI e.g. www.intel.com, and use their search facility.

Table 1.2.1 shows some important Intel microprocessors, the intention being to show the rapid development in terms of speed and complexity. (Intel actually produces many more types.)

Table 1.2.1   *Crude indicators for Intel microprocessors*

Intel chip	Date	MIPS	Width of data bus	Number of transistors
4004	1971	0.06	4	2300
8008	1972	0.06	8	3500
8080	1974	0.64	8	6000
8085	1976	0.37	8	6500
8086	1978	0.33	16	29 000
8088	1979	0.33	16	29 000
80286	1982	1.2	16	134 000
80386SX	1985	5.5	16	275 000
80486DX	1989	20	32	1 200 000
80486SX	1991	13	32	1 185 000
80486DX2	1992	41	32	1 200 000
80486DX4	1994	52	32	1 600 000
Pentium P5	1993	100	64	3 100 000
Pentium P54C	1994	150	64	3 200 000
Pentium MMX	1997	278	64	4 500 000
Pentium Pro	1995	337	64	5 500 000
Pentium II	1997	–	–	7 500 000
Pentium III	1999	–	–	9 500 000
Pentium III	1999	–	–	28 000 000
Pentium 4	2000	–	–	42 000 000
Pentium 4	2002	–	–	55 000 000

Beware!

1. The table shows speed for the earlier chips in *Millions of Instructions Per Second* or MIPS. As explained elsewhere in this chapter, this is a very crude means of testing microprocessor speed and is only included here with this warning. The speed in MIPS of these chips will change if the clock speed is changed and you will notice the clock speed has been left out. This is because comparing chips on clock speed is an even cruder means of evaluating performance. A 100 MHz 80486 is not four times slower than a 400 MHz Pentium, the speed difference is in fact a little tricky to pin down but it is certainly more than eight times slower. Using MIPS for later chips is even more mis-leading so has been left out.

2. The width of the data bus can also be given an inappropriate level of importance when comparing microprocessor performance. An 8-bit microprocessor will take many times longer to perform a 16-bit by 16-bit multiplication with a 32-bit answer than a 16-bit microprocessor, the 8-bit machine will take dozens of instructions, the other will take 1 instruction. Couple this with the fact that the 16-bit machine will perform this instruction in fewer clock cycles and the clock is running faster and you can see the microprocessor speed is indeed tricky to pin down!

Nonetheless, the table shows the remarkable development over nearly 30 years.

Moore's law

In 1965, Gordon Moore was the Research Director of the electronics company Fairchild Semiconductor. Some 3 years later he was to become one of the founders of Intel. He made an interesting prediction based on what had happened up to that time with memory chips (not microprocessors). He noticed that memory capacity doubled in every 18–24 months. He then predicted this would continue, leading to an exponential growth in size and hence computing power. Market trends have shown it to have come true up until now, with memory and with microprocessors; there are predictions that it will fail in the future but these predictions have themselves failed in the past as they have been made many times.

Mathematics in action

What is exponential growth?

It is when the next value in a series is multiplied by a factor, not added to. So if you start with a number, say 1 and multiply it by a factor, say 2, you get an answer of 2. If you then repeat this, the number grows slowly at the start but very soon becomes very fast.

For instance: if you start with 1 and keep multiplying by 2, you get the series 1, 2, 4, 8, 16, 32, 64, 128, 256, 512, 1024 and so on. The speed of increase is best displayed as a graph.

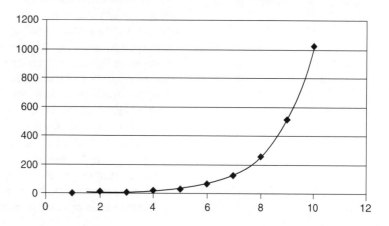

Figure 1.2.1 *Simple exponential growth*

Searching the Internet

Much detailed information on current microprocessor specifications can be seen on the Internet. The problem with giving
too many URLs is that they are not guaranteed to exist after
this book is printed. If you make good use of a search engine,
you will find them very quickly.

There are different types of search engine so:

You could use a *keyword search engine* such as www.google.
com, with a search string of

+microprocessor +history

The + signs show the word must be present (it is like the
boolean AND operator)

You could also use a *subject-based search engine* such as
Yahoo Advanced (search.yahoo.com/search/options) with the
search string

microprocessor history

in the 'all of these words' box.

Finally you could choose a *meta search engine* such as
Metacrawler (www.metacrawler.com/), the search string will be

microprocessor history

make sure the 'all' box is checked.

Be *very* careful who you believe!

1.3 What is a microprocessor?

A microprocessor is a complex circuit built from large number of simple
circuits containing *transistors*, *diodes*, etc. made to perform *logic*. A
Pentium 4 has approximately 55 million transistors, 10 times the Pentium
Pro used as an example here in the first edition of this book! There are
two key properties that a microprocessor has:

It can execute logical instructions in *sequence*

and

It can make *decisions*.

The instructions to carry these out (the program) are separately stored
outside of the circuit in *memory*. The decisions or instructions are very
modest in human terms, they usually take the form something like 'if
number A is bigger than number B then execute instruction K else execute
instruction X' or 'add 6 to number A'. The logical instructions are executed
in sequence by the microprocessor, each is fetched from memory then
executed, one at a time (complex modern microprocessors can execute
several instructions at once). No *single instruction* does anything really
complex like 'move paragraph to the bottom of the document', they all do
relatively simple tasks. Complex tasks are built from hundreds or thousands
of these simple tasks, just like a town is built from thousands of bricks;
the town is complex, the bricks are simple.

All the operations of the microprocessor are controlled by a *clock* which
means that a constant number of pulses or 1s and 0s are fed to the circuit and
each instruction is executed on each pulse. A clock in this sense has nothing

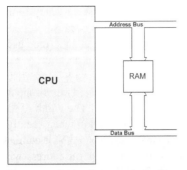

Figure 1.3.1 *Connection of a simple CPU and external RAM*

to do with devices that tell the time! When you see that a Pentium processor has a clock speed of 600 MHz, it means that 600 000 000 clock pulses are supplied to the circuit per second. A quick thought will tell you that if things are happening that fast, why is it that you can watch some operations take some time to execute. The answer is simple, complex tasks are made from a large number of very simple tasks, the simple tasks get executed at a speed hard to relate to human experience but there are *so* many to execute!

In Figure 1.3.1, there are two components, the CPU and the RAM. All the instructions are stored in the RAM and must be loaded one by one into the CPU. After a single instruction has been loaded, the CPU decides what it means, i.e. it *decodes* it, then *executes* the instruction. This is called the *Fetch–Execute cycle*. There is a clock input to the CPU which supplies a series of timed 1s and 0s as a square wave.

The CPU

What follows does *not* describe a real microprocessor. It is a simplified version of the original microprocessors and is presented to demonstrate the way that these devices work. Real microprocessors are more complex but share the same basic way of working.

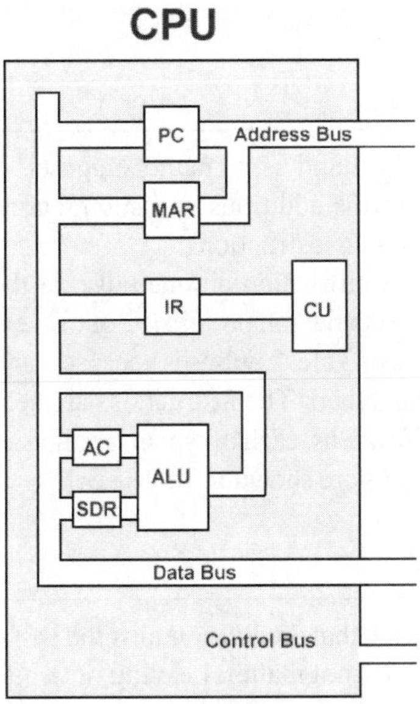

Registers

The CPU contains *registers*. These are circuits that can remember individual numbers for a short time. Figure 1.3.2 shows these:

- The AC register is traditionally known as the *Accumulator*, it is the register where the results of calculations are held.
- The SDR is called the *Store Data Register* and is used to hold data ready for and instruction.
- The IR is the *Instruction Register* and is used to hold the latest instruction fetched from RAM.
- The MAR is the *Memory Address Register* and is used to hold addresses.
- The PC is the *Program Counter* and is used to store the location or address of the next instruction to be fetched.

CPU

Figure 1.3.2 *Diagram of a simplified CPU*

Buses

The components of the CPU and those outside the CPU are connected together using *buses*. A bus is simply a collection of wires, so an 8-bit bus is just eight wires each carrying 1s or 0s. Remember that a byte is 8-bits so an 8-bit bus could carry a single byte of information. For example, the information at one moment *could* be the letter G which formed part of the data being processed by the CPU. ASCII for G is 64 + its position in the alphabet = 71 decimal or 47 hex. If you convert this to binary you get 01000111. If each of the wires takes on the value 1 or 0 in this pattern, the bus could be said to be holding a letter G. There is no way of telling if the pattern 01000111 is a 'G' or not, the 'value' of a piece of data is only applied by the software that is using it.

In this simple microprocessor, the data bus is 8 bits wide so the largest number it can store is $2^8 - 1 = 255$. If it is required, you can write programs to handle larger numbers by breaking them down into 8-bit values. The older 8-bit microprocessors did this and is one reason why they are much slower than modern microprocessors, arithmetic was laborious.

Question 1.3.1

If a microprocessor has a 20-bit address bus, what is the maximum size of RAM this can address?

Question 1.3.2

How many address lines are required to address 64 Mb of RAM?

The address bus is also just 8 bits wide. This causes a much more severe restriction on operations than an 8-bit data bus because you can only have 256 addresses. If some of the instructions need data (they usually do), you may have as little as 100 instructions in your program. When you consider that the main executable of Microsoft Word 97 comprises more than 5 million bytes and that this software needs even more support files to make it work, a 256-byte memory is very small! The width of the data bus and the address bus is an important consideration when specifying a microprocessor. The Pentium microprocessor has a 32-bit address bus and a 64-bit data bus. As $2^{32} = 4\,294\,967\,296$, a 32-bit address will allow $4\,294\,967\,296$ different addresses or 4000 Mb or 4 Gb.

Control unit

The control unit is the 'heart' of the CPU. When fed with an instruction from the IR, the microprocessor responds with the correct action, i.e. the right registers are used and if required, the ALU is brought into use.

Arithmetic and logic unit

The ALU is the *Arithmetic and Logic Unit* and as its name suggests, is where the microprocessor actually performs additions and subtractions and logical operations such as AND and OR instructions.

In this example, the CPU will fetch an instruction on one pulse of the clock, decode it right away and execute the instruction on 1, 2 or 3 of the next clock pulses. The reason it might use 1 or 2 or 3 clock pulses is because some instructions are a little more involved than others. The instructions are held in the RAM in a sequence of numbered locations, each of which is called an address. A possible sequence of instructions are shown in Table 1.3.1.

Fetch–execute cycle

Look carefully at Figure 1.3.3. You will see that the PC contains the value 161. The other registers have values that do not matter. Leaving out quite a lot of detail, the fetch–execute sequence will go like this:

Table 1.3.1   *Program for the simple CPU*

Address in RAM (numbered location)	Code for instruction or data held in RAM	Meaning
161	3A	Load the data at the next address into the AC register
162	23	Number to load, i.e. data not an instruction
163	3D	Load the data at the next address into the SDR register
164	12	Number to load, i.e. data not an instruction
165	8C	Add the numbers in the AC and SDR registers and store the result in the AC register
166	3E	Store the value in the AC register at the RAM address held at the next two addresses, low byte first
167	6E	Low byte of address
168	01	High byte of address
169	3A	Load the data at the next address into the AC register
16A	45	Number to load, i.e. data not an instruction

CPU

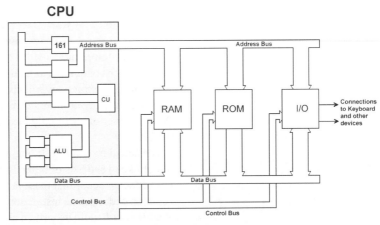

Figure 1.3.3 *The assembled microcomputer*

The fetch part of the fetch–execute sequence

- Instruct the RAM to give the contents of address 161 and place the number found there (3A) into the IR. This is done by putting the value 161 on the address bus and instructing the RAM to read, the value 3A will then appear on the data bus. The control unit provides all the signals for this to happen.
- Allow the IR to feed its value into the control unit.
- The control unit reacts by 'decoding' the instruction 3A which in turn has the effect of putting 162 into the MAR, i.e. the address of the next address where the data is held. The microprocessor is now ready to execute the newly fetched instruction.

Once this is complete, the instruction **Load the data at the next address into the AC register** will be in the CPU, so is the value of the next address but note that it has *not* been executed, i.e. the AC register has not been loaded with the data.

The execute part of the fetch–execute sequence

- Allow the contents of the MAR onto the address bus and instruct the RAM to read. This will result in the value 23 appearing on the data bus.
- Load the contents of the data bus into the AC register.
- Add 1 to the PC ready for the next fetch sequence.

The fetch–execute sequence has now completed and is ready for the next cycle. Remembering this is not a real processor, we can safely ignore some practical details; in this example the fetch sequence took two 'ticks' of the CPU clock and the execute sequence took three ticks. If the clock was running at 1 MHz, i.e. 1 000 000 ticks per second (or better, 1 000 000 1s and 0s), this would have taken 5/1 000 000 seconds or 5 millionths of a second. This is quick in human terms, but all that has happened is that a number has been loaded into a register!

The next instruction in the program is **Load the data at the next address into the SDR register** and this is fetched and executed in a similar way. The next instruction after that is **Add the numbers in the AC and SDR registers and store the result in the AC register**. You should note that this instruction does not have any data associated with it. This means it will take fewer ticks of the clock so will fetch and execute quicker because it does not have to read the RAM a second time.

In general, instructions will take the form of 'what to do' followed by the 'data to do it with' or more formally, *operation code* followed by *operand*. Other instructions will only have the operation code (often shortened to *op code*).

The actual program code and data is of course in binary but we humans do not like to see lists of binary numbers or for that matter, hex numbers. The consequence is that these programs are written down using *mnemonics* for op codes, so the instruction **Load the AC register with the contents of address 14** could be written as the mnemonic **LDA, 14** and the instruction **Add 21 to the contents of the AC register** would be written as the mnemonic **ADD, #21**. The mnemonic **STA, 25** would mean **Store the contents of AC register at address 25**.

A program fragment containing these instructions is:

LDA, 14
ADD, #21
STA, 25

This means:

load whatever data is at address 14 into the AC register
add the value 21
store the result at address 25

When a program is written in the form of

LDA, 14
ADD, #21
STA, 25

it is called assembly language.

Machine code

The program and data in RAM would in reality be just a set of numbers. If you were to write them down as numbers (in hex, decimal or binary, numbers are just numbers!), the resulting code is called *machine code*. This is what is actually run in the microprocessor using the fetch–execute sequence. Everything the CPU executes is machine code; when running Windows, the .EXE or .DLL files are machine codes.

Assembly code

If you write down the same program using mnemonics, the resulting program code is called *assembly code*. The reason is that the mnemonics must be converted or 'assembled' into machine code with another program called an 'assembler'. Writing a program using an assembler is much easier than writing directly in machine code. The sequence would be to use a text editor to type the assembly code then use the assembler to generate the machine code. This is then loaded into the RAM and the program run. With luck it will do what you want it to!

If the assembly language

LDA, 14
ADD, #21
STA, 25

is converted to machine code with an assembler, it might give something like

Address	Machine code
234	3A
235	14
236	8C
237	21
238	3E
239	25

What would be stored is just the machine code, i.e. 3A, 14, 8C, 21, 3E, 25. As you can see, machine code is not easy to read.

Actually writing commercial programs using assembly code (often just called assembler) is difficult but one or two applications in computing are still written this way. An example would be very small but include speed critical parts of an *operating system* or special high-speed animation sections of a game. Most programs are written using high-level languages such as C++ or Visual Basic but eventually, after all the compiling and processing of these languages, everything the CPU executes is machine code. *Absolutely* everything!

Assembly language on real processors

It is not the intention of this book or this unit of the HNC Computing to cover assembly language programming but some understanding of terms such as *16-bit operating system* will need to be explained. It is not at all clear why a 16-bit as against a 32-bit program should be different from each other but the section that follows will show there is a very large difference.

The simple processor shown above is not a real practical device. Several key points were ignored in order to put over the main idea of the fetch–execute sequence and what microprocessors actually do. Unlike the simple processor, real processors have a set of *general-purpose registers*, the ability to multiply and divide, to handle *floating point* (real) arithmetic, but they still fetch then execute instructions in sequence. Pentium processors can fetch more than one instruction at a time, can execute whilst fetching, can store instructions in the processor chip and operate in a very efficient way but still fetches then executes instructions even if the sequence is more complex than presented above.

If you need to write assembly language, you will need to know the *architecture* of the chip that will use the resulting machine code and its instruction set, the list of possible operations the chip will execute. Expertise in writing assembler for a Pentium chip will help you need to write for a MC68040 bit only in a general way. One will not directly transfer to the other in the same way that a C++ program would (or at least should!).

For the sake of comparison, one of the original series of Intel chips, the 8086, had four general-purpose registers called AX, BX, CX and DX so the chip could execute an instruction such as

MOV AX, 8000

which would move (or load) the number 8000 into the AX general-purpose register. This register is 16 bits wide so the largest number it can hold is $2^{16} - 1 = 65\,535$. If you were to multiply 8000 by 8, then the answer of 64 000 will still fit in the AX register, so the instruction

MUL 8

will perform the multiplication and place the answer back in AX.

The problem comes when you try a calculation that results in larger numbers than will fit in a 16-bit register. The instructions

MOV AX, 8000
MUL 9

will not give the correct answer as 8000×9 is greater than 65 535. The solution is to use two registers and hold the answer in two parts but you are still limited to the size of number you can handle in this way. It is quite possible to write routines that handle larger numbers, in fact numbers of

```
            PUSH    DS              ;Save caller's DS and DI
            PUSH    DI
            MOV     DI,DSEG         ;Initialise DS
            MOV     DS,DI
            MOV     NEGIND,0        ;Negative indicator 0
            CMP     DX,0            ;Multiplicand negative?
            JNS     CHKCX           ;No. Go check multiplier
            NOT     AX              ;Yes. 2s-comp. multiplicand
            NOT     DX
            ADD     AX,1
            MDC     DX,0
            NOT     NEGIND          ;and is-comp. indicator
CHKCX:      CMP     CX,0            ;Multiplier negative?
            JNS     GOMUL           ;No. Go multiply
            NOT     BX              ;Yes.2s-comp. multiplier
            NOT     CX
            ADD     BX,1
            ADC     CX,0
            NOT     NEGIND          ;and is-comp. indicator
GOMUL:      CALL    MULU32          ;Perform unsigned mult
            CMP     NEGIND,0        ;Is sign correct?
            JZ      DONE            ;Yes. Exit.
            NOT     AX              ;No. 2s-comp. product
            NOT     BX
            NOT     CX
            NOT     DX
            ADD     AX,1
            ADC     BX,0
            ADC     CX,0
            ADC     DX,0
DONE:       POP     DI              ;Restore caller's registers
            POP     DS
            RET
MULS32:     ENDP
CSEG:       ENDS
            END
```

Program 1.3.1 *8086 code for signed 32-bit multiplication with 64-bit answer.*

any size you choose but they require *routines*, i.e. whole sets of instructions rather than a single instruction.

A 32-bit processor can multiply two 32-bit numbers and give a 64-bit answer in a single instruction, a 16-bit processor will use a set of instructions to achieve the same result. See Program 1.3.1. It may seem that a 32-bit microprocessor is twice as powerful as a 16-bit version but in fact the 32-bit one is very much faster. Suppose you had a 16- and a 32-bit microprocessor that ran at the same clock speed and had the same complexity of instructions, the 32-bit machine would handle larger numbers a great deal quicker. Modern 64-bit machines can of course handle even larger numbers; they also execute each instruction quicker.

The assembly language program presented in Program 1.3.1 multiplies two 32-bit signed numbers and gives a 64-bit result. It is written for the 8086 processor, i.e. a 16-bit machine. It is shown here simply to demonstrate the difference between processors of different bit sizes. On a 32- or 64-bit machine, the same result is achieved using a **single instruction**. For the purposes of this unit, you should not attempt to understand how the program works. (Assembly language programmers will note that the top of the program is missing, the so-called assembler directives, etc. The program is shown here only to make the point between microprocessors, not to demonstrate assembly language itself.)

1.4 More complex processors, CISC and RISC

RISC means *Reduced Instruction Set* and CISC means *Complex Instruction Set* (The final C means Chip or Computing depending on what source material you read!)

In a RISC chip, there are fewer instructions which might lead you to believe the chip was in some way less powerful. There are several factors to consider:

- Fewer instructions mean the physical design in silicon is smaller with fewer electronic component and less complexity than a CISC chip so each instruction can execute quicker, the goal being one instruction per clock cycle.
- Analysis of actual program code written for CISC chips shows that only a small fraction of the large number of CISC instructions are actually used frequently.
- Modern 'RISC' chips have rich instruction sets.
- The Pentium series of CPUs have an architecture that gives, on average, better than one instruction per clock cycle, close to the original goal of RISC design.

In reality, modern CPUs described as RISC have little in common with the original idea of RISC. There are differences in the design approach of the chips and in the way code is written for each chip but the difference is not simple and clear cut.

Pipelining and superscalar architecture

A technique used to increase the performance of CPUs is *pipelining*. This means that the execution of each instruction is broken down into stages so when the second stage of execution is underway, the CPU can start the first stage of the next instruction *in the pipeline*. In this way, instruction execution overlaps; if an instruction takes five clock cycles to execute and there are five instructions in the pipeline, on average, it will take one clock cycle per instruction, providing a dramatic increase in performance. A CPU is *superscalar* when it has more than one pipeline.

1.5 Latest processors

Books such as this are not the best place to have information about the latest processors, the market moves so fast that by the time a book is in print, the market has moved on. The very best way to get easy-to-understand information about the latest technology is via the Internet. Have a look at the manufacturer's website, ARM, Intel, AMD, Cyrix, Motorola, Texas Instruments, etc.

The main developments are still in the quest for speed but recently there has been an increase in the number of application-specific CPUs for video cards, network switches and routers, etc. These chips are optimized for the particular application.

In the past, PCs had a single processor that did all the processing required to complete a task. Modern CPUs are not only very much faster but the total task is now split between the main CPU, graphics processors, CPUs on storage devices, on network cards, etc. so looked at from the viewpoint of the whole task that small computers are designed to undertake, PCs are now true multiprocessor machines.

1.6 Motherboards and expansion buses, PCI, ISA, etc., chipsets, BIOS and the bootup sequence, POST and operating system loader, I/O ports

What happens when you turn on your PC

When you turn on a PC, it takes some time before it is ready for work. It may not seem obvious but most of the software that runs the PC is stored on a disk and when the power is turned on, this must be loaded into memory before it can be used.

With one or two exceptions, everything that happens in a PC is *controlled* by software. The hardware actually performs the tasks but is 'told' what to do by software. This includes the process whereby the software is loaded into memory, so how does the software get into memory as it is software that does the loading? This was a problem for early computers, the very first ones had people loading a *loader* program by hand. When this was run, it could load the rest of the software. In a PC, this code is always present in a chip called the BIOS or *Basic Input Output System* and this starts to execute shortly after power-up. The BIOS is stored as machine code, usually in a device that acts like a ROM but can in fact be changed. Older machines used devices like *EPROMS* (Erasable Programmable Read Only Memories) which as the name implies, can be erased and then programmed. Newer machines use flash memory but the effect is the same, the machine code is there at start-up time.

An aside

The process of starting a computer is called 'booting' after an old philosophical problem that went something like this. *If I pull on your bootstraps, I can lift you off the ground. If you pull just as hard on your own bootstraps, nothing much happens. Why?* The problem is similar because the computer needs a piece of software (a loader) to load the problem, it is like pulling on its own bootstraps, the loader had to come from outside. For this reason, the original loader was called a 'bootstrap' loader and the process of starting a machine was called 'booting up'. It is not the same as turning on the machine, if you do that, all the electronics work but there is nothing to *control* it without software. Control is the central issue.

The first process to occur is the *POST* or *POwer up Self Test*. This code, stored in the BIOS chip, tries to obtain a response from each of the main components, video, RAM, keyboard, etc. As failure of the video may stop error messages appearing on the screen, success or failure of the POST is reported by sound: these are the two 'beeps' you should hear shortly after turning on the PC. Usually, if something is wrong, several beeps are sounded, either long or short beeps, the combination of which indicates what has gone wrong. Different makers use different combinations of sound but most use two beeps to mean all is OK.

The next stage is to initialize the system board and load the *interrupt vectors* into RAM (see the section on interrupts below). Having done this, a check is made for other devices and link the BIOS information in those devices to the main BIOS code. Most devices like video cards, disk controllers, etc. have BIOS code of their own. If you boot different PCs with various devices installed, you will see each BIOS display different text, right at the start of the process. If you have a modern power-saving monitor, it may not have started displaying before it 'warms up' so you may miss this. This is not to be confused with operating system text that appears later.

The next process is the *initial program load*. This is where the BIOS goes to a fixed place on a disk, the first sector, then loads whatever it finds there into memory and starts executing. The first sector is called the boot sector because it contains the bootstrap loader for the operating system to be used. At this point, the BIOS hands over control to the operating system stored on your disk. One of its first tasks is to configure the installed add-on boards using *plug and play*. This means that the hardware interrupts and machine addresses to be associated with each board are determined. (In the olden days, this was done when the board was installed by using switches on each board. It was the cause of much anguish and thankfully is now assigned to the history books!)

The operating system itself now loads using its own loader software. As much as some companies would like you to think otherwise, there are several different operating systems that work well with a standard PC (e.g. linux). The loading from now on is specific to each operating system.

Once this is complete, you can start loading application software and use your PC!

What is an interrupt?

Machine code resides in RAM in a set of addresses so each instruction can be fetched then executed in sequence. Decisions made in software cause the sequence to change, so you could have a decision like 'if A is greater than B, jump to address 3000'. If A is not greater than B, the code will continue at the next address in memory. This kind of execution is fine for small problems but is of little use when a large number of time critical tasks must be controlled. Suppose the code was running through the section that updated the video screen to place the next character in the right place. If during this process, a key was pressed on the keyboard, it would be ignored, the CPU would be busy with its video task. Remember, everything is controlled by software, even keyboard presses. A system designed in this manner (called *Polling*) would be of little use.

The solution adopted very early in the life of computers is to use interrupts. This means the CPU can be signalled to stop doing the current task, give some service to the device that interrupted it, then return to the original task. Usually the interrupting task does not take too long to be serviced, so normal operations continue at a good speed.

Interrupts, an analogy

Imagine you were at home waiting for a friend to call round but were not sure of the exact time she was coming. You could do one of two things. Firstly, you could go to the front door once every minute or so and check to see if she had arrived. That way she would never have to wait more than a minute to be let in. Alternatively, you could install a front door bell, continue with your other tasks until it rings, when it does, you stop what you are doing and answer the door. With luck, she has arrived. The first method is called 'polling' and the second method uses an 'interrupt'. Polling implies that the software executes in a fixed sequence and that each device is looked at during regular intervals. It does mean that if busy, the CPU will not service a task, one that could be important. This is the same as your friend arriving just after you have looked out, you miss her until the next 'polling' event.

In a PC, there are many tasks the system must service, so the CPU is interrupted many times per second. Typical interrupts come from the hard drive, the serial port, network cards, etc. and mean that something has happened that needs attending to. In the analogy of you being at home, this means that while you are waiting for your friend, you put the kettle on. It may boil over if you leave it on the gas, so you choose to use an interrupt, the whistle. There is another interrupt, the telephone; another friend could ring at any time. Of course you must decide in advance, which of these interrupts are the most important, what happens if the kettle boils and the front door bell rings at the same time? In a PC, interrupts have assigned priorities to cope with this problem.

When an interrupt occurs, program execution jumps to the right address in memory then returns when finished. In order to know the right address to jump to, the addresses are stored in a table. If the design of the PC was static, this table could be fixed, but every PC is configurable; you can add devices and services in a very flexible manner. This means the table of interrupt addresses must be changeable. At bootup time, a default set of addresses is copied from the BIOS chip into RAM. Later in the bootup process this can be changed to match the particular devices and programs to be used on your PC. The table of address is called the *interrupt vector*, and is situated at a low address in RAM.

Chipsets

The PC system box has three basic elements: the CPU, the memory system and the I/O subsystem.

The mother board is a PCB (*Printed Circuit Board*) that connects these elements together. In the past, these boards were quite large as there was little in the way of integration between the circuits, indeed the very first IBM PCs were built from 'off the shelf' ICs (*Integrated Circuits*) available for the (then) non-PC market. As the PC market grew, the supporting chips became more specific to their task and became known as *Application Specific ICs* or *ASICs*. Since they worked in sets of chips, they eventually became known as the *chipset*. Names have an odd way of sticking around; modern PCs may have all the functionality in one chip but it is still called a chipset. The function of the chipset is to control the flow of data around the motherboard, provide timing signals, handle DMA (see below) requests and a range of other housekeeping tasks.

The particular chipset available depends on the microprocessor socket or slot type. Each microprocessor has its own socket type so your choice of chipset will depend on the CPU type. Not all manufacturers make boards and chipsets to suit all microprocessors.

Most motherboards have circuits to control the mouse, keyboard, input and output from the serial ports, parallel port, floppy disks, and often the IDE hard disks.

Items not generally included in the chipset are video, sound, networks, NICs and expansion buses such as SCSI (Small Computers Systems Interface) controllers, modems and similar devices. These are fitted as extra boards or externally but a few motherbaords do have on board video or sound, etc.

DMA

DMA is *Direct Memory Access*, a system that allows data to be transferred in blocks. In the earliest pre-PC microcomputers, the process of moving a block of data was achieved by moving a byte at a time. The CPU would fetch the instruction, fetch the data byte, fetch the address to send it to, then send the data byte to its destination. This involved many memory operations per byte. Even the earliest PCs had DMA control, circuits that took over from the CPU and transferred whole blocks of data from devices to RAM, providing a dramatic improvement in performance.

CPU sockets

The microprocessor is fitted into a connector on the motherboard. The earliest microprocessors were built into DIPs (*Dual Inline Packages*) with a line of connecting pins down each on two sides. Modern CPUs have so many connecting pins that the package would be far too large, so the pins are now arranged in several rows or rectangular arrays. As microprocessors have developed so have the connectors.

Motherboard 'form factors'

The size and shape of the motherboard is called the *form factor*. Very old 286-based PCs were called designated AT (meaning Advanced Technology!) and the board form factor was known as the AT board. This form factor was kept for the 486 microprocessors and some early Pentiums. 'Baby AT' boards were smaller than the 'full AT' boards. Most of these boards have ISA (Industry Standard Architecture) expansion slots, the old 8-bit and the slightly newer 16-bit versions. PCI (Peripheral Component Interconnect) expansion slots came later and are much faster than the ISA versions.

Pentium Socket 7 and the Pentium III chips use the ATX (AT eXtended) form factor and these boards will usually have PCI expansion slots, they may also have some 16-bit ISA slots to allow old (or legacy) boards to be fitted. Some boards use a *riser* where all the connectors and expansion slots are plugged in. The motherboard also plugs into this riser. These are designated NLX (New Low profile eXtended).

Motherboard memory sockets

Modern boards have memory slots of various designs to suit RAM chips (DIMM, SODIMM or RIMM), the older ones would use banks of either 32- or 72-pin SIMM sockets. This refers to the size and layout of the RAM chips. The reason the sockets have changed is to accommodate wider buses. Some boards allow some mixing between chip types but most set-ups avoid this complication.

ISA bus

The ISA bus is the Industry Standard Architecture. The oldest version had an 8-bit data bus and ran at 4.77 MHz, this was followed by a 16-bit version. These are the largest of the expansion slots found on all but the very latest motherboards. Old or legacy devices usually fit this slots. Because the bus runs at such a slow speed, data transfers are slow. The requirement for more and more performance has led to the development of faster buses but the ISA bus is still around to support the many legacy boards still in use. Some devices are so slow that no benefit will be obtained by connecting them to a faster bus.

Local buses

Simple machines use a single address and a single data bus controlled by the microprocessor. This leads to a bottleneck because if one device connected to the buses is transferring data, nothing else can happen. Indeed it is odd to think that most of the time, devices in these simple machine are doing nothing at all. PC have a much more complex architecture, many operations can and do happen at the same time. One of the means by which this can happen is to have a bus in addition to the main bus and allow the CPU to have direct access to it. This feature is called a local bus and there are different kinds available in the marketplace. One of the first was the VESA local bus but this has now been superseded by the PCI local bus. PCI is short for Peripheral Component Interconnect and was first introduced in 1993.

This original PCI was a 32-bit bus with a maximum speed of 33 MHz which means that 33 million times a second, a single piece of 32-bit data can flow along the bus to other devices. If it is set to run synchronously with the PC (the usual case), the actual speed is a set fraction of the PC bus speed. In machines that use a bus speed of 100 MHz, the PCI is running at just one-third that speed, 33 MHz. On some motherboards, the PCI bus is set to run asynchronously, i.e. not in time with the PC.

Most motherboards have three or four PCI slots, most will support *bus mastering*. This is where control of the bus is given to devices on the bus and allows data transfers to occur that are not under the direct control of the CPU. The advantage is that data can flow at the full speed of the bus when it is required. An arbitration circuit ensures that no one device can obtain complete control of the bus.

The most common devices found on the PCI bus are video cards, SCSI adapters, and networking cards. Hard disk controllers are on the PCI bus but are connected directly to the motherboard rather than occupying an expansion slot.

You will see the main system bus referred to as a *front side bus*. This is because the bus has two 'sides', one connecting the CPU to the L2 cache and the other, the *back side bus*, connecting the CPU to the main RAM. The back side bus has a typical speed of 66–133 MHz, the front side bus runs at either one-half of the processor speed or the full processor speed. As is the way with computers, the terms front side and back side bus are no longer used by Intel but are still in daily use. More modern terms are given below.

Modern system board layouts

Figure 1.6.1 shows a typical PC board layout.

- The CPU is the Central Processing Unit, i.e. the Pentium or AMD chip.
- The system RAM is the main memory typically fitted as DIMMs or similar.
- The FSB or Front Side Bus is the main communication to/from the CPU. The speed of the FSB is critical to the performance of the whole machine.
- The PCI or Peripheral Component Interconnect Bus is an Intel design to connect adapter cards to the main system.
- The ISA or Industry Standard Architecture Bus is also known as a legacy bus. This is the old, slow 8- or 16-bit bus fitted to original PCs. It has disappeared from some modern boards, it is only included on others to allow the fitting of older devices.
- The AGP or Accelerated Graphics Port is a high-speed link directly to/ from the CPU to allow improved graphics performance. This is missing from some older boards.
- A Bus Bridge is simply a device that 'converts' the signals on one type of bus to another, it will handle speed and signalling differences.

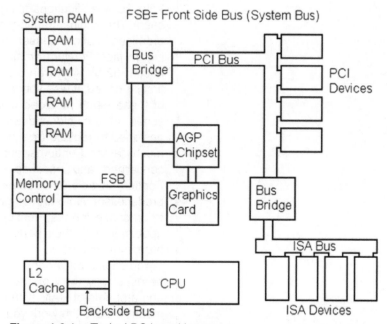

Figure 1.6.1 *Typical PC board layout*

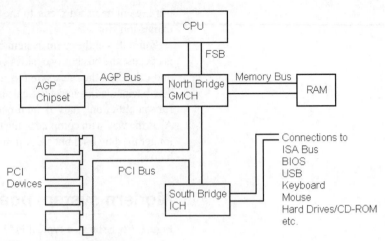

Figure 1.6.2   *PC chipset*

There is another way of looking at a PC motherboard layout. Figure 1.6.2 shows essentially the same PC as in Figure 1.6.1 but in a more modern way. Older PCs were made from numerous chips, assembled to make the complete machine. Modern machines contain most functions in dedicated *chipsets* that are used to connect the CPU with the rest of the machine. This chipset is split into two main parts, the *North Bridge* and the *South Bridge* as in Figure 1.6.2. Intel now calls the South Bridge the *Communications I/O Controller Hub* (C-ICH or just ICH). The North Bridge is now called the *Graphics Memory Control Hub* (GMCH).

The design and speed of the chipset plays a vital role in the overall performance of the machine.

Historical note

With PC specifications things may not always be what they seem. The original Pentium processor with its 64-bit data bus promised to offer PC-users the advantages of 64-bit processing. In fact, Pentium architecture is based on two interconnected 32-bit '486-type processors. When the Pentium was first launched, it was sobering to find that the first generation of these much heralded chips could only just matched the speed of the 'clock doubled' '486 chips that they were designed to replace (real benefits didn't materialize until the much faster Pentiums appeared). As far as memory is concerned and because of its 32-bit address bus, the Pentium is able to address exactly the same range as its predecessor. Not surprisingly, many people who rushed out to purchase the first Pentium-based systems were very disappointed with their performance – there must be a moral here somewhere!

You should be very careful about manufactures claims and be especially wary of 'the numbers', fantastic clock speeds and amounts of RAM. The only real indicator is how fast the machine does the work you want it to perform.

Compatible IDE/ATA (Integrated Drive Electronics/AT Attachment) hard disks (see Section 1.10) can be bus masters. Standard IDE drives use Programmable Input/ Output or PIO mode but bus mastering provides a performance improvement in some circumstances. It does not make everything quicker. Beware, if the hard drive you buy supports bus mastering it does not mean that it will work that way, you must ensure the operating system, motherboard and device drivers also support bus mastering.

AGP

AGP stands for *Accelerated Graphics Port* and is not really a local bus but provides similar benefits, i.e. data can be transferred to and from the AGP without other devices making demands on the circuit. The AGP is entirely independent of the PCI bus on the motherboard.

Even though the PCI bus is fast, the requirement to move very large amounts of data for 3D image effects, texturing, full motion video and ever higher resolution graphics means that the busy PCI bus cannot provide all the speed that is needed.

Graphics cards do a large amount of processing independently of the main CPU and this processing requires memory. Since VRAM (Video Ram) is expensive, the AGP allows the graphics processor to use main memory for these calculations; this results in more data being transferred along a bus from main RAM to the video card, data that is not part of the traffic that 'belongs' to the CPU. The AGP allows this transfer of data without slowing the PCI bus or tying up the CPU.

The original AGP specification was based on the PCI version 2.1 specification, it runs at 66 MHz and uses a 32-bit bus (4-bytes at once). This allows 254 Mbytes/sec. It can be made to run at twice this speed by providing two two data transfers per 66 MHz clock cycle. This is done by changing the way the data is encoded, i.e. by using the rising and falling edges of the 1s and 0s. The latest AGP specification allows data transfers of 2.1 Gbytes/sec .

Peripheral ports

USB

USB stands for *Universal Serial Bus*, a standard being worked on by Compaq, Hewlett Packard, Intel, Lucent, Microsoft, NEC and Philips.

The idea is that peripherals can be plugged in (or removed) whilst the PC is switched on, they do not need to be initialized during the boot up sequence. When a device is plugged in, the operating system recognizes the event and configures the required device driver software.

Many standard PCs are supplied with two USB ports. Attachment of more than two devices is achieved by USB Hubs that allow daisy-chaining, a technique where devices are plugged in one to the next forming a 'chain' thus reducing the amount of cable required. A further reduction in cabling is achieved because USB supplies the power to the devices in the data cable, up to 2.5 watts. Hubs may be cascaded up to five levels deep providing a connection for up to 127 peripheral devices at a transfer rate of either 12 Mb/sec (full-speed) and 1.5 Mb/sec (low-speed). The USB 1.1 standard has been superseded by USB 2.0. This has a raw data rate at 480 Mb/sec, which is 40 times faster than USB 1.1.

Firewire

Firewire is the common name for a standard called IEEE 1394. This is a serial connection aimed at very high data transfer speeds, at least, high for a serial link. Speeds between 100 and 800 Mbits/sec are possible and a speed of 3200 Mbits/sec is promised. Up to 16 devices can be connected via a single Firewire port. It commonly used to attach digital cameras to PCs, one reason being the very simple cable attachment and set-up that is used.

IrDA

This is an infrared serial communication standard that is intended to dispense with cables and run at a maximum of 4 Mbits/sec. IrDA will also work at standard serial speeds to mimic the old RS-232-C serial standard (see below). Since there is a clear possibility of several devices in one place using IrDA and the infrared signal is 'broadcast' around that place, the standard includes techniques similar to those used in networking, to avoid device conflicts and data being sent to the wrong device. It is common to find IrDA on notebook PCs or smaller devices to allow communication with desktop PCs without cabling.

Serial ports

Serial devices have been around for many years. The earliest machines could be connected to devices such as modems or printers using just three wires, a 'send' wire, a 'receive' wire and a signal return wire. Binary 1s and 0s were sent one after the other, i.e. serially. The maximum speed was quite low. To improve speed, extra wires were introduced to allow 'handshaking', signals that allowed or disallowed the sending of data depending in the readiness to receive. These data and handshake lines and the associated timings, etc. were incorporated into a standard called RS-232-C which used a 25-pin 'D' shaped connector. Since only a few of these pins were actually used, IBM introduced a similar 9-pin 'D' connector that is now common on modern PCs. Unfortunately, as a standard that has 'evolved' over the years, the 25-pin connectors are still common as are many different arrangements for interconnecting 25-pin, 9-pin old and new devices. Modern PCs with modern serial devices cause little problem but the use of legacy serial devices with any PC can prove to be problematic. The maximum speed of a serial is currently 115 200 bits/sec. With a simple serial link, each 8-bit byte has a 'start' and 'stop' bit added so using 10 bits/byte. 115 200 bits/sec would then give 11 520 bytes/sec. You may notice that some speeds are given as Mbytes/sec and others as Mbits/sec. This is because the number of extra bits (i.e. not data bits) is variable, depending on the application and the PC industries common practice of quoting the largest number to look attractive in advertisements! Also you should be wary of 'standards'.

Serial ports under Microsoft DOS or Windows have names COM1, COM2, etc. The set-up for these COM (Component Object Model) ports quote the speed in bits/sec, number of data bits, parity and number of stop bits. A typical set-up may be 9600, 8, none, 1. This means 9600 bits per second, 8 data bits, no parity and 1 stop bit. Parity is an old error checking system now little used, it is in the set-up to allow connection with legacy devices. You may see 9600 bits/sec quoted as 9600 Baud but the 'Baud rate' is not the same as bits/sec.

Parallel ports

Most PCs have a single port for the attachment of a local printer. This is a parallel port, i.e. it has control lines and eight data lines, one each for the 8-bits of a byte. Although designed as a single direction port for outputting to printers, some programmers have managed to allow two-way communication. The port is slow by modern standards but as the printers are even slower, no advantage is gained by using a high-speed link.

More modern machines use either an EPP or ECP port. The EPP or Enhanced Parallel Port was designed by Intel, Xircom and Zenith. It allows 500 Kbytes to 2 Mbytes, to be transferred each second, faster than the old Standard Parallel Port, SPP. Microsoft and Hewlett Packard introduced a specification called ECP, Extended Capabilities Port, that was designed to provide improved speed and functionality for printers.

Under Microsoft DOS or Windows, the parallel port is called LPT1 (for Line Printer 1). It is possible to add more parallel ports by plugging expansion cards into the ISA bus, they would then be called LPT2, etc.

1.7 Memory: RAM and ROM

> **Key fact**
>
> **RAM**
>
> RAM is short for *Random Access Memory* and is one of the silliest names in computing! It really refers to the main memory of the PC, it is where most of the software and data is stored when the machine is in use. It is called random access because any byte can be read into the CPU in any order from any address but this is also true of ROM. A better term would be RWM or Read–Write Memory, indeed some people do use this name.
>
> RAM is volatile, it loses it value as soon as the power is lost. That is one reason it takes so long to boot up a machine, once the power is restored, all the software and data must be loaded.

There are many different kinds of RAM on the market, the result of intense competition to satisfy the ever-increasing demands for speed, capacity and low cost. Some of the more important types are described below but a detailed knowledge is not required to fulfil the criteria for this unit of the HNC Computing.

> **Key fact**
>
> **ROM**
>
> Unlike RAM, *Read Only Memory* (ROM) cannot be written to by the CPU but it has the advantage of retaining all the data when the power is lost. It is slower than RAM, i.e. it takes longer for the circuits to present data on the data bus after a read instruction from the CPU. It is ideal for the BIOS. As explained in Section 1.6, computers need software to control the loading of software, so software that is already present is very useful!

Types of RAM

For the purposes of the unit of the HNC Computing, a very detailed knowledge of memory types is not required but knowledge of how RAM works and in particular how this affects system performance is important. The points you should remember from the section below are related to this performance and they should inform your purchasing decisions when buying PCs.

Dynamic RAM or DRAM

This is the main type of RAM fitted to PCs, it is cheap but not as fast as other kinds of RAM. In technology there is nearly always a trade-off between conflicting requirements, in this case it is between cost and speed. DRAM is cheap but slow. It suffers from another problem, many times a second the memory contents need to be refreshed, i.e. the chip will forget or lose its contents unless a read or refresh operation is carried out. This means that separate refresh circuits are needed, adding to the complexity of the board.

Static RAM or SRAM

This kind of RAM holds its data without refresh signals and is faster than DRAM, but in the classic trade-off, SRAM loses on cost. It is implemented with between four and six transistors whereas DRAM is made from one transistor and a capacitor. This may not sound expensive but the six transistors are for just one bit! A byte is 8 bits, so 1 Mb of SRAM would take $6 \times 8 \times 1024 \times 1024 = 50\,331\,648$ transistors! Consider that the latest Pentium microprocessors use about a one-seventh of this, although it is really overstating it somewhat as RAM is much simpler to make than CPUs but the scale of the problem is obvious.

How is memory addressed?

In early microcomputers, RAM was addressed directly, so when an address was placed on the address bus, the RAM chips were read in one go and the data flowed onto the data bus. Modern PCs use a more complex arrangement. If you have a 32-bit address bus, this means there are 32-wires arranged in parallel. As $2^{32} = 4\,294\,967\,296$, you can have $4\,294\,967\,296$ or 4096 Mbytes of data, assuming one address location can hold 1 byte. $4\,294\,967\,296$ in decimal is $100\,000\,000$ in hex. If a hex address of $500\,317$ is applied to the address bus, it means there is the pattern 10100000000001100000111 on the bus, where a '1' is 'on' and a '0' is 'off'. 10100000000001100000111 in binary is $500\,317$ hex.

Memory speed

What do we mean by speed with respect to memory?

It is usually taken as the time for the DRAM chips to respond with a data request measured from the time of the request to the time the data is made available. This is quoted in nanoseconds and typical RAM chips have 60 or 70 ns ratings although some are much quicker. A time of 70 ns seems very fast but consider a 600 MHz Pentium CPU, slow by modern standards. 600 MHz means that 600 000 000 clock cycles occur each second. The time between each one is 1/600 000 000 or 1.67 ns, enough time for 70/1.67 = 42 clock cycles! Clearly, in a Pentium 600 machine, it would not be viable to have the CPU read each instruction one by one from the main memory. This is where memory cache is important.

Mathematics in action

What is a nanosecond?

A nanosecond is 10^{-9} seconds or 1/1 000 000 000 seconds. In language, this is a thousand times shorter than a millionth of a second. In human terms, this is an impossibly short period of time but in computing terms, is an 'everyday' unit of time. Table 1.7.1 shows the factors of 10 and the associated names and symbols. Table 1.7.2 shows the factors of 2, you should notice that some values, for instance 10^3 has the same name as 2^{10}, i.e. kilo. but $2^{20} = 1024$ and $10^3 = 1000$ so there is only an approximate equality.

It is sometimes difficult for humans to get a good mental picture of very large or very small numbers. A technique used to help with this problem is to imagine that 1 second is stretched out over a *whole year* and then to see what happens inside that year. If we take the 600-MHz clock speed as an example and imagine 1 second stretched out over a year. There are 60 seconds per minute, 60 minutes per hour, etc. so in 1 year we get $60 \times 60 \times 24 \times 365 = 31\,536\,000$ or 31.5 million seconds per real year. If 600 000 000 clock pulses occur per real second, we would get 600/31.5 = 19 pulses per stretched out second. In other words, even if we slowed down the Pentium by 31.5 million times, it would still be doing 19 things a second. If we now take a 3 GHz machine, this is 3/0.6 = 5 times faster still, so we would get $19 \times 5 = 95$ things a second!

Nanoseconds and other named fractions

Asynchronous and synchronous DRAM

The DRAM fitted to most older PCs was called *asynchronous*. This means it does not operate in time with, i.e. it is not synchronized with, the system clock signals. This worked satisfactorily with slower machines, but newer machines need better performance. SDRAM or *synchronous* DRAM has its operation tied to the system clock so the timing of what happens is under better control. DRAM chips have typical speeds of 60 or 70 ns whereas SDRAM chips have typical values of 10 or 12 ns, i.e. much faster. Beware of the trap often found in computing, especially regarding speeds. A rating of 10 ns does not mean a system with SDRAM is six times faster than one fitted with 60 ns DRAM. The SDRAM can deliver that much faster but since it is now under the control of system timing,

Question 1.7.1

Assume the average size of a hard disk drive in a PC in the year 2000 is 10 Gb. If Moore's law were applied to average hard drive sizes and continued until the year 2012, what would the average size be in that year?

The answer may surprise you! Answer on page 409.

Table 1.7.1   *Powers of 10 and their names*

Factor of 10	Value	Prefix	Symbol
10^{-18}	0.000 000 000 000 000 001	atto	a
10^{-15}	0.000 000 000 000 001	femto	f
10^{-12}	0.000 000 000 001	pico	p
10^{-9}	0.000 000 001	nano	n
10^{-6}	0.000 001	micro	μ
10^{-3}	0.001	milli	m
10^{-2}	0.01	centi	c
10^{-1}	0.1	deci	d
10	10	deca	da
10^{2}	100	hecto	h
10^{3}	1000	kilo	k
10^{6}	1 000 000	mega	M
10^{9}	1 000 000 000	giga	G
10^{12}	1 000 000 000 000	tera	T
10^{15}	1 000 000 000 000 000	peta	P
10^{18}	1 000 000 000 000 000 000	exa	E
10^{21}	1 000 000 000 000 000 000 000	zetta	Z
10^{24}	1 000 000 000 000 000 000 000 000	yotta	Y

Table 1.7.2   *Powers of 2 and their names*

Power of 2	Number of bytes	Symbol	Name
2^{10}	1024	kb	kilobytes
2^{20}	1 048 576	Mb	megabytes
2^{30}	1 073 741 824	Gb	gigabytes
2^{40}	1 099 511 627 776	Tb	terabytes
2^{50}	1 125 899 906 843 624	Pb	petabytes
2^{60}	1 152 921 504 607 870 976	Eb	exabytes
2^{70}	1 180 591 620 718 458 879 424	Zb	zettabytes
2^{80}	1 208 925 819 615 701 892 530 176	Yb	yottabytes

it may not get access to the bus for long enough so giving a slower effective speed. The settings of the BIOS, especially those that affect system timings, number of wait states, etc. are critical if the maximum performance is to be achieved from the PC. Wait states are when the memory system is told to wait for a clock cycle or more (depending on wait state setting) before acting. The fastest is zero wait states but the RAM in the PC may not be able to keep up. It is quite possible to have all the right hardware fitted to the machine but for it to still not run as fast as it should.

There are several kinds of SDRAM but this unit of the HNC Computing does not require such a level of detail. You may see the following term with respect to RAM types: Extended Data Out (EDO), Burst Extended Data Out (BEDO), Double Data Rate SDRAM (DDR SDRAM), Direct Rambus DRAM (DRDRAM), Synchronous-Link DRAM (SLDRAM).

In several sections of this book you will see warnings about making simple assumptions regarding speed ratings. Be very careful, the actual situation is much more complicated than it appears to be at first. The only real test of a PC is to run real life problems, the speed of sub-systems can become very academic.

Cache memory

As demonstrated above, even fast modern RAM chips cannot deliver anywhere near the speed required to feed a high-speed CPU with data. The solution adopted is to use cache memory.

Analysis of a large number of machine code programs (remember *all* programs run as machine code in the CPU) reveals that most of the time, the next instruction to be executed is next to or very close to the instruction being executed. This means that if a block of the program is copied into a section of high-speed memory, the CPU would be able to access instructions and data very much quicker. The problem is that not all instructions are in the high-speed RAM, the *cache*, so a process must go on 'behind the scenes' to load the correct sections of data from main RAM to the cache. About 90% of the time or even better, the next instruction is already in the cache so only 5% or 10% of memory requests will result in a direct memory read.

On Pentium systems, there are two levels of cache known as L1 and L2. L1 is very high-speed RAM inside the processor chip, L2 is a high-speed RAM cache outside the CPU but still with a high performance. With caching, doubling the speed of the main RAM has little effect on the overall machine performance, the critical speed is how fast the CPU can gain access to the cache.

Virtual memory and the amount of RAM required

If cache memory is very fast, virtual memory is very slow! In old mainframe computers, the main memory was very very expensive. It could be that only 1 kb was fitted (not a 1 Mb!). The programs to be run were much larger so techniques were evolved to have a small amount of code in memory and arrange for pieces of the main program to be loaded from disk only when required. This way programs of any size could be run but as the code pieces were loaded from disk each time, the process was quite slow. This is virtual memory, it is the memory that exists 'virtually', i.e. it is not real. Microsoft uses a similar technique with Windows. Windows needs a fair amount of space for itself and each application you have running needs its own space in memory. In the original PCs there was generally not sufficient RAM so a *swap file* was used. This means that sections of program code in memory that was not needed right away was 'swapped' onto the disk. As far as Windows was concerned, there was now enough memory, but of course, being disk bound, the process is slower. Fitting more RAM to a PC allows Windows to access the swap file less often so dramatically improving performance.

If you were to load a simple operating system (not Windows!) then load and run a single program, the amount of RAM fitted would have no effect whatsoever. The amount of RAM fitted only affects performance when virtual memory techniques are made less necessary. If everything is in RAM, the disk is not accessed to get more data; accessing any part of main RAM takes the same time so no improvement is made by fitting more.

Experiment

You can detect when the swap file is accessed quite often, just keep an eye on the disk drive LED on the front of the PC. If there is much activity when you open a new window, it is likely that the swap file is being accessed.

1.8 Video graphics

Pixels

When a graphical image is shown on a computer screen, it is made up from a large collection of dots. Each of these dots is called a *pixel*, a word which is short for *picture element*.

Pixels are arranged in rows and columns; typical numbers of rows and columns are shown in table below.

Name	Columns	Rows
VGA	640	480
SVGA	800	600
	1024	768
	1280	1024
	1600	1200

The number of pixels per screen is known as the resolution. The higher the number of pixels, the better the resolution or the finer the detail that can be shown.

Each pixel may have just one colour at a time, chosen from a set of colours. Suppose each pixel could be just one from a selection of 256 different colours. This would mean that a number must be assigned to that pixel. If bright red was colour number 37, then that one pixel would be stored as the value 37. Since 1 byte is made up of 8 bits, the largest number that can be stored in 8 bits is 255. If you include the value 0 then it is possible to store 1 of 256 different colour values in 1 byte, or the pixel can be one of 256 different colours. Another way to state this is that $2^8 = 256$.

If you use less memory than 1 byte per pixel, say 4 bits per pixel (half a byte), then you must be content with fewer colours. With 4 bits, the largest number you can store is 15, so (including the value 0) the number of possible colours is 16 or 24. (Half a byte is called a nibble!)

More generally, the number of colours that are available is given by 2^N. If you choose to use 8 bits per pixel then the number of colours is $2^8 = 256$, or with 24 bits per pixel, the number of colours is $2^{24} = 16.7$ million.

Bytes	Bits	Number of colours
¼	2	$2^2 = 4$
½	4	$2^4 = 16$
1	8	$2^8 = 256$
2	16	$2^{16} = 65\,536$ (64 k), Hicolor
3	24	$2^{24} = 16.7$ million, Trucolor

Most video graphics systems use a value of N that divides evenly into bytes, so values of 2, 4, 8, 16 or 24 are common, values such as 3, 5, 7 are not. The table below shows the number of colours available:

The term *colour planes* is sometimes used to describe the power of 2 so a $2^{24} = 16.7$ million colour setting would be described as a 24-bit colour plane. This comes from the design of the original VGA graphics card.

16-bit colour is called *Hicolor*, 24-bit colour is often known as *Trucolor* and is used where the better graphical image quality is required. Some scanners are now offering 30-bit colour although you could not realistically expect the full $2^{30} = 1\,073\,741\,824$ colours!

Consider some realistic limitations of human perception of image quality. If you have 16.7 million colours, can you see all of them? There are several answers to this.

1. Humans can perceive approximately 10 million colours.
2. The phosphors in the monitor cannot reproduce all the colours that you can see, for example, a really convincing brown colour is very hard to make.

3. If you have a screen set to 1024×768 pixels, you have less than 16.7 million pixels. To have enough pixels, to have one each of 16.7 million colours, you would need a resolution of 4730×3547 (maintaining the width to height ratio of 4:3).

The main reason to have 16.7 million colours is not to use them all but to have sufficient shades of each primary colour to reproduce a realistic shaded representation of an object.

Graphics cards

The original design of PCs had no facility to output graphics. The method used get around this problem was to have a separate *video card* or *graphics card* plugged into the main board. This card contained the video RAM and some ROM BIOS that contains the code required to write pixels, etc. More RAM allowed more colours or higher screen resolutions. Modern PCs may have the video card incorporated on the main board or as a separate component.

Modern video cards incorporate a CPU to speed up the graphics process. Imagine this problem: you wish to draw a single line at an angle on the screen and you know the colour and the start and end points of the line. Somehow the position of all the pixels that form the line must also be calculated. If this is done using the main CPU then that CPU is not available for calculating new graphics data so the system is relatively slow. If a CPU on the graphics card is dedicated to this task (known as *vector generation*), the main CPU is available for other calculations so speeding up the process greatly. A better enhancement is obtained when solid in-fill colours are required. A 100 by 100 pixel square needs $100 \times 100 = 10\,000$ pixels to be coloured. When this is done by a dedicated CPU, the main CPU has only to calculate the corner positions, just four points.

Note that non-vertical or non-horizontal lines cannot be quite smooth as they are made up of pixels, a phenomenon known as *aliasing*. The same is true for circles, etc. and extra pixels can be added in different colours to smooth out the line; this is called anti-aliasing. There are a number of algorithms used to calculate these extra pixels which require a fairly large CPU 'overhead' and if not done by the graphics card, would seriously slow down the main tasks of the host PC. A disadvantage of anti-aliasing is that lines, etc. become wider so reducing the apparent crispness of detail in some images (Figure 1.8.1).

Most PCs are now sold with at least SVGA or *Super VGA* graphics cards giving 1024 by 768 screen resolution or better and at least 4 MB of video RAM. If you need more colours, then you have the option to increase the amount of video RAM. A video card set to 1024 by 768 Hicolor requires at least 2 MB, if you want this resolution and 24-bit Trucolor, you need 4 Mb as shown below.

Video RAM (VRAM) is a specialized type of RAM that allows *dual porting*, i.e. it allows the CPU to access the RAM at the same time as the video circuits. If a screen refresh of say 85 Hz is used, the video system must access the RAM 85 times a second. VRAM allows the CPU access during the same time.

Figure 1.8.1 *Illustration of aliased and anti-aliased image*

Video RAM required

A screen resolution of 800×600 pixels will yield $800 \times 600 = 480\,000$ pixels. If each pixel needs half a byte it will allow for 16 colours so the screen will require $480\,000 \times 0.5 = 240\,000$ bytes of storage.

$800 \times 600 \times 256$ colours requires $(800 \times 600 \times 1) = 480\,000$ bytes of storage because each pixel will need 1 byte. $2^8 = 256$ different colour combinations. $480\,000$ is roughly half a Megabyte of RAM.

In general, calculate the storage required for 1 pixel remembering that $2^N =$ number of colours where $N =$ the number of bits required. Next multiply by the number of pixels on the screen.

Display types

The CRT

The glass screen you see uses essentially the same image forming technique as domestic television, the image is made up of several hundred lines of a glowing substance called a 'phosphor'. This substance is made to glow by being 'hit' by a beam of electrons radiating from a point source at the back of the CRT. A fairly sophisticated arrangement of components in the CRT causes the electrons being emitted from the point source to be formed into a thin beam. If the beam were to be kept still, all you would see is a single point of light where the beam hits the phosphor on the inside of the front of the screen. Other components allow this beam to be moved anywhere on the screen, either horizontally or vertically.

A picture is made up by very quickly moving or scanning the beam from one side of the screen to the other in a series of lines that cover the whole of the visible portion of the screen. The detail in the picture is provided by changing the brightness of the fast moving beam. The phosphor has a property that causes it to glow for a little while longer after the beam has passed, this gives the illusion that the screen is evenly illuminated at all times.

Raster scan screens

To display a screen image on a CRT, an electron beam is focused on to the front of the screen; this screen is coated with a material that glows when struck by a stream of electrons. The beam is scanned from left to right to form a line across the screen, a scan line. Once each line is formed, the beam is made to return (or fly back) to the side of the screen and down one line, ready for the next line. Once the bottom of the screen is reached, the beam is moved to the top and the process repeated, each screenful of lines is called a *raster*. A picture is produced by changing the intensity if the beam as it traverses the screen and synchronizing this change with the intensity of the image required (Figure 1.8.2).

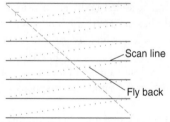

Figure 1.8.2   *Raster scan*

The number of times the raster is repeated per second is called the refresh rate. Slow refresh rates are seen by humans as flickering so rates of at least 72 times a second or 72 Hz are used to display a steady image, 75 Hz is better. Normal TV screens use a raster scan but are slower than 72 Hz, a fact easily seen if you observe a TV screen in your peripheral vision where movement will be more obvious to you. This is even more obvious if you observe this at an electrical retailer's shop where you have many screens at once. If they are arranged down the side of the shop and you look down the centre of the shop slightly away from the TVs, you will see a very marked flicker in your peripheral vision.

Colour screens

Colour CRT screens use three electron beams, one each for red, green and blue parts of the image.

An electron beam does not have a colour. The achieve colour, small areas of the screen are each allocated red, green and blue parts. These small areas are called slots and each of the three electron beams is made to hit exactly the right point, the 'red' beam hits a point that glows red, etc. The distance between each one is called the *slot pitch* or *dot pitch*. Generally, the smaller the slot pitch the sharper the image because there are more points of light to make up the image. Different shades of each colour are made up by varying the relative brightness of each of the red, green and blue parts of each slot.

Slots are only visible by using a powerful magnifying glass close to the screen. They can be observed on video monitors and domestic televisions and it can be seen that different makers use different shaped slots (shadow mask and aperture grille here).

Experiment

Use a magnifier to view a white portion of a monitor. You will see no white dots, only red, green and blue. All the colours you see are made of these three colours simply by mixing them in different amounts with different brightnesses. It can take some time to come to terms with the fact that there are no white portions of the screen. Most of your visual experience is concerned with your brain rather than your eyes, in this case your brain has 'manufactured' the white you see; your eyes are only receiving red, green and blue light.

Experiment

Observe the slots or dots carefully again with a powerful magnifier. Depending on the make of monitor you are using you will see dots or slots. Notice the slots have no effect on the image pixels, slots and pixels are completely different, pixels are a function of the computer graphics system and slots are fixed by the monitor maker. Move the image from side to side with the horizontal adjustments on the monitor. The slots stay still, the pixels move. You must not confuse slots with pixels; each pixel is a picture element and may take up different physical sizes on one computer by changing to different video modes. The number of slots available on one screen is fixed at time of manufacture of the screen. If you compare two video monitors with the same slot pitch but different sizes, the larger one will have more slots across the screen so will show each pixel more clearly. This is the reverse of the rule with domestic televisions, where larger screens show less sharp images.

Interlacing and refresh rates

On TV systems or old PCs, the beam cannot scan all the lines required to maintain a good number of full images per second, hence cannot provide

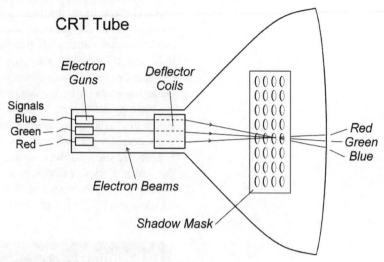

Figure 1.8.3   *Basic layout of a CRT*

an adequate refresh rate. To get around this, a system is used that scans only alternate lines, i.e. lines 1, 3, 5, 7, etc. to the bottom then the beam returns to the top and scans line 2, 4, 6, etc. The result is half the number of full frames per second and is called interlacing; it is the system used on domestic televisions. This is highly undesirable on video monitors as the image can be seen to vibrate slightly. The human response is for the eye to try to keep up with the moving image, a process that leads to sensations of 'tired eyes' because your eye muscles must continuously move your eyes to adjust of the slightly moving image. Better video systems use non-interlaced screens that produce very steady images. Most people now agree that screen refresh rates of 75 Hz or better is required to achieve a good quality, steady image.

Laptop and flat screens

There are many different kinds of LCD screen on the market, but they include:

- passive supertwist nematic displays;
- active-matrix displays.

Passive supertwist nematic displays

Passive supertwist nematic displays make use of a material, a nematic liquid crystal, that is able to change under the application of an electric field. The change in the nematic liquid crystal is in the way that light is polarized when passing through it.

In its normal state with no electric field applied, the polarization of the light that passes through it follows a twisted path. If the liquid crystal is put between two polarizing filters, each one with its axis of polarization at more than 90° to the other, the twisted path of the liquid crystals causes any light from one side to be transmitted out through the other side. When a voltage is applied across the polarizing screens, the light in the liquid crystals no longer travels in a twisted path and so is blocked by one of the polarizing filters. This is used to turn pixels on and off.

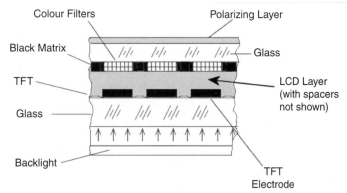

Figure 1.8.4 *Simple diagram of active LCD screen*

Active-matrix displays

Active-matrix displays incorporate transistor to control each pixel on the screen. These TFTs or Thin Film Transistors are made into a matrix, each point in the matrix forms one pixel. Each TFT has opaque parts so not all the area assigned to a pixel is able to produce light. The ratio of the area of light production to the opaque part is called the aperture ratio and is taken as a measure of quality of the screen. A value of 30% is good but a value of 50% is better and this is achieved in the better screens.

The backlight shown is cold cathode fluorescent light source. The light from this is attenuated by the black matrix. The higher the aperture ratio, the brighter the image.

Compared with CRTs, the LCD screens (Figure 1.8.4) found on notebook PCs are:

- physically smaller;
- have lower power consumption (allow batteries to be used);
- lighter;
- display good contrast with bright saturated colours;
- show a crisp image.

There are problems when compared with CRTs; LCD screens have a

- viewing angle;
- slow response time, they are not good for animated games, video etc.;
- high cost, the LCD screen accounts for most of the price difference between a desktop machine and a notebook PC, active LCD dispalys are more expensive than the passive type but produce a much brighter display.

1.9 Printers

What do you need from a printer?

The answer depends of course on the kind of business or task that you are undertaking.

Things to consider are:

- speed of text printing;
- speed of image printing;
- quality of text printing;

- quality of image printing;
- convenience;
- cost of purchase;
- cost of running.

Some of these are easy to assess, i.e. Will the printer produce a good output on normal office quality photocopy paper which is cheap and available everywhere? Is it easy to use and is it supplied with software to allow your computer to communicate with it?

Other factors are not so obvious and advertisements for printers often do not show the real answer; sometimes even the technical specifications do not show the answer. The best solution is to test one or at least see it running.

Print quality

The most commonly used measure of print quality is *resolution* measured in dots per inch (dpi) or dots per mm. Many laser printers have a resolution of 600 dots per inch or approximately 23.6 dots per mm. It is not sufficient to use this resolution as a measure of print quality. Other factors are also important such as how the ink 'sits' on the paper and the sophistication of the printer driver software. At least one major manufacturer of printers claims that the driver software is *more* important than a simple measure of resolution. One feature the use to support this claim is marketed under various names such as 'Resolution Enhancement Technology' or similar. This takes the idea of improving the resolution of individual characters instead of the whole page. The section below shows the large amount of RAM required to store a whole page. If mathematics are used to enhance each letter in a manner similar to anti-aliasing as used in video graphics, sharp letters can be produced by 300 dpi printers with a great saving in the RAM required and the associated processing. It can sometimes be difficult to tell simply by looking at a printed page, the difference between some 300 dpi and 600 dpi printers. Several reputable computer journals and magazines run tests on different printers models. These tests often show that choosing a printer on technical specification, especially the resolution alone, is not a reliable method of printer selection.

Colour reproduction (also see Appendix C, Colour)

The colour of an image on the screen may not closely match the colour of the final printed image. The reason is that one uses coloured phosphors to produce light, the other uses inks and dither patterns to simulate the same colours. Although modern printers do well in matching colours, often much experiment will be required to get the best results for your particular monitor/printer combination.

Memory required

To produce large images, printers need large amounts of RAM.

As each dot on a mono laser can be encoded in just one bit, 1 byte can store 8 dots.

Question 1.9.1

For a 600 dpi printer, how many dots are there on an A4 page and how much RAM will be required to store this data? Allow a 10 mm margin all round. Answer on page 410.

Table 1.9.1 *RAM required for full A4 page with 10 mm margin*

dpi	Dots	Bytes	Kb
300	7 341 900	917 737	896
360	10 572 336	1 321 542	1 291
600	29 367 599	3 670 950	3 585
720	42 289 342	5 286 168	5 162
1200	117 470 395	14 683 799	14 340
1440	169 157 369	21 144 671	20 649

Extending the calculation for other printer resolutions gives the results in the Table 1.9.1. As you can see, if you want a 1440 dpi printer to print a mono full-page image, you need a huge 20 Mb of RAM.

Printer speed

This is an area where great claims are made but real printers often fail to impress. Laser printers and some inkjet printers are quoted as printing 'N pages per minute'. Eight pages per minute is pretty average for a small laser printer but can you really expect eight full pages to be finished after just 1 minute? Probably not. There are several reasons for this.

1. If you are printing images, does the printer or the PC 'rasterize' the image, i.e. turn it into a set of black dots suitable for printing. If this is done in the PC, it will produce a huge amount of data to be downloaded into the printer. The answer to the question above demonstrates just how large the amount of data could be, i.e. about 30 million dots. This is the extreme case of an image size of the page. In some cases this may take a few minutes, preventing the 'eight pages per minute' claim of the manufacturer. If done in the printer, it will probably be faster. See Methods used to control printers below.
2. Does the printer already contain all the fonts you are using? If not, each font will be downloaded which takes time.
3. In the case of a laser, has it warmed up yet?

If you start with a cold printer, i.e. just turned on and have a system where the PC rasterizes images instead of this being done in the printer, the time from when you ask a page to print to the time it is in the out tray may be say 4 minutes. If the manufacturer claims eight pages per minute, it should have been in the tray after less than 8 seconds. The truth is that the speed is quoted as the 'engine speed', i.e. the maximum throughput speed of the actual printing mechanism once the data has been prepared for printing. The quoted speed is almost reached if you measure it once the printer has started producing multiple copies of the same page.

At full speed, even an eight page per minute laser printer will outperform an old dot matrix printer *but* if you time a small print job, say a single invoice, from the time of request to the finished item, dot matrix printers are often faster, they do not suffer from the start up delay found in laser printers. If the task you must solve involves this kind of printing, especially if you need a carbon copy of every document, the old dot matrix machine still perform well.

Be very careful with claims of printer speeds.

Kinds of printer commonly used with PCs

Dot matrix	Cheap and cheerful and quite old fashioned but they are used in point of sale machines or tills and in many businesses for printing invoices at point of sale, simply because dot matrix printers will make carbon copies.
Inkjet	Cheap to buy, very popular for home use with the better models producing convincing photo quality. Will print on many different kinds of media but ink cartridge prices make it expensive to run.
Mono laser	Best quality from reasonably priced printer, makes a good crisp image at a good speed on cheap paper, good life from a toner cartridge.
Colour laser	Makes a good crisp image at a good speed on cheap paper. Machines currently more expensive than mono machines but prices are becoming more realistic.
Thermal wax	Good colours.
Dye sublimation	Close to photographic quality prints. Uses transparent colours allowing good colour reproduction (see Appendix C, Colour).

An aside – hexadecimal and binary numbers

Before continuing with this section, make sure you understand hex (hexadecimal) and binary numbers, you will find these in most technical areas of computing. An introduction is included at the end of this section.

Another aside – ASCII characters

Also before continuing with this section, you will need to understand the ASCII character set. An introduction is also included at the end of this section.

Methods used to control printers

When a computer sends data to a printing device, the data may take one of several forms. This affects the way the programmers must think about how they are to format their data and how to make the best use of the printer's differing functions; it also affects the speed of response as seen by the user. More complex print formatting requires more sophisticated communication with the printer. When you install software on a machine, one task is to load a *Printer Driver*. This piece of software has the task of taking the data from an application including any mark-up that defines formatting, etc. and translating it to the form the printer will accept. Many modern printers will accept all the forms shown below.

Method 1: Send plain ASCII codes to the printer?
The simplest method of outputting data is as a stream of ASCII codes, a set of binary codes that describe each letter. A problem arises when you wish to print graphical images since each pixel must be sent just as a dot, a slow and unsatisfactory process. Another problem arises when you wish to 'control' the printer. One code will send the print carriage back to the left (a Carriage Return, ASCII character 13 decimal, 0D hex), another will advance the paper one line (a Line Feed, ASCII character 10 decimal, 0A hex), but accurate fine resolution control is difficult. Underlining or bold printing is not possible as the printer will print everything it receives. Not a useful method.

Method 2: Send plain ASCII codes to the printer with Escape sequences
This is similar to Method 1 but overcomes the problem of underlining, etc. by using special codes to tell the printer when to underline, print double high, etc. These codes use ASCII character 27 (1B in hex), the *escape*

Question 1.9.2

Referring to the list of ASCII codes and the example above, write down the sequence of codes that should be sent to the printer to

reset the printer,
set italic underlined font,
print the letters 'HNC',
set underline off.

character. For instance, if the word 'CAT' is sent to the printer, the ASCII codes would be 67 65 84, (or 43, 41, 55 in hex) the codes for C, A and T. If you wished to have this underlined you would first send the escape sequence 27 45 1 that is 'ESC','–', '1'. The printer will not try to print these codes, it will simply print everything that comes after it underlined. To turn off the underlining you would send 'ESC', '–', '0'. The full sequence to print an underlined CAT and then to turn off underlining would then be

27, 45, 49, 67, 65, 84, 27, 45, 48, in decimal
1B, 2D, 31, 43, 41, 54, 1B, 2D, 30 in hex

Other examples of escape sequences:

ESC, 'W', 1 to turn on double wide printing, ESC, 'W', 0 to turn it off
ESC, '4', 1 to turn on italic printing, ESC, '5' to release
ESC, '@' resets the printer

Methods 3 and 4: Use a page description language.
The most common method used to talk to modern printers is to *describe* the page layout and contents then send that description to the printer. The printer usually contains its own computer, which interprets the description and forms an image to be printed. This computer is sometimes more powerful than the one used for wordprocessing, etc.!

The page description could be either in the PostScript language or the Hewlett Packard language called *PCL*. However, the when page is described, it must be *rasterized*, i.e. turned into a set of dots; this is the purpose of the computer in the printer. It is possible to do this in the main PC but this slows down the PC as far as the user is concerned and generates huge amounts of data to be downloaded to the printer, further slowing down the process.

The advantage gained by using a page description language is much better control of the printed image. For instance, the original software does not need to know how to place each dot needed to form a line; only where the line starts and ends, the printer works out the placement of each dot in the line, i.e. it generates the whole line from just the end point data. This also means that the printer can hold the shape of each letter in each size (called *fonts*), so the image of each letter does not need to be sent to the printer. If unusual letters are required, they can be sent to the printer hence allowing almost unlimited printing of characters and graphics images.

Examples of both PostScript and PCL are attached.

PCL is based on or evolved from an advanced series of escape sequences but PostScript is a stack-based computer language that may be written 'by hand' or interpreted by other software. You could if you wished write programs in PostScript. Software is available (such as Ghost Script) that will form an on-screen image of the document just by using the PostScript information. A feature of PostScript is that it is not dependant on the printer resolution. This means that if you send a PostScript file to a low-resolution printer it will be rendered according to that printer. If you send the same file to a high-resolution machine you get the same image in the same proportion but looking much sharper. This is the method of choice for many DTP operations. The image is composed on a PC and checked on a local laser printer but the file is sent to a professional typesetter who would use a printer with many times the resolution.

The use of a page description language allows much better control of the printed image and is most suitable for everyday office use but do not forget that not all printers are attached to PCs or bigger machines. The printers in point of sale machines that produce till receipts still need to be controlled as do numerous other small printing devices and many of these are still dot matrix printers. Many businesses choose to keep their dot matrix printers for printing invoices instead of using laser printers, they are simple, robust and very fast for small print jobs because they do not have a long start up time.

Hex or ASCII dumps from four methods

The hexdumps shown below are what were the outputs from Wordperfect 5.1 with different printers set-up. The data in the wordprocessor was just '**This is some sample text, some of it is underlined, some of it is not**.' A dump implies that a data file has been printed in a raw state as hex bytes and as readable ASCII, with no formatting or special treatment. It is used to inspect raw data and is often very useful to help understand what has gone on or gone wrong with a process. Most dumps are like these, with 16 bytes shown in hex and the same 16 bytes shown in the right hand column in readable ASCII with CTRL characters or other non-printable characters shown as dots.

It is clear that it is *not* important to remember details shown here, just that different printers accept data in different forms to achieve similar results.

1. As printed on a printer *with no ability to format text*. Note that all underline codes, etc. are missing, only plain ASCII is present. 0D is the Carriage Return and 0A is the Line Feed character.

```
0D 0D 0A 0D 0A 0D 0A 0D 0A 0D 0A 0D 0A 20 20 20 ............
20 20 20 20 20 20 20 54 68 69 73 20 69 73 20 73 This is s
6F 6D 65 20 73 61 6D 70 6C 65 20 74 65 78 74 2C ome sample text,
20 73 6F 6D 65 20 6F 66 20 69 74 20 69 73 20 75 some of it is u
6E 64 65 72 6C 69 6E 65 64 2C 20 73 6F 6D 65 20 nderlined, some
6F 66 20 69 74 20 69 73 0D 20 20 20 20 20 20 20 of it is.
```

2. As printed on a Panasonic 1123 printer emulating a Epson LQ-850 24 pin dot-matrix printer using escape sequence control. The escape sequences are not the same as the examples above, each printer uses its own which is why a separate *printer driver* must be loaded on your machine to work properly with your printer. A printer driver 'knows' the sequences for the relevant printer.

```
1B 40 1B 36 1B 74 01 1B 52 00 1B 32 1B 6B 06 1B .@.6.t..R..2.k..
21 02 1B 78 01 1B 43 42 1B 2B FF 0A 0D 1B 2B 95 !..x..CB.+ÿ... + •
0A 0D 1B 24 3C 00 54 68 69 73 1B 24 55 00 69 73 ...$<.This.$U.is
1B 24 62 00 73 6F 6D 65 1B 24 7D 00 73 61 6D 70 .$b.some.$}.samp
6C 65 1B 24 A1 00 74 65 78 74 2C 1B 24 BB 00 73 le.$¡.text,.$≫.s
6F 6D 65 1B 24 D6 00 6F 66 66 1B 24 E4 00 69 74 1B ome.$Ö.of.$ä.it.
24 F0 00 69 73 1B 24 FD 00 75 6E 64 65 72 6C 69 $∂.is.$ÿ.underli
6E 65 64 2C 1B 24 38 01 73 6F 6D 65 1B 24 53 01 ned,.$8.some.$S.
6F 66 1B 24 61 01 69 74 1B 24 6D 01 69 73 1B 24 of.$a.it.$m.is.$
7A 01 6E 6F 74 2E 1B 24 BB 00 1B 2D 01 20 20 20 z.not..$≫..-.
20 20 20 20 20 20 20 20 20 20 20 20 20 20 20 20
```

3. As printed on a Hewlett Packard LaserJet 5L Printer using the page description language PCL5. Printer control languages actually send a great deal of data to the printer. The text printed was 'This is some sample text, some of it is underlined, some of it is not.' which is only 70 bytes long but the output to the printer produced 504 bytes of data. Note how each escape (1B hex) is followed by a sequence of control bytes, followed by the text to be printed.

```
1B 25 2D 31 32 33 34 35 58 40 50 4A 4C 20 52 44    .%-12345X"PJL RD
59 4D 53 47 20 44 49 53 50 4C 41 59 20 3D 20 22    YMSG DISPLAY = "
57 6F 72 64 50 65 72 66 65 63 74 20 4A 6F 62 22    WordPerfect Job"
0D 0A 40 50 4A 4C 20 53 45 54 20 52 45 53 4F 4C    ..@PJL SET RESOL
55 54 49 4F 4E 20 3D 20 36 30 30 0D 0A 40 50 4A    UTION = 600..@PJ
4C 20 45 4E 54 45 52 20 4C 41 4E 47 55 41 47 45    L ENTER LANGUAGE
20 3D 20 50 43 4C 0D 0A 1B 26 6C 31 6F 30 6F 31    = PCL...&l1o0o1
74 30 6C 36 64 31 58 1B 2A 72 30 46 1B 2A 63 31    t0l6d1X.*r0F.*c1
30 30 47 1B 2A 76 32 54 1B 26 6C 30 4F 1B 26 61    00G.*v2T.&l0O.&a
30 50 1B 26 6C 30 45 1B 39 1B 2A 70 30 58 1B 2A    0P.&l0E.9.*p0X.*
70 30 59 1B 28 31 30 55 1B 28 73 31 70 31 32 76    p0Y.(10U.(s1p12v
73 62 34 31 34 38 54 1B 26 6C 32 61 30 45 1B 26    sb4148T.&l2a0E.&
6C 32 68 30 45 1B 39 1B 26 6C 30 4F 1B 26 61 30    l2h0E.9.&l0O.&a0
50 1B 26 6C 30 45 1B 39 1B 2A 70 30 58 1B 2A 70    P.&l0E.9.*p0X.*p
30 59 1B 2A 70 33 33 38 59 1B 2A 70 32 32 30 58    0Y.*p338Y.*p220X
54 68 69 73 1B 2A 70 33 33 34 58 69 73 1B 2A 70    This.*p334Xis.*p
33 38 38 58 73 6F 6D 65 1B 2A 70 35 32 39 58 73    388Xsome.*p529Xs
61 6D 70 6C 65 1B 2A 70 37 30 39 58 74 65 78 74    ample.*p709Xtext
2C 1B 2A 70 38 33 34 58 1B 26 64 44 73 6F 6D 65    ,.*p834X.&dDsome
1B 2A 70 39 37 35 58 6F 66 1B 2A 70 31 30 33 39    .*p975Xof.*p1039
58 69 74 1B 2A 70 31 30 38 36 58 69 73 1B 2A 70    Xit.*p1086Xis.*p
31 31 34 30 58 75 6E 64 65 72 6C 69 6E 65 64 1B    1140Xunderlined.
26 64 40 2C 1B 2A 70 31 34 31 35 58 73 6F 6D 65    &d@,.*p1415Xsome
1B 2A 70 31 35 35 36 58 6F 66 1B 2A 70 31 36 32    .*p1556Xof.*p162
30 58 69 74 1B 2A 70 31 36 36 37 58 69 73 1B 2A    0Xit.*p1667Xis.*
70 31 37 32 31 58 6E 6F 74 2E 0C 1B 26 6C 31 68    p1721Xnot...&l1h
30 45 1B 2A 72 42 1B 26 6C 30 6C 31 68 30 0E 30    0E.*rB.&l0p1l1h0
6F 30 45 1B 28 38 55 1B 28 73 70 31 30 68 31 32    oO.(8U.(sp10h12
76 73 62 33 54 1B 26 64 40 1B 45 1B 25 2D 31 32    vsb3T.&d@.E.%-12
33 34 35 58 40 50 4A 4C 20 52 44 59 4D 53 47 20    345X@PJL RDYMSG
44 49 53 50 4C 41 59 20 3D 20 22 22 0D 0A 1B 25    DISPLAY = ""...%
```

4. As printed on a Apple LaserWriter *PostScript Printer*. Printer control languages but especially PostScript actually send a great deal of data to the printer. The text printed was '*This is some sample text, some of it is underlined, some of it is not.*' which is only 70 bytes long but the output to the printer produced 13 867 bytes of data using PostScript from the wordprocessor used, Wordperfect 5.1. When set as 10 point Courier in Word 97, this page description prints on eight A4 pages! What is shown here is only some of the data actually sent to the printer in PostScript, much of it has been left out for clarity. You can see that there is no need for a hexdump as the data is sent as a computer language in plain ASCII, i.e. a description of the results rather than the actual page.

```
%!PS-Adobe
/wpdict   120 dict def
wpdict    begin
/bdef     {bind def} bind def

/bflg     false def
/Bfont    0 def
/bon      false def
.
.
.
```

much of the 13 867 bytes of the PostScript file removed to save space.

```
.
.
.
letter usertime 5000 add {dup usertime lt {pop exit} if} loop statusdict
/manualfeed true put usertime 5000 add {dup usertime lt {pop exit} if}
loop _bp 0 13200 10200 _ornt /HelveticaR 600 _ff
0 13200 10200 _ornt
/_r  { sflg {/_t {0 rmoveto}bdef /ron false def}
     { /_S /show load def /_t {0 rmoveto}bdef /ron false def}ifelse
   }bdef
1200 11849 _m
(This)_S 67 _t
```

```
(is)_S 67 _t
(some)_S 67 _t
(sample)_S 67 _t
(text,)_S 67 _t
_U
(some)_S 67 _t
(of)_S 67 _t
(it)_S 67 _t
(is)_S 67 _t
(underlined)_S _u (,)_S 67 _t

(some)_S 67 _t
(of)_S 67 _t
(it)_S 67 _t
(is)_S 67 _t
(not.)_S _ep
statusdict /manualfeed false put _ed end end
```

1.10 Hard drives

The hard drive in a PC employs a rotating disk or disks. These disks are coated with a material that has certain magnetic properties that are persistent, i.e. once changed they stay that way for a long period until changed again. This is all that is required to store data as 1s and 0s.

The purpose of this part of the book is to provide help with the specification of devices, so the precise details of how the various types of hard drive actually work will be ignored. The most important points to note are:

- capacity;
- performance;
- cost;
- reliability;
- compatibility with other systems/components.

Although we shall ignore the fine detail, some understanding of how a drive works is required to properly understand factors in the performance of a drive. The disk rotates at a constant speed and a *read/write head* is moved to nearly any point over the surface. If fed with the correct signals, this read/write head is able to affect the magnetic coating of the disk to store a binary 1 or a binary 0 or of course to read 1s and 0s from the disk. Clearly the speed at which this read/write head can be moved over the disk surface and the speed at which it rotates will have an affect on the speed of operation. The read/write head is usually mounted on a radial arm that can swing across the disk surface as shown in Figure 1.10.1. Multiple disks are mounted one about the other and are called 'platters'. Each has two surfaces so a six platter drive will have 12 read/write heads as shown in Figure 1.10.2.

Disks are formatted into *tracks* and *sectors*. This is a process controlled by software that writes data onto the disk to allow control. Each track is concentric, the number of tracks depends on the bit density achievable on the disk, i.e. how much data can be stored in a small area. A sector is part of a track, it is usually numbered and it contains data and error checking code called a CRC. CRC is short for *Cyclic Redundancy Check*, it is used to test if data loaded from the disk has become corrupted in some way. If a drive has multiple disks or platters, the tracks are called cylinders, the read/write heads mounted on the actuator arm all move together so all the tracks of the same number are one above the other.

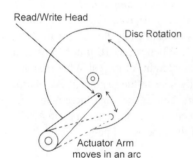

Figure 1.10.1 *Layout of simple disk drive*

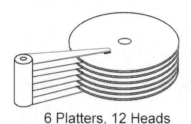

6 Platters, 12 Heads

Figure 1.10.2 *Platters and heads*

Disk performance

Amongst all the performance data for a drive that is available, there are two figures that are the most prominent, the *data transfer rate* and *average access time*.

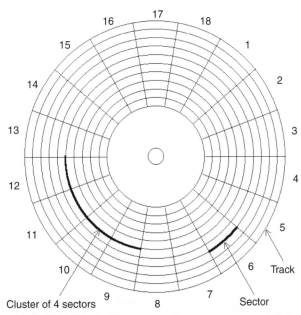

Figure 1.10.3 *Simple arrangement of tracks, sectors and clusters on a disk*

Data transfer rate

The data transfer rate is the speed that data may be read from the drive once it is spinning, the read/write head is correctly positioned and data is flowing, i.e. it is a measure that does not take into account the time to set up the reading process. Really old drives gave values of about 0.6 Mbytes/sec but newer drive can deliver 80 Mbytes/sec or more, about 130 times faster! Advertisers will often quote a *peak* transfer rate, the speed that can be achieved for a short time only. This figure is misleading, it is better to consider the *sustained transfer rate*, the speed the drive can deliver over an extended period, for instance, the time it takes to load a large file into RAM.

Average access time

If a request is made to the drive to supply data from a certain position on the disk, in all probability, the read/write head will not be in the correct place to start the read process. It must wait until the disk has rotated to the correct sector and be placed over the correct track or cylinder. It must then wait for a short time to 'settle' or for any residual movement to stop. If you measured the time it took to complete this whole process, it would not give you a useful figure as the distance the read/write head or the disk had to travel will affect the value obtained. To get around this problem, the process is tried many times; the read/write head is positioned at a random point, a data request is made and this is repeated a thousand times or more to obtain an average time. If a drive has an average access time of say 10 ms, it simply means that on average, the time from a data request to the time the data starts to flow is 10 milliseconds or 10^{-2} seconds, it tells you nothing about how fast the data will flow after that.

To get this time in proportion, consider of a disk that rotates at 3600 rev/min. 3600 rev/min = 60 rev/sec so 1 revolution takes 1/60 second or about 17 ms. Draw an imaginary line through the centre of the disk and through the centre of the read/write head; this line will cut the disk in half. Calling the halves A and B, now consider that on average, the sector that will be needed next will have a 50% chance of being in half A and a 50% chance of being in half B. It follows that the average time to access any sector will be approximately the time taken to rotate half a revolution providing the average is taken over a large number of data accesses. In this case you might expect a drive that rotates at 3600 rev/min to have an average access time of $17/2 = 8.5$ ms. The actual values are slower than this because the actuator arm travel has to be taken into account as does the 'settling time'.

If a drive has a modest data transfer rate but a fast average access time, you can be sure the advertisers will concentrate on the access time. They will say that 'drive x has a time of 8 ms which is faster than the competition value of 10 ms'. The problem you need to consider with buying or specifying drives is 'will I see a difference if I buy the 8 ms drive?' The answer depends on much more than this simple number.

In what follows, take track and cylinder to mean the same thing. Various ploys are used to improve disk performance. One is to increase the rotational speed but this is limited to the speed at which the read/write head and the associated circuits can cope with the data. Too fast and whole rotations are missed until the sector comes round again. Another ploy is to interleave sector numbering. If sector 8 is being loaded, it is a good guess that the next one that will be requested is sector 9. The trouble that once sector 8 has past the read/write head it may be just too late to request sector 9 so a complete rotation is lost. The answer is to number the sectors so they are 'interleaved', i.e. sector 9 is not next to sector 8 but is the next but one. Now when reading sector 8, after is has past, there is enough time within one rotation to request sector 9. A third ploy is called cylinder skewing. In a problem related to the need to interleave, the read/write head must change track at some point to get to the next sector. If the sector numbering goes say 0–25 then 0–25 in the same pattern on the next track, any read that needs sectors 23, 24, 25 then 0, 1, 2, etc. on the next track will result in waiting a full rotation between sectors 25 and 0 as the time it takes to move the actuator arm with the read/write head to the next track is too slow. Again, a full rotation is missed. Cylinder skewing simply aligns each sector 0 on a track differently from its closest neighbour, i.e. it is skewed. The result is a performance increase because the data can be read uninterrupted by track changes.

Disk addressing

The actual sectors on a disk are addressed according to the *cylinder* (or track of one disk), head number and sector number. This is called *CHS addressing* and is what happens inside the drive. Outside and as far as the operating system is concerned, the sectors are most often addressed by their *Logical Block Address* or LBA. The LBA is a simple number starting from 0 and counting all the available sectors. The drive hardware translates the LBA into the actual CHS. This has great advantages over the older system when the operating system itself used CHS, each drive had to be installed according to the number of heads, cylinders and sectors, the sector size (usually 512 bytes) and a few other parameters. You can see these old types listed in the BIOS of a PC as drive type 1 to drive type 46. Type 47 drives are those that are 'user definable'. Thankfully, all that is history. Logical Block Addressing means that drive makers are free to optimize their drives, have any combination of number of heads, cylinders, sectors, etc. and still be compatible with the PC and the operating system. Looked at another way, it places the responsibility of optimum use of the disk with the disk maker not the operating system programmer.

Disk cache

A disk can seem to be very fast if disk caching is present and active. This is a technique that copies sections of the disk into a buffer area in RAM on the assumption that it will be needed. If a subsequent data request for what is already in the cache, it is loaded from there so giving a very fast response. The disk cache can be either on the hard drive itself or in main RAM, if it is on the hard drive the maximum speed it limited by the drive interface, if it is main RAM, it is only limited by the RAM system itself.

Partitioning the disk

In the past, individual physical disks were addressed directly as single devices. This is often inconvenient so modern disks can be divided into logical sections called partitions. In this way a single physical drive can appear to be several different drives. Original DOS drives had a 16-bit FAT which imposes a size limit by having $2^{16} = 65\,536$ addressable elements. As explained below, the only way to address larger disks with a 16-bit FAT is to use cluster sizes greater than 1. This results in inefficient use of disk space so partitioning a larger disk into smaller logical drives can make more efficient use of the disk space, each partition will have its own FAT. The same efficient use of the disk space can be achieved by using a 32-bit FAT. Many people find that multiple disk partitions are a convenient way of organizing their software and data.

Drive interfaces

An important factor in determining disk performance is the *interface* used to connect the drive to the PC. The two competing interfaces that dominate the PC market are *IDE/ATA* and *SCSI*. Broadly, IDE/ATA drives offer a good speed at low cost, SCSI offers higher speed and the ability to address other devices but at a higher price. For this reason, most PCs are fitted with IDE/ATA interfaces but those required for performance critical applications are fitted with SCSI drives.

Key fact

'Standards'

First a note about names and 'standards' in the computing business. A 'standard' is really an agreement usually written and published by a approved organization. International bodies such as the ISO do a great deal in this area. There exists a problem in the computing industry, there are many '*de facto*' standards, i.e. standards that exist 'in fact' but have not been agreed internationally, they are simply adopted. This approach is fine except that anyone can modify the 'standard' and still claim they are conforming. This leads to an ever growing list of 'standard' names which can and often does lead to confusion. This is especially true with disk drive interfaces.

IDE/ATA interface

You will see many adverts for *IDE drives*, a term that was originally used to differentiate the old drives that used a separate controller board from the (then) new *Integrated Drive Electronics* (IDE) drives. The trouble is, other devices also have 'integral' electronics so the term is of little use. Drives that are called IDE are really using the 'AT Attachment' standard so should be called ATA but most adverts use the term IDE. IDE/ATA is by far the most popular interface commonly available but variations are also known as ATA, EIDE, ATA-2, Fast ATA or Ultra ATA. The ATA Packet Interface or ATAPI is an extension that allows connection to CD-ROM drives, etc.

Original ATA

The original IDE/ATA supported two hard disks that worked with 'Programmable I/O' or PIO modes and DMA.

ATA-2

With increasing performance demands the next standard, ATA-2 was brought out to support faster PIO, LBA and several other enhancements that need not concern us here. Ignoring a few minor details, ATA-2 is the same as Fast ATA, Fast ATA-2, or Enhanced IDE (EIDE). The differences are those between different manufactures and is an example of a 'standard' being applied differently!

ATA-3

ATA-3 is an improvement to ATA-2 that introduces Self-Monitoring Analysis and Reporting Technology (SMART). Although often confused with it, ATA-3 is not the same as Ultra ATA.

Ultra ATA

Ultra ATA (also called F, ATA-33, DMA-33, etc.) is an even faster interface that uses a 33.3 Mbytes/sec transfer mode using DMA. Ultra ATA is backwards compatible with previous ATA interfaces, so if you fit an Ultra ATA drive to a board that does not support the faster mode, it will still work at the slower speed.

ATAPI

The original ATA would not support CD-ROM drivers or floppy disks so the *ATA Packet Interface* (ATAPI) was introduced to bring the advantage of one standard to cover all the common drives. To make this work, an ATAPI driver must be installed; this is a piece of software called a 'device driver', and it communicates with devices using 'packets' of data. This is because CD-ROMs are quite unlike hard drives in their method of working so software makes up the difference.

PIO

IDE/ATA drives support both PIO and DMA transfer modes. Programmed I/O (PIO) is performed by the main CPU, it requires no support software but ties up the CPU when I/O is in progress. There are several PIO 'modes', each newer than the last, the fastest of which is supported by the latest IDE/ATA drives. As a performance comparison these modes gives maximum transfer rates of

PIO Mode 0	3.3 Mbytes/sec
PIO Mode 1	5.2 Mbytes/sec
PIO Mode 2	8.3 Mbytes/sec
PIO Mode 3	11.1 Mbytes/sec
PIO Mode 4	16.6 Mbytes/sec

DMA

Direct memory access or DMA achieves data transfer without the CPU, either using the old (and rather limited) DMA chips fitted as standard to all PCs or using bus mastering of the PCI bus.

DMA Mode

Single word 0	2.1 Mbytes/sec (no longer used)
Single word 1	4.2 Mbytes/sec (no longer used)
Single word 2	8.3 Mbytes/sec (no longer used)
Multiword 0	4.2 Mbytes/sec
Multiword 1	13.3 Mbytes/sec
Multiword 2	16.6 Mbytes/sec
Multiword 3	33.3 Mbytes/sec (DMA-33)

Do not think that PIO mode 4 and DMA Multiword 2 will give the same overall performance. Both achieve 16.6 Mbytes/sec but the PIO mode ties up the CPU whereas the DMA mode allows the CPU to complete other tasks at the same time, for instance, if an AGP device is fitted. However, an average user will probably not see this performance improvement, it will only be when heavy demands are made on the disk that such things will be useful. The disadvantage of using bus mastering is the added complexity of getting the devices and associated software to work properly.

Small Computer Systems Interface

In contrast with ATA, the Small Computer Systems Interface (SCSI) interface did not start in the PC world nor is it a disk drive interface, it is a standard that is used in Unix machines and others to achieve a fast and flexible means of data transfer between devices. Hard disks are only one of a range of devices that are 'skuzzy' compatible.

SCSI suffers from a similar problem to IDE/ATA, there are too many standards or names giving rise to considerable confusion in the marketplace.

There are main standards, SCSI-1, SCSI-2 and SCSI-3, that are compatible, i.e. older devices that conform to SCSI-1 will work on SCSI-2 adapters.

Table 1.10.1   *Main SCSI parameters*

	Bus width	Transfer rate Mbyte/sec	Bus speed MHz	Number of devices per bus
Regular SCSI-1	8 bits	4.77	5	8
Wide SCSI-2	16 bits	$2 \times 4.77 = 9.54$	5	16
Fast SCSI-2	8 bits	$2 \times 4.77 = 9.54$	10	8
Fast wide SCSI-2	16 bits	$2 \times 9.54 = 19$	10	16
Ultra SCSI-3	8 bits	$2 \times 9.54 = 19$	20	8
Ultra wide SCSI-3	16 bits	$2 \times 19 = 38$	20	16

SCSI-1

SCSI-1 defined a basic 8-bit bus (now called a 'narrow' bus), a 5 MHz bus and 4.77 Mbyte/sec transfer rate.

SCSI-2

SCSI-2 is an extension of SCSI-1 giving a 10 MHz bus, an increased bus width from the original 8-bit SCSI bus to 16 bits and support for 16 devices. It also defines new higher-density connections; unfortunately SCSI has suffered from a large range of 'standard' cables. If you look at hardware suppliers catalogues, you will see a large range of them! A 32-bit bus is defined and is called very wide SCSI but is not in common use.

SCSI-3

SCSI-3 is yet another extension giving a 20 MHz bus, improved Cabling enabling 'wide' SCSI (i.e. not 8 bit!) and for the first time, SCSI-3 contains the new serial SCSI, also called Firewire.

There are three different bus speeds used in SCSI, 5, 10 and 20 MHz, there is the slow and fast SCSI, all this gives rise to some confusion in the marketplace to add to the problems with cabling.

Table 1.10.1 shows a summary of SCSI speeds.

SCSI adapters

Because SCSI is an interface standard rather than a disk drive interface, there is no point in building the SCSI interface into the drive as is the practice with IDE/ATA drives.

The interface is usually on an expansion or accessory card connected either to the (old) ISA bus or more usually to the PCI bus. This expansion card is called a host adapter. Expansion cards connected to the PCI local bus support the use of bus mastering.

Comparative performance of SCSI and IDE/ATA

Some people will say that 'SCSI is better than IDE'. Whilst it is possible to demonstrate that SCSI is faster in some circumstances, in practice the difference is harder to pin down.

- The actual disk drives spin at comparable speeds so the time to get to and access a sector should be the same.

- The fastest SCSI bus is the ultra wide SCSI, which has a maximum transfer rate of 40 Mbytes/sec. This is better than the best IDE/ATA rate of 33 Mbytes/sec. As 40 is only 20% faster than 33, it is unlikely the difference will be spotted except when using demanding applications and they are being timed. It must also be remembered that 40 Mbytes/sec is the maximum of the SCSI interface and not necessarily that of the drive and interface together.
- The SCSI interface has a high 'overhead', i.e. it is much more complex than the IDE/ATA interface; more processing takes place. For this reason, if you ran a comparison of a single IDE/ATA drive running simple tasks against a SCSI drive fitted in an otherwise identical machine, the IDE/ATA drive may well perform better because the interface can react quicker.
- SCSI allows multitasking unlike ATA, so in set-ups with multiple disks that require simultaneous access, SCSI will handle multiple tasks better.
- In PCs fitted with IDE/ATA drives that support bus mastering, the difference between SCSI and IDE/ATA is less marked. In practice, not that many IDE/ATA drives are actually using bus mastering but this situation is likely to change as better device drivers and drives become available.

In summary, for PCs with single drives for desktop use, specify IDE/ATA because it is fast and cheap. For PCs with multiple disks that run demanding tasks or are used as a server, use SCSI.

Size limits

There are various factors that limit the size of disk that can be handled in a given PC. Most modern PCs take drives that are large enough for common applications and plenty of data but if you need more information it can be found on www.pcguide.com/ref/hdd/bios/size.htm.

High-level formatting

Operating systems must use at least one method to keep track of files on a disk. Although disks are formatted with tracks and sectors (the so-called low-level format), there is nothing about this structure that organizes files and directories (directories are called folders in Windows). This organization of files and directories is a function of the operating system, i.e. it is controlled entirely by software, the hardware plays no part at all in the *organization* although clearly it actually executes the task.

There are many different ways to arrange this organization but it is not the intention of this part of the book to describe them all. The section in Appendix D describes one of the simplest and almost certainly the most common, Microsoft DOS File Allocation Table. Operating systems like Windows NT are able to read and write to different disk filing systems whereas older operating systems use only their own. The purpose of the appendix is simply to illustrate the problems that must be solved.

1.11 CD-ROM and DVD drives

CDs work by storing large numbers of 1s and 0s as 'pits' in an optically reflective surface. Unlike hard drives, the 'tracks' are one continuous spiral and the rotational speed of the disk is adjusted to give a constant linear speed past the read head. This is called CLV or *Constant Linear*

Velocity. Hard drives use CAV or *Constant Angular Velocity*, i.e. the rotational speed is constant and the nearer the outside the read/write head is, the faster the linear speed past the head. You can hear the CD-ROM drive change speed as it works, indicating that the read head is moving in or out.

There are many different formats of CD, they conform to standards that are in 'books' named after colours, so you get 'orange book' for CD-R and CD-RW disks or 'red book' for audio or CD-DA disks. This unit of the HNC Computing does not cover such detail except that a drive must conform to a given standard to be useful. For instance, if you buy a CD-RW compatible drive, it will play CD-DA (audio) disks but beware, not all drives support all formats. The actual situation in the marketplace is far from standardized. Likewise, DVD is far from having common standards that are 'standard', i.e. work universally. DVD now stands for *Digital Versatile Disk* but did not start out like that, it was called a *Digital Video Disk*, an indication of the lack of standardization. The original format was for video data but now sound and data are to be found on DVD. Hopefully the 'standards' will become more standard in the near future. Older CD-ROM drives cannot read more modern formats.

Speed

You will have seen advertisements for '×32' or '×40' CD-ROM drives. This refers to the original speed of 150 Kbytes/sec drive. A '40 times' or '×40' drive should deliver a data transfer rate of $150 \times 40 = 6000$ Kbytes/sec or 5.86 Mbytes/sec. The drive listed below is a '×48' version so will provide $150 \times 48 = 7200$ Kbytes/sec. Do not be fooled by this number. It is the maximum the drive can deliver not the actual rate you will get once the drive has spun up to speed, the head has found the data you want and it has started flowing.

The average access time, just like hard drives, is the average time it takes to start delivering data after a data request has been made. Again, this figure is often misleading. Unlike hard drives, CD-ROM drives stop rotating soon after use, so if you measure the actual access time from a stationary disk, the result will be in whole seconds! The spin-up time increases as the 'times' speed increases to a '×48' drive will take longer to spin up to the high speed it needs before the data starts flowing. If your application accesses the CD infrequently, the spin-up time will dominate the average access time but will not figure in the specification at all.

A typical CD-ROM specification would look like this:

1. ATAPI-IDE interface
2. Supports Enhanced-IDE
3. ATAPI compatible
4. Supports ISO 9660 (High Sierra), CD-I, VCD, Multisession
5. Photo CD, CD+, CD-extra, i-trax, CD-UDF, CD-R, CD-RW
6. CD-DA, CD-ROM (mode 1 and 2) format
7. Supports Multiread, CD-RW format
8. Supports Multiread function packet writing format
9. Supports Digital Audio Extraction
10. High-speed audio playback
11. Supports Ultra-DMA mode 2

12. 48× speed drive with maximum 7200 Kbytes/sec transfer rate
13. Average access time: less than 80 ms.

Points 1, 2, 3 and 11 refer to the ATA interface that the drive can use. (See the section on hard drives.)

Points 4–10 refer to the format of CDs to be used. It will play audio disks, record on CD-R and CD-RW disks, play the Kodak Photo CDs, etc.

Point 12 gives the 'times' speed.

Point 13 gives the average access time in milliseconds.

DVD speeds are not the same as CD-ROM speeds, so a '×6' DVD is not slower than the '×48' CD-ROM. A '×6' DVD should be able to deliver 8100 Kbytes/sec or six times 1350 Kbytes/sec. At this rate a DVD will be 8100/150 = 54 times the CD-ROM speed. Note from the specification below that when reading CD-ROMs and not DVDs, the data transfer rate is a lot lower.

A typical DVD specification would look like this:

1. 6 × (8100 Kbytes/sec) maximum speed at DVD-ROM drive
2. 32 × (4800 Kbytes/sec) maximum speed at CD-ROM drive
3. ATAPI/E-IDE interface
4. Supports PIO mode 4/Multiword DMA mode 2/Ultra-DMA 33
5. Compatible with CD-DA, CD-ROM/XA, Karaoke, CD/Video CD, CD-I/FMV, Single/Multisession photo CD, Enhanced CD and CD-RW
6. Interface type: E-IDE/ATAPI
7. Data transfer rate: 8100 Kbytes/sec maximum at DVD-ROM drive, 4800 Kbytes/sec maximum at CD-ROM drive
8. Average access time: 120 ms at DVD-ROM drive, 90 ms at CD-ROM drive
9. Disk formats: DVD single layer/dual layer, DVD-R, DVD-RW, CD-ROM, CD-ROM/XA, CD-R (CD-WO), CD-I/FMV, Single/Multisession photo CD, Enhanced CD.

Compare this specification with the one for the CD-ROM

CD-ROMs and DVDs either use the ATAPI or SCSI interface. SCSI is better for CD-RW because it offers multitasking and therefore does not interfere with the flow of data to the disk. If you are recording with a CD-RW disk on an ATAPI interface, it is often better not to use the PC for any other task as the recording process is time critical. If other tasks are running that might slow down the flow of data to the writing software, *buffer under-runs* can occur. CDs need a constant stream of data when writing. This data is stored temporarily in a buffer (a piece of memory), ready to write to the disk. If this buffer runs out of data, the disk cannot be fed with a constant stream so the writing process fails. This is called a buffer under-run.

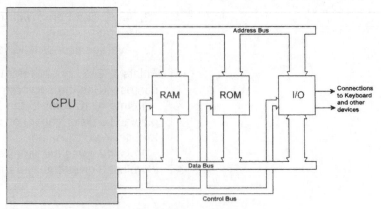

Figure 1.12.1 *A simple microcomputer architecture*

1.12 Computer performance

A human model of CPU performance

The classical model of a simple microcomputer is shown in the diagram below. The effect of this design may not be obvious from the start but the most important thing to notice is that the Central Processor (CPU) is separate from the memory (RAM). This results in the unfortunate fact that the program to be run must be fetched into the processor before the CPU knows what to do and it must be fetched in pieces. With normal programs, in no sense is the whole program ever found inside the CPU. This has quite a profound effect on the performance of the microcomputer because no matter how fast the CPU executes each instruction, the speed at which instructions are fetched from the RAM may well limit the speed at which the whole program is executed.

In this simple model, the processor fetches one instruction, decodes it, then executes it. It then fetches the next instruction, decodes and executes it and so on in an 'endless' sequence. Newer processors fetch instructions a few at a time and these can be executing whilst the processor fetches some more at the same time. Although this provides a very large increase in speed over the old designs, the fact remains that instructions in RAM must be fetched before they can be executed.

Computer performance, an analogy

Warning. Analogies such as this cannot be taken too far. For it to be of use, the humans involved are *not* using their own intelligence, they are simply following instructions blindly, acting as parts of a machine.

Imagine you were in a room with your friend, Fred and you are to perform a calculation. You are the processor, the 'CPU', Fred is the memory or RAM. You must ignore the fact that have intelligence and remember that you do not know what job is required of you; you can add, divide, multiply, keep a note of where you put answers, etc. but you cannot see the whole problem. Your friend Fred, in the same room, knows that a job must be completed but he does not know how to do it, all he knows is that the instructions are written down. He can read the written list of instructions from a reference book. It might go something like this.

Fred opens a tax reference book, finds the correct part then reads to you:

1. take the salary of £20 000;
2. subtract £5400;
3. remember what is left;
4. subtract 23% of this amount;
5. if 6% of what is left over is greater than £1250 then subtract £1250 otherwise subtract 6%;
6. Finally add £5400 to what is left;
7. divide it by 12;
8. tell me the result.

Points to note

The formal list of instructions is the program, it contains the problem.
You are the 'CPU', you do the calculating but do not have a complete picture of the problem.
The *written list* of instructions is the 'RAM'.
Your friend Fred is the connection between the RAM and you, i.e. he is the 'Bus'.

Now consider these points:

1. On a second run through the program, you perform the individual calculations faster but Fred reads them at the same speed, would the overall problem be solved quicker? No it would not, the speed is limited by either the 'RAM' speed or the 'Bus' speed even though you, the CPU, is now quicker.
2. On a third run through the program, if Fred reads the next instruction before you have finished the previous calculation, the speed of execution of the whole problem is now limited by the 'CPU' speed.
3. As a reminder, do not take this analogy too far!

Simple and some more complex computers are like this, the speed of execution depends on more than the speed of the processor. The message is, when you buy a PC, do not be overawed by the processor clock speed, the speed of the whole machine relies on more than this.

Caching

In old PCs with simple processors, the speed was limited more by the RAM because the processor could run faster. Processor design far outstripped the improvements in RAM speed. Modern PCs have RAM that is not all that much faster. How can they offer such a large increase in performance? This is achieved by *caching*. In our analogy, if Fred were to write the program down on a convenient piece of paper before execution then put the main book away, he would be able to access the 'program' quicker rather than looking it up in a book. Of course larger problems would not fit on his piece of paper but most of the time a useful speed increase would be achieved. Attached to a modern processor, there is a small amount of high-speed RAM that is used for this purpose, it is much faster than the main RAM. This is called level 1 or L1 caching.

A second and even better speed increase could be achieved by copying parts of the program onto smaller pieces of paper in your hand, i.e. in the 'CPU'. These are only small pieces of paper but the execution speed is now limited by how fast you can do the calculations, you need not wait for Fred to read them. The problem is that not all the program can be on your piece of paper. Fred must ensure that the next part of the program is available when you need it by copying it whilst you are doing the actual calculations. This is level 2 or L2 caching and is one of the reasons why modern machines are so fast. Caching is what squirrels do, in autumn they hide acorns in a cache for use later on in the winter. This is a similar idea because instructions are put into a cache for use a little later on.

Clock speed

The next thing to consider is the clock speed. In our analogy, the clock speed is roughly equivalent to the time that elapsed between the execution of each simple instruction. A processor does things step by step at a constant speed so if you have a 2 GHz processor, this is doing simple things 2000 million times a second. Although in human terms this seems impossibly fast, remember that each thing that is being done is as simple as 'add 3' or 'store a number', nothing as complex as 'check this spelling'. It does not matter what software is running, it is all made up of very simple machine level instructions called Machine Code. That includes Windows! When Windows is running, the processor cannot tell as all it does is to execute millions of simple instructions. A different analogy is one of bricks making up a building. If you imagine the detail required to understand how a single brick takes part in a building, when you consider Windows in the same analogy you would look at the design of a whole town not just a brick. Machine Code, as far as the processor is concerned, is just a vast array of 'bricks', Windows is the whole town.

What is meant by the term 'speed' in a computer?

If you look at advertisements you will find that companies selling computers quote the CPU speed and expect people to know how fast the machine is from that. For instance, you may think that a 2 GHz Pentium-based PC is 'faster' than a 1.7 GHz Pentium PC. The trouble is that it is often not true. The time taken by a computer to complete a task depends on many factors.

What most non-technical people mean by speed is 'how fast the computer will do a task just for me'. Many of these people would not know or care about the CPU speed. One of these users might be using a large database in which case the main speed of the 'computer' will be limited by the disk drive and memory systems. Another user may be playing a game, the speed here is at least partly limited by the video system.

Imagine you had to describe the complete performance of a car with just *one number*, is it possible? No, in real life it is not possible to define just one such number or *performance indicator*. A Formula 1 racing car may be able to reach 200 mph but if used on a rough farm track competing in a rally it would go several yards before getting stuck in the mud, even a Tractor would be faster! The problem is not just the power of the car, it is the whole design of the vehicle. One car may go very fast in a straight line but slowly around corners, a different car may do well on the corners but slow down the straight. Could you predict which one would win a race without knowing if the race track had lots of corners? No. The problem with defining the speed of the computer is much more complex even than this; you must realize that just quoting the CPU clock speed is almost useless as a measure of speed. There is perhaps one exception to this, modern PCs with faster CPUs tend to be fitted with faster subsystems so may be faster almost by default.

The speed of the processor

If a PC has a Pentium 2 GHz processor fitted it means that the chip is *clocked* or pulsed 2000 million times a second. On almost each one of these clock cycles, a low-level or machine instruction is completed. A typical instruction may be 'store number in memory' or 'add one number'. This means the number of machine level instructions performed per second is *roughly* 2000 million or 2000 MIPS. Something complicated like putting a single character on the screen takes more than one instruction, a task like moving a paragraph in a wordprocessor takes hundreds of machine instructions. Clearly the faster the CPU executes these instructions the better but there is a problem, the instructions are stored in memory so if the CPU needs them in a hurry, the memory system must be able to supply them at speed. The problem is, it can't! To be affordable, the RAM fitted to most machines is far too slow to supply instructions to the CPU. The solution is to copy a block of instructions to a 'cache' and the CPU looks in the cache for them. This cache is faster than the RAM and can (nearly) keep up with the CPU. Defining processor speed in MIPS is only a very crude measure of speed.

MIPS is an acronym for million instructions per second. An old measure of a computer's speed and power, MIPS measures roughly the number of machine instructions that a computer can execute in 1 second. However, different instructions require more or less time than others, and there is no standard method for measuring MIPS. In addition, MIPS refers only to the CPU speed, whereas real applications are generally limited by other factors, such as I/O speed. A machine with a high MIPS rating, therefore, might not run a particular application any faster than a machine with a low MIPS rating. For all these reasons, MIPS ratings are not used often anymore. In fact, some people jokingly claim that MIPS really stands for Meaningless Indicator of Performance.

Some processors have a Complex Instruction Set (CISC) and some have a Reduced Instruction Set (RISC). You could compare the speed of two processors with the same clock speed, one a RISC chip and the other a CISC chip. The problem is that such a comparison of the MIPS is completely meaningless unless you happen to want to sell computers to a gullible public and are happy telling straight lies! The reason is that a single instruction in a RISC processor may achieve more than a single instruction in the CISC processor so you find that a 30 MHz RISC machine executes a whole program faster than a 100 MHz CISC machine. The lesson is, do not compare clock speeds unless the processor has more or less the same design.

The speed of the internal buses

The computer uses *buses* to communicate between devices. These are simply collections of wires that transmit the pattern of 1s and 0s that represent the data and instructions. These buses operate on a clocked system, i.e. many times a second a signal is generated in the chipset that sets off one operation at a time. The buses in common PCs all operate slower than the CPU, typically 'only' 100 MHz or 100 million times a second. The result is that only a certain amount of data can be transmitted per second no matter how fast the CPU. This data may be on its way to the disk drive or the video system and hence some tasks are limited by the bus speed.

The speed of the disk drive system

Disks spin at a fixed speed so the maximum rate at which data can be delivered to or from a disk is partly the result of this speed. If you fit a faster CPU, the rate at which the data comes from a disk drive is not affected.

The speed of the video system

To view the result of running a program, the video system must display a large collection of dots called *pixels*. A screen with a resolution of 1024 by 768 is showing over ¾ of a million pixels, each one must be handled by the video system. If you increase the screen resolution to 1280 by 1024 you will now have over 1.3 million pixels or 66% more so it must take more time to compute the colour of each one. The video system in modern machines have their own dedicated set of chips to do this but some video systems are faster than others, this is not affected by the speed of the CPU.

The speed set in the power save system

If you have ever worked with a laptop computer you will have noticed that to save battery life the disk slows down after a short period of inactivity. If you want your machine to do a task, the disk must then spin up to speed before it starts. This will give the impression that the machine is quite slow, regardless of the speed of the CPU.

Summary

The only effective measure of speed is to run tasks that you require of the computer and to compare one machine with another. Some performance charts in computer journals demonstrate this technique. They would typically run these tasks:

- A large spreadsheet that requires loading and recalculation.
- Transformation of a large graphics image.
- Running a standard database enquiry on a large database.

The results are then displayed as a table. It is often the case that one machine will outperform the others in one task but not others.

Beware of adverts!

Other terms found in describing speed

- FLOPS = *Floating Point Operations per Second*, a common benchmark measurement for rating the speed of microprocessors. As we have seen, the CPU speed alone does not tell you everything about the performance of a whole computer.
- MFLOPS = Mega FLOPS or Million FLOPS, GFLOPS = Giga FLOPS or 1000 Million Flops (1 000 000 000), TFLOPS = Tera FLOPS or Million Million Flops (1 000 000 000 000). Floating-point numbers are those with decimal fractions. Integers whole numbers only.

Floating-point operations include any operations that involve fractional numbers. Such operations, which take much longer to compute than integer operations, occur often in some applications. Most modern microprocessors include a *floating-point unit* (FPU), which is a specialized part of the microprocessor responsible for executing floating-point operations. The FLOPS measurement, therefore, actually measures the speed of the FPU. One of the most common benchmark tests used to measure FLOPS is called Linpack. Many experts feel that FLOPS is not a relevant measurement because it fails to take into account factors such as the condition under which the microprocessor is running (e.g. heavy or light loads) and which exact operations are included as floating-point operations. For this reason, a consortium of vendors created the Standard Performance Evaluation Corporation (SPEC), which provides more meaningful benchmark values. Their Web URL is www.specbench.org/contents.html but many of the ideas shown are very technical and are not part of this unit.

1.13 User requirements

When considering the specification of PCs and associated equipment, there is more to consider than the machine itself. How do you know if you need the wonderful model on sale for £2000 or the lesser model selling for £500? A very large reason for the ever increasing power of computers being purchased is caused by 'upgradeitus'. Some people will buy the latest computer/software simply because it is available. Operating systems like Windows are very hungry for disk space and RAM and work very slowly unless run in a very powerful machine. People often lose sight of the fact that Windows and many Windows applications offer features most do not even realize are present let alone use on need. In a competitive commercial environment, a sound knowledge of why computers and software are specified is very important. There is no real point in upgrading a system just because it becomes available. As an example, if an application in one office is running perfectly well using an old 80286 PC running MSDOS and a dot-matrix printer, why change it? What *need* is there to change? Simply upgrading the computer is very easy as is upgrading the software but successfully running and paying for the change in work practice and staff training is often very expensive and can be difficult.

Cost of ownership

In order to own and run computers in a business for a period of time, the following items of value must be considered:

- Hardware
- Software licences
- Staff training

- Installation and maintenance
- Business specific data and documents
- Staff experience and knowledge

Which of these is higher? After working for some time, much data is generated in the normal course of the business and much knowledge and experience of the computer systems is built up in the staff. After a very short time, this data and staff knowledge is much more valuable than the costs of the computers. Although the ongoing cost of IT support and maintenance is high, the value of the staff knowledge is probably greater. The cost of the hardware is often the lowest of these and its value falls to zero in a very short time.

It is not sensible to upgrade unless there is a clear business need.

Over the last few years, companies like Microsoft, Lotus, Corel, etc. have put more and more features into their software. This has resulted in the perceived 'need' to upgrade the machines and staff training, often without any real thought. It is interesting to note that the 'Cost of ownership' issue has become very prominent in recent times and that these software companies have started to change their policies, making their software easier to use rather than having more features that require ever more powerful machines.

The graph below (Figure 1.13.1) shows typical proportions of the cost of ownership found in many companies. The cost of the machines themselves is just a fifth of the total. Simply upgrading machines, then the software often causes grief for no real benefit to the organization because the extra training required and the cost of data conversion outweigh any benefits of newer machines. It makes sense to 'over specify' for a new installation so the machines will perform well for a reasonable period but it does not always make sense to upgrade when new hardware or software become available.

General guidelines

Microprocessor

Do not get overawed by CPU clock speeds. In practice, you are very unlikely to see the difference between a 1.7 and a 2 GHz machine, 2 is

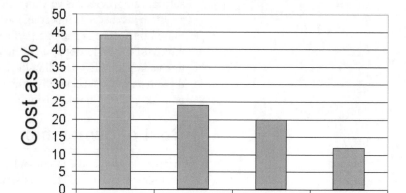

Figure 1.13.1   *An analysis of the cost of ownership*

only $2/1.7 = 1.176$ or about 18% faster and the overall speed of a machine is a result of much more than the CPU speed. Machines fitted with faster CPUs are generally fitted with faster sub-systems at the same time so naïve users may be fooled into thinking it is all due to the heavily advertised processor 'inside'.

RAM

If running Microsoft Windows as a desktop operating system, performance improves up to about 128 Mbytes of RAM. Fitting above this is not likely to show a marked improvement unless the applications to be run all need simultaneous open windows or are themselves very demanding on memory. Running a PC as a server is very different but is not in the scope of this part of the book. You will probably not see much difference between the latest RAM types unless you enjoy running benchmark software or timing long tasks with a stopwatch.

Video

The amount of RAM fitted to the video card depends on what you need the machine for. Running standard office applications does not require animated 3D so you calculate the RAM required from the resolution you intend to set. Many people do not like the highest resolution set for office applications, they cannot see the screen fonts, so if the target is the typical 800×600 you will see no benefit from an 8 Mbyte video card. If you plan 3D applications and high-speed animated games, more video RAM the better but you will only see the benefit if the software designers make use of the hardware. More memory will have no effect on older software.

Monitor

Buy a good one! For the overall experience of using a PC, it is better to have a good stable image with crisp resolution and well-saturated colours than something that is a few percent faster. Spend the money you save by not specifying the 'latest, fastest processor' on the monitor. Users will thank you for it. If you run a price comparison on machines with the latest CPU you will see the price rise dramatically towards the faster end of the market. If one machine is 50% more expensive but only 20% faster, spend the difference on the monitor.

Disk drive

A while ago it was thought you could not buy a disk that was too large! This was mainly due to the ever increasing size of the software and data files. Now that MP3, graphics and video are becoming more important, it looks like the demand for disk space will now be caused more by your data than the software. At one extreme, if you are only using the machine for typing plain text and you type at a good 'office' speed of 45 words a minute all day and all night, 7 days a week without a break for 40 years, apart from being tired and hungry, you will still only generate less than 5 Gbytes of data! At the other extreme, you are likely to fill a 60 Gbytes drive very quickly if you store MP3, graphics and video files. One hour of full broadcast quality video can be stored on a 10 Gbyte drive. The best option is to go for size and only buy the more expensive fast drives if the applications *really* need it.

Floppy disk drive

Almost every PC has one, it is hardly ever used but as soon as you specify a machine without a floppy drive, someone will arrive with an important file on a floppy.

CD-ROM

Almost all PCs are fitted with a CD-ROM or DVD drive. CD-R is now cheap and is an excellent system for backups of key data. Unless the budget is very tight, specify a CD-RW compatible drive wherever possible and use it for CD-R writing. DVD drives are gaining acceptance and offer much larger capacity but most software is still distributed on CD. Speed is only an issue if you will use the drive as a continuous source of data; software installation speed is not seriously limited by CD-ROM drive speed. Buy quality rather than speed.

Sound

Specify the cheapest possible sound if the system is for office use. Most users turn it off after a while, especially if the office is open plan. If you need good quality sound to support games or to edit music, etc., it is better to output sound to a sound system than to spend on expensive PC speakers. In this case, buy a high quality sound card and leave the speakers in the shop.

Modem

Modems will soon be a thing of the past, at least that will be true if most people use broadband ADSL or cable modem connections. People who use laptops 'on the move' from hotel rooms, etc. will still need a modem, at least until these places have broadband connections. Most offices use a direct LAN connection. Until this happens, 56K modems are adequate. Buy quality and avoid the 'plain wrapper' kind.

A Modem is a 'MOdulator–DEModulator'. In English to *modulate* means to change (like modify). The old telephone system (known to some as POTS, *Plain Old Telephone System!*) could carry only analogue sound signals. It was not possible to put a digital signal through such a system. Modern digital telephone systems are very different but Modems were designed for the POTS. A modem modulated a sound with digital information and de-modulated this sound for the received signals. The speed of a modem is given in bits/second, most are now 56 Kbits/sec. As each byte is encoded in either 9 or 10 bits, this means a 56K modem will transmit about 5.6 Kbytes of data per second in an ideal world. Real world rates are nearly always slower and having CPUs that are claimed to 'speed up the Internet' will make no difference at all!

Printer

Printers. For home or SOHO use, inkjets are fine; they are expensive to run if your output is high and are not as reliable as laser printers. For office use, the only real choice is a laser printer, they are fast, quiet and reasonably cheap to run. Even for small offices, a printer with a large paper capacity will be appreciated by the users. (SOHO means *Small Office Home Office*.)

How to specify and buy a computer

First, clearly specify why you need a computer, what do you want to do with it and who needs to be able to share your data. Next, decide on your budget.

The next step is to decide on what software you will need to satisfy your business needs and only then to specify what hardware is required to run that software. It is a great mistake to think 'I will need a 3 GHz Pentium' just because they are available and heavily advertised.

Make sure that your user's or customer's requirements are *fully* met. For instance, one customer of the author (a travel tour operator) still uses a mixture of '486' and Pentium 100 machines running Windows 95 and 98. This is simply because, (1) they still work, (2) the specific software and hardware they use will not run under Windows XP. Specifying modern PCs may be a mistake. Even if you convince the hardware vendor to supply without Microsoft operating systems, the hardware sub-systems may not be compatible with the software, e.g. you may not be able to get Windows 98 (required for some old software) to run modern hardware. Even if you manage to get a modern machine and to 'upgrade' their old software, now you have an increased training cost to get staff to use the new system. Some customers are now very resistant to 'upgrading'.

Due to the ever increasing efficiency of hardware production and changes in far east economies, the actual costs of hardware are getting lower and lower. This means that the 'lowest' specification of some computer components now on sale is more than adequate for most people. For example, many machines now come with a disk drive with a 60 Gb capacity as standard. If you only need a wordprocessor this will meet your needs for a very long time. Some people seem to think that if they specify a 120 Gb drive the machine will be 'better' in some respect. This is not true. Many machines are fast enough for normal business activities and more speed is simply not required. Many people find that to run Windows 98 and Word 97 on a Pentium 266 with 32 Mb RAM fitted is quite adequate, why specify any more. In any case, what would you mean by 'more speed' in respect of a wordprocessor, always assuming that a 2 GHz Pentium is somehow 'faster', will it enable you to type faster?

Consider these typical applications running:

- Wordprocessing
- Spreadsheets
- Databases
- Graphic arts
- Technical design

Now consider these things that would appear on a list of components when specifying a computer.

- Disk speed
- Disk capacity
- Video resolution
- Video RAM size
- Monitor size
- Monitor resolution

- Monitor slot pitch
- Monitor refresh rate
- Main RAM size
- Processor type
- Processor clock speed
- Internal bus speed
- Internal bus type
- Motherboard features, buses, expansion slots, etc.

Now write down what is required (allowing for future expansion) rather than what you might 'like' to have. You will find that if you focus more on quality than on performance, the benefits will be higher. Clearly you need a machine that has sufficient performance but you should next consider:

- Cost/budget
- Performance
- Expandability
- Ergonomics, i.e. how well the components 'fit' with the people who will use them
- Needs of specific or specialist software, e.g. Autocad

Some people are specifying notebook computers in place of desktop machines, but you should consider these points that notebooks:

- cost at least 50% more for the same 'power', often twice as much;
- sometimes will not run some specialist software;
- are not as reliable as desktop machines, they are easy to damage;
- are not as expandable or configurable as desktops;
- are very portable (so thieves love them);
- have LCD screen (that many people prefer);
- newer versions of software make ever more demands on the hardware, notebooks go out of date quicker.

Now consider the questions shown in the sample assignment below and discuss your thoughts with your lecturer and fellow students. Keep your mind focused on what is *needed* not on what is desirable or what you may see advertised as 'The Computer Deal of the Century!'

Exercise 1.13.1

Sample assignment tasks

You are asked to specify computers for the six users below. For each of the users listed, choose a suitable machine and justify your choice. You should give a detailed explanation choices in terms of: cost, capabilities, performance and upgrade path.

The simplest way is to list the items fitted or specified in your chosen machine and explain the significance of each item and how it relates to the users' requirements. Write down the machine specification as a list of components in the same way you would present it to a supplier.

User 1

This company supplies artwork, graphics, etc. to the advertising industry, especially the glossy magazine trade. Their main expertise is in photo retouching using very high-resolution images. They only need machines for five graphic artists, the management function in the company is already computerized.

User 2

A small college runs 200 standalone PCs. A network company has offered a sponsorship deal and supplied a full network with cabling and servers to support the college provided that the college upgrades the users' machines. The current 200 machines are to be scrapped. The plan is to run Windows, MS Office and similar software on each user machine but with the user files stored on the servers; they have an extremely tight budget where every penny counts. You must achieve the cheapest possible machine that will run the software.

User 3

The PA to the finance director of a large shipping company requires a machine to do wordprocessing and e-mail. All the other computerized functions in the company are already running elsewhere.

User 4

A very experienced design engineer working on petrochemical plant designs has been on an Autocad course. The projects she works on involve 3D drawings of very complex pipework, etc. During the course of the next year, she will employ two assistants to computerize the existing paper drawings and to use Autocad themselves, so she needs three new networked PCs to run Autocad. The application requires that large amounts of data are stored and that the hidden line removal and other performance critical functions in Autocad are used to full effect.

User 5

A local private genealogy society has computer links to help in their research, they use an old PC with a 56 Kb/sec modem. To reduce costs and speed up enquiries, they have decided to start a large database of family genealogy details. The eventual size of the database may be 200 Gbytes with requirements to have at least one level of backup. Funds are very tight but users will require a good service. To limit the expenditure, only one member will use the machine at a time, linked via a fixed modem on a pre-arranged time slot.

User 6

A financial accountant uses spreadsheets to model the financial behaviour of companies. The spreadsheets are very large and she is hoping to make them even larger but is impatient with the recalculation time obtained with her current computer.

2 Systems analysis

Summary

The aim of this unit is to give students the ability to compare the different lifecycle models. It provides a foundation of systems analysis and design by covering requirements analysis techniques for a variety of applications used within the computing industry. The unit also covers the data and functional modelling which students can be expected to use. It also provides an opportunity for students to implement a data model using a proprietary database. In order to develop modern systems analysis requirements the chapter encourages the use of software development, documentation and implementation tools, which are used within the computing industry today.

Introduction

The development of modern software systems requires a thorough understanding of systems analysis and design methods to ensure the end product is produced efficiently on time and within budget. The concept of requirements analysis skills for both commercial and technical applications needs to be professionally implemented to ensure the product specification meets the needs of the customer. Systems analysis provides an underlying structure for developing the key skills required within the field of software engineering.

In this chapter we will be concentrating on why different software development techniques are required in the analysis/design process.

You will learn how to apply software analysis techniques for a given 'real world' specification based on an appropriate lifecycle model.

You will learn about different approaches to analysis and make comparisons about different models that are used within the systems analysis environment today.

An important aspect is to learn about the techniques involved in 'fact finding' for a systems investigation and how to record/present follow-up documentation for a prospective customer.

In order to implement the analysis model the you will learn about basic data modelling techniques, including functional modelling development and graphical representations (e.g. entity-relationship diagrams) and to implement such designs into a simple rational database systems.

The importance of good quality documentation is emphasized within the chapter. It looks at different ways of presenting information using text and graphical applications. The use of a commercial CASE tool application is used to demonstrate and test graphical models.

This chapter is designed to integrate analysis techniques with practical applications in order for you to use information technology to document, analyse, design and implement systems being investigated.

2.1 Systems analysis lifecycle

It has often been a problem for software developers to produce a quality product that fully satisfies the needs of the customer. Far too often the software product is delivered late and over budget. In order to improve the production of software systems several analysis and design techniques have been developed. These range from simple graphical techniques through to formal mathematical structures.

Several problems have been associated with the development of software systems, these include:

- Complexity
- Size
- Cost
- Deadlines
- Project management
- Environment issues

Software is classified as an 'invisible medium', you do not see what you are getting until very late in the development process. This is why it is important to apply a thorough-analysis strategy in order to ensure that you are developing a quality product that meets its specified aims.

Traditional lifecycle

The traditional lifecycle, or the waterfall method as it is sometimes called, represents the steps a project follows from its conception through to its termination. It starts with the customers' requirements followed by several activities each resulting in a set of documents (Figure 2.1.1).

Figure 2.1.1 shows a typical lifecycle layout.

The initial stages, requirements analysis and specification form the overall analysis phases and specify 'what' the system is to do. Design then follows where a solution to the problem is formulated, followed by the coding and maintenance stages. Verification and validation form the quality assurance role and act over the whole lifecycle.

The requirements analysis activity receives the 'user requirements' document as input and its main aim is to analyse its contents to ensure it is correctly structured and understood by all parties. It extracts from the customer the requirements that are needed for the software system to be developed. This output of this activity is to produce a precise document, the negotiated statement of requirements, which the system can then be designed on.

Specification then follows by taking the negotiated statement of requirements as input and develops a model as to what the system is to do. This activity is still analysing the problem and is not concerned with providing a solution. There will still be heavy interaction with the customer during this stage to ensure the output documentation, the system specification, is accurate.

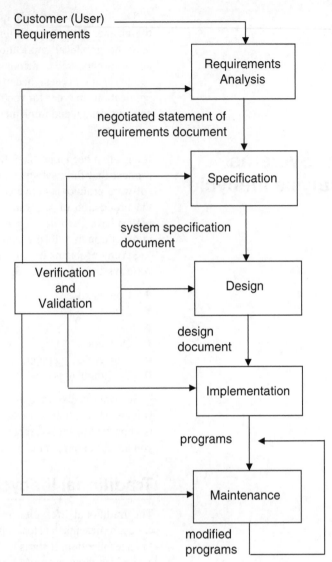

Figure 2.1.1   *Traditional lifecycle model*

Next comes the design activity that takes the system specification as its input document and sets about providing a solution to the problem. This stage is concerned with how the system is going to operate and will use structure or class diagrams that specify components within a given programming environment. Some developers may also use a Program Design Language (PDL) which provides the code lines that can be implemented into a high-level programming language. The output of this activity is the design documentation that provides a basis for implementation.

The implementation activity takes the design documentation and codes it into a designated programming language. The output of this activity are the programs that execute the required system.

The final activity is maintenance that provides support for the developed programs. Many will contain 'bugs' that need to be rectified in order for the system to work correctly and meet the full requirements of the end user. Maintenance also provides the opportunity to upgrade software systems as the need arises. Many companies will offer software maintenance contracts which provide users with the opportunity to upgrade

Question 2.1.1

With reference to the traditional lifecycle model:

1. What are the main activities associated with the traditional lifecycle?
2. What documents result from each activity?
3. What is the role of the verification and validation activity?
4. Why is it sometimes called a waterfall model?

systems when new updates become available. The output documentation of this activity will be modified programs.

Verification and validation provides the quality assurance activity that acts over the whole lifecycle of the project and ensures the end product reaches an acceptable level of quality. Validation ensures that the output from each activity meets the user requirements. Verification ensures the project is being built in the correct way and the output of each activity is a correct conversion as an input to the next stage.

The above description shows why the traditional lifecycle is sometimes called the 'waterfall model', this is because the output of one activity 'flows' directly into the next activity, like a waterfall.

Prototyping

We know from the world of engineering that a manufacturer will develop a prototype model before mass producing the final product. So why not apply this concept to the development of a software product? This is what the pioneers of prototyping have set out to achieve by attempting to demonstrate how a system or a component of a computer-based information system will function in its environment.

Users find such demonstrations very helpful in visualizing what proposed systems will do for them. They often find it difficult to accurately access what they are getting from a system by reading large requirements specifications.

Prototyping can result in a set of requirements that are better understood by the user and is more likely to be complete and accurate. Its advantages are that it is dynamic, flexible and provides a collaborative methodology that both aid the end user of the product and the development team.

However, if prototyping is good why is not used by more developers? Two main reasons are shown below:

1. Lack of suitable prototyping tools.
2. Lack of means of managing the prototyping process.

Some benefits of developing a prototype

- Misunderstandings between software developers and users may be identified as the system functions are demonstrated.
- Missing user services may be detected.
- Difficult to use or confusing user services may be identified and refined.
- Software development staff may find incomplete and/or inconsistent requirements as the prototype is developed.
- A working, albeit limited, system is available quickly to demonstrate the feasibility and usefulness of the application to management.
- The prototype serves as a basis for writing the specification for a production quality system.

Ince and Hekmatpour (1987) stated other uses:

- It can be used for training users before the production-quality system has been delivered.
- It can be used during system testing. The same tests can be applied to the prototype and the final system and results compared.

Boehm (1984) specified four stages in the prototype development:

- Establish prototype objectives.
- Select functions for prototype inclusion and make decisions on what non-functional functions must be prototyped.
- Develop the prototype.
- Evaluate the prototype system.

The major technical problems associated with prototyping revolve around the need for rapid software development. However, non-technical problems have meant that 'rapid prototyping' is still not widely used, except in data processing system development. Some of these management problems are:

- Planning, costing and estimating a prototyping project is outside the experience of most project managers.
- Procedures for configuration management are unsuitable for controlling rapid change inherent in prototyping.
- Management pressures to reach swift conclusions may result in inappropriate requirements.

Types of prototyping models

Exploratory programming

This method is based on producing an initial basic model that is shown to the customer for any comments, then refining the model until its reaches an acceptable system. This model may have an advantage for developers who have previously developed a similar system from which the initial model can be produced. Figure 2.1.2 shows the layout for the exploratory programming cycle.

The system uses an iterative process to refine the initial model. The success of this approach lies in how rapidly the developer can process these iterations in order to advance to model towards its end goal.

Exploratory programming tends to result in a system that is not well defined. There is going to be a lot of 'change' going on within the software

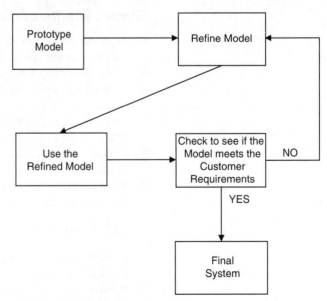

Figure 2.1.2   *Exploratory programming*

that can lead to errors being produced. This often results in problems with maintenance that can be costly and time consuming especially for large-scale systems. Verification is also a problem as it checks the project against its original specification which is not clearly defined.

Students will often start with this approach without realizing it. Given an assignment a student may start with a basic model and refine it by adding additional components until they have satisfied the requirements. More often this is not achieved by accident and a tested analysis and design has not been adopted.

Throwaway prototyping

This method starts with an initial model, a prototype, which is checked with the customer to ascertain its correctness then developers start to build the final product from the beginning. The prototype is 'thrownaway'. It is used as an aid to understanding and does not form part of the final product. Because it is only an experimental system all non-functional requirements can be ignored.

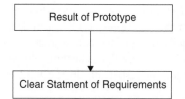

The initial model or prototype may also have some of the functional requirements missing. The use of a front end graphical user interface can be ignored and systems that handle error recovery do not need to be included at this stage.

Figure 2.1.3 shows a typical layout for a 'throwaway' prototype system. The prototype is developed from an outline specification and presented to the customer to ensure they are satisfied with its functional objectives.

The diagram starts with the prototype that is evaluated to ascertain a full system specification. Once this has been achieved the prototype is thrown away and work starts on the full version.

There are several problems with this method:

1. Often many important functions are left out to aid the speed of the development prototype.
2. We have seen with the traditional lifecycle that the negotiated statement of requirements can form the basis of a contract between the customer and developer. This model is incomplete at the prototype stage and therefore cannot be an adequate basis for such a contract.

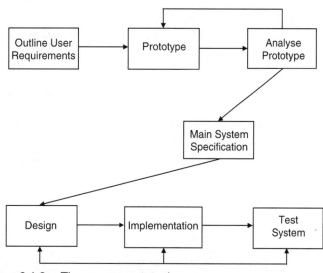

Figure 2.1.3   *Throwaway prototyping*

3. It does not consider non-functional requirements.
4. The user has a restricted use of the prototype model which can lead to a false impression as to how the system will function.

Having stated these problems this method does have its advantages, e.g. concept of a prototype gives the customer an early view of the product. As systems grow even more complex, there becomes a problem in developing a full specification from scratch. It is expected that the concepts of prototyping will grow even though they introduce problems of their own.

Reverse engineering

This is not strictly a prototype method, but often comes under that heading in many texts. It starts with some completed code (or a complete system) that may be used as a base for a current project which is developed to meet the needs of the new specification. Figure 2.1.4 shown below shows this process in action.

The main objective of this model is to use lines of code that are already written and may be useful for the new application. The code is then reconstructed to suit the user requirements of the new system.

This activity contains the essence of code reuse that is becoming more popular in current programming paradigms, especially in the field of object-oriented designs.

The existing code is more likely to be successful if it is properly documented and has been designed in the systematic way as the new project.

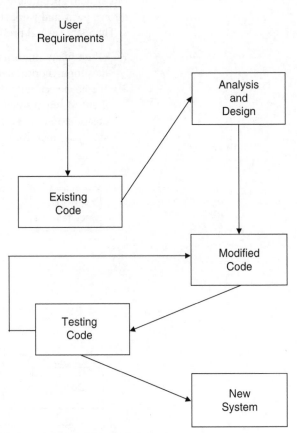

Figure 2.1.4   *Reverse engineering.*

Question 2.1.2

1. What is a software prototype?
2. What stages are involved in software prototype development?
3. Describe in your own words:
   (a) exploratory programming;
   (b) throwaway prototyping;
   (c) reverse engineering.
4. Specify four problems that may arise through prototyping methods.
5. What do you think are the main advantages of prototyping?

Object-oriented analysis

There has been a massive increase in the use of object-oriented programming languages over the last decade. Although not new, languages like C++ and Java have had a greater influence within system applications especially those associated with Internet design and management.

Introduction to the world of objects

Objects model real-world or fake-world entities. Anything we can see, interact with or quantify in some way can be classified as an object. Objects are therefore real things with unique properties and each has its own set of characteristics.

The essential characteristics of objects are (Booch, 1991):

- Its STATE
- Its BEHAVIOUR
- Its IDENTITY.

Characteristics within the world of objects

Encapsulation allows for certain data types and methods to be hidden from the user. This provides for a binding of data structures and methods into a class of objects. The result of this is a more efficient programming structure with a reduction in the possibility of data becoming corrupted. In languages like C++ and Java these are classified as *private* members and the *public* methods provide access into the class. Encapsulation is also known as information hiding. Encapsulation applies specifically to objects whilst information hiding can be used in any software application.

The interface between a user and a class is provided via the 'class methods' which accept the parameters (arguments) that send and receive the messages for the object to act on. This is layout is shown below in Figure 2.1.5.

The reason for allowing messages or arguments to have access only via their designated methods aids the process of reuse of constructed class structures. This has a benefit for the developers of systems when it comes to the concept of 'change' or designing a new system that can make use of the existing structures.

Inheritance allows for one class to inherent the characteristics of another class. Developers can exploit the property of inheritance by

class: example

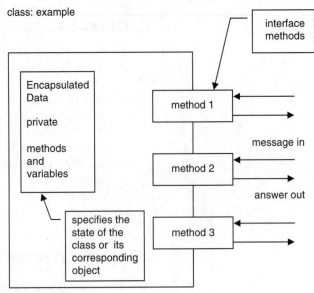

Figure 2.1.5   *Class method interface diagram*

creating an 'ancestor' class that has attributes and behaviours that are appropriate for its own execution and reusing the ancestor class to describe new ones.

For example, if we have constructed a class called circle and we want to create a new class called cylinder, then cylinder can be designed as an 'ancestor' of circle as it describes some of the properties for cylinder. For example, to calculate the volume of a cylinder the area of a circle is required, therefore the new class, cylinder, can obtain this information from circle and just add a method to multiply the length to the area in order to calculate the volume of a cylinder.

Polymorphism is the ability for a number of classes to share names of methods. The methods, that are named the same, behave appropriately to the particular class for which they were designed.

Object analysis

This activity takes the 'negotiated statement of requirements' and analyses its contents to determine its classes and associations. This is usually achieved by constructing a class-association diagram that depicts the systems to be developed. The class-association diagram can be used a graphical representation of the overall system or subsystem.

Classes

Object-programming languages contain class structures that represent a template for objects. A class definition is the means by which objects are designed.

For C++ we are given the definition:

An object is an instance of a class

Similar definitions are inherent within other object languages like Smalltalk and Java. Since the class design is a type definition for objects, an instance is a member of a class, i.e. an object.

Class structures can be classified as:

1. *Tangible* – these represent physical entities out there in the real world. Some examples are: car, bus, house, aeroplane, college, classroom, etc.
2. *Roles* – these represent the roles that people or other parties play in the application area. Some examples are: student, policeman, sailor, workman, etc.
3. *Events* – these relate to particular circumstance like a happening or an incidence. Some examples: party, enrolment, lecture, booking, etc.
4. *Units* – these represent organizational units with the application area. For example, if we are designing a college system an example of a unit would be a department.

While these classifications are useful, the overall purpose of the analysis activity is to identify classes where the behaviour of objects is significant.

Associations

An association is a connection between two objects that is significant for the application area being developed. If we take Dog and Cat as two objects then an appropriate association between them could be chases. For example, Dog chases Cat or Tutor lecturers Students. One point about syntax at this stage, it is customary to use uppercase first letters to represent objects.

Associations can be classified as one to one, one to many and many to many. These concepts will be covered in more detail later in the chapter.

Responsibilities

These describe the behaviour of an object in terms of the responsibilities that affect its overall requirements for an intended system. They can take two forms:

- Responsibilities for recording information.
- Responsibilities for carrying out a prescribed task.

The way objects work

To the user of applications objects are considered as 'black box' components. They operate by receiving a message and respond with an answer. The object that sends a message is called the receiver. An example is outlined in Figure 2.1.6.

Question 2.1.3

1. What is the main factor why object development is popular?
2. What is meant by the following terms:
   (a) encapsulation?
   (b) inheritance?
   (c) polymorphism?
3. How are objects defined?
4. What are main aims of object-oriented analysis?
5. What provides a communication route to an object?

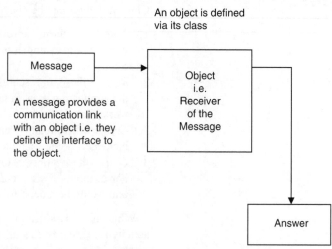

An object is defined
via its class

Message

A message provides a
communication link
with an object i.e. they
define the interface to
the object.

Object
i.e.
Receiver
of the
Message

Answer

Figure 2.1.6   *Object structure*

Evaluation of models

The use of a required model depends on a number of factors. Is the specification for a system that requires function, object or data modelling. Is the project to be implemented into a high-level language like C/C++, Pascal etc. and if so, does it need to be structured via a visual environment. Is the application going to be developed within a database environment like Access and programmed using VB. There are so many questions and the solution often depends on what you are skilled in and what resources are available to you.

The other main factor is the availability of systems analysis tools that you need to develop the specification. A lot of these tools allow for the graphical models to be developed following set procedures and checked for syntax and semantic correctness. But they are expensive and take a lot of training to use and often you have to make do with standard graphical packages that allow the diagrams to be completed without the added advantage of in-built testing facilities.

The traditional lifecycle is gradually giving way to other models, but its inherent concepts should not be ignored. A number of software houses have been using the model, or a variation of it, for several years with very successful outcomes.

However, there is a greater emphasis on object and data modelling within industry today and these facts may provide you with the choice of which technique you use to analyse the system. You will need to provide a constructive base on which the design and implementation of the project can be developed.

Question 2.1.4

Your local college requires a management information system to handle student admissions.

From this specification extract suggest a possible method for analysis. Explain why you have chosen this method.

2.2 Systems analysis tools and techniques

Yourdon data flow diagrams

The Yourdon Structured Method or YSM has been in use for several years and like most of the analysis models on the market today it primarily uses graphical techniques to structure the 'negotiated statement of requirements' into a coherent framework. This framework still needs to be understood by the customer so the basic structure is simple in its presentation and has the advantage that a single diagram can show what is on several pages of written text.

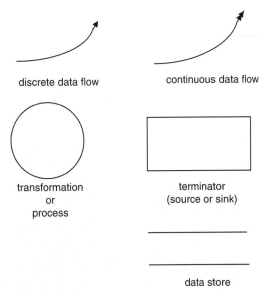

Figure 2.2.1 *Yourdon DFD symbols*

The data flow diagram or DFD is the first graphical technique used to analyse what the system is to do. Figure 2.2.1 contains the symbols used within the analysis process.

It is hierarchical in structure and all diagrams start with a 'top level' design called a 'context diagram'. This diagram contains one process only that represents the whole of the system. Its main objective is to show where the main data sources are coming from and where the output data is going. The input data originates from a 'source' terminator(s) and the output data is sent to a 'sink' terminator(s).

Example 2.2.1

Construct a context diagram for a system that calculates the standard deviation for a given set of examination grades. The grades should be in the range 0–100 and entered through the keyboard via an operator. If the operator enters an incorrect value a suitable message is to be displayed on the monitor. The standard deviation values are to be printed out so the operator can send the results to the appropriate person.
   Suggested solution:

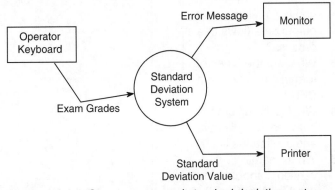

Figure 2.2.2 *Context mean and standard deviation system*

The solid directed lines represent the flow of data. A single arrow at the end depicts a discrete flow of data that arrive at their destination at discrete intervals in time.

A continuous data flow continually sends data to its destination. The process or transformation uses the data that arrives and processes it in some way to produce an output.

Some basic rules:

1. Context diagrams contain one process only.
2. A process must have at least one input and one output.
3. All data flows are named with a noun.
4. Processes must be labelled with text which suggests how the data is transformed.
5. Data flows and processes should be uniquely named.
6. A process cannot originate data.
7. Data flowing to a terminator can only come from a process.
8. A diagram should be numbered and contain an explanatory caption.

Once the context diagram has been completed the next step is to refine it by creating a child. Children are only created through processes so there can only be one child from a context diagram. A child diagram should not contain more than seven processes to avoid complexity. If this is starting to appear likely then further children of the process would need to be created. The term for this is known as 'functional decomposition' and is achieved through data flow diagram refinement.

For a large-scale project the following steps are required:

- Create a context diagram.
- Refine the process in the context diagram to describe its component data flows, processes and stores.
- Refine each process into another data flow diagram.
- Repeat this process until the required level of detail is obtained.
- Complete the process specifications for the final processes.
- Check all diagrams for consistency and syntax requirements.

Question 2.2.1

With reference to the context diagram:

1. How many processes can a context diagram contain?
2. What is minimum number of input and output data flows to a process?
3. What are the types of terminators used in a DFD?
4. What is the difference between a discrete and continuous flow?
5. What naming convention should be used for data flows?

Example 2.2.2

From the solution given in Example 2.2.1 refine the context diagram to produce child that adequately models the system. Suggested solution:

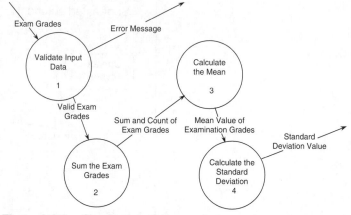

Figure 2.2.3 *Standard deviation system*

Important rule

The flows that go in and out of the process being refined must be the same flows that appear in the child diagram. This is classified as parent–child balancing and if the two diagrams do not match an error will be evident in the design.

The above example required only one child to provide an analysis model of the system. Note that it is not necessary to show the original terminators in the child diagram.

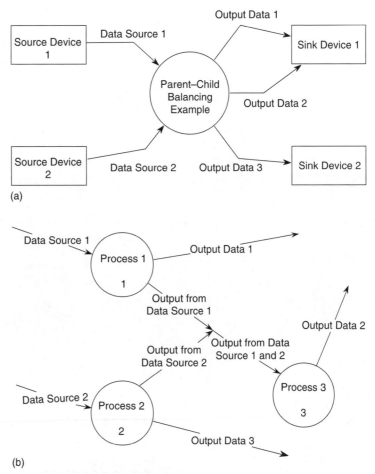

(a)

(b)

Figure 2.2.4 *(a) Context parent–child balancing example (b) Parent–child balancing (child)*

Example 2.2.3

Below are the requirements for making vegetable soup.

A 'vegetable soup' is to be made with three main ingredients. These are to be potatoes, onions and broccoli. The vegetables are contained in a vegetable rack and they need to be prepared before they are ready for use. You then need to add water to a saucepan and slightly boil the potatoes first. Next you need to add appropriate condiments with the onions and broccoli. They then need to be cooked for a prescribed time and when ready the soup is to be served in a bowl.

1.   Complete a CONTEXT diagram to model the specification.
2.   Refine the context diagram so it fully specifies the system.

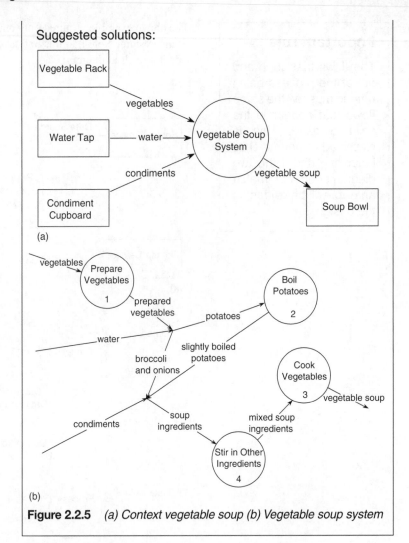

Suggested solutions:

(a)

(b)

Figure 2.2.5 *(a) Context vegetable soup (b) Vegetable soup system*

The role of stores

Data stores are storage areas that are internal to a system that is being modelled. These stores often represent the basic building blocks of a database system and from which a entity-relationship diagram can be constructed. The direction of the data flow lines is important as it depicts whether the store is read only, write only or read/write. This is shown diagrammatically in Figure 2.2.6.

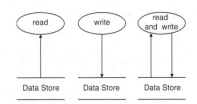

Figure 2.2.6

Example 2.2.4

Example containing stores – Bernese Coach Company

Below is an extract from a system specification.

The Bernese Coach Company requires a computer-based system to handle customer enquires. The customer enquires that need to be answered are:

- give the travel price between any two destinations;
- for a given route display the coach number;

- display the time each coach leaves for a specified destination;
- print the routes which are offering special party bookings.

An booking clerk is to operate the system by typing in one of the four commands, the command needs to be validated to ensure it is correct. The system uses a database called 'Coach Details' that contains all the information specified above.

1. Draw a context diagram to represent the proposed system.
2. Refine the context diagram by producing a child of the main process in order to develop a solution. Keep the diagram simple, remember a good DFD should not contain any more than seven processes.

Suggested solution:

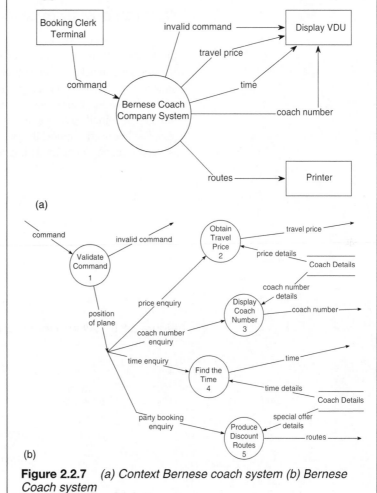

Figure 2.2.7 *(a) Context Bernese coach system (b) Bernese Coach system*

In order to ensure the developer has as much information as possible, some DFD development tools allow for a process specification to be created as a final transformation refinement. The process specification contains information about the flows in and out of the transformation and its body contains a high-level specification in structured English describing what is happening inside. An example from the Standard Deviation System is shown below.

```
@ IN = Valid Exam Grades
@ OUT = Sum & Count of Exam Grades

@ PSPEC 0.2 Sum the Exam Grades

On receiving the Valid Exam Grades do:
        Iterate to calculate the Sum and Count of Exam Grades
Output these values to the next process
@
```

Note that the body is in semi-formal English and it must contain the data flow names that flow in and out of the process.

Output flows from processes

If a process produces more than one output then the way this is depicted on the DFD will give the developer information about whether all the data items are produced at the same time or if just one of this. This 'and' and 'or' situation is shown in the diagrams below. Figure 2.2.8 shows a process where the outputs can be considered as alternatives and Figure 2.2.9 shows the outputs initially as a single flow then splitting into the output data components. The need to model the parsing of data flow into its alternative forms is a common one when modelling the essential characteristics of a system.

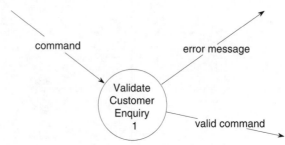

Figure 2.2.8   *Alternative output flows*

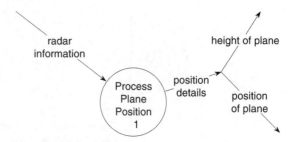

Figure 2.2.9   *Single output flow parsing into two flows*

Input flows to processes

If a number of data flows are required by one process then they should merge before they reach that process. This reduces the complexity of the diagram structure and shows at a glance to the developer that all the input data items are required for the process to carry out its transformation. Figure 2.2.10 outlines this procedure.

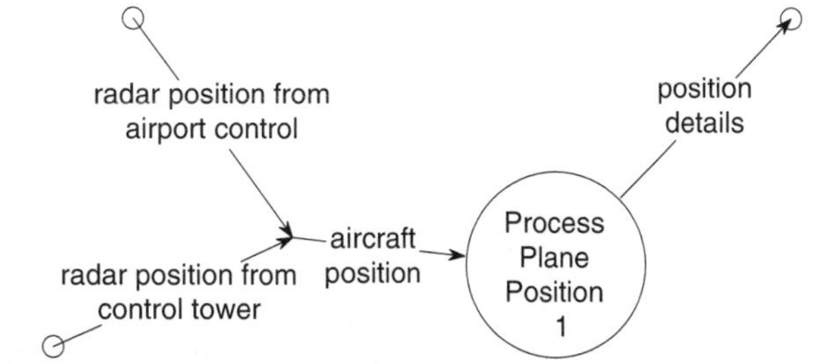

Figure 2.2.10 *Merging of input data flows*

Some graphical analysis tools allow for the splitting of flows to carried out by 'group nodes' that need to be fully clarified via a text directive. Using Select Yourdon this is achieved by creating a BNF (Backus–Naur Format) specification. The syntax that is used is shown in the left column.

From diagram 14 a suitable BNF structure could be:

- *height of plane + position of plane* stating that both are outputs from *position details* stressing the **and** condition.
- [*height of plane/position of plane*] stating that either could be outputs from *position details* stressing the **or** condition.

These techniques are further refinements from those discussed above and allow a better structuring of the diagram which is both easier to read and more accurate in its content.

Validating the DFD

The following list highlights the important points for validating a DFD system:

- Does each circle or process precisely state the transformation? (make sure each process contains a verb).
- Is all the data shown? and at the correct level.
- After refinement does the net input and output data flows match those in the parent diagram?
- Can the DFD be remodelled to make it easier to follow? Remember the maximum number of processes a diagram should contain is seven.
- You should not have the same name for a data flow that enters a process and a data flow that leaves it. Remember the action of a process is to transform the data, i.e. convert it from one form to another. Also all data flows should have unique names
- Have you refined each process as far as it will go? If so have you completed an appropriate process specification? Remember a process specification is the final child to be created

Remember a DFD is detailed at customer level. It specifies what the system is to do by providing a graphical specification, which is still open for discussion with the customer, to ensure it is a correct representation of the negotiated statement of requirements.

Link between data flow diagrams and entity-relationship diagrams

In order to develop a model that requires a relational database component the required DFD needs to be further refined. An example of this is outlined below. Further details of developing entity-relationships are given within the Data Modelling section of this chapter.

DFD (with stores)

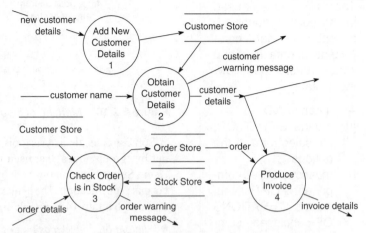

Figure 2.2.11 *Customer order system data flow diagram*

Figure 2.2.11 shows a proposed customer order system. The facilities allow Customer Services to add new customer details, find the customer details given the name of the customer and to produce an invoice for the customer if the item(s) required are in stock. Notice that there are four stores that have some relationships between them. The relationships that exist between the data flow diagram stores is shown below:

Store	Relationship	Store
Customer	Places	Order
Order	For	Stock
Order	Creates	Invoice

The degree of each relationship needs to be defined, for example:

A Customer can place one to many Orders and each Order is received from a single customer. This gives a 1:n relationship between Customer and Order.
An Order can be for 1 to many Stock items and each Stock item is for a single order. This gives a 1:n relationship between Order and Stock.
Each Order produces a single Invoice and each Invoice is for a single Order. This gives a 1:1 relationship between Order and Invoice.

The resulting entity-relationship (E-R) diagram is shown in Figure 2.2.12.

Question 2.2.3

What is the link between a data flow diagram and an entity-relationship diagram?

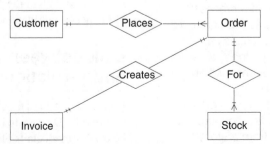

Figure 2.2.12 *E-R diagram for the customer order system*

Exercise 2.2.1

The Bailey & Bess Dog Kennels

Below is an extract from a system specification for a computerized system to be installed in the Bailey & Bess Dog Kennels.

A computer system is required to replace the paperwork system currently in use by the kennels. The system needs to book in dogs that come to stay at the kennels and book them out when their stay is finished. The system needs to take advance bookings so the receptionist needs to be able to look up if there are kennels available for a specified period. Some of the kennels are reserved for quarantine animals and these are not available for short stay dogs. A number of options need to be available to the receptionist in order to maintain the booking system. These include:

- display the available kennels for a specified period;
- display which kennels have been reserved for quarantine use;
- print a report giving details of who has pre-booked;
- display what dogs are in the kennels at the present time;
- print the names, address and telephone numbers of people who currently have dogs in the kennels.

In order to ensure the reliability of the system an error message is to be displayed if the receptionist enters an incorrect command.

1. Draw a context diagram to represent the proposed system.
2. Refine the context diagram to produce a solution to the problem.
3. For the final transformations produce appropriate process specifications.
4. Check your diagrams to make sure they are syntactically and semantically correct.

Exercise 2.2.2

For the College Management Information System specified in Exercise 2.3.1 complete a DFD process to include the following steps:

1. Draw a context diagram to represent the proposed system.
2. Refine the context diagram to produce a solution to the problem.
3. For the final transformations produce appropriate process specifications.
4. Check your diagrams to make sure they are syntactically and semantically correct.

SSADM

Introduction

SSADM (Structured Systems Analysis and Design Method) is a widely used system analysis and design development tool and is often specified as a requirement for government computing projects. Developed within the UK it is increasingly being adopted by the public sector throughout Europe. SSADM is in the public domain, and is formally specified in British Standard BS7738.

Objectives of SSADM

SSADM divides an application development project into modules, stages, steps, and tasks, and provides a framework for describing projects in a fashion suited to managing the project. SSADM's objectives are to:

- Improve project management and control.
- Make more effective use of experienced and inexperienced development staff.

- Develop better quality systems.
- Make projects resilient to the loss of staff.
- Enable projects to be supported by computer-based tools such as Computer Aided Software Engineering (CASE) systems.
- Establish a framework for good communications between participants in a project.

SSADM covers those aspects of the lifecycle of a system from the feasibility study stage to the production of a physical design; it is generally used in conjunction with other methods, such as PRINCE, which is concerned with the broader aspects of project management.

Outline of SSADM

In detail, SSADM sets out a cascade or waterfall view of systems development, in which there are a series of steps, each of which leads to the next step.
SSADM's steps, or stages, are:

- Feasibility – Feasibility Study Module.
- Investigation of the current environment – Requirements Analysis Module.
- Business systems options – Requirements Analysis Module.
- Definition of requirements – Requirements Specification Module.
- Technical system options – Logical Systems Specification Module.
- Logical design – Logical Systems Specification Module.
- Physical design – Physical Design Module.

For each stage, SSADM sets out a series of techniques and procedures, and conventions for recording and communicating information pertaining to these – both in textual and diagrammatic form. SSADM is a very comprehensive model, and a characteristic of the method is that projects may use only those elements of SSADM appropriate to the project. SSADM is supported by a number of CASE (Computer Aided Software Engineering) tool providers.

Each stage is divided up into a sequence of numbered steps which in turn are divided into numbered tasks. For example, step 010 is specified for 'Prepare for the Feasibility Study'.

An outline of this structure is shown in Figure 2.2.13.

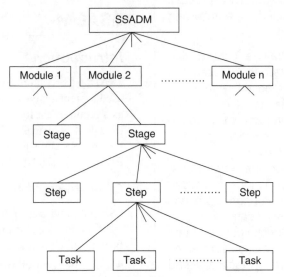

Figure 2.2.13 *Structure of the SSADM model*

Diagrammatic techniques used within SSADM

- Data flow modelling
- Logical data modelling
- Entity/event modelling
- Enquiry access paths
- I/O structuring
- Dialogue design
- Logical database process design.

Non-diagrammatic techniques used within SSADM

- Relational data analysis
- Requirements definition
- Function definition
- Formulation of options
- Specification prototyping.

Background to the SSADM lifecycle (Version 4)

Stage 0 Feasibility Study

This forms the first stage in the lifecycle and its objectives are:

- to decide whether to proceed to a full specification;
- to decide whether to proceed in a different direction from that envisaged in the initial documentation.

Figure 2.2.14 shows the steps taken during this stage.

Several options for taking the project forward to a full analysis and factors like weighing benefits against cost are considered. It may be found that the project is not feasible and abandoned at this stage.

Stage 1 Investigation of the current environment

It the new system is intended to be a replacement for an existing system then an investigation will be carried out as a vehicle for uncovering user requirements. The following points outline what can be achieved during this stage.

- Retained functionality – what functions are still required in the new system?
- User confidence – demonstrates the developers ability to understand the current system and their ability to ascertain the requirements for the new system.
- Identification of requirements – this is thought by many developers of systems to be the most efficient way of ascertaining the requirements of a new system. It provides opportunities for the developers to discuss problems with users of the current system and how they would like changes to be made in the new system.
- Familiarization – this gives the developer a chance to become familiar with the environment under investigation.
- Project scoping – the scope and complexity of the proposed system can often be obtained efficiently from the current system.

Figure 2.2.15 outlines the stage.

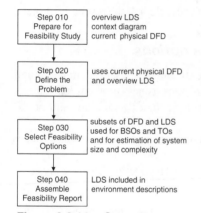

Figure 2.2.14 *Stage 0 – feasibility*

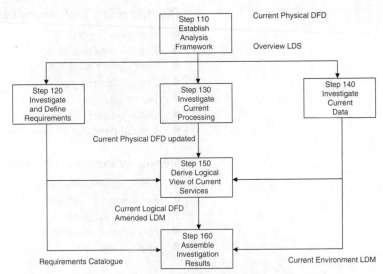

Figure 2.2.15   *Stage 1 – investigation of the current environment*

The output of this stage is a comprehensive set of user requirements which provides a documentary base for developing the rest of the project.

Stage 2 Business systems options

Here we examine the comprehensive statement of user requirements and put together several options for solving the business problem. The objective of this stage is to define business (or logical) solutions and not to describe the technical environment.

Figure 2.2.16 shows the path taken during the Business System Option (BSO).

The SSADM tasks carried out in step 210 (Define Business Systems Options) are:

1. Task 10 – establish minimum requirements for the proposed system.
2. Task 20 – produce outlines for a number of BSO normally about 6.
3. Task 30 – discuss the outlines with the users to produce a shortlist.
4. Task 40 – carry out a cost benefit and impact analysis for each short listed BSO.

Step 220 is the remit to select the BSO to be fully investigated for the new system. This will depend on a number of factors like the internal standards and circumstances of the project. It will involve the project team and user representative body to explain each option clearly and highlight its strengths and weaknesses. The final output of this stage is a comprehensive document that specifies why the proposed option has been chosen and acts as a bases for the final system.

Stage 3 Definition of requirements

This is the centre of the project where the user requirements are refined into a detailed and precise specification of 'what' the system is to do. Figure 2.2.17 outlines the steps taken during this stage.

The order of events through this stage need to be carefully planned. Steps 310 and 320 can be carried out in parallel. Step 310 feeds into Step 330 and Step 320 feeds into Step 340. Step 350 may not begin until

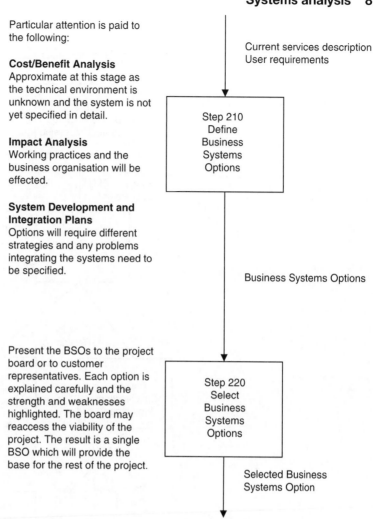

Particular attention is paid to
the following:

Cost/Benefit Analysis
Approximate at this stage as
the technical environment is
unknown and the system is not
yet specified in detail.

Impact Analysis
Working practices and the
business organisation will be
effected.

**System Development and
Integration Plans**
Options will require different
strategies and any problems
integrating the systems need to
be specified.

Present the BSOs to the project
board or to customer
representatives. Each option is
explained carefully and the
strength and weaknesses
highlighted. The board may
reaccess the viability of the
project. The result is a single
BSO which will provide the
base for the rest of the project.

Current services description
User requirements

Step 210
Define
Business
Systems
Options

Business Systems Options

Step 220
Select
Business
Systems
Options

Selected Business
Systems Option

Figure 2.2.16   *Business systems options (BSOs)*

Step 310 and Step 330 have been completed. Steps 330 and 340 are a trigger for Step 360.

The requirements catalogue remains the centre document throughout this stage. It contains the functional and non-functional requirements which are updated as the stage develops. The Logical Data Model (LDM) is modified using the technique of relational data analysis and will continue to provide a descriptive outline of the business rules and data requirements. The Data Flow Method (DFM) is an invaluable aid for system processing and communicating with the customer or end user of the product. It is refined up to the middle of the stage where more rigorous and detailed models are used to link the processing elements together. It will remain a useful reference document and will be included in the complete document set and used for consistency checks within the project.

The main objectives of the Definition of Requirements stage are:

● to provide a Requirements Specification Document for the development of a Logical Requirements Specification (LRS) to satisfy the needs of the customer or end user;

● to set out measurable acceptance criteria for the progress of the product.

Stage 3 moves from the process of analysis into the realms of design by specifying what the required system is to do.

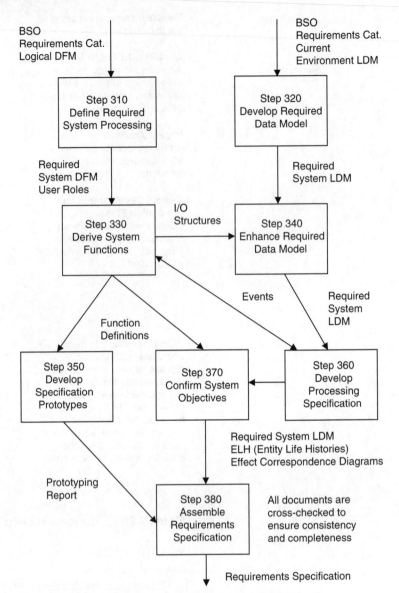

Figure 2.2.17   *Stage 3 – Definition of requirements*

Stage 4 Technical system options

This stage is carried out in parallel to Stage 5 (Logical Design). The main objectives are:

● to identify and specify ways of physically implementing the Requirements Specification;
● to provide a means of validation for the non-functional requirements that are to be incorporated into the proposed environment.

Figure 2.2.18 shows the steps taken during this activity:
   The stage will need to plan and develop information in four main areas:

1. Technical Environment – this will cover issues of specific hardware and software configuration and implementation.
2. Development Strategy – who will develop the application, e.g. will the use of sub-contractors be required or will it be developed totally in-house?

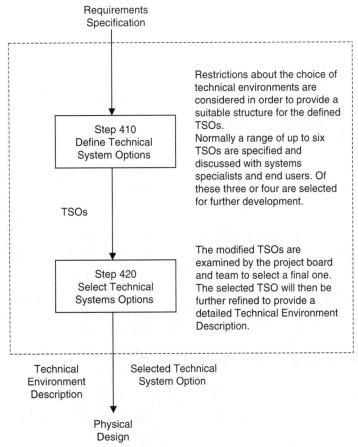

Figure 2.2.18 *Stage 4 – technical systems options (TSO)*`

3. Organizational Impact – this could include social issues like working practices or is it going to effect an existing project that is under production?
4. System Functionality – this would be handled in the BSO stage, but there may need to be some changes made in light of the technical requirements of the system.

The output of this stage is to determine the final implementation environment that the system is to run in. This includes the Technical Environment Description and the selected Technical System Option (TSO).

Stage 5 Logical Design

In this stage the developers will take the system design process as far as possible without referencing any technical environment issues. The resulting design will have a logical structure that is independent of any particular platform. It will act as a model for 'how' the system is to implement the user requirements without having any physical constraints. Figure 2.2.19 outlines the steps taken throughout this stage.

The main objectives of Stage 5 are therefore:

● to create a logical specification of the system;
● to define the update and enquiry processing and the dialogues of the new system;
● to validate and ensure integrity of the processes created.

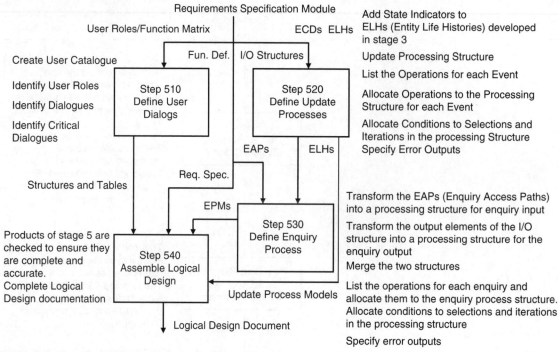

Fun. Def. | I/O Structures

Add State Indicators to ELHs (Entity Life Histories) developed in stage 3
Update Processing Structure
List the Operations for each Event
Allocate Operations to the Processing Structure for each Event
Allocate Conditions to Selections and Iterations in the processing Structure
Specify Error Outputs

Transform the EAPs (Enquiry Access Paths) into a processing structure for enquiry input
Transform the output elements of the I/O structure into a processing structure for the enquiry output
Merge the two structures

List the operations for each enquiry and allocate them to the enquiry process structure. Allocate conditions to selections and iterations in the processing structure
Specify error outputs

Figure 2.2.19   *Stage 5 – logical*

The final step of this stage is to produce a Logical Design Document that will cover all the products of Stage 5 and will provide an accurate base to be carried through to the Physical Design stage.

Stage 6 Physical design

This stage translates the Logical Design method created in Stage 5 and the Technical Environment Options created in Stage 4 into a full Physical Design. The steps involved are outlined in Figure 2.2.20.

Question 2.2.4

1. State the seven stages used in the SSADM lifecycle.
2. What are the main objectives of the Feasibility Study?
3. Specify the requirements of the first step (210) in the Business Options stage.
4. Specify the main requirements of Stage 3 (Definition of Requirements).
5. Within Stage 4 what is a Technical Environment Description?

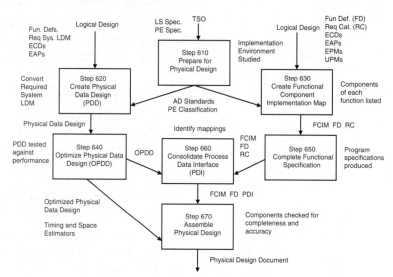

Figure 2.2.20   *Stage 6 – physical design*

The main objectives of Stage 6 are:

- to specify the physical data, processes, input and outputs using the features of a physical environment and employing quality standards;
- to establish a design which provides all that is needed to construct the system in a specified environment.

The end step of this activity involves checking the system for completeness and consistency before the final Physical Design is published. Once this has been accepted the developers can move on to implementing the design to provide a full working application to meet the needs of the original user requirements where it all started.

SSADM modelling techniques

Data flow modelling

Like other data flow diagram conventions the SSADM methods is hierarchical in structure which starts with a 'context diagram'. The context diagram shows the entire system in a single process with data flowing between it and entities that represent the outside world.

Data flow modelling is used in the early stages of the SSADM model to:

- show the sources and receivers of the data into and out of the system;
- define the processes that transform or act on data;
- specify the flows of data around the system;
- show the storage requirements for the data within the system;
- provide a communication document between the developer of the system and the end user;
- outline the current environment;
- form the basis for the functional definition.

SSADM uses four main symbols to construct data flow diagrams. These are shown in Figure 2.2.21.

1. External entities

These represent real things like people, organizations, transport animals of other computer systems that supply or receive data into the system. They acts as sources and sinks for the data that is required to initiate the system and receive the end result.

The name given to an external entity refers to a 'type' not an 'occurrence' of the entity. It is a generic type, e.g. an occurrence of College Administrator would be Sheila or Jack.

2. Processes

Processes represent the activities to be carried out and are trigged by data being passed to them. They represent a high-level abstraction in user terms and do not equate directly with computer code. The process refers to the business activity that it supports.

Generally data flow diagrams that contain processes only show them transforming or changing data during the activity. There may be exceptions where the process acting on input data needs to produce enquiry information or reports.

The name given should be brief but still specify the transformation to be carried out, i.e. specify the processing to be carried out. The unique

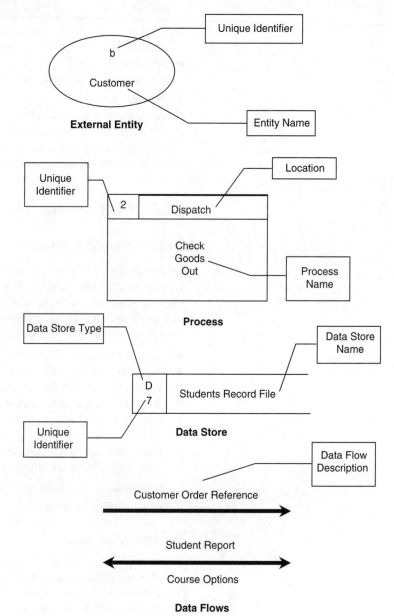

Figure 2.2.21   *Data flow diagram symbols*

identifier is not a sequence number, like all data flow diagrams the sequence of events is not specified.

Like the Yourdon data flow diagrams the processes for the SSADM model can be refined or decomposed to produce lower level diagrams (children) containing additional data to more accurately represent the activity. This process starts with a context diagram and refinement continues until no further decomposition is possible.

The final processes are classified as 'Elementary Processes' which contain an asterisk in the lower right-hand corner of the box. For each Elementary Process an Elementary Process Description will be completed summarizing its operations and activities. An outline of an Elementary Process Description is shown below:

Elementary process description
Process ID: 1
Process name: check course availability and register student Description: Details about a new student are received from the college administrator for admissions. The course file is then examined to find a particular course that the student is qualified to join. Once a course is found this information also with the student details is passed on to the student file where it is permanently stored.

3. Data store

These are stores for holding data within the system. There are four types of store:

- **D:** This is a computerized data store that holds computerized data within the system being defined. For example, a computer-held purchase order file.
- **M:** This is a manual data store within the organization that the system is being developed for. For example, a filing cabinet, archive library, etc.
- **T(M):** This is a manual transient data store. This represents a temporary data store where data is held until it is read once only. After being read once the store is then removed or deleted. For example, pigeon hole, desk in-tray, etc.
- **T:** This is a computerized transient data store. This represents a temporary storage area for data passing through the system. For example, it may be necessary to temporarily save data for an input enquiry before it is fully processed. Also if searching for a number of stored items they can temporarily stored before being displayed to the user.

The name given to a data store must reflect what it contains. There is no good just calling something 'Data Store' as this does not specify its contents. A better name would be 'Student File' as this gives a clue as to the contents of the store.

4. Data flows

Data flows use arrows to show the direction and name of the data flowing around the system. They specify the inputs and outputs to processes and data stores and highlight the information passing around the system as whole acting as links between other objects within the DFD.

Listed below are the components that can be directly connected by data flows:

- Two processes
- A data store and a process
- A process and an externals entity.

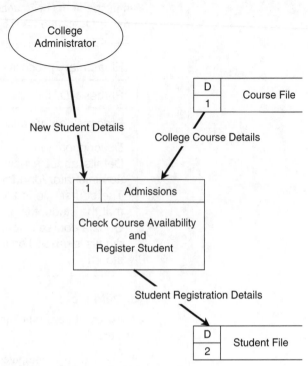

Figure 2.2.22   *College admission system*

What is not allowed:

- You cannot connect an external entity directly to a data store with a data flow.
- You cannot connect two data stores together with a data flow.

As shown in Figure 2.2.21 flows can be unidirectional or bidirectional and they must contain real data required to support the system. When obtaining information from a data store it is not necessary to show a flow going to the store that may contain a unique key to find a record. We only need to show data that is of interest in specifying what the business activity is to do.

All data flows should contain a uniquely label which clearly states the flow occurring. For example, names like Customer Order, Student Enquiry should be used not abbreviated names like My Junk or In Data, as these do not give a clue as to the contents of the data flow.

Combining the components

By putting together the different components we can construct a picture of how data is passing through the system. The Data Flow Diagram (DFD) extract shown in Figure 2.2.22 illustrates the following activities.

1. College Administrator sends new student details to the Admissions section.
2. These are checked to find a suitable course which has vacancies.
3. Student registration details are then permanently stored in the College Student File.

During the early stages of the feasibility study (Step 010) we are only concerned with modelling the physical flows of data in the current model, it is a high level abstraction only. DFDs therefore provide an early representation of the system that provides a base for defining the problem along with any necessary LDM.

Logical modelling

The physical data flow diagram provides a model of how data is processed throughout the system and how data is actually stored. It does not tell the developer or user anything about the underlying meaning or structure of that data. An SSADM LDM provides a way of graphically representing what the data information is really about, its rules and how it interacts with other information within the system.

Logical Data Modelling (LDM) consists of two parts:

- Logical Data Structure (LDS)
- Set of associated textual descriptions:
  - entity descriptions;
  - relationship descriptions;
  - attribute descriptions;
  - grouped Domain descriptions.

LDS is based on:

- Entities
- Attributes
- Relationships.

As the concept of LDS closely follows that of Data Modelling the concepts outlined above will be discussed in more detail in Section 2.4.

A LDM can be used to represent both the underlying processing of data within a current system and the required data structure of proposed new systems.

Question 2.2.5

1. What is the function of a process within an SSADM data flow diagram?
2. What is an elementary process and how is it designated?
3. Specify what is not allowed when adding data flows to a DFD model.
4. Name the component that acts as a source for the data flowing into a system.
5. What are the main components of the Logical Data Model?

Example 2.2.5

The Morgan Show Company is responsible for running a series of canine exhibitions that include a number of associated seminars. A system needs to be designed that receives visitors in the foyer where a Registration Clerk checks their personal details and if they have made an advance booking. The visitor details are then added to an entry list that contains details of people who are currently in the exhibition. Once the visitors have been registered they are passed on to the Seminar Organizer who determines what seminars the visitor wishes to attend and adds the details to a seminar list. Finally visitors receive a pass from the Seminar Organizer that contains their personal details and any associated seminars that they wish to attend.

Question:
Complete an outline SSADM data flow diagram that represents the system.

Suggested solution:

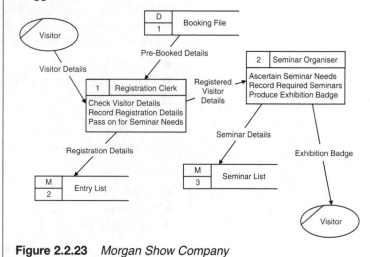

Figure 2.2.23 *Morgan Show Company*

Exercise 2.2.3

The Bess & Bailey Department Store has the facility to handle customers orders 'in house' and if the item they require is in stock it is delivered to their home. An Order Clerk is designated to attend to the customers as they enter the store. The Order Clerk assists the customer in choosing the required item and then checks via the Warehouse Manager to ascertain if it is stock. The Warehouse Manager looks up the details of the required item from the stock database and if they are available, records the customer details (name and address) and raises a dispatch note which is sent to the customer's home.

Question:
Complete an outline SSADM data flow diagram that represents the Bess & Bailey Department Store system.

Object-oriented analysis (OOA) development

Class association diagrams

Object-oriented analysis is concerned with analysing the 'negotiated statement of requirements' to ascertain the required classes to be developed and any relating associations, responsibilities and collaborations.

Some general points:

- A class describes the behaviour of a set of objects of some kind.
- Objects are classified as instances of a class and can be associated to other objects. This is termed as an *association* between the classes for which the objects are instances.

- All classes have an internal state with an appropriate behaviour associated with them. This can be described in a set of *responsibilities* which specify a part of the overall behaviour of the intended system.
- In order to fulfil their responsibilities objects *collaborate* with other objects.

The first stage for any developer is to take the 'negotiated statements of requirements' and ascertain any classes (which represent objects) within the structure. These need to be analysed to find out if they are required in the model or not. The final list of objects then form a base for the development process to continue.

When analysing a negotiated statement of requirements we need to first identify classes and associations that are present. There are two general issues that need to be made clear:

1. It is difficult in the first instance to establish all the class and associations that exist within the document. It takes practice in order to become proficient in obtaining this data and analysis will improve with experience.
2. When first establishing the classes and then the associations it must not be forgotten that both are interconnected. Considering what classes are needed helps in identifying what associations exist between the classes.

Identifying classes

In identifying classes we are identifying the components whose behaviour is significant in application area under analysis. It is a first and foremost requirement for a good understanding of the application area to be developed. If we take a banking cash machine system then Customer or Cash are obvious class structures that would need to be considered. Remember that class structures can come in different formats (tangible, roles, events and units) which need further add to the problem of class identification.

In order to analyse the requirements to determine the classes present, you should consider the 'nouns' or 'noun phrases' that occur within the text. When finding these they should be underlined in order to highlight their presence.

Take the extract below:

> In the college there are a number of rooms, some of these may be classrooms and contain students whilst others are non-teaching rooms or staff rooms. Each classroom in use contains a lecturer who is responsible for the course content being taught. Some of the lecturers are assigned course tutor roles with the responsibility of organizing the curriculum content of the subject areas.

By using the process of *textual analysis* the requirements can be scanned and any likely class candidates can be emphasized (or underlined).

Looking at the extract above we get:

> In the <u>college</u> there are a number of <u>rooms</u>, some of these may be <u>classrooms</u> and contain <u>students</u> whilst others are <u>non-teaching</u> *rooms* or <u>staff rooms</u>. Each <u>classroom</u> in use contains a <u>lecturer</u> who is responsible for the *course content* being taught. Some of the *lecturers*

Question 2.2.6

1. What is the link between a Class and an Object?
2. What format of class structure does Student and Library come under?

are assigned *course tutor* roles with the responsibility of organizing the *curriculum content* of the *subject areas*.

We can see that a number of likely candidates for classes to be developed have been underlined. But are all of these classes going to be required in the final model? This is where a thorough understanding of the negotiated statement of requirements is essential that is backed up with experience in developing object models.

Associations

As we have already learned an association is a connection between two objects that is significant for the application area under development.

Figure 2.2.24 shows one Lecturer object (Bailey), five Student objects (Peters, Jones, Watson, Collins and Davies) and five associations. The diagram only gives a limited view in what it is trying to express and requires what is called an *association type* to describe a group of associations with a common structure and meaning.

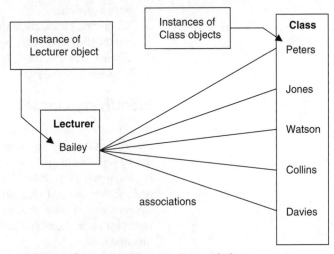

Figure 2.2.24   *Object instances and associations*

An association type has two important properties:

- A name which reflects the meaning of the association. This is often expressed as a verb, e.g. the association name between Lecturer and Class could be 'tutors' (A lecturer tutors class).
- The association will need to show multiplicity that relates to the degree between objects. These can be one to one, one to many and many to many. This is donated by the use of a block blob on the many end of the association line. The association multiplicity between Lecturer and Class is shown in Figure 2.2.25.

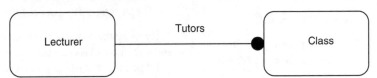

Figure 2.2.25   *The tutors one to many association type*

When reading the diagram it stresses the multiplicity with respect to Class (i.e. there is one Lecturer object and many Class objects), but the diagram must also be considered in the other direction where Class is just concerned with one Lecturer object.

Question 2.2.7

Draw diagrams (similar to the one in Figure 2.2.25) by selecting objects of your own choice to represent associations that are classified as:

1. classified as one to one;
2. classified as many to many.

Give a brief description for each diagram explaining the association type.

Invariants

Taking the example below:

> A Lecturer may lecture several Students and Students may be taught by a number of Lecturers that are members of the same Course Team as the Course Tutor.

This is saying that lecturers who lecture students must be from the same course team as the course tutor. This is known as an invariant and must always be true for the classes and associations being developed.

An invariant is a rule that places a constraint on the allowable instances of classes and associations.

Responsibilities

These need to be specified for the classes being developed. Shown below are two examples one for a Student class and one for a Course class that need to record data as part of their operational behaviour.

Class: Student
Responsibilities:
Recording the student name, enrolment number and course

Class: Course
Responsibilities:
Recording the course name, curriculum content, formal prerequisites

An example where the responsibility is designed to carry out a prescribed task is shown below.

Class: Sensor
Responsibilities:
To set off the temperature and pressure warning systems if they become dangerous

Identifying associations

One way of achieving this is to use a class-association matrix which takes the classes that have been identified and pairs them together to establish if an association, that is relevant to the application area under development, exists.

For specifying small to medium size object models a useful approach for identifying associations is to use a matrix structure which is shown in Figure 2.2.26. The diagram specifies a class-association matrix for classes that are established for a typical college system.

	Principal	Vice Principal	Head of Department	Section Managers	Lecturer	Student	Administrator
Principal		X					
Vice Principal	X		X				
Head of Department		X		X	X		X
Section Managers			X		X		X
Lecturer			X	X		X	X
Student					X		X
Administrator			X	X	X	X	

The X's signify that an association exists between classes

Figure 2.2.26   *Class-association matrix*

The wording of an association between classes plays an important role in determining its category. For example:

A work schedule is organized by a lecturer *for a* student.

The words *for a* suggest that an association exists between Lecturer and Student which would emphasize a one aspect of a one-to-many association. If we had a statement like:

Work schedules are organized by lecturers and *used by* students.

Here the words *used by* signify a many multiplicity association with respect to the work schedules.

Inheritance

We have seen that inheritance is an important attribute of object-oriented analysis and this concept need to be clearly specified on the class-association diagram. A college, e.g. will have many employees, the principal, vice principal, senior managers, lecturers, maintenance staff, security and administration staff. They all inherent common attributes, e.g. they all have names, addresses, national insurance numbers, etc., but they will differ in respect to their precise roles and their associations with other class members. A graphical representation is shown in Figure 2.2.27.

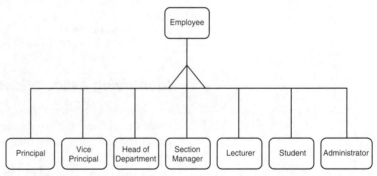

Figure 2.2.27   *Class-association diagram showing inherited classes*

In some texts this inheritance relationship is known as a 'is-a-kind-of' relationship. The semantics of this diagram specifies the behaviour of each inherited class in two ways. For example, an instance of Lecturer has its behaviour defined in two ways; the part of the behaviour that is unique for lecturers and the part common to all employees defined in the Employee class.

Developing a class-association diagram

The following example develops the concept of a class-association model by taking part of a negotiated statement of requirements, analysing its content to ascertain the classes and associations and produces a graphical representation.

Remember a class is a set of objects that share a common structure and a common behaviour. An object has state, behaviour and identity.

Example 2.2.6

Part of a negotiated statement of requirements for the Carabaz Dog Breeding Kennels is shown below:

> The kennels need to keep and maintain information about the dogs they keeps and the progress of breeding when the required dogs become available. The dogs are organized into breeds; each dog belonging to a breed and a breed contains many dogs. There are two sorts of dog; a dog (males) and a bitch (female). It is important for the kennels to maintain a record for the breeding background of all the dogs. A dog (male) can mate many times a year, whereas a bitch (female) can only mate once (when they come into season). A mating will hopefully produce many puppy births.

We first need to perform a textual analysis of the requirements in order to determine the candidate objects for the classes. Possible classes are:

> The <u>kennels</u> needs to keep and maintain <u>information</u> about the <u>dogs</u> it keeps and the progress of breeding when the required <u>dogs</u> become available. The <u>dogs</u> are organized into <u>breeds</u>; each dog belonging to a <u>breed</u> and a <u>breed</u> contains many <u>dogs</u>. There are two sorts of <u>dog</u>; a <u>dog</u> (<u>males</u>) and a <u>bitch</u> (<u>female</u>). It is important for the <u>kennels</u> to maintain a <u>record</u> for the breeding background of all the <u>dogs</u>. A <u>dog</u> (<u>male</u>) can <u>mate</u> many times a <u>year</u>, whereas a <u>bitch</u> (<u>female</u>) can only <u>mate</u> once (when they come into <u>season</u>). A <u>mating</u> will hopefully produce many <u>puppy</u> births.

The Candidate Objects are:

> Kennels, Information, Dogs, Breeds, Dog (Male), Bitch (Female), Record, Mate, Season, Year and Puppy.

From this list we need to eliminate any:

- Redundant classes – where two words mean the same thing you need to choose the one that is more descriptive.
- Irrelevant classes – those that have nothing directly to do with the problem.
- Vague classes – those that are not specific enough and need to be more closely defined before they can be developed.

The eliminated candidate objects are:

> Information, Record, Season and Year – which are not directly relevant at this stage to represent the requirements of the system.

This leaves the revised list of candidate objects:

Kennels, Dogs, Breeds, Dog (Male), Bitch (Female), Puppy and Mate

these represent the requirements for the kennel's breeding program and will form the bases of the class-association diagram.

Possible associations are between:

Kennels and Breed (one to many association, as each breed belongs to the kennels and the kennels has many breeds)

Breed and Dog (one to many association, as one each dog belongs to a breed and breeds contain many dogs)

Dog (male) and Mate (one to many association, as a dog can mate many times)

Bitch (female) and Mate (one to one as bitches can only mate once during – when they are in season)

Puppy and Mate (one to many association, as a single mating can produce several puppies)

Inheritance

Dog (male), Bitch (female) and Puppy are all types of Dog and therefore inherit some common characteristics as well as individual ones.

Responsibilities

```
Class: Kennels
"There is only one instance of this class, it is the
orchestrating instance"
Class: Breed
Responsibilities: Record the types of breed
Class: Dog
Responsibilities: Record the name, breed, sex and age
of the dogs
Class: Dog (male)
(inherits from dog)
Responsibilities: Record the date of last mating
Class: Bitch (female)
(inherits from dog)
Responsibilities: Record the date of last season
Class: Puppy
(inherits from dog)
Responsibilities: Record name of new puppies
Class: Mate
Responsibilities: Record the mating details for each
litter
```

Class-association diagram

Figure 2.2.28 represents an understanding of the application area to be developed. It represents the way things are related to one and other and ensures that we fully understand what is required before designing a solution. It still open for discussion with the customer, or end user, to ensure it is an accurate model for the functional requirements of the system.

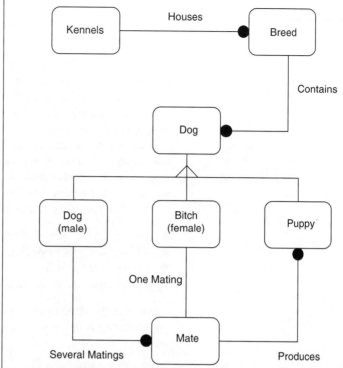

Figure 2.2.28   *Class-association diagram for the Carabaz Dog Breeding Kennels*

Question 2.2.8

1. What are you looking for when you carry out the process of textual analysis?
2. Give a graphical illustration showing an example of inheritance.
3. What is an invariant?
4. What method can be used to identify associations?
5. When carrying out textual analysis on a problem statement, what does a redundant class mean?

Exercise 2.2.4

The following is an extract from a negotiated statement of requirements:

An organizer needs to keep and update information on a seminar devoted to canine health. The seminar is made up of several sessions, each run by different speakers. The speakers running the sessions have to produce a booklet for their own slot. Each session has a chairperson and that person is only allocated this role once. Information about the speakers who produce the booklets needs to be recorded; each booklet is written by one speaker only and speakers are only required to produce one booklet. For the seminar presentation purposes, a person can be a chairperson or a speaker.

1. Perform a textual analysis to ascertain any candidate objects.
2. Select the required classes to be presented.
3. Ascertain any associations that exist.
4. Specify the inheritance factors contained within the text.
5. Produce associated text to outline the class responsibilities.
6. Complete a class-association diagram.

UML

Introduction

The Unified Modelling Language (UML) is the industry-standard language for specifying, visualizing, constructing and documenting the artefacts of software systems. Using UML, programmers and application architects can make a blueprint of a project, which, in turn, makes the actual software development process easier.

UML was created at Rational Software by methodologists Grady Booch, Ivar Jacobson and Jim Rumbaugh with input from other leading methodologists, many software vendors, as well as end users. Its aim is to unify the various existing systems into a best-of-breed modelling language.

The UML technique can be used to model the following processes:

- Business process modelling with use cases
- Class and object modelling
- Component modelling
- Distribution and deployment modelling.

As already stated there is an increase in the use of object-oriented programming languages, so UML can provide an alternative model for analysis.

UML claims

- Is sufficiently expressive to represent and connect the concepts of abstraction within software development across a number of domains which include:
  - information systems;
  - real time systems;
  - web systems.
- It can handle the modelling of business processes:
  - their logical and physical software models;
  - provide references to their implementation.
- It is not complex:
  - the unified modelling language is built from a small number of concepts applied consistently across a number of modelling problems.

Basic components of UML

- UML specification contains a notation guide, semantics and appendices
- UML notation and semantics describe:
  - class diagrams;
  - object diagrams;
  - use case diagrams;
  - behaviour diagrams;
    - state diagrams
    - activity diagrams
    - sequence diagrams
    - collaboration diagrams
  - implementation diagrams
    - component diagram
    - deployment diagram

UML is free for all to use within their given applications. This helps to establish its usage within industry where software companies can use it within their own methods and developers of computer aided software engineering applications are free to develop associated tools.

Question 2.2.9

1. Where does UML originate from?
2. What are stated advantages of using the UML modelling process?

Objects and classes

One of the main advantages of UML is that it provides an excellent foundation for object-oriented analysis and design. UML defines an object as:

> An entity with a well-defined boundary and identity, encapsulates state and behaviour. State is represented by attributes and relationships, behaviour is represented by operations and methods. An object is an instance of a class.

UML consolidates a set of core modelling techniques that are generally accepted across many current development applications. Its inherent object structure is ideally suited for implementation into modern languages like C++ and Java.

UML diagram structures

1. Use case diagram

To determine the system boundaries and the high level requirements for the system a 'use case' diagram is constructed. It shows the 'actors' in the system and the general services that they require. Stick people normally represent the actors and the services are represented by ellipses. These diagrams originate from Jacobsen who was one of the three original developers of UML.

Definition for a use case diagram:

> A sequence of actions that the system performs, yields an observable result of value to a particular actor

They are used for:

- providing scenarios that illustrate prototypical use case instances. An instance of the use case class;
- providing an overall picture of systems functionality and user requirements.

An example of 'use case' model is shown in Figure 2.2.29.
A use case diagram has the following advantages:

- Capture requirements from users' perspective – it provides a diagrammatic base for user involvement and validation.
- Helps manage delivery – prioritize use cases to define processes for delivery and help estimate requirements.
- Progresses the development – can identify objects and provides a base for user manuals and test plans.
- Improve quality – aids tracing of requirements and identifies faults earlier.

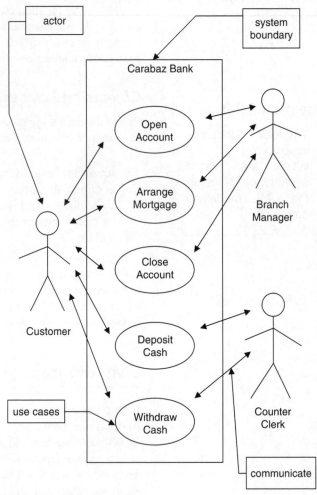

Figure 2.2.29   *A use case diagram*

Question 2.2.10

1. Specify two advantages for creating a 'use case' diagram.
2. Draw a 'use case' diagram to represent the following scenario:

A patient attends a consultation at the hospital and is seen by a specialist about a medical problem. This results in an operation being performed by a surgeon (not the specialist) who is also an expert in area of the medical problem. The operation is serious and the patient needs to recover in the recovery ward where the surgeon and doctors can monitor his/her progress. Once they are satisfied the patient is transferred to a general ward where the doctors and nurses can finally nurse the patient back to full health.

2. Class and object diagrams

Class and object diagrams capture most of the static structure and relationships of classes and objects. They do not handle the dynamic aspect of their behaviour, this is modelled in either state diagrams, sequence diagrams, collaboration diagrams or activity diagrams.

Class diagram

A class is a group of things with similar attributes and behaviour. A class diagram represents 'things' that are handled in the system. A simple example is shown in Figure 2.2.30.

Figure 2.2.30   *Example of a class diagram*

Object diagram

This is a variation of the class diagram and uses similar notation. It differs in the fact that it shows a number of object instances of a class instead of just classes. Figure 2.2.31 shows a class diagram containing Student and Computer classes, this is then expanded to produce an object diagram which shows a Student instance 'Jones' and two Computer instances 'Library PC' and 'Room 801'.

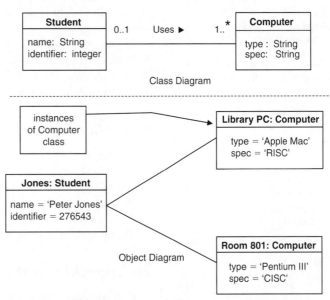

Figure 2.2.31   *Object diagram developed from Class diagram*

Objects diagrams are used to exemplify a complex class diagram by showing what the actual instances and relationships look like. They may also be used as part of a collaboration diagram which specifies the dynamic collaboration between objects.

Class diagram syntax

The class box can be split into three compartments as shown in Figure 2.2.32. The syntax used in the compartments is independent of the programming language used, although some developers like to incorporate program specific structures like Pascal, C++ or Java.

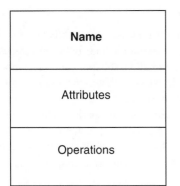

Figure 2.2.32   *Class compartments*

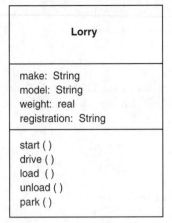

Figure 2.2.33 *Lorry class example*

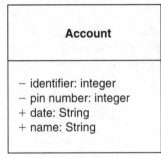

Figure 2.2.34 *Visibility of attributes*

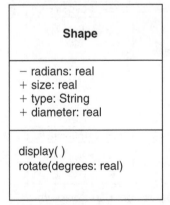

Figure 2.2.35 *Class operation example*

Figure 2.2.36 *An example of an association*

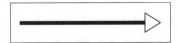

Figure 2.2.37 *An example of a generalization*

Figure 2.2.33 gives an example of this for a class Lorry with attributes Make, Model, Weight and Registration, followed by the operations start( ), drive( ), stop( ), load( ), unload( ), park( ).

Name compartment

This contains the name of the class and is typed in *bold* and is centred. The name should relate directly to the class it represents and be meaningful. Often a noun is used like Customer, Student, Manager, etc.

Attribute compartment

Typical attribute types are integer, real, Boolean, enumeration and String, etc. which can be specific for certain programming languages. Attributes can be expressed as 'public' which can be viewed and used from outside the class. The encapsulated attributes are defined as 'private' and can only be viewed and accessed from within the class they are declared in. To denote the difference between these the following notation is used:

- − (minus sign) specifies a private attribute;
- + (plus sign) specifies a public attribute.

An example is shown in Figure 2.2.34 that contains two private (encapsulated) attributes *identifier* and *pin number* and two public attributes *date* and *name*.

In some variations of the model, a *protected* type can also be used which is similar to the *private* type except that all inherited classes can also view and use the data. The term used for these attribute definitions is *visibility*, i.e. an attribute visible and it can be referenced by other classes.

Operation (action) compartment

These are used to manipulate the attributes to perform certain actions. Figure 2.2.35 shows two operations, *display( )* and *rotate(degrees: real)*. These will look familiar to you especially if you have been programming in languages like C++ and Java where functions and methods are integral parts of the language.

The operations describe what a class can do and what services it offers.

Relationships within UML

Class diagrams consist of classes and the relationships between them. The relationships can be described as:

1. *Association* – a connection between two classes or an object of those classes. An association represents a semantic link between classes that can be unidirectional or bidirectional. Graphically an association is shown as a solid line, possibly directed, with a name and showing multiplicity. An example is shown in Figure 2.2.36.
2. *Generalization* – a relationship between a more general and a more specific element. This relationship is used to define inheritance (to model derived classes from a parent class). Graphically this is shown as a solid line with an arrowhead that points to the parent. An example is shown in Figure 2.2.37.
3. *Dependency* – this specifies a relationship between two elements one being dependent and the other independent. A change in the

Figure 2.2.38 *An example of a dependency*

Figure 2.2.39 *An example of a refinement*

independent element will affect the dependent element. Graphically this is shown as a dashed line and may be labelled. An example is shown in Figure 2.2.38.

4. *Refinement* – a relationship between two descriptions of the same thing, but at different levels of development. Graphically (see Figure 2.2.39) this is shown as a dashed line with a hollow triangle between the two elements.

Association structure

An association occurs where classes depend on, or interact with, one and other. They define the routes for sending messages and relate to the operations that objects must meet in order to carry out their responsibilities. An association name must be expressed so that it describes its exact relationship between classes. A filled arrow that specifies the direction of the association may also follow it. The name normally contains a verb that expresses the association, e.g. *Takes a*, *Placed with*, *Employs'*, etc. These are found during the textual analysis process where verb and verb phrases are identified. An example of associations between two classes is shown in Figure 2.2.40.

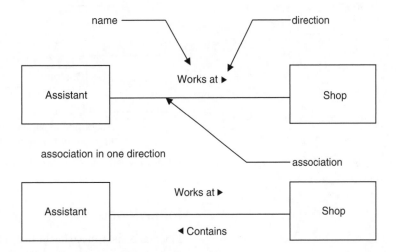

Figure 2.2.40 *Class association syntax*

If a class participates in the association then it has a specific role in the relationship. Figure 2.2.41, an Assistant has the role of employee and the Shop has the role of a counter.

Most texts and the OMG (Object Management Group) UML specification outline several types of association, but for the level of work required for this 'system's analysis' unit what is classified as a normal association will generally handle its specified aims.

Figure 2.2.41 *Association role relationship*

Question 2.2.11

1. What is the difference between a class diagram and an object diagram?
2. What does *visibility* of attributes mean? Give two examples.
3. What is the *operation* compartment of a class diagram for?
4. Specify the four types of relationships that exist between classes.
5. What do associations define?

Question 2.2.12

Draw a simple class diagram to represent the relationship between a Lecturer and Tutorial group. Add a suitable name, direction and multiplicity.

Multiplicity

It is sometimes necessary to show how objects are linked across instances of an association. This is termed multiplicity (i.e. the number of objects involved in an association), examples of which are shown below:

- 0..1 (zero to one)
- 0..* or just * (zero to many)
- 1..* (one to many)
- x..y (x to y where x and y are integer values i.e. 7..14)
- n (exact number i.e. 5, 4, 47, etc.)

Combinations of these can be used to specify more complex multiplicities which can be expressed within list structures.

If an association is shown to have a 'many' multiplicity side then an alternative way of specifying how individual objects can be found may be used. This is then termed as a 'qualified association' and is donated by an identifier enclosed in a box that is applied to the class that uses it. An example of this structure is shown in Figure 2.2.42, where customers have unique identifiers that allow them to be referenced by the Accounts.

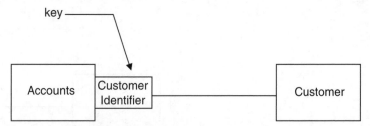

Accounts class uses the unique Customer Identifier
key to identify individual Customer objects

Figure 2.2.42   *Qualified association*

Inheritance

Inheritance is a mechanism that allows classes to inherit characteristics through a tree type structure. At the top of a tree is a superclass that contains all the common characteristics required by the subclasses underneath it. The subclasses can then use the characteristics (i.e. inherit them) from the superclass plus any additional ones that they declare within themselves. Inheritance operates at class level and is the kind of relationship that centres on the activity of classification. Multiple inheritance can be shown by producing further levels, i.e. producing subclasses of subclasses.

Inheritance can be approached in two ways: through *specialization* or *generalization*. Specialization involves examining a particular class for different ways in which its member objects can be split into subclasses which have their own individual characteristics. Generalization involves searching for different classes that have the same characteristics in common and grouping those characteristics into a superclass. For example, if we wanted two classes, *circle* and *sphere* then they have some common attributes like radius, diameter, etc. which can be grouped in a superclass called *Shape*. Here we have used generalization to abstract common characteristics of circle and sphere into a task superclass. The symbol used for a generalization is shown in diagram 40.

Aggregation

This is split into two categories: aggregation and composition (or composite aggregation). The former is a special case of an association and signifies a 'part-of' relationship between classes or objects. Diagrammatically a hollow diamond is used at the end of the association to signify that aggregation exists between classes. For a college system, a Department is part of the whole College. This representation is shown in Figure 2.2.43.

Figure 2.2.43 *Aggregation*

An aggregation operates at object level, unlike inheritance which operates at class level. The tree structure used is similar to that used with inheritance apart from the diamond present at the superclass end. This can lead to some confusion and you need to remember that an aggregation tree is composed of objects that are part of an aggregate object, whereas a generalization tree is composed of classes that describe a single object.

A composition (composite aggregation) indicates that any part of an object 'live' inside a unique whole. That is, the part will live or die together with the whole. Diagrammatically this is represented by a black diamond and is shown in Figure 2.2.44 where a Statement 'lives' inside the Transaction and if the Transaction is destroyed, the Statement will die along with in.

Figure 2.2.44 *Composite aggregation*

A composition owns its parts, therefore the multiplicity on its whole side must be zero or one (0..1) and the multiplicity on the part side may be any value (*).

Responsibilities

A responsibility is normally expressed in terms of obligations to other elements. It is normally expressed as a string and attached to a class in its own name compartment. Figure 2.2.45 gives an example of a classifier symbol with a list of responsibilities.

A good starting point for modelling classes is to specify the responsibilities using a natural English structure. Each class will have at least one responsibility ranging to only a few for well-structured classes. Never allow a class to have an excessive number of responsibilities otherwise it may lead to modelling problems and a complex interpretation that is difficult to validate. As you refine a class model the responsibilities can be transformed into attributes and operations.

Navigability

In more detailed diagrams it is advantageous to show the direction of the association between classes. Graphically this is shown by using open

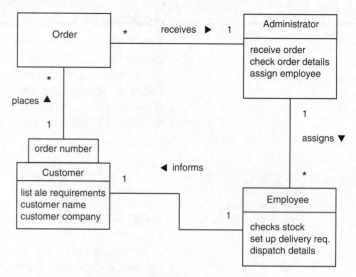

Classes with required responsibilities

Administrator	
Responsibilities	Collaborations
Receive an order from a customer	Customer
Check the order details	Order
Assign employee to handle the order	Employee

Figure 2.2.45   *Bailey Ale company class diagram*

headed arrow that points to the class that is navigable. For example, if we had two classes *Order* and *Customer* and the arrow points to the customer class then we can say that *Order* has the responsibility to tell you which customer it is for, but the *Customer* has no reciprocal ability to tell you which order it has. The lines can have the same multiplicity as ordinary associations and can be shown as unidirectional or bidirectional. They express information that are more useful for implementation and specification diagrams.

General comment

For a first-level abstraction we should not spend too much time looking for attributes and operations as these can be added as the project develops. For a general view that is understandable to the customer or end user, the responsibilities can give a clearer picture of the required behaviour for the classes. The initial class diagram should be kept simple and it does not need to fix the actual implementation, but provide a base for discussion and future development.

A class diagram only gives a static view of the classes in the system and does not give us any information about how the system behaves dynamically, i.e. what happens over time as the system is executed. In order to express these concepts UML uses the following diagrams:

- sequence diagrams;
- collaboration diagrams;
- state diagrams;
- activity diagrams.

Sequence and collaboration diagrams are different ways of specifying the messages that pass between classes over time periods. State diagrams show how objects of a class change state when acted on by certain events. Activity diagrams are similar to state diagrams but are more appropriate to systems that change state as a result of an internal event as opposed to an external one. An example of a sequence diagram is shown in Figure 2.2.46.

Question 2.2.13

1. What is a composite aggregation? How is this symbolized on a class diagram?
2. How are responsibilities recorded on a class diagram?
3. What is the difference between inheritance and aggregation?

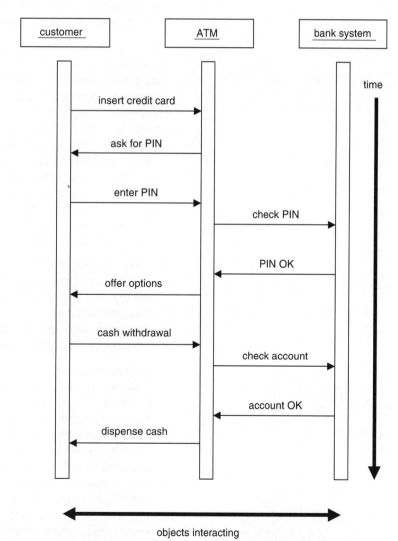

Figure 2.2.46 *Sequence diagram for an Automatic Teller Machine system*

Example 2.2.7

The following is an extract from a negotiated statement of requirements:

The Bailey Ale Company is a small independent brewing company that produces a selection of real ales. The company requires a system to process a customer order for a consignment of ales. The company has a designated administrator who receives the customer order and assigns an employee to check the assignment and feedback the availability to the customer.

The ale supplied to the customer is part of a consignment that comes in three types:

- *Mild Brew* – which is brewed to 3.4% alcohol with a specific gravity of 1.024 and a low sugar content.
- *Vicars Tibble* – which is brewed to 5.3% alcohol with a specific gravity of 1.037 and a medium sugar content.
- *Bailey Gut Rot* – which is brewed to 8.1% alcohol with a specific gravity of 1.098 and a high sugar content.

The management responsibilities of the administrator are to receive customer orders, check the order details and assign an employee to process the order. Each order is given a unique 'order number' by the customer and specifies the ale required for the consignment, along with the customer name and company. On receiving the cleared order, the employee responsible for processing it, checks the consignment details to ensure the ale is in stock, sets up delivery requirements and informs the customer that the order is being dispatched. The employee then activates the consignment requirements. The consignment responsibilities are to list the number and type of ale ordered along with the cost breakdown.

Take the following steps to analyse the requirements:
1. Carry out a textual analysis to ascertain the classes that are relevant for the Bailey Ale Company.
2. Ascertain the associations between classes.
3. Ascertain the responsibilities for each class.
4. Draw a class diagram to represent the system.

Suggested solutions:
1. Relevant classes are: Customer, Order, Administrator, Employee, Consignment, Ale, Mild Brew (Ale), Vicars Tibble (Ale) and Bailey Gut Rot (Ale)
2. Associations come from statements like: *Administrator receives a customer order* which specifies a *receives* association in the direction from Order to Administrator.
3. At a high level it is a good idea to specify the responsibilities for each class, i.e. the responsibilities of Employee are to check the ale is in stock, sets up delivery requirements and provide dispatch details for the customer.
4. Please see Figure 2.2.47.

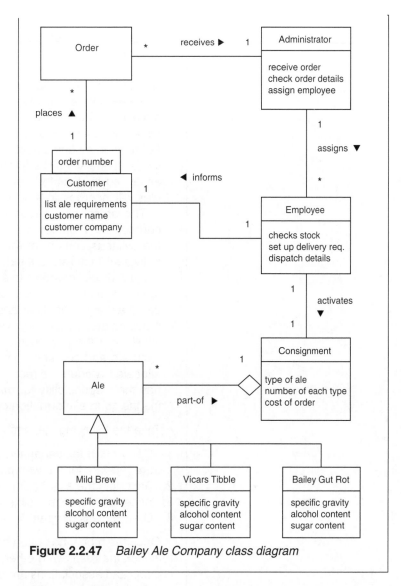

Figure 2.2.47   *Bailey Ale Company class diagram*

UML summary

UML is a modelling language, not a method or methodology. It defines a number of diagrams and the meaning of those diagrams. It does not describe the steps used to develop the software which carries out certain tasks and the full implementation requirements. It is a blueprint for developers so they know exactly what they need to build and for project managers as an aid to cost estimation. It is also a bridge between technical developers and non-technical users and provides an opportunity for developers to ascertain the exact requirements the users have for the proposed system. The idea behind UML is that it is method independent.

Exercise 2.2.5

The following is an extract of a negotiated statement of requirements:

The Bernese College wants to improve its marketing strategy by setting up an Intranet web site primarily to contain a computerized prospectus. The prospectus will contain course information that can be viewed by lecturers, managers, non-teaching staff and students. The college courses are made up of modules that are classified at three different levels; foundation, intermediate and advanced. Students will take 3 years (full-time) to complete the course starting at the foundation level first. Foundation modules need to be assessed by incorporating level one key skills, intermediate modules need to be assessed by directed coursework and advanced modules will incorporate 'A' level examinations.

The prospectus needs to provide a list of lecturers, courses and modules with a more detailed description of the syllabus content of the modules. Information about individual lecturers should include their location, main subject disciplines and telephone extension as well as the modules that the lecturer tutors. Each course is allocated a unique identifier and is made up of a number of modules at the required level. The management responsibilities of the prospectus need to add and/or remove lecturers and courses from the system. Each course is allocated a course director, who is also a lecture, who has the responsibility for running the course and updating the course information contained in the prospectus.

Take the following steps to analyse the requirements:

1. Carry out a textual analysis to ascertain the classes that are relevant for the web page prospectus system.
2. Ascertain the association between classes.
3. Ascertain the responsibilities for each class.
4. Draw a class diagram to represent the system.

Once the model has been completed it would be beneficial to check the result with other group members to ensure the classes and associations are accurate representations of the requirements.

2.3 Systems investigation

Requirements analysis an introduction

The starting point for any project is a document that originates from a customer or a user of the proposed system, known as the customer or user requirements. The document, which is usually written in a natural language, can range in size from a few pages to a large booklet. It is often the case that someone who is not a computing system specialist produces this document. This results in a document that needs to be analysed to ensure the main requirements are clearly specified and fully meet the needs of the customer. The document also needs to be fully understood by the developers of the product so the resulting system can be constructed to its full potential.

The requirements analysis activity aims to produce a specification that is:

- clear,
- concise,

- unambiguous,
- understandable to the customer or end user.

The development team needs to analyse the user requirements to produce the following specifications:

- functional requirements,
- non-functional requirements,
- hardware,
- user training arrangements,
- software support,
- criteria for acceptability.

Functional requirements

These specify the main functions that are inherent in the user requirements. They specify what the customer wants the system to do by highlighting the main aims within the document.

Non-functional requirements

These are often known as constraints that provide information about the limitation on the system. For example, 'the response time for the customer enquiry must be within 3 seconds', or 'the program is to run on the company PC network structure which operates via a Novell operating system'.

Non-functional requirements either specify the characteristics of a system, e.g. specifying the time it takes to receive a response or the speed of operation of a certain system, or they govern the development process by specifying a certain programming language.

Example 2.3.1

A local squash club needs a computer system to allocate the use of its courts. The players need to book in at a reception where the operator can check on the availability of the courts. The operator can type in commands to:

- Display all the courts that club owns and whether they are operational.
- Display the courts that are available to use.
- Display who is playing at the current time.
- Enter data for people who want to play currently.
- Enter data for people who need to pre-book a court.

The system also needs to inform the operator when the time is up, for players on a particular court. The system is to be implemented on the clubs existing PC network that operates using Pentium II machines running at 266 MHz with 2.4 Gb disk drives (less than 0.3 Gb available) and 32 Mb RAM running under Windows 95.

From this extract we need to ascertain the functional and non-functional requirements.

Functional requirements

1. Display all the courts that club owns and whether they are operational.

2. Display the courts that are available to use.
3. Display who is playing at the current time.
4. Enter data for people who want to play currently.
5. Enter data for people who need to pre-book a court.
6. Inform the operator when the time is up, for players on a particular court.

Non-functional requirements

1. System to run on Pentium II machines.
2. Machines restricted to a processor speed of 333 MHz.
3. Limited disk drive space as only 0.3 Gb is available.
4. Restricted RAM memory of only 32 Mb.
5. Operating system is running under Windows 95.

It can be seen from the functional requirements that the use of bullet points helps in finding main objectives, but in most cases this is not the case and the text has to be thoroughly examined for these items. This is the case in the next example where an extract from a user specification is given with no obvious indication of the functional or non-functional requirements. This unfortunately is the norm for most user requirement documentation.

Question 2.3.1

Examine the fragment from a user requirements document shown below and identify the functional and non-functional requirements.

A system needs to monitor and display the temperatures in all the cold store units within the company. It needs to detect any adverse change in temperature that would indicate a fault within the cold store machinery. At selected intervals the system should write temperature data to a database which the engineers can use as a check for the correct running of the cold stores. The system is to be implemented on the company computer system where only 1 Mb of memory is available. The company computer is running on a VAX VMS operating system. As memory is a problem and the data needs to be kept for an indefinite period, the system should periodically archive the database files to a magnetic tape system.

It is often the case that the user requirements contain the following properties.

Functional and non-functional requirements are not obviously separated

Many user requirements documents are not structured into neat categories that are easily separated into the required specifications. The document takes a lot of analysing, to first find the required functions and separate them as required.

The user requirements document contains ambiguous statements

As the customer uses a natural language to complete the requirements it is open to ambiguities within its structure. As the specification requires a high level of precision to outline the main requirements, structures like the one shown below need to be clarified.

> A system needs to check on the speed and temperature of a specified mechanism. Flashing red and green lights are to be used to display this information to the user.

The second sentence is ambiguous, as it is not clear as to the way the lights should operate. Do both have two lights? Red for a warning and green for OK or is there one light for each of them that uniquely identifies them?

Such ambiguities need to be addressed by the development team and if necessary the customer needs to be involved to ensure the resulting specification meets their original aims.

From the squash club example above we find:

> The system also needs to inform the operator when the time is up for players on a particular court.

Now how is the system going to inform the user, is it going to be an audible signal or visual message, or both. This again needs to be clarified to satisfy the requirements for the squash club.

The user requirements may contain omissions

As many systems are very large it is more likely that the user requirements may contain omissions. If we take the squash club example above, there is a mention of the operator entering several commands, but what happens if the operator enters a wrong command? A suitable warning message should be given and the option of re-entering the command should be offered to the operator.

Platitudes need to be clarified

These relate to meaningless statements, for example:

> The system should be easy to use and help should be given to the operator

This does not mean anything to the developer. It needs to be expressed in concrete terms to include facts like a Graphical User Interface, or a Menu driven interface is to be used to supply helpful information to the user.

Remove any extraneous detail

Remove any unnecessary statements that are not directly part of the final requirements.

For example, a supermarket database system does not need to contain details about precise input sequences that need to be entered when checking the database for certain stock items. This level of detail can be left to the design and implementation activities.

Properties that are important to both the developer and customer should not be hidden under unnecessary data. So remove any 'waffle' that is not essential to ensure only precise statements remain.

The output documentation from the requirements analysis activity should be presented at the same level of detail throughout. At this stage the document should be at a level that is still understandable by the customer but contains precise detail to build the next phase of analysis. It should not contain any design detail at this stage, e.g. it can contain statements like student file of pressure control, but not terms like direct access file system or a recursive loop structure.

It provides the written component for the system specification and a base to develop the documentation further using appropriate graphical or mathematical modelling tools. The end product of these activities, which comprise the system analysis components, is clear, concise set of documents backed up with precise models that are both semantically and syntactically correct.

To sum up, the negotiated statement of requirements should contain, in an unambiguous way, what the proposed system is to do, its functions and what the limitations on the developer are. It is a description of 'what' a system is to do in application terms. It is the key document on which all subsequent activities in the software project depend. In legal terms it may provide a basis for a contract between the customer and the developer.

Question 2.3.2

1. What is a platitude?
2. What is meant by an omission? Give an example
3. Why is it important to remove ambiguous statements?
4. What is extraneous detail?
5. What is the final objective of the requirements analysis document?

Techniques used within the requirements analysis process

In order to ascertain what is required from a system, there needs to be a lot of interaction with the customer or end user of the product. This interaction can take on many forms, e.g. interviews, observations, investigations, questionnaires and meetings. These need to be carefully planned in order to make the most efficient use of the time spent during the analysis and produce the desired results.

Interviews

All interviews need to be carefully planned in order to ensure that all the required information is obtained in the most efficient time from the customer or potential end user of the product. The interview need to be formal and conducted to a carefully thought out agenda that contains checklists and questions that are to be put to the interviewee. The questions need to draw out such issues like the functional objectives, completion deadlines and acceptability criteria.

In order to get a full picture of what is required it may be necessary to conduct interviews with several members of the organization. This ensures that points that may have been forgotten by one interviewee may have been specified by another. It is always important for an interviewer to step back from an interview and to apply his/her experience in order to fully evaluate the responses.

The interviewer should provide feedback in terms of his/her own understanding to clarify concepts in order to ensure the conclusions are reached.

Main objectives of an interview:

- Ascertain the customer needs and desires.
- Clarify the priorities for the proposed project.
- Find out about the current system and associated personnel.
- Determine the environment to which the system must be interfaced to.
- How staff will accept change when implementing the new system.
- Support requirements for installing and using the new application.
- Staff responsibilities within the organization.

The interviewer must always show interest in, and thoroughly listen to, what is being said by the interviewee.

Interviews allow users to make their experiences and feeling part of the analysis process. This is an essential characteristic of analysis and one that should be continued throughout this stage.

Observations

This allows for the developer to spend time in the environment in which the system is to be implemented. This practice familiarizes the developer with the needs of the system and provides an opportunity to pinpoint problems and additional requirements that may need to be added. It provides a basis for a conceptual model which can be used as a design for the final product. An example of an observation could involve the system developer travelling to a North Sea Oil Rig to look at the environment for a proposed 'safety warning system'.

Investigations

These involve the developer actually functioning as part of the system. It has the advantage that the developer gains a clearer insight as to what the proposed system is to do, but can have the disadvantage that the investigation may move into the area of how things should be as opposed to how they are now. The developer at this stage does not want to move away from the concept of analysis, i.e. ascertain what the system is to do, into the areas of design and implementation.

Questionnaires

This activity needs to determine the same objectives as the interview. The questionnaire or survey needs to be carefully structured so that it is easy to complete, and provides all the necessary feedback that is required. A good questionnaire will be laid out so the person completing it just has to tick a box in response to a question. If it is being sent to a large market then the developer of the product could consider the returned forms computer analysed. There should be a place for additional information so the potential user can insert additional requirement details as necessary to complement the rest of the form.

Example 2.3.2

Extract from a questionnaire

In order for us to ascertain your requirements for the proposed 'Shirt Packing System' kindly **tick** the response box to the left of the question.

Do you want the system to display the number [   ] 01
of shirts packed
Do you want the system to state when a target [   ] 02
number is reached
- ...
- ...
- ...

If you have any additional information please indicate
below:
....
....

Meetings

In most cases a proposed project will start with a 'kick-off' meeting. The meeting will be attended by all parties associated with the system to be developed and it should be formally structured to a specified agenda. Below is a preparation list for setting up a meeting.

- Has a venue that is convenient for all parties been booked?
- Are the rooming facilities appropriate for the needs of the meeting?
- Have all parties been sent an agenda and location guide?
- Has tea/coffee or lunch been booked as required?
- The venue provides other facilities like toilets, telephones, etc.

A suitable chairperson needs to be appointed, this will normally be a company manager of the systems house appointed to develop the product. Other people from the company should include the Project Manager, Team Leaders and appropriate Analysts responsible for the systems analysis of the project. The rest of the members should be made up from company staff who proposed the product and should include the IT Manager, Senior Staff and end users of the application. It may be necessary in some cases to bring in a third party to provide an independent view and give advice on external issues if the need arises. An example could be a representative of the Tax Office if a Payroll System was being proposed.

Further meetings will follow this format as the development lifecycle progresses. They provide a fundamental structure for quality standards to be maintained by interactive feedback to project members and the end user of the product.

Documentation

Good documentation is an essential component during the development and use of a software product. We have seen the scarce when the year 2000 problems came to light and many systems using older software had inadequate documentation and code structures that provided no support comments. People were brought out of retirement and given substantial inducements to check the systems which cost the industry millions of pounds.

Question 2.3.3

1. What are the main objectives of an interview?
2. Why is it necessary to use a questionnaire?
3. What is the main disadvantage of an investigation?
4. Why members should attend a typical progress meeting?
5. What should an agenda contain for a specified meeting?

To aid reading, documents should be easy to understand, be clear and concise and diagrams used to aid the explanation process. We have already seen a number of techniques used within this chapter, two common tools are:

- data flow diagrams (DFD);
- flow charts (FC).

The DFD graphically describes the flow of data within an organization. It can be used to document existing systems or plan new ones. An FC is an analytical tool used to describe some aspects of an information system in an unambiguous way. Some flow chart examples are listed below:

- document flowchart – illustrates the flow of documents and information between the areas of responsibility within an organization;
- system flowcharts – specify the relationship among the input, processing and output areas of an information system;
- progress flowcharts – outline the specific logic requirements that are to perform a process outlined in the system flowchart.

DFDs emphasize the flow of data and its associated influence on a system, whereas a flowchart specifies the flow of documents or records that contain the data. DFDs also have a limited number of symbols whereas flowcharts may use many symbols that show a greater detail of events.

Other document tools may require the data to be set out in a tabular format, e.g. the use of decision tables that represent the logic characteristics of software or hardware and possible, define any alternative actions.

Standards play a large role in the development and presentation of documents. Some example headings for a software test document using the ANSI/IEEE standard 829 are outlined below:

- test plan identifier
- introduction
- test item
- features to be tested
- approach
- pass/fail criteria
- suspension criteria and resumption requirements
- test deliverables
- testing tasks
- environmental needs
- responsibilities
- staffing and training needs
- risk contingencies
- approvals.

The International Standards Organization (ISO) also lays down guidelines, which help to produce documentation to the highest professional standards.

Good documentation is essential not only for the initial success of a project but for future maintenance requirements. It is what the customer sees. Poor documentation can reflect badly on the developing software company and may affect the future success of the product.

Exercise 2.3.1

College Management Information System

This exercise requires you to work in groups in order to carry out a simulation of a complete requirements analysis.

Below is an extract of a user requirements document:

A college admissions system is to be specified. Details for new students are entered by the operator and then stored on a student file. The required course is then checked against the course database to ensure it is available. If the required course is available the enrolment proceeds with details entered into a registered file, if the course is not available a suitable message is displayed on the operator's console. An invoice for the appropriate fees is to be produced for the students whose course is available.

The system needs to produce partially completed enrolment forms for continuing students at the start of each academic year.

Information about existing college courses should be printed for students who were not able to find an appropriate course during the previous year's enrolment.

The system is run on the existing college apple network system where only 300 Kb of disk space is available. In order to speed up events, the system should respond in less than 1 second and be easy for the operator to use.

Required steps:

1. Within your allocated groups, organize and carry out a meeting to analysis the information. The meeting should have a specified agenda and minutes written.
2. Ascertain from the information the following:
   - Functional requirements
   - Non-functional requirements
   - Any obvious omissions
   - Platitudes
3. Construct a suitable set of questions that can provide a basis for an interview with the customer.

2.4 Functional and data modelling

Functional modelling an introduction

When developing a functional model the developer needs to ascertain the main components (functions) that are inherent within the stated specification. The main functions can then be modelled using a structure chart method that shows the flow of information around the system. Some techniques used to further design the diagrammatic models are outlined below:

- Process descriptions
- Pre and post-condition structures
- Operation schemas
- Decision trees or tables.

Functional modelling in action

Problem outline

The 'Fiddle VAT Holiday Company' wants a computer system to ascertain how much a customer needs to pay for a holiday. The customer can only pay by cash and the holiday sales assistant needs to be able to complete the following:

- select a holiday destination
- select the number of weeks for the holiday (after these two have been entered the system displays the total CASH price)
- the assistant then enters the total cash tendered by the customer (the total change is then displayed, followed by the individual cash denominations of the change to be given, i.e. the number of £10, £5, £2, etc.)

This means that the sales assistant knows exactly what change to give the customer as the company does not have an automatic till system in place.

The system is to be displayed on a modern visual interface that helps the assistant select required options and reduces the risk of error input.

In order to break down, the main functional components of a Structure Chart need to be developed. This is shown in Figure 2.4.1.

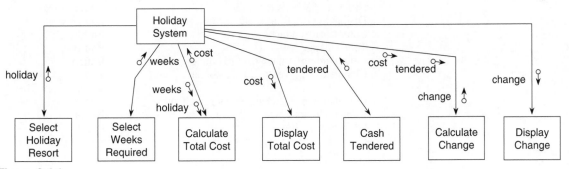

Figure 2.4.1

Process descriptions

Select Holiday Resort – Assistant to select a holiday destination from a predefined list of countries. As the list is already defined no error checking is required. The result of the selection is a string variable.

Select Weeks Required – Assistant to select the number of weeks required from a defined list. Assume that only whole weeks are available and no error checking is required. The result of the selection is a string which needs to be converted to an integer for the cost calculation.

Calculate Total Cost – This calculation is based on the number of weeks and the destination. The table below gives prices, e.g. countries that can be selected from the list.

Country	Cost per week
France	250.75
Germany	225.25
Greece	282.55
Italy	371.50
Portugal	325.60
Spain	199.99
Switzerland	465.50
Turkey	345.77

Cash tendered – The assistant enters the amount tendered by the customer. It will return a string which will need to be converted to a float. A check will need to be made to ensure that it is enough to cover the holiday cost. If it is not enough a suitable message is to be displayed.

Calculate Change – This process will calculate the change required and the actual change denominations that the assistant is to give the customer.

Display Change – The total change will need to be converted to a string before displaying and the resulting change denominations to be given to the customer, each will need their own text display area.

Function implementation

The system is to be implemented into a visual programming environment as its rapid application development tools and resulting user interface suit the company requirements. The table below outlines the main functions and the suggested widgets that could implement them.

Functions	Operational widgets
Required holiday countries	Combo Box
Number of Weeks for Holiday	Combo Box
Displaying the Total Cost	Edit Box
Enter Cash Tendered	Edit Box
Total Change	Edit Box
Calculation of Total Cost of Holiday	Button
Change to be given to the Customer	Edit Boxes (10 in all starting from £10)
Calculation of the change denominations	Button
Closing the interface	Button
User information	Labels

Implementation (Delphi)

In this case Borland Delphi has been chosen to implement the above functional requirements.

An example interface is shown in Figure 2.4.2.

Question 2.4.1

Complete the actual coding for this interface using an appropriate visual programming application.

Exercise 2.4.1

The Fiddle VAT Holiday Company outlined above wants an additional system to help with currency exchange. This system needs to contain a list of countries that are holiday destinations. The assistant needs to be able to:

- select a country from a list and press a button to display the currency of the country and its current exchange rate;
- enter the amount of currency that the customer wants to convert and press to button to show the foreign exchange amount;
- press a button to display which countries use the 'Euro' currency;
- select a country from a list and display the national flag of that country.

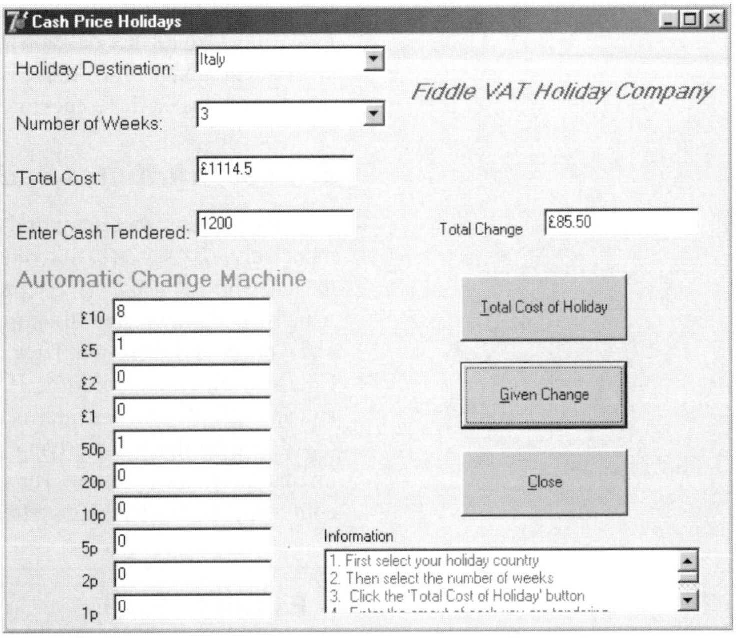

Figure 2.4.2

Data modelling

Introduction

A database is a collection of data that is required to be stored or retrieved within a specified system. The production of the data flow diagram will produce a number of stores that contain data to be used or data to be saved by the associated processes. The data flow diagram does not, however, give any further information about the precise nature of the stores and their relationships with other stores. This is where the process of data modelling comes in with the aim to provide additional graphical representations that adequately model the system to be developed.

In a number of data flow diagrams the layout of the stores is repeated to aid clarification and in some cases different stores will contain the same data items. Without any further analysis this problem will lead to implementation with a set of files that contain repeated data. This is often termed as redundant data and can lead to the following problems:

- The need for additional secondary storage is to reduce wasteful of resources and to reduce the efficiency of the final product.
- Updating becomes a problem because the system needs to ensure that if one set of data is updated then the others must also be changed to reflect this modification. This is to ensure consistency of file data throughout the system.

There may be situations where other relationships exist between data that has to be saved and acted an in the system. For example, in a college application it would be natural to keep data about courses offered, the number that have vacancies and the maximum group size for each course. In addition, it would also keep information about students and employees of the college like managers, lecturers and administration staff. We can see that there is a relationship between courses and students, also between lectures and students and these must be recorded. This main aim of data modelling is to further develop the data flow structure in order to produce an efficient model which reduces redundancy and shows the relationships that exist between different stores.

Entities, attributes and relationships

All data can represent items and things from the real world. Within a data model an *entity* is used to describe the objects which represent 'things' from the real world. An *entity type* represents a collection of similar properties in which we are interested. Examples of entity types are Student, Lecturer and Course and these will have their own occurrences. An example of a Course occurrence would be HNC Computing or A level mathematics and an example of a Lecturer occurrence could be Peter Brown.

All entities have underlying *attributes* that represent the associated internal properties present. The example shown below takes a 'customer entity type' from a banking system and lists some of its possible attributes.

Example 2.4.1

Customer (*AccountNumber*, Name, Address, Telephone-Number, Balance, OverDraft)

The first attribute provides a unique access route to the entity and this is sometimes termed a candidate identifier that is underlined to emphasize this point. There may be more than one candidate identifier where either, or one, of them provides unique access to the entity type they are described in. We can see that the entity can provide a basis for a *record* structure and the attributes form the required *fields*.

Question 2.4.2

Set up a table to list all the instances of the *Studies* relationship given in Figure 2.4.3.

Finally we need to consider the way things are related and this is achieved by specifying the *relationships* that exist between entities. A relationship is an association between entities and can be based on a number of factors like ownership, structure, location and inheritance. For example, we could have entity types, Student and Course and a suitable relationship could be Studies, i.e. A Student *Studies* Course. An example of relationships between entities is shown in Figure 2.4.3.

Figure 2.4.3 clearly shows examples of relationship instances, e.g. Bailey *Studies Intro. to programming* is an instance of a relationship or an association between precisely two entities.

Just like other modelling techniques discussed in the chapter Entities and Relationship types should be given meaningful names. Entities should be named with a noun and kept singular (i.e. it is *Student* not *Students*) and relationships named with a verb. One important characteristic of relationships is that they contain a degree association that can be one of the following:

- One-to-one (denoted 1:1) – each instance of one entity type is associated with one instance of another entity. For example, the entity *College* is associated with one *Principal* entity. The *College* has exactly one *Principal* and one *Principal* is appointed to exactly one *College*.
- One-to-many (denoted 1:*n*) – one instance of the first entity type may be associated with more than one instance of the second entity type.

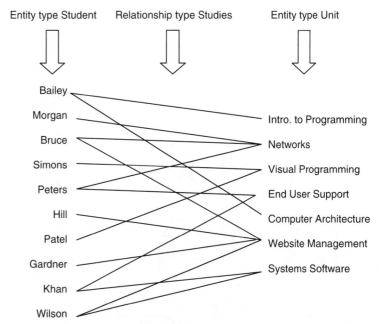

Figure 2.4.3 *A relationship between entities*

For example, a college *Head of Department* is in charge of many *Lecturers* and *Lecturers* have one boss the *Head of Department*.

● Many-to-many (denoted *m:n*) – many instances of the first entity type may be associated to many instances of the second entity type. For example, a *Lecturer* may tutor many *Students* and *Students* will have many *Lecturers* for their course.

Entity-relationship diagrams

Entity-relationship (E-R) diagrams provide a graphical data model to show the layout of proposed entities and their relationships. They can be constructed from data flow diagrams or directly from user requirements. Either way they provide a model which is still open for discussion with the developer and end user to ensure the components match the requirements. Most modelling tools on the market will also provide a means for syntax checking and the creation of required attribute lists for the specified entities. There are few components used in an E-R diagram, these are listed in Figure 2.4.4.

The E-R diagram forms part of a conceptual model which obtains its information from a real-world source and extracts the patterns of data that are used within the organization that the system is being developed for. It is normally carried out without reference to 'how' the system will be implemented. The output of this stage is to produce a conceptual model or the data components that satisfy the requirements of the customer or end user.

An example of a simple E-R diagram is shown in Figure 2.4.5.

Figure 2.4.5 contains the following relations:

● *Registers for* – A student may take many examinations but each examination paper is taken by one student, hence the 1:*n* relationship.
● *Is on* – A course can contain many students but students can only enrol on one course, hence the 1:*n* relationship.
● *Is for* – Courses contain many examination papers and many examinations have been organized for each course.

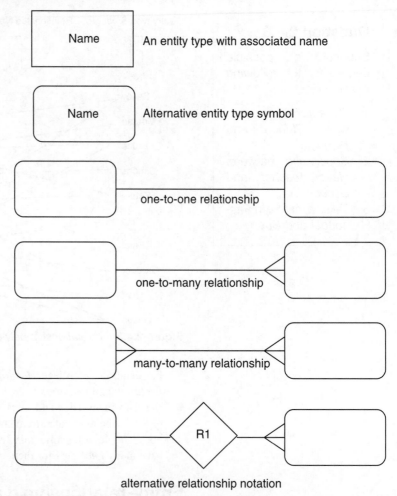

Figure 2.4.4   *Components used in E-R diagrams*

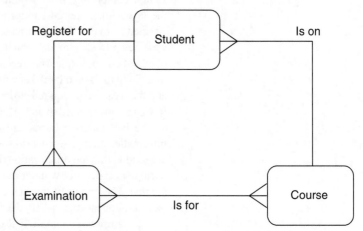

Figure 2.4.5   *An E-R diagram for a student examination system*

Although the definition of relationships looks unnecessary complex, the description needs to be expressed from the view of each entity in order to ascertain its exact degree value.

In some cases developers will replace an *m:n* relationship with two 1:*n* relationships. This has the advantage that the implementation of the

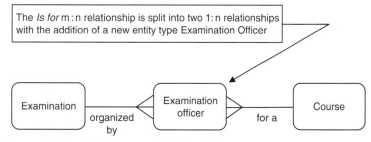

Figure 2.4.6 *Splitting a m:n relationship*

model will easily fit into the structure of a modern relational database application. An example of this procedure is shown in Figure 2.4.6.

Using CASE tools

When modelling, a data system is a good idea to use a case tool application for its construction. Most of these offer good checking facilities which ensure they are syntactically correct and provide a range of templates which allow quick access to the required diagram symbols. They are ideally suited to implement the change and so corrections or modification can be implemented directly across all the created diagrams. Data dictionaries allow the developer to add additional information relevant to any particular graphical component. This end result is a precise document that can easily be checked for semantic correctness and modifications can be implemented without major modifications.

The main problem with such case tools is that they are generally expensive, but they can be used with a number of different models. Example 2.4.2 was constructed using the Select Yourdon CASE tool application version 4.2.0. It can also be used to construct data flow diagrams, state transition diagrams, Jackson charts, Constantine diagrams, structure charts as well as associated specifications and dictionaries.

Attribute diagram

An attribute diagram shows the attributes, or data items, that are associated with a particular entity. The diagram consists of the entity in question, its attributes, and domains. A domain is a graphical representation of the set of possible values an attribute can take. For example, the attribute arrival could belong to the domain of time.

Attributes are represented as links between the entity and domains. All attribute links will have a cardinal value at either end (1:1, 1:*n* or *m:n*). Any of the attribute names may be underlined to indicate that they are prime attributes. The prime attribute(s) will represent the unique identifier field(s) that allow access to the specified entity. Most CASE tool applications will allow an attribute diagram to be developed as a child of an entity.

Question 2.4.4

1. What are the main components used in a E-R diagram?
2. What is a relationship? Specify the different degrees associated with relationships.
3. Suggest some suitable attributes for an entity type student.

Example 2.4.2

Below is an extract from a negotiated statement of requirements:

As part of the new animal passport scheme the port authorities need a system to monitor the movement of animals. The system is to be initially developed as a prototype to provide information on animals of the type dog only. These are then to be classified into breeds and only two breeds are to be registered the Bernese Mountain Dog and the Australian Shepherd Dog.

Questions:
1. Analyse the text to ascertain the relevant entities.
2. Establish any relationships between entities and their degrees.
3. Complete an E-R diagram.
4. For the Bernese Mountain Dog entity type construct an attribute diagram.

Suggested solution:
1. Possible entities are: Animal, Dog, Breed and Bernese Mountain Dog and Australian Shepherd.
2. Relationships are:
   Type of between Animal and Dog. This is a 1:*n* relationship as there is only one dog animal but many dogs will go through the system.
   Contains between Dog and Breed. This is a 1:*n* relationship as a dog entity type contains many breeds but there is only one instance of each breed.
   Are part of between the Bernese Mountain Dogs and Australian Shepherd Dogs and Breed. This is a 1:*n* relationship as there is a single breed for each group of dogs and a breed contains many dogs.

Note: You will notice that the diagrams are displaying some additional symbols not yet mentioned. The little circle before the many fork means a zero-to-many association (as opposed to a one-to-many). The two little dashes on the single lines indicate a strictly 'only-one' relationship. Figure 2.4.7 has been created as a child of the entity Bernese Mountain Dog in

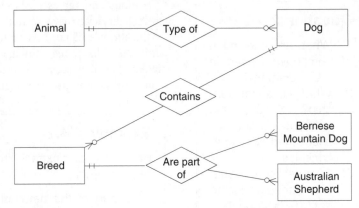

Figure 2.4.7   *E-R prototype model for animal passport system*

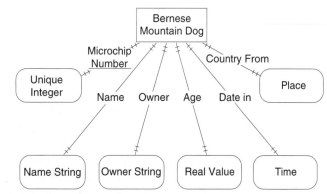

Figure 2.4.8 *Attributes for a Bernese Mountain Dog*

Figure 2.4.8. Both have been checked for syntax correctness, an example check report is shown below:

```
Project: C:\MYDOCU~1\SELECT\SYSTEM\DTATA1\
Title: Data Flow Example
Date: 21-Aug-2000 Time: 12:4

Checking DOG2.DAT
No Errors detected, No Warnings given.
--------End of report--------
```

Exercise 2.4.2

Below is an extract from a negotiated statement of requirements:

The Morgan Software house employs a number of programmers. Each programmer is allocated with their own terminal and they work on one or more systems at the same time. Each office within the company can contain up to 10 terminals and each terminal has its own operational manual as their specification is different. Each office has a manager who is in charge of the programmers in that office.

Questions:
1. Analyse the text to ascertain the relevant entities.
2. Establish any relationships between entities and their degrees.
3. Complete an E-R diagram.
4. Construct attribute diagrams for each entity selected.

Implementing a database

Before we start to implement database models we need to consider so basic building blocks. We have seen the concept of entities, attributes and relationships, so how do these fit into a modern database application tool? In order to answer this, we first need to start with some basic terminology and then look at the initial building blocks to create a working database application.

Relational database

A database is simply a collection of data, in our case stored electronically. It has no formal definition and is sometimes used to describe data file made up of records and fields contained in tables. In order to implement the real word relationships developed in the data model a 'relational database' needs to provide a means of linking sets of table data together in order to establish the relationships. A relational database is therefore a collection of tables roughly equivalent to a collection of records that are related by the data stored jointly in their fields.

Tables

A table is a collection of data relevant to a specific entity, e.g. students or lecturers. A separate table is used for each topic which means the data is only stored once which improves efficiency and reduces data entries. Tables are organized into columns (these represent the field data) and rows (these represent the records).

Forms

Forms are used to help you to input and manipulate data which includes:

- Data-entry form to enter data into a table;
- Switchboard form to open other forms or reports;
- Custom dialog box to accept user input and carry out an associated action.

Queries

Use queries to view, use and analyse data in various ways. They can also be used as a source of records for form and reports.

Reports

A report is an effective way to present your data in a printed format. You have control over everything that is on a report, so you can display what information you want and how you want to see it.

Macro

A macro is a set of one or more actions that each performs a particular operation. Macros can help you automate tasks like opening a form, printing a report etc., by just pressing a designated command button.

Example 2.4.3

Creating simple data tables

This exercise involves two entity types, *Customer* and *Product*. There is a relationship between them, *Orders*, which allows customers to order many products, but each product is only for one customer.

1. Create an entity-relationship diagram to represent this system

Figure 2.4.9 *E-R between Customer and Product*

2. Consider some suitable attributes for each entity (*Customer* and *Product*). Some examples are shown in Figures 2.4.10 and 2.4.11.

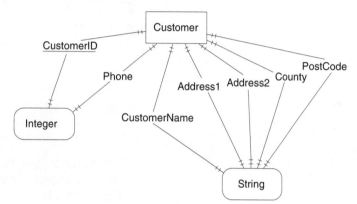

Figure 2.4.10 *Attribute diagram for Customer*

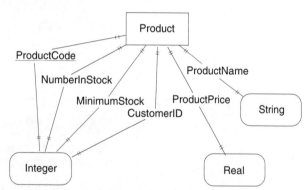

Figure 2.4.11 *Attribute diagram for Product*

3. For each entity create database tables by entering some example field data under each specified attribute. The examples shown below in Figures 2.4.12 and 2.4.13 have been created in Access 2000, but the same table construction could have been implemented in any commercial database application.

Note: If you have not created database tables before then use the 'database wizard' to construct the tables with the appropriate field names. Use the 'help' option to find out more about this facility and any alternative examples.

Figure 2.4.12 *Customer table*

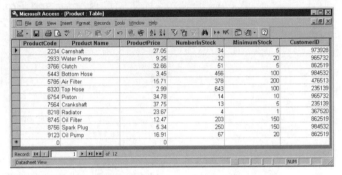

Figure 2.4.13 *Product table*

4. For the Customer table change the column layout so that the customers names are shown in ascending order (Figure 2.4.14).

Figure 2.4.14 *Customer table showing the CustomerName column in ascending order*

Note: this should be a simple operation, just click on the column to be ordered (the CustomerName field) and select the ascending order button.

5. Apply a filter to a sort to list all the customers that live in Surrey (Figure 2.4.15).

Figure 2.4.15 *Filter applied to show the customers who live in Surrey*

Note: in Access this is achieved by selecting the Records, Filter, Advanced Filter/Sort menu. The result is shown in Figure 2.4.16 which has its criteria set as the string *Surrey* and is activated by clicking the *Apply Filter* button.

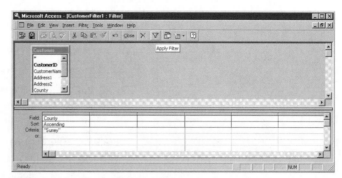

Figure 2.4.16   *Applying a filter to a sort*

6. Display a 'form view' of a particular record from the customer table and change a field data entry for the first address line. This is achieved in Access by selecting the record to be viewed from the customer table and then clicking the down arrow next to the New Object button and selecting Autoform. An example form is shown in Figure 2.4.17.

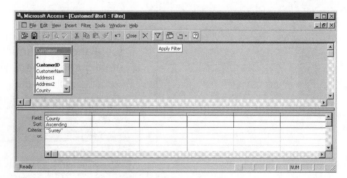

Figure 2.4.17   *A database form*

Then view the whole table to ensure the change has taken place. Figure 2.4.18 shows the change made to the address1 field (the street number and name have been altered).

Note: Forms are used to enter, view and change data. They are usually used to improve the way the data is displayed on the screen. The arrows at the bottom of the form can be used to navigate through the table entries.

7. Add a new record to the Customer table. There should be no problems here, just add a new record in the next

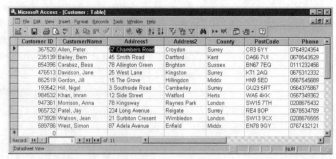

Figure 2.4.18 *Customer table showing the modified address for the first record*

available row. Figure 2.4.19 shows the new record inserted with the list still sorted in name order.

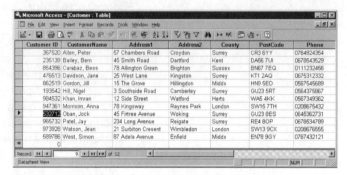

Figure 2.4.19 *New record added for Jock Oban*

8. Show that a relationship exists between the Customer table and the Product table that represents the 1:*n* degree highlighted in the E-R model (Figure 2.4.20).

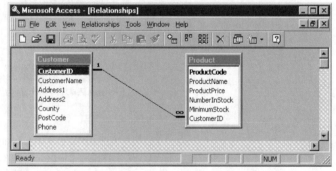

Figure 2.4.20 *1:n relationship between Customer and Product*

Note: you can build relationships between tables by *dragging* from a field in one table to another field in a second table. In our example we have dragged from the CustomerID field name in the Customer table to the CustomerID field in the Products table. This is achieved by clicking the left mouse button over the first field name in the customer table and holding it down whilst dragging to the second table and releasing over the required field. In Access releasing the mouse button results in the following dialog box in Figure 2.4.21 being displayed.

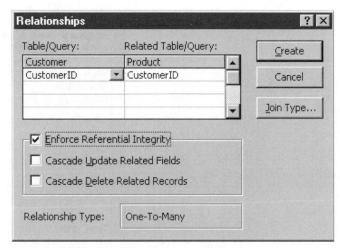

Figure 2.4.21 *Setting up relationships in Access*

In the join Join Properties dialogue box you can specify the type of join that you want Access to create in new queries. Because Access is a relational database, queries can be used from more than one table at a time. As we have seen, if the database contains tables with related data, the relationships can be easily defined.

It is customary for the matching fields to have the same name as in our example of Customer and Product tables. In the Customers table, the CustomersID field is the primary field and relates to the CustomerID in the Products table that is classified as a foreign key.

The various types of relationships are as follows:

- *Inherited* – for attaching tables from another Access database. The original relationships of the attached database can be used in the current database.
- *Referential* – for enforcing relationships between records according to certain rules, when you add or delete records in related tables belonging to the same database. For example, you can only add records to a related table, if the matching record already exists in the primary table, and you cannot delete a record from a primary table if matching records exist in a related table.

9. You create a query so that you can ask questions about data in the database tables. By far the most common operation is to produce a subset of the data held in a table. Produce a subset from the Product table containing only the product name and price (Figure 2.4.22).

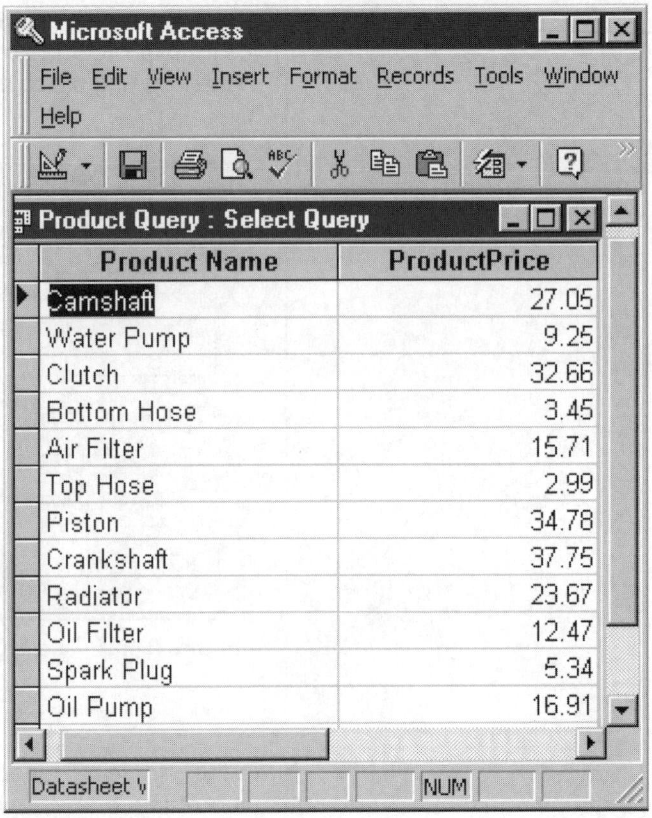

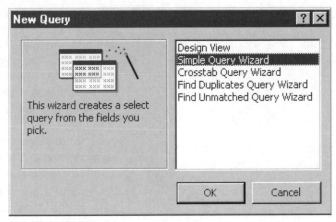

Figure 2.4.22   *Query on product table*

To do this, load the database and in the Database window click the queries tab, followed by the *New* button which opens the *New Query* dialogue box. The resulting dialog box is displayed:

Figure 2.4.23   *New query dialog box*

Selecting the Simple Query Wizard, displays the following:

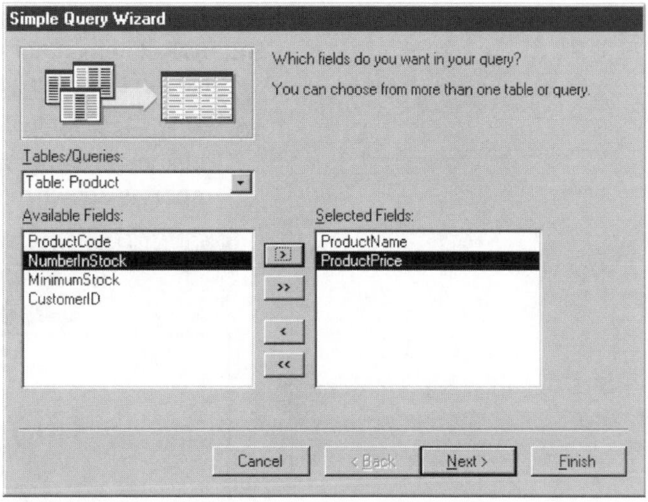

Figure 2.4.24   *Simple query wizard with selected fields required for the subset*

The required table is then selected with the associated fields required for the subset. On pressing the *Next* button, another dialogue box asks if you want a detailed report or a summary. Pressing *Next* again takes you to the final dialogue box which asks you for the name of the query.

Types of queries

The query that we have created so far, is known as a select query, which is the most common type of query. However with Access you can an create and use other types of queries, as follows:

- Crosstab query – used to present data with row and column headings, just like a spreadsheet. It can be used to summarize large amounts of data in a more readable form.
- Action query – used to make changes to many records in one operation. For example, you might want to remove all records from a given table that meet a certain criteria. Obviously this type of query has to be used with care.
- Union query – used to match fields from two or more tables.
- Pass through query – Used to pass commands to SQL.
- Data-definition query – used to delete, create and change tables in an Access database using SQL statements.

SQL stands for Structured Query Language, often used to query, update and manage relational databases. Each query created by Access has an associated SQL statement that defines the action of that query. Thus if you are familiar with SQL, you can use it to view and modify queries, or use it to set form and report properties. An alternative to these actions is to use a QBE (Query By Example) grid which is easier to initially structure. If you design union queries, or data definition queries, then you must use SQL statements, as these kind of queries cannot be designed with the QBE grid. Finally, to create a sub-query, you use the QBE grid, but you enter SQL SELECT statement for criteria, these issues will be covered in detail in the Data Analysis and Database Design unit.

10. Produce a *report* from the Customer table showing the customer name and telephone number. An example report is shown in Figure 2.4.25.

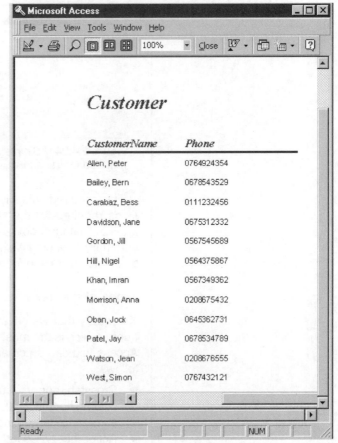

Figure 2.4.25   *Report from the Customer table showing the Customer Name and telephone number*

A report is like a query in that it can summarize data, but its output is in a form that is more suitable for printing. In Access a basic report is set up from the Database box and selecting the Reports tab. From there you can follow the wizards (similar to queries) to set up the required report.

Exercise 2.4.3

Below is an extract from a college management information system:

A Course Director is responsible for a number of Students and each Student is allocated a single Course Director.

Your task is to analyse and implement the scenario to produce a simple relational database for the specified entities. In order to achieve this the following steps need to be followed:

1. Complete a entity-relationship diagram to represent this model.
2. For the suggested attributes tabled below, complete corresponding attribute diagrams.

	Course director	Student
Attribute(Key)	CourseDirectorID	StudentID
Attribute 2	CourseDirectorName	StudentName
Attribute 3	RoomNumber	StudentCourse
Attribute 4	PhoneExtension	StudentAge
Attribute 5	Email	CourseDirectorID
Attribute 6	Faculty	

3. Set up a database system containing two *tables* (Course Director and Student) by adding suitable data under each attribute heading. You should complete at least 10 student records and 5 course director records.
4. Practice *sorting* the data into ascending order by selecting alternative columns (i.e. by the name column).
5. Apply a *filter* to display only the records that fit a selected criteria, i.e. all the student surnames that start with an 'S'.
6. Display a *form* view of a particular record from either table and change a field data entry. View the whole table to ensure the change has taken place.
7. Add a *new record* to the student table
8. Link the two tables together to establish a *relationship* between them. Use the CourseDirectorID field from each table to set up the link and ensure the correct degree is shown (this should be the same as the original E-R diagram)
9. Set up a *query* so as to summarize the student names and their corresponding courses from the Student table.
10. Produce a printed *report* to show the Course Directors name and e-mail address from the appropriate table.

Question 2.4.5

1. In an attribute diagram the resulting domains are shown (i.e. String, Integer, Real, etc.). How are these domains specified within a database application?
2. What is a *form* used for when implementing a database application?
3. What are *queries* used for?
4. What is the main difference between a *query* and a *report*?
5. What is a *database wizard* and how does it help you to implement your required database model?

This aim of these exercises is to provide the link between analysis, design and implementation. It only covers the basics of database implementations but provides a foundation for future development in the application area. This will be covered in detail within the Data Analysis and Database Design unit. At this Stage 1 must stress the need for thoroughly researching and documenting the work carried out. This not only ensures a disciplined approach to the task but instils a professional ethos which is characteristic for the production of quality software systems.

3 Programming concepts

Summary

Edexcel suggest a 3GL, a '3rd generation language' rather than a more modern visually oriented programming environment. Pascal has been used in the part of the book partly because it is a 'traditional' teaching language and partly to satisfy the requirements of a 3GL as stated above. Modern visual languages provide many more features and enable Rapid Application Development (RAD), but the aim of this unit is to teach principles of programming rather than the production of commercial programs.

Introduction

The Edexcel unit states: Centres may choose any appropriate language as a vehicle for developing this unit but for HNC/D Computing, a 3GL would be expected. Programs should be written to defined quality standards and problem-solving tools (structure diagrams, pseudo code, etc.) should be used. Emphasis should be placed on the need for modularity and an indication should be given of the link between modularity and object-based development.

This chapter introduces the main concepts involved with producing simple programs. No prior knowledge is assumed as some students on Higher National programmes of study do not have any experience in writing program code. Confusion has arisen in the past regarding 'level' of programming units because chapters such as this present the same material for courses at different levels. The difference lies in the time allocated to learning, the amount of support given and the standard of assessment; it does not lie in the subject content.

3.1 High-level languages

In general, software for computers is produced from a *high-level language*. Assembly language is a *low-level language* and as described in Chapter 2, each line in the code translates almost exactly to an op-code in the resulting *machine code*. It is considered that machine code is a *1st generation language* as the original machines were programmed using straight machine code. As this is slow and is very prone to errors, assemblers were produced to make life easier. Assemblers are considered to be *2nd generation languages*. *3rd generation languages* use text that looks a little more like plain language, this is converted by a relatively complex system into machine code. Remember, whatever language used to write software, the code executed by the processor is machine code. Always!

Well known early 3rd generation languages are Fortran (FORmula TRANslation), COBOL (Common Business Oriented Language) and BASIC (Beginners All-purpose Symbolic Instruction Code). All predictions that these will be outclassed by more modern languages have so far proved to be in accurate! These more modern 3rd generation languages are C, C++ and Java, very powerful languages but not ideally suited to the beginner programmer. All these have been designed to suit given classes of problem, Fortran to solve more mathematical problems, COBOL for Business applications, etc. Pascal is a 3rd generation language that was specifically designed to teach the ideas of programming, it has little or no commercial use. It does allow the development of programming ideas in a more formal way than BASIC, this formal way is favoured in the development of larger projects. Whilst BASIC is a general-purpose language, it allows some sloppy programming practices that lead to bugs that are hard to find.

An aside

Bugs are errors in the program. There is a nice story about why they are called 'bugs'. It says that Grace Murray Hopper, the designer of COBOL, first used the term to describe the removal of a moth (a 'bug') from a Mark II Aiken Relay Calculator, a primitive computer, although she did not do it herself. There is a problem with this nice story, is it probably not true! At the very least, the story may have a *bug* in it!

See http://www.jamesshuggins.com/h/tek1/first_computer_ bug.htm

An aside

ALGOL is a programming language that was in use in the 1960s on large commercial machines, before the age of PCs. ALGOL was written by a team of people that included Professor Niklaus Wirth from the Swiss Federal Institute of Technology.

In order to achieve a better language that encouraged well *structured* and well organized programs, Wirth designed *Pascal* in about 1971. From the start, it was intended as a teaching language. Pascal added the capability to define new data types out of simpler existing types. It supported dynamic data structures, i.e. data structures which can change while a program is running.

3.2 How does a 3rd generation language work?

In Pascal, you can do a task (called *something* here, it does not matter what it is) 10 times using the code:

```
for counter:=1 to 10 do {something};
```

Table 3.2.1 shows the same problem written in Pascal, assembler and machine code.

By reading the Pascal, even non-programmers could guess what was happening, the assembler code is not so easy to read and the machine

Table 3.2.1 *Simple program*

Pascal	for counter:=1 to 10 do {something};
Assembler	L1: mov al,1 {something} dec al cmp al,10 jne L1
Machine code as hex bytes	B0 01FE C8 3C 0A 75 F8
Machine code in binary	10110000 00000001 11111110 11001000 00111100 00001010 01110101 11111000

code nearly impossible unless you remember all the hex bytes. As for the binary … ! It is all the same problem, count to 10.

Suppose the {something} was a task that was already written, i.e. it was available in machine code. Assuming the typed code has been stored on disk, the business of converting a Pascal program is now split into the following steps:

1. Check that all the words and symbols in the Pascal code are correct, i.e. 'for' is not spelt 'four', the ':=' sign is not just a '=' on its own, etc.
2. Make sure that all the words and symbols are in a meaningful order.
3. *Compile* the Pascal code into what looks like assembler code. This code is called *Object Code.*
4. *Link* this code with the prewritten code, in this case, the code that did {something}.
5. Write this linked code as a finished executable file. This is the finished *machine code.*

Notice that when the Pascal is converted to the assembler like code, it does not 'know' how to do the task called {something}. If for instance, the code for {something} needed to read a file of data, the Pascal code does not 'know' how to open and read a file. This ability is contained within prewritten *library files* that are supplied with the Pascal *Compiler*, i.e. the compiler converts the Pascal code then a separate process *links* this code with the prewritten library code. In the past, this *linker* software was supplied separately from the compiler; in the case of the Pascal system you are likely to use, the linking stage is largely hidden.

In this way, library files of object code can be written in (almost) any language, so providing a means to reuse software.

3.3 First steps in Pascal programming

You will need a compiler!

> **An aside**
>
> Turbo Pascal is a common Pascal compiler supplied by Borland and runs under DOS. Unfortunately, the version that runs under Windows has been discontinued. Borland Turbo Pascal version 7.0 is still available but an *almost* identical version is available free of charge. It is called Free Pascal and is available from http://www.freepascal.org/fpc.html to suit most operating systems. For the purposes of this book, the Free Pascal version is to be preferred as it comes with good quality disk based help files and unlike Turbo Pascal, it is available for a range of operating systems.
>
> If you need Borland Turbo Pascal 7.0, see details on http://www.borland.com/pascal/

The section above outlined the stages in producing an executable program using Pascal. These are:

- edit the program text using a text editor;
- compile the code;
- link with library files;
- load and execute the program for testing.

In both Free Pascal and Borland Turbo Pascal, all these stages are built into what they call an *Integrated Development Environment* or *IDE*. Whilst this makes program development easier, you should not forget what is going on 'behind the scenes', i.e. the generation of machine code to suit the processor and operating system of your computer.

The Pascal IDE

Refer to your local centre to find out how to start the software. For a default installation of Pascal, under Windows, open a DOS window and type fp (or tp if using Borland) you should get the *IDE* as shown here:

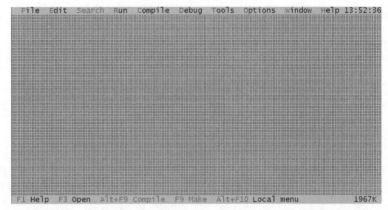

Figure 3.3.1   *Free Pascal IDE, identical with Turbo Pascal*

This presents the main menu options.

To create a new program, press ALT then F for File and choose N for New. You should get the screen as shown here:

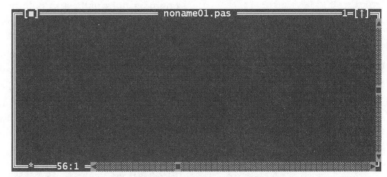

Figure 3.3.2   *A program window ready to enter Pascal text*

Now type in the program code below and remember to save it as 'prog3_1' by pressing the F2 key.

Program 3.1

```
program prog3_1(input,output);
begin
    writeln('Hello World');
end.
```

Points to notice

- The first line finishes with a ';' character, so does the third line.
- The last line has a '.' after the word *end*.
- The program is called prog3.1 but the top line shows it as prog3_1 as a '.' is not allowed in the program name.
- The third line is indented using the TAB key.

So far, nothing has happened beyond editing and saving the code, the IDE has acted only as a *text editor*. The next stage is to compile and link your code to make it executable. Do this from the IDE by pressing ALT and C then choosing C for *Compile* (or just pressing the hot key ALT F9). You should get 'Compile successful, press any key'. Remember, the linking stage has been hidden by the IDE. If the compilation was successful, you now have an executable program. To run it, press ALT and R and choose *Run*. The screen will blink as the program runs then jumps right back to the IDE, so fast you cannot see your output! To actually see the output screen, press ALT F5. To get back to the IDE, press ALT F5 again. In the IDE, you can *toggle* the user output screen with ALT F5 at anytime.

The output screen should look something like:

```
Free Pascal IDE Version 0.9.1
Hello World
```

This is probably the most famous program in computing, known as 'hello world', it is used to present almost every programming language available.

If things go wrong:
Typical errors are
Forgetting the ';' or the '.'
Spelling the words incorrectly

If you have one of these, you will get a compiler error that says 'Compile failed' then give you a suggestion of what has gone wrong. *Warning*! The compiler does its best to help but sometimes gets it wrong! *Take compiler error messages as a guide only*. The error message will be in a new window.

Look at the top right hand side of any window and you will see a number like 1 or 2, etc. You can always activate a window by pressing ALT and that number. Jump back to the window with your code in it, correct the error and recompile and run. You can close a window by clicking on the small square at top left as shown in Figure 3.3.3.

Now try a slightly longer program:

Program 3.2

```
program prog3_2(input,output);
var counter:integer;

begin
for counter:=1 to 10 do
    writeln('I love computing');
end.
```

Start a new program with ALT F then New and type in this new program. Press F2 to save it as prog3_2. Compile it, run it, then look at the output screen, you should have 'I love computing' 10 times on the screen together with the output of the last program.

Window
number

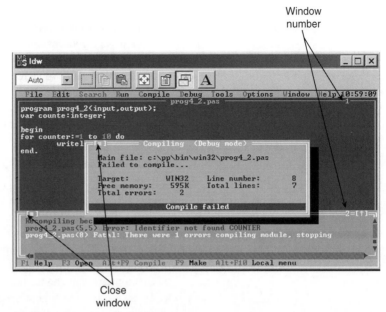

Close
window

Figure 3.3.3 *'Compile failed' window*

To get rid of the previous output screen, first add the lines

```
uses crt;
```

and

```
clrscr;
```

as in the listing for Program 3_3.

Program 3.3

```
program prog3_3(input,output);
uses crt; {adds a library file containing
                monitor control routines}
var counter:integer;

begin
clrscr; {clear the screen}
for counter:=1 to 10 do
        writeln('I love computing');
end.
```

Resave it, recompile and run it. Your output screen should now show just the output from this program, 10 repeats of 'I love computing'.

The line *clrscr* is short for Clear Screen. The line *uses crt* adds a *unit*, in this case the crt unit. After compiling the code, the system links with a library file: this crt unit is an additional library file that contains the prewritten code that 'knows' how to clear the monitor screen.

An aside

CRT is an old name that refers to a Cathode Ray Tube, the device now called a monitor or VDU.

Points to notice

- Each Pascal *statement* ends with a ';' character (there are a few exceptions to this).
- You can put a new line, tabs, spaces, etc. in a Pascal statement to make it more readable. These are known as *white space* characters and are ignored by the compiler.

- Text inside { } brackets (often called braces) is also ignored by the compiler. They are used for comments in the program code. It is considered very good practice to put plenty if comments in your code. This makes it easier to understand your code, especially when looking at it sometime after you wrote it and it makes it easier for someone else to understand it. If you work in a programming team, your colleagues will thank you for good comments.
- The program uses TAB characters for indentation, also to make the program easy to read.

Consider the same Program 3.3 presented below:

```
program prog3_3(input,output); uses crt; {adds a library
file containing monitor control routines} var counter:
integer; begin clrscr; {clear the screen} for counter:=1
to 10 do writeln('I love computing');end.
```

It will compile as before but is much harder to read!

Having run these programs, look in the file system directory where you saved them. You should find files called prog3_1.exe, prog3_2.exe, etc. These are the executable machine code programs, the files that are run by the system to produce your output.

Note on program layout style

You will see many references in this book to indentation, white space and comments to make your program easier to read. You may find that longer programs get so indented that lines run off the right hand side of the paper. If this is likely, use the options menu, choose environment then editor. Change the tab size to 4 instead of the standard 8.

Another layout feature that is used for the same reason is the *case* of the reserved words and identifiers; upper case letters are CAPITALS, lower case are small letters.

Pascal is not *case conscious*, i.e. it will not react differently with WRITELN or writeln or Writeln. In some Pascal works, you will see all the reserved words and identifiers in upper case. In this book, all the code is presented in lower case in readiness for C/C++. These languages are case conscious and (nearly) all the code is in lower case. For this reason, it is considered far better to become familiar with good layout to show *program structure*. If you are more comfortable using upper case for reserved words and identifiers then you should do it consistently. Some examinations in programming require consistency rather than either upper or lower case code.

An aside

In the old way of printing with individual lead characters being set by hand into a frame, the lead capital letters were stored in a box, or case, that was above the case that stored the smaller letters. It has become standard language to refer to letters as upper or lower case from where they were stored in the printing works!

3.4 Elements of Pascal 1

Below presented are some elements of Pascal that will be used to develop the next set of programs. The point of the Software Development unit is to understand programs and how they are developed, not to master Pascal as a subject. For this reason, no attempt has been made to provide a comprehensive guide to Pascal, it is simply a means to an end.

It is strongly recommended that you obtain a copy of Free Pascal from http://www.freepascal.org/fpc.html as the documentation that comes with it contains a great deal that is helpful. In particular, they supply a file called *fpctoc.htm* that is placed in the \doc directory inside wherever the software is installed (C:\pp by default). If you open this file in your web browser and follow the *reference* link, much useful information will be found.

Elements introduced here:

- Identifiers, reserved words.
- Variables of type: integer, real, string and char.
- Predefined functions and procedures: write, writeln, readln, val, trunc.
- Program structure: repeat..until.
- Data validation.
- White space and indentation.

Identifiers and reserved words

Pascal uses *identifiers*. These identify something that has meaning, for instance, the identifier *writeln* used in the first program is the identifier to use when you wish to output to the screen followed by a *new line* character. When you write a Pascal program, you can define your own identifiers, the first is usually the program name such as prog3_3. You must conform to the Pascal rules when naming identifiers, i.e.

- No spaces.
- No punctuation marks, all characters must be letters, numbers or '_' that is used to look like a space.
- The first character must be a letter.
- You must not use one that is a Pascal *reserved word*. In Free Pascal, the complete list of these reserved words are: *absolute, and, array, asm, begin, break, case, const, constructor, continue, destructor, div, do, downto, else, end, file, for, function, goto, if, implementation, in, inherited, inline, interface, label, mod, nil, not, object, of, on, operator, or, packed, procedure, program, record, repeat, self, set, shl, shr, string, then, to, type, unit, until, uses, var, while, with, xor, dispose, exit, false, new, true.*
- You can reuse identifiers such as *writeln* but it would be a little silly as you would not then be able to use the writeln feature of the language!

So the following are allowed:

- tax
- income
- person_age
- counter
- list8

The following will be thrown out by the compiler:

- 8list (the first character is not a letter)
- person_age?
- tax%

and you will get a compiler error such as the one shown in Figure 3.4.1.

Variables

Make sure you understand the section concerned with binary and floating point numbers before you read this. Pascal uses both these methods for storing numbers. It can also store type *string*. Not part of the original Pascal definition, it is now well understood to be part of every Pascal implementation. A string is simply a set of ASCII characters. Variables of type char are just single ASCII characters.

Figure 3.4.1   *Bad identifier*

Table 3.4.1   *Free Pascal supported real types*

Type	Range	Significant digits	Size in bytes
Single	1.5E − 45 to 3.4E38	7–8	4
Real	5.0E − 324 to 1.7E308	15–16	8
Double	5.0E − 324 to 1.7E308	15–16	8
Extended	1.9E − 4951 to 1.1E4932	19–20	10
Comp	−2E64 + 1 to 2E63 − 1	19–20	8

Table 3.4.2   *Free Pascal supported integer types*

Type	Range	Size in bytes
Byte	0 to 255	1
Shortint	−128 to 127	1
Integer	−32768 to 32767	2
Word	0 to 65535	2
Longint	−2147483648 to 2147483647	4
Cardinal	0 to 4294967295	4
Int64	−9223372036854775808 to 9223372036854775807	8
QWord	0 to 18446744073709551615	8

A variable is a named value that must be of a given *type*. Pascal supports a number of variable types, but three are introduced here, type *integer*, stored as a simple *binary number*, type *real*, stored as a *floating-point number* and type *string*, a set of ASCII characters. Tables 3.4.1 and 3.4.2 shows the range of both numeric types.

It is not important for you to remember the *exact* limitations but it is *very important* that you realize that every variable has limitations; integers are limited in range and have no fractions, real (floating point) types have a limited range and are not always accurate.

In situations where you cannot have superscripts to show powers, is to write 5E6 to mean 5×10^6 or 5 with 6 zeros = 5 000 000. Pascal uses this notation; the E stands for Exponent. For instance, variables of type real can store numbers from 5.0×10^{-324} to 1.7×10^{308} but only to 15 or 16 significant digits. Type integer can store numbers from −32768 to +32767 (-2^{15} to ($2^{15} - 1$)), a 16-bit number with the first bit used to denote + or −.

Different implementations of Pascal support variables differ in detail. The ones supported by Free Pascal are shown in Tables 3.4.1 and 3.4.2.

To use a variable, you must first *declare* it with a *statement* like:

```
var counter:integer;
```

Points to note
- The whole statement ends with a ';' character.
- The reserved word var is used to denote that this statement declares a variable.
- The identifier called counter, chosen by the programmer, obeys the rules for identifiers above.

You can declare several variables in the same line as long as they are all of the same type and the identifiers separated with commas. For example:

```
var totaltax, taxable_pay, salary:real;
```

Points to note in Program 3.3
- The first line is (nearly) always the same <program> <your choice of name> <(input, output)>. Both Free Pascal and Turbo Pascal allow you leave out the whole line or just the '(input, output)' part.
- The second part of the program contains all the *declarations*.
- The last part of the program contains the *main program block*, with *begin* at the start and *end.* at the end. The word end. will only be found as the very last word in a Pascal program, the word end; (with a ; not a .) will be used many times.

So the structure for a simple Pascal program is:

```
Program yourname(input, output);
Declarations
Main program block
```

Predefined Pascal functions and procedures

Pascal supplied with a number of *predefined functions and procedures*.

A *function* is some code that does a job then gives you an answer in return that you can assign to something. For example, the *trunc* function converts a real type to an integer type, it does the conversion and gives you an answer. It could be used like this: `y=trunc(x);` where the answer is stored in variable y.

A *procedure* is a code that does a job but does not give you an answer, for instance, the *writeln* procedure outputs data but does not return a value.

The Pascal functions and procedures *write, writeln, readln, val* and *trunc* presented here will be used to develop the next few programs.

The procedures *write* and *writeln* both output data, usually to the screen (unless you tell them to output elsewhere). The difference is that *writeln* outputs a newline at the finish, *write* does not.

Examples

You can put a whole line of *variables* or *constants* in a write or writeln statement.

The *readln* function reads or inputs data (usually from the keyboard unless you tell it otherwise) but waits for the *enter key* to be pressed at the end of the input. The enter key generates a new line.

Table 3.4.3

write(x);	Outputs the variable x
write(x,y);	Outputs both the variables *x* and *y* with no space between
writeln('Total Tax= ', tax);	Outputs the *string constant* 'Total Tax= ' then the value of the variable *tax*. It will only output the space inside the ' ' marks
writeln('Total Tax= ', tax);	The same as above, the extra spaces before the variable *tax* are ignored They are *white space* characters

The *val* procedure val is used to convert a *string* to a numerical type which can be of type real or type integer.

The *trunc* function is used to convert a real type to an integer type by cutting off the fractional part of the real and storing the returning number.

Program 3.4   *Program that uses some of the above functions and procedures*

```
program prog3_4(input,output);
var     x:integer;
        name:string;
begin
write('What is your name? ');
readln(name);
write('Hello ',name,' now please give me a number with no
fractions ');
readln(x);
writeln('Thanks, you answered ',x);
end.
```

When you run this program, it simply asks your name with a readln procedure then *echos* the numerical answer you give at the `readln(x);` line.

Run the program again but this time type in a number with a decimal point. The program should crash with an error message similar to the one below.

Figure 3.4.2   *Input error*

Points to note

- The program crashes if you type a value with a decimal point as Pascal interprets this as a *floating point* input. This is not the correct variable type for the variable x which is an integer.
- Pascal is said to be a *strongly typed* language and this is one aspect of strong typing, it means the rules about variable types are enforced. Some programming languages, notably those based on BASIC, do not enforce data typing as strongly as does Pascal.
- If you run program 3.4 and type 'two' instead of '2', it will crash again for similar reasons, 'two' is a *string*, a set of ASCII characters.

Program 3.5   *A way around the program crashing*

```
program prog3_5(input,output);
var     errorcode:integer;
        y:real;
        name,numberstr:string;

begin
write('What is your name? ');
readln(name);
write('Hello ',name,' now please give me a number ');
readln(numberstr);
val(numberstr,y,errorcode);
writeln('Thanks, you answered ',y:0:3);
end.
```

Points to note

- The programs are getting longer and harder to read as there is little in the way of white space characters.
- The required input, a number, is now achieved using a *string* type. This will prevent the program from crashing if the user types in an inappropriate value. Try running the program and entering different kind of clearly wrong data such as 'two' or 2.A. In these cases, the program outputs 0 as the value. This is not accurate but is better than allowing the program to crash.
- The code: 0:3 in the last line specifies the output format of the real variable y. This will be covered at the end of this section.

Repeat of Program 3.5 with more white space, better indentation and comments

```
program prog3_5(input,output);
{start of declaration section}

var     errorcode:integer;
        y:real;
        name,numberstr:string;
{end of declaration section}

{start of main program block}

begin
        write('What is your name? ');
        readln(name);

        write('Hello ',name,' now please give me a
          number ');
        readln(numberstr);

        {now convert the input string with the val
          procedure}
```

```
                    {errorcode will contain a non-zero value}
                    {if the conversion fails}
                    val(numberstr,y,errorcode);

                    writeln('Thanks, you answered',y:0:3);
end.
```

Points to note

The text is now easier to read:

- It has better comments.
- The indentation clearly marks the start and end of the main program block. As your programs get longer and more complex, you will find that a small amount of effort setting out the program will be of great benefit.
- The val procedure requires three *parameters*. The first is the string to be converted to a number, the second is the variable that will hold that number and the last is an error code. This will contain zero if all goes well or a non-zero number indicating where in the string conversion failed. The next program will make use of this.

Program 3.5   *An improvement on the last program*

```
program prog3_5(input,output);
{start of declaration section}

var     errorcode:integer;
        y:real;
        name,numberstr:string;
{end of declaration section}

{start of main program block}

begin
        write('What is your name? ');
        readln(name);

        repeat
                write('Hello ',name,' now please give me a
                    number ');
                readln(numberstr);

                {now convert the input string with the val
                    procedure}
                {errorcode will contain a non-zero value
                    if the}
                {conversion fails}
                val(numberstr,y,errorcode);
        until errorcode=0;

        writeln('Thanks, you answered ',y:0:3);
end.
```

The program now has a *repeat..until loop*. This will cause the program to go on and on executing all the code inside the words *repeat* and *until* until the *condition* specified after the word until is true. In this case, the variable *errorcode* will only be 0 when the conversion to a number has worked, i.e. the input of a number has been valid. This is a example of *data validation*. Consider most (not all!) commercial programs. Will they crash if you make an invalid input or give an error message? Program crashes are a Bad Thing, error messages should be seen as useful.

Points to note

- The indentation makes the position and meaning of the repeat..until loop much clearer or easier to see.

- the input of the numerical value is now much more reliable as it will accept as input any keyboard characters, errors are *trapped* by the code.

Program 3.6 *An addition to the last program using the* trunc *procedure*

```
program prog3_6(input,output);
{start of declaration section}

var    errorcode:integer;
       y:real;
       name,numberstr:string;
{end of declaration section}

{start of main program block}

begin
    write('What is your name? ');
    readln(name);

       repeat
             write('Hello ',name,' now please give me a
                number ');
             readln(numberstr);

             {now convert the input string with the val
               procedure}
             {errorcode will contain a non-zero value if
               the }
                {conversion fails}
                val(numberstr,y,errorcode);
       until errorcode=0;

       writeln('Thanks, you answered ',y:0:3);

       writeln('The integer part of you number was ',
         trunc(y));
end.
```

Points to note
- The final program in this section, Program 3.6 introduces two more ideas. First, it uses the trunc function to convert a real type into an integer type. Second, use is made of Pascal's ability to have a function or expression as a parameter for a procedure. The example here is the last writeln:

```
writeln('The integer part of you number was ',
trunc(y));
```

The conversion using *trunc* is itself a parameter for the *writeln* procedure.
- It could have been done in two lines like this

```
x:=trunc(y)
writeln('The integer part of you number was ',x);
```

Providing x was an integer type.

Formatting numbers in write or writeln statements

When Pascal executes statement like

```
writeln('Your tax= ',tax);
```

it uses the exponential format for variables of type real unless you tell it otherwise.

In this example, if the variable tax had the value 13.34, Pascal would output 1.334000000000000E + 001 which means 1.334 times 10^1. If the value was 1344, the output would be 1.334000000000000E+003 or 1.334×10^3.

If you want a normal decimal output, use the *format specifier* for type real immediately after the variable name as in

```
writeln('Your tax= ',tax:0:2);
```

The :0 means 'use any number of screen columns', the :2 means 'use two decimal places'.

If you had used the format specifier :8:4, it would mean use eight screen columns and four decimal places.

You can use a *format specifier* with type integer as well but with only one part as in

```
writeln('Your service in whole years= ',service:5);
```

This will output the integer service using 5 screen columns.

3.5 Elements of Pascal 1: practice

The following programs use only the elements introduced in *Elements of Pascal 1*.

Elements introduced were:

- Identifiers, reserved words.
- Variable of type: integer, real, string and char.
- Predefined functions and procedures: write, writeln, readln, val, trunc.
- Program structure: repeat..until.
- Data validation.
- White space and indentation.

Write programs to suit the tasks below

Program 3.7   *Calculate the area of a rectangle. Ask the user for the length of each side and output the result with two decimal places. Do not put any data validation in place.*

Possible answer

```
program prog3_7(input, output);
var side1,side2,area:real;

begin
        {get the size of the rectangle }
        write('Please type the length of side 1 ');
        readln(side1);
        write('and now the length of side 2 ');
        readln(side2);

        {now calculate the answer}
        area:=side1*side2;

        {now output the answer }
        writeln('The area = ',area:0:2);
end.
```

Points to note
- Format specifier :0:2 to give any number of screen columns and two decimal places.
- Sensible variable names.

Program 3.8 *Calculate the foreign currency equivalent to UK pounds. Ask the user for the exchange rate and the amount to be converted. Do not put any data validation in place.*

Possible answer

```
program prog3_8(input, output);
var amount,exchangerate:real;

begin
    write('What is the exchange rate? ');
    readln(exchangerate);
    write('What amount of currency to convert? ');
    readln(amount);

    {now output the result}
    write(amount:0:2, ' equals ',amount*exchangerate:0:2,
                                ' pounds ');
end.
```

Points to note
- Statements can be split across lines with any number of white space characters.
- Use of write instead of writeln when getting user input.
- The final writeln can contain the calculation.

Program 3.9 *Calculate the area of a circle given the formula Area = 3.14159*diameter*diameter. Do not put any data validation in place.*

Possible answer

```
program prog3_9(input, output);
var diameter,area:real;

begin
        write('What is the diameter? ');
        readln(diameter);

        {calculate the result}
        area:=3.14159*diameter*diameter;

        {now output the result}
        writeln('When diameter= ',diameter:0:2,
                ', area= ',area:0:2);
end.
```

Points to note
- Inside the statement writeln('When   diameter= ', diameter:0:2, ', area= ',area:0:2); there is a comma inside the ' ' marks to be output.
- Format specifier :0:2

Program 3.10 *Calculate the temperature in degrees F given the formula degrees C = (F − 32)*(5/9). Be careful about precedence levels when using subtraction and multiplication. Do not put any data validation in place.*

Possible answer

```
program prog3_10;
var degreesF, degreesC:real;

begin
        write('What is the temperature in degrees F ');
        readln(degreesF);
```

```
                    {calculate the answer}
                    degreesC:=(degreesF-32)*5/9;

                    writeln(degreesF:0:2, 'F = ',degreesC:0:2, 'C ');
        end.
```

Points to note
- The (input, output) has been left off in the first line. Although not standard Pascal, it is normal practice in both Free Pascal and Turbo Pascal.
- Use of brackets to ensure the subtraction occurs before the multiplication.

Programs 3.11–3.14
Add some data validation to all four programs 3.7–3.10 to prevent the programs crashing if the user types inappropriate data.

Possible answers Program 3.11, modified Program 3.7

```
program prog3_11(input, output);
var side1,side2,area:real;
    errorcode:integer;
    inputstr:string;

begin
        {get the size of the rectangle}
        repeat
                write(' Please type the length of
                  side 1 ');
                readln(inputstr);
                val(inputstr,side1,errorcode);
        until errorcode=0;

        repeat
                write('and now the length of side 2 ');
                readln(inputstr);
                val(inputstr,side2,errorcode);
        until errorcode=0;

        { now calculate the answer}

        area:=side1*side2;

        {now output the answer}
        writeln('The area = ',area:0:2);
end.
```

Possible answers Program 3.12, modified program 3.8

```
program prog3_12(input, output);
var amount,exchangerate:real;
    inputstr:string;
    errorcode:integer;

begin
     repeat
             write('What is the exchange rate? ');
             readln(inputstr);
             val(inputstr,exchangerate,errorcode);
     until errorcode=0;

     repeat
             write('What amount of currency to
               convert? ');
             readln(inputstr);
             val(inputstr,amount,errorcode);
     until errorcode=0;
```

```
                            {now output the result}
                            write(amount:0:2, ' equals ',amount*
                               exchangerate:0:2,' pounds');
              end.
```

Possible answers Program 3.13, modified Program 3.9

```
program prog3_9(input, output);
var    diameter,area:real;
       inputstr:string;
       errorcode:integer;

begin
       repeat
           write('What is the diameter? ');
           readln(inputstr);
           val(inputstr,diameter,errorcode);
       until errorcode=0;

       {calculate the result}
       area:=3.14159*diameter*diameter;

       {now output the result}
       writeln('When diameter= ',diameter:0:2,
          ', area= ',area:0:2);
end.
```

Possible answers Program 3.14, modified Program 3.10

```
program prog3_14;
var     degreesF, degreesC:real;
        inputstr:string;
        errorcode:integer;

begin
      repeat
          write('What is the temperature in degrees F ');
          readln(inputstr);
          val(inputstr,degreesF,errorcode);
      until errorcode=0;

          {calculate the answer}
          degreesC:=(degreesF-32)*5/9;

          writeln(degreesF:0:2, 'F = ',degreesC:0:2, 'C ');
end.
```

Points to note, Programs 3.11–3.14
- The data validation is basically the same in all cases, each write/ readln pair of statements is enclosed inside a repeat..until loop, the data is read as a string and converted.
- You could add uses crt; and clrscr; as found in program 3.3. to clear the screen for each program.

3.6 Elements of Pascal 2

Below presented are some more elements of Pascal that will be used to develop the next set of programs.

Elements introduced here:

- Assignment
- Expressions and operators
- If..then..else statement and boolean variables
- Compound statements
- Case statement

- For..to/downto statement
- While..do statement
- Repeat..until statement
- Constants

Variable assignment

In *Elements of Pascal 1*, assignment was used to give a variable a name without explanation.

Assignment effectively means 'store a value in a variable'. Unfortunately, the symbols used in many programming languages cause some confusion.

In Pascal, if you want the variable x to take on the value 12, you would write:

```
x:=12;
```

This *assignment statement* ends with a ';' in the usual way and the assignment *operator*, ':=' is used to tell the compiler to generate code to store the value 12 *in memory* at a *location* (or *address*) that Pascal remembers as 'x'.

The confusion comes in some languages (e.g. BASIC) where the same assignment task is written as x = 12, i.e. the '=' on its own is used. What would be better to write is x⇐12, i.e. x with an arrow pointing to the left. It would then read easily as 'x is assigned the value 12' and not be confused with the 'equals' sign. The problem is that standard keyboards do not generate a left pointing arrow, it is not an ASCII character. Although it works on some machines it is not standard. (The S in ASCII stands for Standard)

[please set the x⇐12 as an x with a left pointing arrow then the 12]

The problem gets worse when you consider a very common operation, adding 1 to a variable. In Pascal, this can be written as x:=x+1; clearly x cannot equal x + 1. When you read Pascal programs and see an assignment, it is best to say 'x is assigned', not 'x equals'.

An aside

When Pascal assigns a value to a variable, it must do two things.

1. It must 'know' where to store it in memory. During compilation, when Pascal comes across a declaration statement like

   ```
   var x:integer;
   ```

   it finds 2 bytes of space in memory (2 bytes for a 16-bit integer) then 'remembers' where that place is.
2. When an assignment is required, the value is stored in the correct location.
   It would generate code something like

   ```
   MOV [SI], AX
   ```

> assuming the value 12 is in the AX register and the SI register already *points* to the address of the variable x.
>
> The main point to understand is that the value 12 gets *stored in memory* at a *location* (or *address*) that Pascal remembers as 'x'.

Variable can be assigned values from more than simple constants, for example:

Table 3.6.1

x:=12;	Simple assignment of a constant 12
x:=y;	Simple assignment of another variable. Because Pascal is *strongly typed*, the assigned variable must be compatible with x within the Pascal rules, i.e. integer types, real types, etc. but not mixed
x:=y + 12;	x is assigned the value of an *expression*, i.e. a piece of code that must be evaluated before assignment takes place.
x:=(salary − tax)*taxrate;	x is assigned the value of a more complex *expression*
x:=trunc(y);	x is assigned the value of a *function*
x:=trunc(tax) + trunc(taxallowance)/12;	x is assigned the value of a *expression* that contains a *function*

The value to the right of the assignment operator ':=' must evaluate to be type compatible with the variable. If x was of type integer, the following code would not compile:

```
x:=25.4*size_in_mm;
```

because the code will generate a type real result. If x were type real, there would be no problem.

Expressions and operators

An *expression* is a piece of code that must be evaluated before assignment takes place. You can use functions in expressions but not procedures, functions return a value that can be used in the expression, procedures do not.

Expressions are evaluated according to normal rules of arithmetic, i.e. BoDMAS, which if you remember from school means Brackets of Divide Multiply Add Subtract. Ignoring the old word for multiply (of, because 7 *of* 6 = 42 the same as 7*6), the expression evaluator will:

Work out the values inside brackets first
Perform divisions and multiplications next
The additions and subtractions.

In fact it is a little more involved, but just remembering BoDMAS will help. The actual precedence (importance) of the operators is shown in Table 3.6.2, the highest precedence comes first.

Table 3.6.2   *Precedence of operators*

Operator	Precedence	Category
Not, @	Highest (first)	Unary operators
* / div mod and shl shr	Second	Multiplying operators
+ − or xor	Third	Adding operators
< <> <> <= >=	Lowest (last)	Relational operators

where the *operators* are:

*	multiply	+	add
/	divide	−	subtract
div	integer divide (no fractions or remainder)	or	logical or bitwise *or* operation
		xor	logical or bitwise *xor* operation
mod	remainder after integer divide	<	less than
and	logical or bitwise *and* operation	<=	less than or equal to
shl	logical or bitwise shift left (effectively divides by 2)	>	greater than
		>=	greater than or equal to
shr	logical or bitwise shift right (effectively multiplies by 2)	<>	not equal to

Constants

A very important aim is to make the program code easier to read. Pascal supports *constants* to help in this respect. A typical use for a constant is below:

```
program demo(input, output);
const daysinyear=365;
var monthlysalary,annualsalary:real;

begin
      { some code left out for clarity }
      monthlysalary:=annualsalary / daysinyear;

      { the rest of the program left out for clarity }
end.
```

Points to note
- The declaration of constants is usually before the declaration of variables.
- If used throughout a long program, any change need only be made once, in the declaration.
- If the use of constants makes the code easier to read and understand then you should use them, if not, leave them out.

If..then..else statement and boolean variables

The *if* statement is used to control what code is executed, e.g.

```
if (name= 'Fred') then writeln('Hello Fred');
```

The part between the *if* and the *then* must evaluate to *true* or *false*. It may be an expression or a *boolean* variable. A *boolean variable* is one that can be just true or false, nothing else.
Typical code is:

```
if (salary>taxfreepay) then tax:=salary*taxrate;
```

where (`salary>taxfreepay`) has only the value *true* or *false*, the expression does not evaluate to a number. Either salary is greater than the taxfreepay or it is not. If the expression evaluates to false, the code on the right of the *then* reserved word is not executed.

It is often useful to add the else clause to the if statement, for example:

```
if (age<16)
     then
             childsfare:=true
     else
             childsfare:=false;
```

Points to notice

- There is no ';' after the line `childsfare:=true` because the ';' character means *end of statement*.
- The indentation and white space makes the code much easier to read.
- The assignments are to a *boolean* variable but can be any valid Pascal statement.
- The code after the *else* clause is only executed if the expression evaluates to false.

An aside

George Boole was born on 2 November 1815 in Lincoln, Lincolnshire, England.

He went to school in Lincoln but at the age of 12 he had become very skilled at Latin, so much so that it provoked an argument. He translated an ode by the Latin poet Horace that was published by his proud father. His schoolmaster disputed that any 12-year old could have written with such depth. The schoolmaster was wrong.

From the age of 16 Boole was an assistant teacher. He maintained his interest in languages and intended to enter the Church but from 1835 he began to study mathematics on his own. He began publishing in the Cambridge Mathematical Journal and was awarded the Royal Medal from the Royal Society for his work on the solution of differential equations.

In 1849, Boole was appointed to the chair of mathematics at Queens College, Cork. He taught there for the rest of his life, gaining a reputation as an outstanding and dedicated teacher.

In 1854 he published '*An investigation into the Laws of Thought, on Which are founded the Mathematical Theories of Logic and Probabilities*'. Boole had reduced logic to simple algebra and it began the algebra of logic called *Boolean algebra*.

He died on 8 December 1864 in Ballintemple, County Cork, Ireland, aged just 49.

Compound statements

A statement is one piece of code that ends with a ';' character. It is often required to 'join' several statements together to make them act as one statement. This is done with *begin* and *end;* as in the example below.

```
if (salary>taxfreepay) then
    begin
        writeln(Salary will be taxed');
        tax:=salary*taxrate;
    end;
```

If the expression after the *if* evaluates to true, both the statements here will be executed, they have become a *compound statement*. You can make many statements into a compound statement, however, if you have too many, it is probable that rewriting the code with a better structure will make it clearer and easier to read and understand.

If you had written

```
if (salary>taxfreepay) then
            writeln(Salary will be taxed');
            tax:=salary*taxrate;
```

The line `writeln(Salary will be taxed');` will only be executed *if (salary>taxfreepay)* evaluates as true *but* the line `tax:=salary*taxrate;` will *always* be executed because it does not 'belong' to the *if* statement. This is a very common mistake in Pascal programs. If you want more than one statement to be executed as a result of a decision, they must be made into a single compound statement with a *begin end;* pair.

Points to notice
- At the risk of being too emphatic, the white space and indentation make the code easier to read and understand. This is especially true if you forget to type *begin* and *end;* to make it into a compound statement. After you become more practised, the indentation will reflect the program logic and you will be able to see such errors very quickly. People who think they can add the indentation later to finish off a program are making a fundamental mistake. The indentation, comments and white space are used to help you write the program in the first place, to aid understanding.
- There is a ';' character after the line `tax:=salary*taxrate;`, i.e. the line before *end;* It is possible to leave this off as *end;* marks the end of the compound statement. It does no harm to leave one there!

Case statement

The case statement acts like many *if* statements in line.
For example:

```
case choice of
    'a' :writeln('You pressed the a key');
    'b' :writeln('You pressed the b key');
    'c' :writeln('You pressed the c key');
    'd' :writeln('You pressed the d key');
else
    writeln('Invalid key pressed');
end;
```

In this statement, the variable *choice* is expected to have the value 'a' or 'b' or 'c' or 'd'. The appropriate writeln is executed depending on this value or a suitable error message is displayed.

Points to notice

- In place of a variable you can have an *expression*
- The statement ends with *end;*
- You could have written the same logic with a set of *if* statements. There is not a clear choice whether you choose *case* or a set of *if* statements, it is a matter of style. Some languages do not support *case*

More complex case statements are possible, for example

```
Case choice of
 'a','e','i','o','u' : writeln ('vowel pressed');
else
  writeln ('key was not a vowel');
end;
```

where choice can have any value from 'a', 'e', 'i', 'o' or 'u'. If any other value is entered, the statement in the *else* clause is executed. The variable choice would be of type char.

You could also write a case statement with the case constants in a range like this:

```
case choice of
'a'..'m':writeln('Thank you');
else
writeln('That was not correct');
end;
```

The clause 'a'.. 'm' is evaluated as any ASCII character between 'a' and 'm'. The variable choice would be of type char.

For..to/downto statement

If you need to execute a statement a known number of times, you can use the construction below the *for loop*.

```
for count:=1 to 10 do {something};
```

which takes the variable count (an integer type, not a real type) from the value 1 to the value 10 and executes the code, in this case, 10 times.

You could use variables as in

```
for i:=start to finish do {something};
```

or expressions as in

```
for y:=(x-1) to (x+20) do{something};
```

You can also count down just by changing *to* to *downto* as in

```
for count:=100 downto 20 do {something};
```

As an example of a *for loop*, here is a program that will write the 13 times table

```
program timestable(input,output);
var count,table:integer;

begin
        table:=13;

        for count:=1 to 12 do
                writeln(count, 'times', table, ' = ',
                  count*table);
end.
```

Points to note

- The writeln statement uses several parameters separated with commas.
- Only the spaces inside the ' ' marks are significant in the writeln statement.
- If you wish several statements to be executed by the for loop, they must be made into a compound statement.

While..do statement

This is another loop but one that is more flexible than the *for loop*. Its construction is

while <condition> do {something}

It is more flexible because the condition can be anything that evaluates to a *boolean*, i.e. true or false, it need not be based on numbers. While the loop is running, the condition that determines when it is finished must have the chance to change, otherwise the loop will go on forever. The usual rule applies about compound statements.

For example:

```
x:=1;
while x<=100 do
      begin
              writeln(x);
              x:=x+23;
      end;
```

This will write the sequence 1, 24, 47, 70, 93.

Points to note

- Indentation!
- If you missed the statement x:=x+23; the loop would go on forever.
- You could have achieved the same output with a for loop but this is easier to understand.

Repeat..until loop

This is another loop. The main difference from a *while loop* is that the condition that terminates the loop is at the end not at the beginning. The only important difference therefore, is that a *repeat loop* will always execute at least once, a *while loop* has the possibility that it will not execute at all, depending on the condition.

For instance, the code

```
x:=1;
repeat
      writeln(x);
      x:=x+23;
until x>=100;
```

will generate the same number sequence as in the *while loop* example. Some programming languages do not support *repeat loops*, as the same effect can be achieved using the right conditions and a *while loop*.

Points to note

- The repeat loop does not need the begin end; pair to make a compound statement. Some people see this as an inconsistency in Pascal.

- Unless you indent the code, it is even harder to see where the repeat..until loop is in a long program.

3.7 Elements of Pascal 2: Practice

The following programs use the elements introduced in *Elements of Pascal 2*.

Elements introduced were:

- Assignment
- Expressions and operators
- If..then..else statement and boolean variables
- Compound statements
- Case statement
- For..to/downto statement
- While..do statement
- Repeat..until statement
- Constants

Write programs to suit the tasks below

Program 3.15 *Modify program 3.14 to*
- *Output an error message if non-numeric input is typed.*
- *Prevent temperatures below −459 F being entered.*

Possible answer (modifications shown in **bold**)

```
program prog3_15;
var     degreesF, degreesC:real;
      inputstr:string;
        errorcode:integer;
        temp_in_range:boolean;

begin
        repeat
            write('What is the temperature in
              degrees F');
            readln(inputstr);
                val(inputstr,degreesF,errorcode);

                {new lines for program 3.15}
                if errorcode<>0 then writeln('Error in
                  input');
                if (degreesF< -459) then
                        temp_in_range:=false
                        else
                        temp_in_range:=true;

        until (errorcode=0) and (temp_in_range);

        {calculate the answer}
        degreesC:=(degreesF-32)*5/9;

        writeln(degreesF:0:2, 'F = ',degreesC:0:2, 'C ');
end.
```

Points to note
- The error message is produced by an *if* statement testing the value of the variable *errorcode*.
- The program uses a boolean variable; the value is set to *true* or *false* depending on the temperature entered. If below −459, the boolean temp_in_range is set to false, any temperature above that, temp_in_range is set to true.

- The line

  ```
  until (errorcode=0) and (temp_in_range);
  ```

  could have been written as

  ```
  until (errorcode=0) and (temp_in_range=true);
  ```

  i.e. the last expression tested explicitly against the value *true*. In general with programming languages, this is not required, as the expression evaluator only comes back with true or false so a simple boolean variable is all that is required.

- Try removing the brackets from the line `until (errorcode=0) and (temp_in_range);` and then try to recompile the program. The missing brackets may be wrong but the error message is less than helpful! See Figure 3.7.1. Do not always believe compiler error messages!

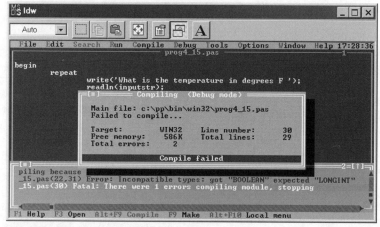

Figure 3.7.1   *Program 3_15 compilation failure*

Program 3.16   *Write a program that outputs the area of either a circle or a rectangle. The program should have the following features. Take an input of a single keyboard character, R for rectangle and C for circle (allow r for R and c for C).*
Data validation for all inputs

Possible answer

```
program prog3_16(input, output);
var    diameter,side1,side2,area:real;
       errorcode:integer;
       inputstr:string;
       choice:char;

begin
     writeln('Press C for circle or R for rectangle');
     writeln('Then press ENTER');
     repeat
          writeln('Choice?');
          readln(choice);
     until (choice='c') or (choice='C') or (choice='r')
               or (choice='R');

     case choice of

     'c','C':
          begin
```

```
                        repeat
                            write('What is the diameter? ');
                            readln(inputstr);
                            val(inputstr,diameter,errorcode);
                        until errorcode=0;

                        {calculate the result}
                        area:=3.14159*diameter*diameter;

                        {now output the result}
                        writeln('When diameter= ',diameter:0:2,
                                ',area= ',area:0:2);
                    end;
            'r','R':
                    begin
                        {get the size of the rectangle}
                        repeat
                            write('Please type the length of
                                side 1 ');
                            readln(inputstr);
                            val(inputstr,side1,errorcode);
                        until errorcode=0;

                        repeat
                            write('and now the length of
                                side 2 ');
                            readln(inputstr);
                            val(inputstr,side2,errorcode);
                        until errorcode=0;

                        {now calculate the answer}

                        area:=side1*side2;

                        {now output the answer}
                            writeln('The area = ',area:0:2);
                    end;
            end;
        end;
end.
```

Points to notice

- The *end;* reserved word is underneath the beginning of the statement it belongs to.
- The variable choice is of type *char*.
- The validation of the key press could be done in a more elegant way, more of that later.
- The choice between rectangle and circle is done via a *case* statement.
- The case statement uses compound statements delimited with *begin* and *end.*
- The same program is presented below without white space, indentation or comments. Which is easier to read? Program code layout is done to help *you*.

```
program prog3_16(input, output);
var diameter,side1,side2,area:real;
errorcode:integer;
inputstr:string;
choice:char;
begin
writeln('Press C for circle or R for rectangle');
writeln('Then press ENTER');
repeat
writeln('Choice? ');
readln(choice);
```

```
until (choice='c') or (choice='C') or (choice='r') or
   (choice='R');
case choice of
'c','C':
begin
repeat
write('What is the diameter? ');
readln(inputstr);
val(inputstr,diameter,errorcode);
until errorcode=0;
area:=3.14159*diameter*diameter;
writeln('When diameter= ',diameter:0:2,
',area= ',area:0:2);
end;
'r','R':
begin
repeat
write('Please type the length of side 1 ');
readln(inputstr);
val(inputstr,side1,errorcode);
until errorcode=0;
repeat
write('and now the length of side 2 ');
readln(inputstr);
val(inputstr,side2,errorcode);
until errorcode=0;
area:=side1*side2;
writeln('The area = ',area:0:2);
end;
end;
end.
```

Program 3.17   *Write a program to input the age of six people and output the average age. Use data validation to cope with bad inputs. Clear the screen as the first instruction.*

Possible answer

```
program prog3_17;
uses crt;

var total,age,average:real;
    counter,errorcode:integer;
    inputstr:string;

begin
    clrscr;
    total:=0; {initialise the variable to ensure it
              contains 0}

    for counter:=1 to 6 do
        begin
            {validate the input}
            repeat
                write('What is the age of person ',
                            counter, ' ');
                readln(inputstr);
                val(inputstr,age,errorcode);
            until errorcode=0;
            total:=total+age;
        end;
    average:=total/6;

    writeln('The average age= ',average:0:2,' years');
end.
```

Points to notice

- The line write(`What is the age of person', counter, ` '); has a quoted space at the end to provide space between the value of variable counter and the user input.
- The *for loop* uses a compound statement.
- Each input is added in turn with the line total:=total+age;.
- The variable *total* has been initialized to zero with the line total:=0;.

Initializing variables

Since the act of declaring a variable simply asks the compiler to find space in memory for the value, if there is already some (unknown) value at that address, the variable may appear to take on that value. It is good practice therefore to set all variables to known values. This will help you to be ready for languages that do not initialize them for you, e.g. C/C++. In some languages (e.g. BASIC) this step is not required because each variable is always set to zero at compilation time.

As an experiment, try this program.

```
var x:real;
begin
      writeln(x:0:3);
end.
```

As the variable x has not been initialized, it may output any number, depending on two things:

- Whether your Pascal compiler initializes variables.
- What is currently in your computer's memory, a freshly booted system may output 0.000 because there is the value 0 at the address used to store the value of variable x. A machine that has been used for a few different programs without a reboot may output whatever value happens to be at the location where x is stored.

Program 3.18 *Write a program that calculates the average age of an unknown number of people. Use data validation to cope with bad inputs. Clear the screen as the first instruction.*

Possible answer

```
program prog3_18;
uses crt;
var total,age,average:real;
    counter,errorcode:integer;
    inputstr:string;
begin
    clrscr;
    total:=0; {initialise the variable to ensure it
                contains 0}

    age:=0;
    counter:=1;

    while age<>-1 do {use -1 as a sentinel value to
       end the loop}
          begin
                {validate the input}
                repeat
                    write('What is the age of
                       person ', counter, ' ');
```

```
                                        readln(inputstr);
                                        val(inputstr,age,errorcode);
                              until errorcode=0;

                              if (age<>-1) then
                                        begin
                                                total:=total+age;
                                                counter:=counter+1;
                                        end;
                    end;
            average:=total/(counter-1);

            writeln('The average age of ',counter-1,
                        ' people was ',average:0:2,' years');
end.
```

Points to note

- Use is made of a *while loop* because the number of ages to average was unknown at *compile time*. A *repeat..until loop* could have been used.
- The counter was initialized to 1 not 0.
- A *sentinel value* has been used to terminate the loop, in this case −1. The assumption is made that −1 is not a valid age!

3.8   Elements of Pascal 3

Below presented are some more elements of Pascal that will be used to develop the next set of programs.

Elements introduced here:

- More predefined functions and procedures.
- User defined procedures.
- User defined functions.
- Scope of variables.
- Parameter passing by value and by reference.

More predefined functions and procedures

The documentation that comes with Turbo Pascal or Free Pascal lists a large number of predefined functions and procedures. Some of these are standard Pascal such as writeln or readln, some are not standard Pascal. No distinction is made here between the two.

Some useful string functions are:

Table 3.8.1

Name	Example	What is does
chr	y:=chr(65);	returns ASCII character, in this case, 'A'
lowercase	name:=lowercase(name);	returns a string in lowercase
upcase	name:=upcase(name);	returns a string in uppercase
copy	s:=copy('ABCDEFGH', x,count);	returns a substring starting at position x, count bytes long.
str	str(x,outputstr);	converts number x into a string
length	y:=length(name);	gives the length of a string

Some useful numerical functions are:

Table 3.8.2

Name	Example	What it does
abs	y:=abs(value);	gives absolute value of argument, i.e. removes the minus sign
int	y:=int(x);	returns the integer part of a type real
odd	x:=odd(y);	returns true if y is odd, false if y = true
pi	area:=pi*d*d;	returns the value of Pi = 3.1415926535897932385
power	y:=power(10,2)	returns base to power x, in this case, $10^2 = 100$
random	y:=random(x);	returns a random number $>= 0$ and $<x$. Always generates the same random numbers unless randomize is used first
randomize	randomize;	generates a new seed value for the random number generator
round	y:=round(x);	rounds x to nearest integer
frac	y:=frac(x);	returns the fractional part of x
sqr	y:=sqr(counter);	returns square of its argument. Warning, this means square root in other languages!
sqrt	y:=sqrt(x);	returns square root of x

Making programs modular

As you can see from Program 3.16 onwards, when programs get longer, they get harder to understand. One way to make programs easier to write, read, understand and make more reliable is to split them into smaller pieces and write/test each piece on its own.

The two main methods of splitting standard Pascal programs into pieces are to write *procedures* and *functions*. You will recall that a *function* is some code that does a job then gives you an answer in return and that a *procedure* is a code that does a job but does not give you such an answer.

You have already used procedures like writeln and val and functions like trunc. Their use is like this:

```
writeln(x);
```

or

```
val(inputstr,age,errocode);
```

and you often use *functions* by *assignment* or as part of an *expression* like this:

```
y:=trunc(x);
```

or

```
if trunc(tax) > maxvalue then taxfree:=4000;
```

Pascal provides the means to write your own functions and procedures.

A user defined procedure

To a procedure that displays a welcome message is *declared* like this:

```
procedure welcome;
var name:string;

begin
    write('Hello, what is your name? ');
    readln(name);
    writeln('Welcome ',name, '. Please press the ENTER
      key to continue');
    readln; {a readln on its own simply waits for
      enter, any input is "thown away"}
end;
```

The structure is similar to that of a program, the first line starts with the reserved word *procedure*, this is followed by a *user defined identifier* that follows the standard Pascal rules already described. This is followed by an optional *parameter list*. This parameter list is missing from the welcome example but will appear shortly.

To *use* the declaration above is very easy, you simply type welcome, i.e. the procedure name. That way it can be used as often as you like.

Program 3.19   *This is Program 3.9 repeated but with the addition of the* procedure declaration *and its* procedure call *(when it is used) shown in* **bold**.

```
program prog3_19(input, output);
var diameter,area:real;

procedure welcome;
var name:string;

begin
    write('Hello, what is your name? ');
    readln(name);
    writeln('Welcome ',name,
        '. Please press the ENTER key to continue');
    readln; {a readln on its own simply waits for
      enter, any input is "thown away"}
end;

begin {start of main program block}
    welcome; {call the procedure defined above}
    write('What is the diameter? ');
    readln(diameter);

    {calculate the result}
    area:=pi*diameter*diameter;

    {now output the result}
    writeln('When diameter= ',diameter:0:2,
', area= ',area:0:2);
end.
```

Points to notice

- The procedure declaration belongs in the declaration section of the main program.

  The structure for a Pascal program with procedures or functions is:

```
Program yourname(input, output);
Declarations {including declarations of procedures
  and functions}
Main program block
```

- The procedure declaration has the same structure as a simple program declaration.
- The procedure is *called* by name with the line *welcome*;
- You can have many statements in a procedure but remember, the point of a procedure (or a function) is to split the code into easily managed pieces, so long procedures are probably a sign of a badly designed program.
- You can have variables (or indeed other procedures) declared inside a procedure. The variable *name* is defined inside the *welcome* procedure.
- The first code statement to be executed is the first statement in the *main program block*, even if there are declarations of executable code 'above it' in the declaration section.
- The statement `area:=pi*diameter*diameter;` uses the function *pi* in place of 3.1415926535897932385.

An aside

Some people seem to think that a large number of decimal places must be a Good Thing. Taking pi as 3.1415926535897932385 implies that the calculation you are performing implies an accuracy to 19 decimal places. Suppose the calculation was for the area of a circular piece of concrete to be laid for the erection of a flagpole. The concrete is to be 10 m diameter. The area is *approximately* pi*5*5 = 78.5398163397448309616 because the value of pi can never be set down with perfect precision, it is an *irrational number*. Now consider the answer against another problem. An atom is roughly 10^{-10} m diameter so a square 1 atom by 1 atom is $10^{-10} \times 10^{-10} = 1 \times 10^{-18}$ so the calculation of the concrete area is 10 times more 'accurate' than a square 1 atom by 1 atom!

A second procedure, passing by value

If you split a program into pieces, there must be a mechanism for the pieces to share data. One of the best ways is to 'send' that data to the procedure (or function) when you call it. You have already used this form with `writeln('Hello ' , name);` the data is sent, or more correctly *passed* to the procedure in the constant 'Hello' and the variable *name*. Pascal supports two ways to pass variables to procedures, *by value* or *by reference*. They are used in different ways as will be shown here.

```
program prog3_20;
var i,j:integer;

procedure doit(x:integer);
var y:integer;
begin
    writeln('You passed the value ',x,' to this
      procedure');
    x:=x*2; {multiply the local value by 2}
    writeln('Twice the value is ',x);
    y:=51;
    writeln('The local variable y = ', y);
    writeln('But you cannot see it outside of this
      procedure!');
end;
```

```
begin {start of main program block}
      writeln('This is the first piece of code to be
        executed');
      i:=12;
      doit(i);
      j:=34;
      doit(j);
end.
```

This program outputs:

```
This is the first piece of code to be executed
You passed the value 12 to this procedure
Twice the value is 24
The local variable y = 51
But you cannot see it outside of this procedure!
You passed the value 34 to this procedure
Twice the value is 68
The local variable y = 51
But you cannot see it outside of this procedure!
```

Points to note

- The variable x is *passed by value* to the procedure. This means that it is 'called' x *inside* the procedure but you can pass any type compatible variable to it. In the main program block, the variables i and j are passed to the procedure *doit* and Pascal places a *copy* of the value into variable x for its own internal use.
- The value x is changed inside the procedure with the line `x:=x*2;` but it has no effect on the variable that was passed. So when the procedure was called with doit(j); the value in variable j was copied to variable x inside the procedure but variable j was not affected.
- The variable x is not visible outside the procedure. The variable y, declared inside procedure doit is also not visible outside the procedure *doit*. These are called *local variables*.

A third procedure, passing by reference

```
program prog3_21;
var i,j:integer;

procedure changeit(var z:integer);
var y:integer;
begin
      writeln('You passed the value ',z,' to this
        procedure');
      z:=z*2; {multiply the local value by 2}
      writeln('Twice the value is ',z, ' inside the
        procedure');
end;

begin {start of main program block}
      writeln('This is the first piece of code to be
        executed');
      i:=12;
      writeln('Variable i = ',i);
      changeit(i);
      writeln('Variable i = ',i);
      j:=34;
      writeln('Variable j = ',j);
```

```
        changeit(j);
        writeln('Variable j = ',j);
end.
```

This program outputs:

```
This is the first piece of code to be executed
Variable i = 12
You passed the value 12 to this procedure
Twice the value is 24 inside the procedure
Variable i = 24
Variable j = 34
You passed the value 34 to this procedure
Twice the value is 68 inside the procedure
Variable j = 68
```

Points to note
- The syntax of the procedure declaration changes just a little, there is the reserved word *var* in the *parameter list*. The parameter list is the part inside the brackets of the declaration. Apart from that, the declaration is the same.
- When passing by reference, the variable passed to the procedure *can* be changed.
- In the main program block, the variable i starts with a value of 12. This is passed by reference to the procedure but it is 'called' z inside the procedure. When z is changed by the line z:=z*2;, the variable i is also changed. You have already used a procedure in this form. In the programs that used val(inputstr,age,errorcode), the variables *age* and *errorcode* are *passed by reference* as they are changed inside the procedure.
- Look at the program output, you will see that both variable i and variable j have been changed by the procedure.
- The variable types to be passed are declared in the parameter list, other local variables are declared in the procedure's declaration block, in this case the variable y.

A user defined function

Functions are declared in the same place as procedures, in the declaration block, using a similar syntax. The difference is that a function needs to *return a value* and that value will have a *type*. Remember, Pascal is a *strongly typed* language. You can also pass variables to functions in a parameter list just like procedures. You can pass by *value* or pass by *reference* but normal practice would be to pass by value as the function itself returns a value.

A simple user defined function:

```
function twice(x:integer):integer;

begin
    twice:=x*2;
end;
```

In this simple function, a variable is passed by value to the function twice and the function will return a value of type integer.

It is used in assignments or expressions like this:

```
y:=twice(x); {used in an assignment}
if z=twice(score) then writeln('Good!'); {used as an
    expression}
```

An aside

The mechanism used when passing by reference is to send the *address* of the variable. When a variable is declared, Pascal finds free space in memory (RAM) and keeps a 'note' of where it is, i.e. it *points* to the address in memory. When passing by reference, this address is passed to the procedure, not a copy of the data, so the variable inside the procedure *points to the same place*. The reason that variables passed by reference can be changed is that there is only one address where the value is stored.

Points to note

- The return value of this function is of type integer and is made to return by assigning a value to the function name in the line `twice:=x*2;` inside the function declaration.
- The variable type passed to the function does not need to be the same as the return type.

Program 3.22   *A second example function. Outputs the times table of choice.*

```
program prog3_22;
var i,counter:integer;

function getnumber(lower,upper:integer):integer;
var inputstr:string;
      errorcode:integer;
      x:integer;

begin
      repeat
            write('Type a value between ',lower,' and ',
                        upper,' inclusive');
            readln(inputstr);
            val(inputstr,x,errorcode);
      until ((errorcode=0) and (x>=lower) and
        (x<=upper));
      getnumber:=x;
end;

begin {start of main program block}
        counter:=getnumber(2,12);
        for i:=1 to 12 do
                writeln(i,' times',counter,
                    ' = ',i*counter);

end.
```

Points to note

- The function getnumber is declared with two variables of type integer in the parameter list.
- The function validates the input for non-numeric input and an upper and lower value.

Scope of variables

So far, variables declared in procedures have been referred to as *local*. This means that the variable has no meaning outside of the procedure. Variables declared in the main program are said to be *global* and can be used anywhere. The term applied to this is *scope*, the scope of a variable is local or global.

In Program 3.22, the variable x is declared inside the procedure *getnumber*. As an experiment, try adding the line `writeln(x);` in the main program block. You will find that the program will not compile, the compiler will give the error message 'Identifier not found x', because x is *out of scope*.

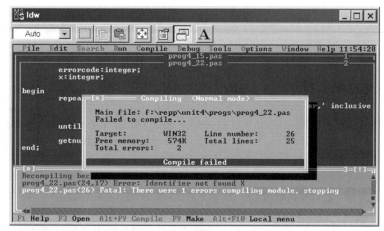

Figure 3.8.1   *Compiler error message*

How to confuse a programmer with variable scope

You could define a global variable x in the main program block and another local variable also called x inside a procedure. If you then had a statement like `writeln(x);`, in which x is being referred to? In fact the local one has precedence as the following experiment will confirm. The global x has a value of 90, the local x has a value of 34. Inside the procedure dummy, both variables are *visible*, i.e. they are both in scope but the local one has precedence, the writeln statement outputs 34.

Small program experiment

```
var x:integer; {a global variable}
procedure dummy;
var x:integer; {a local variable}

begin
    x:=34;
    writeln('X= ',x);
end;
begin
    x:=90;
    dummy;
end.
```

You can confuse many programmers with this problem! The solution is to have the lowest possible number of global variable (none at all is best!). Another solution is to use a naming convention. One such convention is to use L as the first letter in every local variable name and G in front of every global name. Many programmers find that this leads to ugly variable names so will not use it.

It is an excellent idea to write small experiments like the one above to ensure you understand particular points. They only take a few moments to put together and is a powerful way to improve your understanding.

Why have local and global variables?

In larger programming projects, the overall task of writing the code is spilt between more than one person. If only global variables were used, there would have to be a systems that avoided variable names clashing in different parts of the program. For instance, if you used counter as a variable in your code and someone else used counter inside a procedure that was used by your code, the value of the variable would at the very least be confusing. In reality, the value would not be as either programmer had planned. It is much better to have a piece of code, a procedure or function, that stands on its own without relying on the value of a global variable. Values that must be supplied for the procedure or function to work are passed by value or by reference as described above.

3.9 Elements of Pascal 3: Practice

The following programs use the elements introduced in *Elements of Pascal 3*.

Elements introduced here:

- More predefined functions and procedures.
- User defined procedures.
- User defined functions.
- Scope of variables.
- Parameter passing by value and by reference.

Write programs, procedures and functions to suit the tasks below. To test a function or procedure, write the simplest possible main program block.

Program 3.23 *A function that returns a string in Title Case, i.e. all lower case but first letters in uppercase. It should convert 'this is a test string' to 'This Is A Test String'.*

Possible answer (does not run in Turbo Pascal, no *lowercase* function)

```
program prog3_23;

function titlecase(name:string):string;
    {returns string with first letter=capitals}

var       p,i:integer;
          ch:string;
          done:boolean;
          convert_to_caps:boolean;
          outputstr:string;

begin
    name:=lowercase(name); {first ensure everything is
      lowercase}
    done:=false;
    repeat {a loop to ensure that any leading spaces
      are removed}
        if copy(name,1,1)=' ' {if first char is a
          space}
            then
                    {get rest of string only}
                    name:=copy(name,2,length(name)-1)
            else
                    {assign boolean to end the loop}
                    done:=true;
    until done;

    convert_to_caps:=true; {initialise boolean for use
      in for loop}
    outputstr:=' '; {initialise string to null
                        ready to build output string}
```

```
        for i:=1 to length(name) do {look at each
          character in string}
              begin
                    ch:=copy(name,i,1); {get one char at a
                       time}
                    if convert_to_caps=true
                          then
                          begin
                                {add upper case char to
                                   output string}
                                outputstr:=concat(outputstr,
                                   upcase(ch));
                                {set boolean ready for next
                                   time}
                                convert_to_caps:=false;
                          end
                          else
                          begin
                                {add lower case char to
                                   output string}
                                outputstr:=concat
                                   (outputstr,ch);
                          end;

                    {see if next char must be capital}
                    if ch=' ' then convert_to_caps:=true;
              end;
        titlecase:=outputstr; {assign finished string to
          the function}
end;

begin {start of main program block}
      {simply to test function output}
      writeln(titlecase('this is a test string'));
end.
```

This program outputs

```
This is A Test String
```

Program 3.24 *A procedure to ask a simple question to be used to build an arithmetic test program. The question is 'What is x + y' where x + y = a maximum number you specify. You should pass a boolean variable by reference and specify the maximum answer.*

Possible answer

```
program prog3_24;
var rightanswer:boolean;

procedure showquestion(maxanswer:integer;
var    correct:boolean);
var    answer,errorcode,num1,num2:integer;
             inputstr:string;

begin
      randomize; {so that the random numbers are always
        different.}
            {Leave this line out for program testing
               then}
            {all the random numbers will be the same
               each}
            {time the program runs}
```

```
        num1:=random(maxanswer);
        num2:=random(maxanswer-num1);
        repeat
              writeln('What is ',num1,' + ',num2,' ?');
              readln(inputstr);
              val(inputstr,answer,errorcode);
        until errorcode = 0;

        if answer=(num1+num2) then correct:=true
          else correct:=false;
end;

begin {start of main program block}

{very simple program to test procedure}
showquestion(1200,rightanswer);
if rightanswer then writeln('Well done')
  else writeln('Wrong');
end.
```

Points to notice

- The procedure generates the possible numbers to be added, num1 and num2 based on a random number.
- The element in the parameter list var correct:boolean declares the variable *correct* by reference, i.e. it can be changed inside the procedure and the changed value is available once the procedure is finished.

3.10 Design of larger programs

The programs presented so far have been small enough to cope with or without thinking too hard about the design. This is normal for small programs but most commercial applications require programs of significant size and complexity.

How to design a product for a customer

1. The first requirement is to find out exactly what the customer wants. It is hard to believe but, it is at this stage that most design projects fail. People who do not find out what the customer wants usually land up designing something based on a false idea. The writing of the *customer* or *user's specification* involves writing down the customer's needs in non-technical terms.
2. Once the customer specification is done, you can write out the *technical specification*. The technical specification defines performance and other technical details.
3. Once the technical specification is complete you can write out a list of possible solutions. At this stage of the design process you should *not* attempt to *evaluate* any of the solutions. If you are using the design team to arrive at a possible solution, meetings should disallow any adverse comments about other people's suggested design solution. The idea here is to encourage the entire team to be imaginative. This way allows new ideas to be considered. If a climate of derision is allowed to exist, people tend to be too wary to suggest new and possibly better ways of doing things.
4. Having decided on the whole range of solutions, one solution is selected for further work.

5. In the case of programming, there are often at least two aspects to design, often more:
   - what the computer user sees on the computer output, known as the *Human Computer Interface* or *HCI*;
   - the internal processes of the software.

   These two aspects are often designed and written by separate teams. For instance, if the program was a database application, the manipulation of the data is best left to a database specialist and the design of the user screens is best left to someone with the greatest experience in designing user interfaces. The screen designer needs to know little about databases and database design and need only to concern themselves with screen design. One useful benefit from this technique is that the screen designer can produce a prototype before the rest of the software is finished. It can then be approved by the customer before any more work is done. Most people would call this *prototyping* although is usual with computing, this word can have other meanings.

6. Once the prototypes and the final programme are complete, the software is tested. If it is found not to perform to the technical specifications, designers go back to Stage 4 or even Stage 3, depending on what has failed.

This process can be summarized as

1. Define customer needs
2. Define technical needs
3. List possible solutions
4. Detailed design
5. Prototyping
6. Evaluation and testing

These ideas do not apply to software design alone, this design scheme can be used to design almost anything.

You should notice that detailed design does not start until Stage 4.

The scheme outlined above does not take account of the use of *top down design* or *bottom up design*.

Top down design is where you start with the whole problem in mind, you consider all the larger aspects first. Once these are clear, you concentrate on the next level of detail and so on until you have designed all the elements.

As an example of top down design, consider the design of a car. (a real design would of course be more detailed but the purpose here is to describe the process not the car!)

The point about top down design is that details such as the engine, layout of the wheels, etc. are not decided first, the whole problem is considered, then progressively refined.

Table 3.10.1

Determine the needs of the customer	Four adult seats, space for their luggage, have maximum safety features, be able to cope with rough country roads and be able to run on fuel available anywhere
Write technical specification	Size and shape of seating and internal space, determination of possible weight and hence the power output of the engine, determination of the ground clearance to cope with rough roads, definition of fuel type based on survey of what kinds are available worldwide (i.e. do not assume it is a petrol engine!)

(contd)

List possible solutions	4 wheel drive, 2 wheel drive either front or back, tracked vehicle (remember, at this stage no one is allowed to make adverse comments about a possible solution!). Normal piston engine, rotary engine, turbine, steam engine. Fuel diesel, petrol or LPG.
The actual design	A Landrover!
Prototyping	Make a 4 wheel drive for testing on a test track
Testing	Ensure that the car meets the customers needs.

Bottom up design is the opposite of top down. In this method, important details are decided first then more and more is added until the whole product is finished. This is a very poor technique for something like a car, the result is often a lovely engine mounted in an ugly car without space for all the passengers. You may well have travelled in one!

In contrast, bottom up design is useful for some programming problems. Consider a program that takes a scanned image of some text and converts it to editable text. This is known as *Optical Character Recognition* or *OCR*. The finished product must be easy to use, be able to take input from all sorts of graphics devices/files, etc., just the kind of complex product that should result from top down design. There is however a key problem here, this is able to recognize the characters reliably with an acceptable error rate. Until this problem is cracked, the rest of the project is not required. Early attempts at OCR failed at the recognition stage. A product of this nature could first be designed by concentrating on the key problem, the recognition. Once this has been achieved, the rest of the program code can be built around it. This process, starting with a detailed part of the product, is called bottom up design. It suits small design tasks that may have difficult technical features, it does not suit larger and more complex products.

Most professional designers actually use both techniques. Although top down design is usually preferred because it concentrates on customers needs first then produces a solution, some problems need a detailed treatment first.

More formal techniques used to develop business software are described elsewhere in the book.

3.11 Translating a design into code

For smaller projects or the components of larger projects, use can be made of *stepwise refinement* and *pseudo code*.

Stepwise refinement

In order to design an efficient solution to a given problem, it is best to break the task down into manageable parts. As an example consider the task below. Assume that both the customer specification, i.e. what the customer wants and the technical specification have been completed. (*This problem is only to illustrate the idea of stepwise refinement, it is not intended to be a guide to income tax!*)

You are asked to write a program that calculates income tax, national insurance, etc. not for a company, just for individuals.

Define customer needs: done by agreement with the customer. She needs a small program that will act as a handy tax calculator to give away with her main product, an employment advice package. She would like users to type in their annual salary and their tax allowance issued by the Inland Revenue, the program will then *estimate* their annual tax. It has been accepted that actual tax calculations can be complex, the program will act as a tax estimator only.

Define technical needs: done in consultation with a tax specialist, all the complex aspects of tax to be left out, only a simple PAYE calculation to be completed. The specification would include details such as the data to be validated, age range only 16–100, marital status: married, single, divorced, widowed, separated, etc.

List possible solutions: Your first task would be to find out the relevant taxation rules and rates for income tax and national insurance, etc. before you could proceed. These are available from the Inland Revenue web-page at www.inlandrevenue.gov.uk. There are few possible solutions as the rules have been laid down elsewhere.

Detailed design: You discover that you need at least these details: age, gender, marital status, salary and tax allowance from the user and the 'tax bands', currently 10%, 22% and 40% charged at various levels of salary. You also discover that the tax bands and the salary levels are often changed so cannot be fixed in your program.

You could write the program such that when a value has been calculated, the result is output straight away. This is a style of coding that will eventually lead to an over complex program so should be avoided. It would be better to break the program into three pieces which are:

- Get user details
- Do the calculations
- Output the result

These can be represented on a diagram like this:

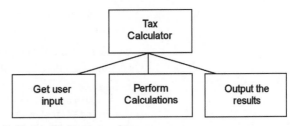

Figure 3.11.1 *Main parts of tax program*

There is not yet sufficient detail to write code, so each of the three parts are broken down even more.

The *Get user input* section can then be broken down or *refined* into more pieces, i.e. the get and validate user input. The validation is done to conform the validation rules set out in the *technical specification*.

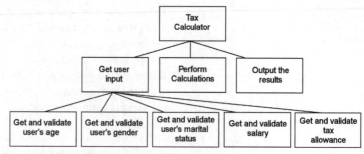

Figure 3.11.2   *First stage of stepwise refinement*

Likewise, the *Perform Calculations* section can be broken down into more pieces:

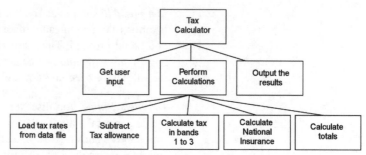

Figure 3.11.3   *Second stage of stepwise refinement*

In this program, the *Output results* section is already simple enough so does not need further refinement.

When finished, the process of stepwise refinement should leave you with tasks that can be written as program code.

Pseudo code

You could now take each task from your stepwise refinement and write *pseudo code*. Pseudo code is not a real programming language but is an 'English like' representation of a real language. It will translate *approximately* line by line to a real language.

For instance, the pseudo code:

Repeat

    Obtain user's age from keyboard
until age is in range 16 to100

would be used as the pseudo code for the *Get and validate users age* section. This may translate into the Pascal

```
repeat
     write('Please give your age in years ');
     readln(inputstr);
     val(inputstr,age,errorcode);
until (errorcode=0) and (age>=16) and (age<=100);
```

Each task is written in this way until the whole program is coded.

Evaluation and testing: The finished program is then tested to see if it conforms to both the customer and technical specifications.

A typical technique used for this testing is to prepare *test data* and to set it out as shown below. In this case, the test data would be constructed with the aid of a tax specialist to ensure it is correct.

Table 3.11.1 *Tax calculator test data*

Inputs	Age	Gender	Marital	Salary	Tax allowance
	34	M	S	23 000	4535
Expected outputs	Tax band 1 188	Tax band 2 3648.70	Tax band 3 0	Total tax 3836.70	NI 1380
Actual outputs	Tax band 1 188	Tax band 2 3648.70	Tax band 3 0	Total tax 3836.70	NI 1231
Output valid?	Yes	Yes	Yes	Yes	No

The test data has previously calculated values. You can see that the table has space for *inputs* and the *expected results*, when these input values are used together with a space to show if the outputs are correct. In this example, the value for NI (National Insurance) is not correct, indicating a problem with the coding.

Well designed test data is valuable for program testing, the test data should include:

- Normal input values, i.e. ages, salaries, etc. in the usual range.
- Invalid inputs to check on the validation routines.
- Values at the extremes of the validation ranges. This will discover such errors as

  when you put

  ```
  until (age>16) and (age<100)
  ```

  when you meant to put

  until (age$>=$16) and (age$<=$100)

  as in this case, an input of the age 16 would have been thrown out as invalid.

A number of these tests should be performed to show that your program is performing to specification.

3.12 Debugging inside the IDE

Both Free Pascal and Borland Turbo Pascal offer a debugger. This is a tool that 'stops' the execution of the program at a *breakpoint* then displays the value of a *watch*. Figure 3.12.1 shows Program 3.17 with the debugger turned on and a *watch* set for the variable *total*. The program is running but has stopped at the *breakpoint* which is set on the line

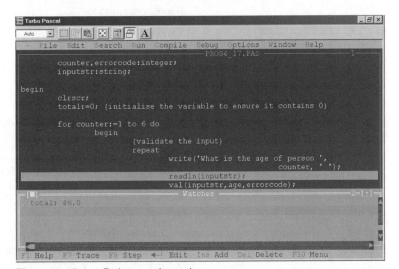

Figure 3.12.1 *Debug and watch screen*

`readln(inputstr);`. This allows inspection of the watch set on the variable total. Breakpoints and watches are set in the Debug menu.

In this example, the variable total is showing the expected result but 'bugs' can be found using this technique.

Trace tables

The expected value of a variable can be set out in a *trace table* then made use of the *debugger* to see if the variable actually has the right values. For instance, if a program had the code

```
repeat
        {do something}
        x:=x+0.001;
until x=10;
```

it may well fail. You will remember from the section on floating point numbers that repeatedly adding a value like 0.001 to a floating point number may well give inaccurate results. The loop here will only finish when x = 10 *exactly*. It may well be that because of the floating point error, x will never be exactly 10, only very near. Unfortunately, computers do not 'think' so when it would be obvious to a human that the calculation should finish, the computer will go on and on round the loop. If you set a breakpoint in the loop and watch the variable x, you may find that instead of producing a sequence like

9.996
9.997
9.998
9.999
10.000

as you may expect, it actually produces

9.9960000000001
9.9970000000001
9.9980000000001
9.9990000000001
10.0000000000001
10.0010000000001
10.0020000000001

showing why the loop did not finish, i.e. the variable never actually *equalled* 10.

The solution is to write `until  (x>=10);`, then it will terminate properly.

The *trace table* would show this

Table 3.12.1   *Trace table*

Variable x	Expected	Actual
	9.996	9.9960000000001
	9.997	9.9970000000001
	9.998	9.9980000000001
	9.999	9.9990000000001
	10.000	10.0000000000001
	10.001	10.0010000000001
	10.002	10.0020000000001
	etc.	

3.13 Prototyping

In terms of say a car or an aircraft, the word *prototype* means a finished product that is used to test the complete design. In programming, the word protype is used in a different sense. It usually means that the user interface is designed so that the customer can see what the finished product will look like but the software will not perform every aspect of its specification. In the case of the small tax calculator above, this could be used as a prototype for a more complete tax calculator, the program 'works' but does not take into account many of the real life income tax details.

If you consider a software designed to run under Microsoft Windows, the language of choice for many people would be C++ as it very powerful and can generate fast and efficient code. One trouble with C++ is the effort required to produce the 'windows' that make up the user interface. In this case, it is quite possible to use a different language to make the prototype. Visual Basic has strengths in this area, it is known as a Rapid Application Development (RAD) language. The prototypes for customer approval would be made using Visual Basic but once approved, the same user interface would be built using C++ or other more powerful language.

3.14 Program documentation

When software is developed, it is usually carried out by a team of people. This implies that there must be adequate documentation and communication between the team members, their customers and outside consultants, etc.

This is especially important when a team member leaves the team as others will now have to maintain code that they did not write themselves.

As a minimum, this documentation should include the following

- Customer specification
- Technical specification
- Details of algorithms and heuristics used
- Version history
- Bug reports
- User guide

Details of algorithms and heuristics used. An *algorithm* is a set of rules that defines how a problem may be solved. It is a set of 'do this, then this, then this' rules that allows either a satisfactory answer or a report that such an answer is not possible. A *heuristic* is different; some problems are not solvable using algorithms, i.e. no set of rules exist to solve the problem. There are some classes of problem where 'an educated guess' is made at the answer and this answer is tested for accuracy. If it is not sufficiently accurate, an updated guess is made and the process repeated either until a satisfactory answer is obtained or until it is clear that such an answer is not possible.

Version history. The version history is where changes to the software are noted. It is usual to have two version numbers for example, 'version 6.3'. The 6 refers to the 6th major revision of the software and the .3 refers to the 3rd bug fix or minor improvement made in the software. The full version history will record exactly what has been changed and why the change was made.

Bug reports. A bug report is where a user will report a fault found in the software. To be really useful, all reports should include exactly how the bug was found and list any other factors that may affect the software such as the version of the operating system in use, hardware details, etc.

User guide. The user guide should tell the user all that is required to use the software to its fullest extent. It must be written with the user not the programmer in mind, i.e. it should not assume prior knowledge of the software. Really good application software such as a wordprocessor should be useable without reading the user guide but this is rarely achieved.

4   Concepts of database design

Summary

The aim of this chapter is to provide students with an insight into database design and technologies. The chapter provides an introduction into the history of storage mechanisms and how databases have evolved, examination of data models and how they have supported users in the understanding and communicating of data set knowledge. The role of database management systems (DBMSs) will also be examined in terms of its function and architecture. The chapter also provides examples of database uses in real-life contexts.

Students are expected to design their own database in order to meet the criteria of the qualification specifications, this chapter will therefore introduce students to database software and the tools and techniques for development.

Introduction

Databases play an integral role in the majority of business systems. Their ability to store and manipulate data has enabled organizations across a range of commercial, financial, academic, industrial and medical domains to keep accurate and up-to-date data about their customer, client and patient base.

Databases have evolved from being just a flat-file storage tool to a fully relational management and information system that can analyse, predict and demonstrate certain levels of intelligence.

This chapter takes a holistic view of how databases have evolved, design and methodology issues and the uses of databases within real-life contexts. This chapter is also designed to support students with their own database designs by introducing the use of database applications software tools and techniques.

4.1 Database environments

To fully appreciate the contribution that databases have made in terms of data storage, manipulation and management, an insight into the history of database development and an overview of the environment in which they operate will be examined.

This chapter looks at how databases have evolved, and the users that have contributed to these advancements. The development, functions and features of database management systems (DBMSs) and examples of the use of databases in real-life contexts.

What is a database?

Many definitions exist in terms of describing a database, some of which include: 'an electronic version of a filing cabinet', 'a computerized record-keeping system' and 'a shared collection of logically related data and a description of the data, designed to meet the information needs of an individual or organization.'

Primarily a database is a combined storage and manipulation tool that forms the backbone to many organizational IT systems. Databases are used because they can:

- Process data fast and efficiently.
- Process large volumes of data.
- Reduce data redundancy due to its centralized approach.
- Reduce repetitiveness of tasks for end users.
- Create a secure data environment.

Because of these qualities databases can be seen operating in a number of environments such as:

- Carrying out credit checks – see case study.
- Surfing the Internet.
- Checking flight availability at a travel agents.
- Stock control at a supermarket.
- Confirming patient details at a surgery.

It is hard to imagine what life was like without databases, however, data storage has always been achievable through alternative, manual methods and although not as efficient, their contribution to electronic storage is invaluable.

Case study – credit agencies

Credit agencies are used by a number of retail, banking and financial institutes to check the credit rating of consumers that want to take out a loan, mortgage or credit facilities on goods and services. In order for an organization to assess a consumer's ability to honour payments a credit check is carried out. The process of checking a credit rating is based upon a scoring system where historical data, personal finances and stability are assessed. The more points accumulated that greater the chance of being approved for credit.

Credit agencies gather this information from a variety of sources such as electoral rolls, public opinion surveys, other organizations and agencies. This information is stored on a database for quick reference and sold onto organizations requiring credit check services. In conjunction, updated information about credit check status, approvals and rejections are passed back to the credit agency.

Storage systems

Data storage has always been possible through the use of manual systems consisting of in-trays, filing cabinets and index cards, etc., extending to file-based systems through to electronic storage systems such as databases and DBMS.

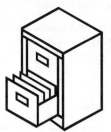

Manual storage data storage includes card index systems, in-trays and filing cabinets. Easy to access but with limited storage and no capabilities of cross-referencing.

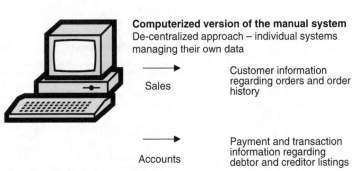

Computerized version of the manual system
De-centralized approach – individual systems managing their own data

Sales → Customer information regarding orders and order history

Accounts → Payment and transaction information regarding debtor and creditor listings

Fully electronic centralized storage system
Database approach where all data is centrally deposited thus allowing easy access

Figure 4.1.2   *Storage evolution*

Each generation of storage, manual through to electronic have contributed in some way to creating a more improved and faster way of storing and manipulating data.

The benefits of a manual system include its simplicity and hard copy formats, the limitations however include:

- inability to handle and process large volumes of data;
- inadequate cross-referencing;
- physical storage capacities;
- security.

These limitations generating the need for a more efficient system. However, the underlying principles of manual storage – having individual data files stored in specific filing cabinets worked quite well in some areas, so therefore the next generation of storage was modelled on this. File-based systems being an early attempt to computerize the manual system.

File-based systems

The file-based system uses application programs to define and manage data, and it is modelled around the concept of decentralization. Within an organization each functional department generates their own data sets, this data would then be electronically stored, manipulated and accessed by personnel within that functional area. Figure 4.1.3 illustrates a typical file-based system.

This decentralized approach to data storage can create a number of problems that include:

- repetition of data within individual systems and across different systems;
- segregation of data in different systems;

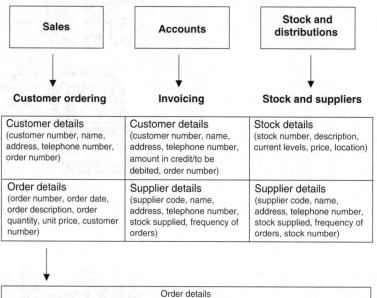

Figure 4.1.3   *File-based systems*

- possible incompatibility issues;
- data dependencies;
- static application framework.

Data repetition can be seen within Figure 4.1.3.

Questions 4.1.1

1. What are the benefits of using a database approach to storing, retrieving and manipulating data?
2. What are the limitations of a file-based approach?
3. What are the key issues of a decentralized approach to data storage?
4. For the following environments provide an overview of how a database could be used:
   - College or university
   - Hospital
   - Supermarket
5. Progression from manual through to file-based and electronic data storage has evolved over the years. What are the fundamental concepts of each stage and how has each stage of evolvement contributed to the next?

Activity one – database technology

Why use a database – this activity can be used to identify a range of organizations that use databases and how it has improved their systems, increased efficiency and reduced costs, etc.

Task one

Using the Internet, identify current developments in database technology and examine the historical progression of data structures and how they have contributed to today's technology.

Task two

Provide an analysis on how file-based management systems have contributed to the framework of database structures and developments.

4.2 Data models

Databases have evolved from users and developers being able to understand the semantics of data sets and communicating this understanding clearly and logically. To facilitate this, a specific data model/s can be used as a framework for examining and understanding the entities, attributes and relationships between data sets. A data model can therefore help users to understand the meaning of data, and to convey this understanding easily to other users.

Data models consist of three elements:

- a structural element;
- a manipulative/interrogative element;
- set of integrity rules (possibly).

These elements all contributing to representing data in a way that is understandable to end users.

Data models can be broken down into three categories, these include:

1. Object-based models: entity-relationship, semantic, object-orientated and functional.
2. Record-based models: hierarchical, network and relational.
3. Physical data models.

Object-based models

Object-based models focus on concepts such as entities, attributes and relationships. The entity-relationship model encompassing these concepts and thus emerging as one of the main techniques in the design of conceptual databases. The object-orientated model builds upon the foundations of the entity-relationship model by describing actions associated with an object and how it behaves.

The diagrammatic aspect of entity-relationship modelling is referred to as 'entity-relationship diagrams (ERDs)'. The ERD having four main components that consists of:

1. Entities
2. Relationships
3. Degree
4. Optionality

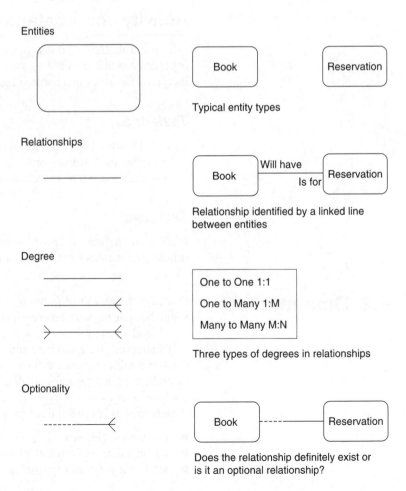

Entities

Typical entity types

Relationships

Relationship identified by a linked line between entities

Degree

One to One 1:1

One to Many 1:M

Many to Many M:N

Three types of degrees in relationships

Optionality

Does the relationship definitely exist or is it an optional relationship?

Entities

Entities provide the source, recipient and storage mechanism for information that is held on the system. They are distinct objects (people, events, places, things or events) that are represented within a database. For example, typical entities for the following systems include:

Library system

Entities	Book
	Lender
	Reservation
	Issue
	Edition

Hotel system

Entities	Booking
	Guest
	Room
	Tab
	Enquiry

Airline system

Entities	Flight
	Ticket
	Seat
	Booking
	Destination

Each entity will have a set of attributes, the attributes describing some aspect of the object that is to be recorded. For example, within the library system, an object exists – book, the ways to describe the book/object are the attributes.

Entity:	Book
Attributes:	*ISBN Number*
	Title
	Author
	Publisher
	Publication date

Each set of attributes within that entity should have a unique field that provides easy identification to the entity type. In the case of the entity type 'book' the unique key field is that of 'ISBN Number'. The unique field or 'primary key' will ensure that although two books may have the same title or author, no two books will have the same ISBN number.

Relationships

A relationship provides the link between entities. The relationship between two entities could be misinterpreted, therefore labels are attached at the beginning and at the end of the relationship link to inform parties exactly what the nature of the relationship is. For example if you had two entities, book and author linked as illustrated:

Example of entity-relationships

the nature of the relationship could be any of the following:

- An author can write a book, therefore the book belongs to an author.
- An author can refer to a book, therefore the book is in reference by an author.
- An author can buy a book, therefore the book is bought by an author.
- An author can review a book, therefore the book is reviewed by an author.

The actual relationship that exists in this scenario is that an author reviews a book and the book has been reviewed by an author.

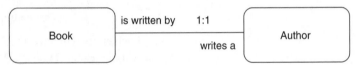

Degree

There are three possible degrees of any entity-relationship; these include:

- One to one 1:1 – which denotes that only one occurrence of each entity is used by the adjoining entity.

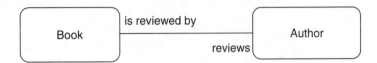

A single author writes a single book

- One to many 1:M – which denotes that a single occurrence of one entity is linked to more than one occurrence of the adjoining entity.

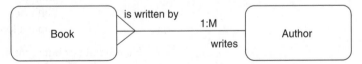

A single author writes a number of books

- Many to many M:N – which denotes that many occurrences of one entity is linked to more than one occurrence of the adjoining entity.

An author can write a number of books and
books can have more than one author

Although M:N relationships are common, the notation of linking two entities directly is adjusted and a link entity is used to connect the two.

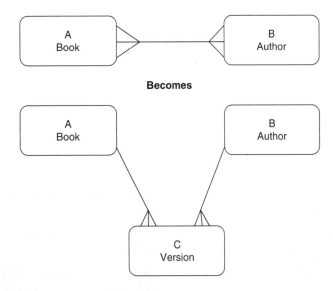

Becomes

In this scenario an author can write a number of versions of a book, and a book can have a number of versions that have been written by an author.

Optionality

There are two status types given to a relationship, firstly those that definitely happen or exist and secondly those that may happen or exist, this second status being referred to as 'optional'.

A dashed rather than a solid link denotes optionality in a relationship.

In this scenario an author may or may not decide to write a book.

Record-based models

Record-based models consist of a number of fixed-format records. Each record type defining a fixed number of fields of fixed length.

Record-based models have advanced over the years from the earlier generation of the hierarchical and CODASYL (network) model through to the more current and versatile relational model.

Hierarchical model

The hierarchical data model is so-called because of the way in which the data is arranged. Based on tree structure with a single table as the root and the tables forming the branches as shown in Figure 4.2.9.

The relationships within this structure are described as parents and children, where a parent can have multiple children but a child can have only one parent. The way in parents and children are linked together is through the use of 'pointers'. A parent will have a list of pointers extending to each of their children.

The child parent rule assures that data is systematically accessible. In terms of navigation, to get to a low-level table you would start at the root and work down the tree until you reach the target.

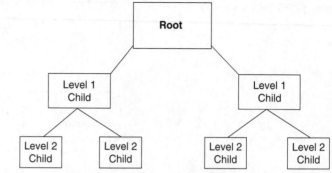

Figure 4.2.9   *Hierarchical data model*

There are a number of problems with the hierarchical structure these include:

- The user must have a good knowledge about how the tree is structured in order to find anything.
- A record cannot be added to a child table until it has already been incorporated into the parent table.
- Repetition of data within the database.
- Data redundancy due to the fact that a hierarchical database can cope with 1:M relationships but not M:N relationships because a child can have only one parent.

As a result of these problems a different data model was designed to overcome some of the defects attributed to the hierarchical structure.

The network database model

The model originates from the Conference on Data Systems Languages (CODASYL) and was designed to solve some of the more serious problems attributed to the hierarchical database model.

There are similarities between the two models however, instead of using a single-parent tree hierarchy the network model uses set theory to provide a tree-like structure with the exception of the child tables can have more than one parent, thus supporting many-to-many relationships.

The design of the network database looks like several trees that share branches, so that children can have multiple parents and vice versa as shown in Figure 4.2.10.

Although an improvement on the hierarchical model, the network model still had some intrinsic problems. The major problem being that the model was difficult to implement and maintain, most implementations

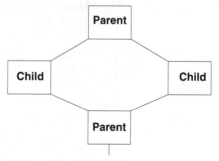

Figure 4.2.10   *Network model structure*

being used by computer programmers and not end users. A less complex database model was required that could be used by real end users, thus giving birth to the relational database model.

The relational database model

The relational database model was developed from the work carried out by Dr. E.F. Codd at IBM in the late 1960s. This new model looked for ways to solve the problems with the existing models.

Central to the relational database model is the concept of a table (relation) in which data is stored. Each table is made up of records (tuples) and fields (attributes). Each table has a unique name that can be used by the database to find the underlying table. Unlike previous models that have a defined hierarchy there is no specific navigational mapping. The relational model works on the basis that any manipulation of data is carried out via the data values themselves. Therefore, to retrieve a row from a table you would compare the value stored within a particular column for that row to some search criteria.

An example of this can be seen in the following, if you wanted to search for all the rows from the 'bookings' table that had 'Milan' in the 'destination' column the database might return a list as shown in Table 4.2.1.

Data from a retrieved row can then be used to query another table. For example, you may want to know which customer has booked a break to Milan on 23-January-03. By using the 'booking number' from this query as the keyword in the new query, you could look in the 'customer table' and look for the row where the booking number M/457789 to find the customer name.

This query methodology makes the relational model a lot simpler to understand. Other benefits of this model include:

● Provides useful tools for database administration (the tables can store actual data and be used as a means for generating meta-data).
● Logical rather than physical representation.
● Use of tables allows for structural and data independence.
● Allows for more effective design strategies.

All of these combined benefits have secured the relational database as being a firm favourite within academic, medical, government, financial, commercial and industrial domains.

Physical models

Physical data models describe the way in which data is stored on a computer to include record structures, orderings of records and access paths. The most common models include the Unifying model and Frame memory.

Table 4.2.1 *Relational database search query example*

Destination	Booking number	Date	Airline
Milan	M/457789	23-January-03	BMI
Milan	M/283999	31-January-03	British Airways
Milan	M/452766	22-February-03	British Airways
Milan	M384002	17-April-03	KLM

What does it mean?
Meta-data: data about a table and the field names that form the database structure, access rights, integrity and data validation rules, etc.

4.3 Users within a database environment

There are a number of roles that can be identified within a database environment. People taking on these roles varying in expertise from novices that use the databases through to technical experts that design and mould the system.

The database environment extends from procedures and standards, through to systems software to include application programs, operating systems and DBMS through to the hardware. At each juncture there is some input from humans ensuring that:

1. the database is being designed correctly to agreed specifications;
2. the programs are being written in accordance to end user needs;
3. the user interface is designed for the needs of the end user;
4. the data, storage and manipulation facilities are accessible;
5. the database is running correctly;
6. the software and hardware supporting the database system is compatible and operating without conflicts.

The people involved with this process include analysts, programmers, designers, database administrators, system administrators and end users as shown in Table 4.3.1. Collectively they ensure that the database performs within the boundaries of its specification.

Table 4.3.1

Analysts	→	Identifies the initial need and feasibility of a database within a given environment
Programmers	→	Work within the boundaries of a given specification to ensure that the database is functional for the end user
Designers	→	Identifies the data and constraints on the data that is to be stored and takes the logical data model and decides how it can be physically executed
Database administrators	→	Manages and controls the DBMS and its data. Responsible for the data resource, security, and the development and maintenance of standards, policies
System administrators	→	Manages and controls the hardware that supports the DBMS. Responsible for upgrades, back-up and recovery procedures and risk management
End users	→	Use the database to store and process data and information

What does it mean?
DBMS – Database Management System (See Section 4.5).

Questions 4.3.1

There are a number of users that have a role in database administration, management, design and end use.

1. How do each of the following people contribute to systems and database development:
   - database administrators
   - designers
   - programmers
2. Which of the people listed in Table 4.3.1 have hardware, software or integrated roles?

4.4 Database case studies

There is a diverse use of databases across a range of organizational sectors. Some databases are used purely to store customer or client information, others have a more specific purpose and some even carry a high commercial value.

Research activity

Select two organizations that use databases, either integrated within their main information system or discretely, and carry out the following research activities:

1. Provide an overview of the organization and the role of the database – does it support a single or multiple functional area? Is it fully integrated with other applications or used independently?
2. Has the database improved the working environment for end users and if so, how?
3. What database support is available and is this internally or externally resourced?
4. What provisions are in place to ensure that the database remains dynamic and grows with the organizations needs?

4.5 Database management systems

A DBMS is the software that allows an organization to centralize its data, thus providing an efficient, accessible and secure environment to the stored data through the use of application programs. The DBMS acts as an interface between application programs and the physical data files as illustrated in Figure 4.5.1.

Components of a database management system

There are three major components to a DBMS these include:

- Data definition language
- Data manipulation language
- Data dictionary

The data definition language (DDL) is the formal language used by programmers to specify the content and structure of the database. DDL is a descriptive language that is used to outline the entities required for the application and the relationships that may exist between them.

The data manipulation language (DML) is a specialized language that is used in conjunction with other generation programming languages to manipulate the data within the database. The language contains commands that allow end users and programmers to extract data from the database in order to carry out end user requests and enable applications development. The most prominent DML is Structured Query Language (SQL).

The final component of a DBMS is the data dictionary. This is an automated or manual file that stores definitions of data elements and characteristics such as usage, ownership, authorization and security. Many data dictionaries can produce lists and reports of data utilization, groupings, program locations and so on. Most data dictionaries are passive; they simply report. More advanced types are considered to be active when a change in the dictionary is automatically utilized by any related programs. For example, to change a telephone number from six to eight digits, you could simply enter the change in the dictionary without having to modify and recompile all of the application programs using 'telephone numbers'.

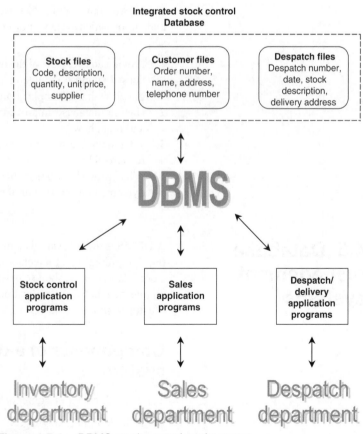

Figure 4.5.1   *DBMS stock control environment*

Functions of a database management system

Codd (1982) identifies a number of functions and services that a full-scale DBMS should provide these include:

- Data storage, retrieval and update – fundamental functions of a DBMS.
- User-accessible catalogue/data dictionary – repository information system that describes the data within the database.
- Transaction support – ensures that that any actions that are carried out on the database are consistent by updating all or none of them.
- Concurrency control services – ensure that the database is updated correctly when multiple users are updating the database simultaneously.
- Authorization services*– allowing only authorized users access to the database.
- Recovery services – mechanism for recovering the database in the event of an accident.
- Data communication support – ability to integrate with communication software.
- Integrity services – a mechanism/s to ensure that the data and any changes made to the data in the database follow certain rule.
- Services that promote data independence – inclusion of facilities that support the independence of programs from the actual structure of the database.
- Utility services – should include utility programs, e.g. monitoring and import facilities and statistical programs.

Benefits and limitations of DBMSs

DBMS like any software has a range of benefits and limitations as shown in Table 4.5.1.

Table 4.5.1   *DBMS – benefits and limitations*

Benefits		Limitations	
Manages data redundancy more effectively than file-based systems	Integration of files reduces duplication of data	Complexity	The level of functionality expected makes the DBMS quite complex
Improved security	Ability to set up security measures, e.g. passwords to restrict user entry	Costs	Associated costs include updating hardware, training, staffing, security
Data consistency	By managing data redundancy inconsistencies are greatly reduced	Greater risk of system failure	By centralizing resources the system becomes more venerable
Sharing of data	Centralized approach allows multiple user access to shared data resources	Reduced performance	In comparison to a specialist file-based system a DBMS is more generalized
Addresses internal conflict requirements between functional departments	No single department would have ownership to the data – equal access	Size	Takes up large volumes of space because of its complexity

There are other advantages and disadvantages associated with a DBMS however the main ones are listed above. For many organizations the main advantages would centre on the ability to centralize, share and reduce data redundancy and the main disadvantages would be the size and cost of maintaining a DBMS.

Data storage

Using a DBMS to store and manipulate data and information may result in continuous investment in technology and the latest technological resources.

The cost of updating data in terms of required storage is dependant upon a number of factors including current resources, current configuration (standalone or networked environment), amount of data to be processed, composition of the data to be processed (numerical, text or graphics), amount of historical data to be retained.

DBMS storage requirements will differ between user types and organizations. For example, a home user might require 20 gigabytes (Gb) as an entry level for storing data. A small organization with three or four standalone computers might require a minimum of 40 Gb on each. A small networked organization with up to ten computers running via a server could have anything up to 500 Gb. A large networked organization running up to 50 computers without individual local drives could require terabyte (Tb) storage.

Storage measurements

Bit	Smallest unit of measurement	Single binary digit 0 or 1
Byte	Made up of 8 bits, amount of space required to hold a single character	Value between 0 and 255
Kilobyte (Kb)	Equivalent to 1000 characters	Approximately 1000 bytes
Megabyte (Mb)	Equivalent to 1 million characters	Approximately 1000 kilobytes
Gigabyte (Gb)	Equivalent to 1 billion characters	Approximately 1000 megabytes
Terabyte (Tb)	Equivalent to 1 thousand billion characters	Approximately 1000 gigabytes

More recently vaster storage capacities have become available to include:

Petabyte	10^{15}	1 000 000 000 000 000	Approximately 1000 terabytes
Exabyte	10^{18}	1 000 000 000 000 000 000	Approximately 1000 petabytes
Zettabyte	10^{21}	1 000 000 000 000 000 000 000	Approximately 1000 exabytes
Yottabyte	10^{24}	1 000 000 000 000 000 000 000 000	Approximately 1000 zettabytes

The need to buy more storage can be an on-going expense for organizations. For some continuous updates are required almost on a weekly basis where storage release is granted by suppliers to meet demand.

Managing terabytes of data

Phone Calls Galore

> Mark Francis, enterprise architecture director at AT&T, manages several terabytes of information. One of his biggest data stores is a multiterabyte mainframe DB2 database containing phone-call details. When an AT&T customer makes a call, the switching equipment automatically inserts a new row in the huge database.

Barry Nance
Computerworld 23 April 2001

DBMS software

There is a range of software that supports the functions of DBMS, the major contenders are:

- Oracle
- Informix
- IBM with DB2
- Microsoft with SQL Server

However, traditional DBMS is being challenged by newer object-orientated DBMS such as O2, Object Store and Objectivity, etc.

Questions 4.5.1

1. What are the key components of a DBMS?
2. The three components of a DBMS are:
   - Data definition language
   - Data manipulation language
   - Data dictionary

   Identify the main features of each component?
3. Codd (1982) identifies a number of functions and services that a full-scale DBMS should provide. Produce a table and order each of the functions and services in terms of what you believe to be of most importance. Justify why you have ordered these accordingly.

4.6 Data manipulation

There is a wide range of database software available on the market. Some software is designed specifically for database management systems providing the interface between the application programs and the physical files such as Informix and Oracle. Other database software is more front end, orientated towards the end user. Database software is designed to provide the end user with a number of tools to allow for quick and easy data manipulation, one of the most commercially available being Microsoft Access™.

The majority of database software will provide the end user with a range of the following tools and facilities:

- Formatting functions
- Query and filter facilities

- Validation functions
- Analysis tools

Formatting functions

Customizing the appearance of a database and tailoring it to end users needs is one of the requirements that may need to be facilitated by a database designer. The complexity of databases and the underlying tools that are used to set up relationships and queries used to interrogate the data are transparent to the end user. The end user needs these facilities to perform searches and updates, etc. but they do not need to know about the underlying semantics.

Customizing a database can provide clarity and aid understanding of the task requirements, project an element of professionalism and provide an interactive, user friendly interface for all levels of end user.

Within Microsoft Access™ the majority of data entry will be done in 'form view', therefore changing the colour of the text, border colours and background or adding new features to each control on a form will make the database more individual and hopefully aid the navigation process. It is also possible to customize the toolbars and copy formats between controls.

Query and filter facilities

Microsoft Access™ has a number of query capabilities that fall into the category of Query-By-Example (QBE). QBE is used by entering example values directly into a query template and identifying the results in terms of the answer to a query. QBE can be used to ask questions about information held in one or more tables and to specify the fields that you want to appear in the answer. QBE can also be used to perform operations such as inserting and deleting records in tables, modifying the values of fields and creating new fields and tables.

Within Microsoft Access™ there are a number of queries that can be performed these include:

- *Select query* – The most common type of query is the 'select query'. The function of the query is to retrieve data from one or more tables and display the results in a datasheet.
- *Totals query* – It is useful to interrogate data and ask questions about groups of data such as 'how many students are enrolled on a particular course?' 'What is the average grade per cohort?' 'How many students went on to do another course following completion?' Totals queries can be used to perform calculations on groups of records. The types of calculation that can be performed include: Sum, Avg, Min, Max and Count.
- *Crosstab query* – The crosstab query can be used to summarize data in a compact spreadsheet format. An example of a crosstab query can be seen in the 'analysis tools' section.
- *Parameter query* – A parameter query displays one or more predefined dialog boxes that prompt the user for a parameter value(s). Parameter queries are created by entering a prompt (enclosed in square brackets) in the 'criteria' cell for each field that is to be used as a parameter.
- *Find duplication query* – This query determines whether or not duplicate records exist within a table, or whether or not records in a table share the same value.

- *Find unmatched query* – This query finds records in one table that do not have related records in another table.
- *Action query* – This query includes delete, append, update and make-table queries. The query can make changes in just one operation.
- *Autolookup query* – This query will automatically fill in certain field values for a new record. When a value is entered in the join field in the query or in a form based on the query, Microsoft Access™ looks up and fills in existing information related to that value.
- *SQL query* – Used to modify all the other queries identified and to set the properties of forms and reports.

Validation functions

There are a number of validation checks that can be carried out during the stages of database design and testing to ensure that data that is being entered and processed within the system is complete, these include:

Check	*Purpose*
Presence check	To ensure that certain fields of information have been entered, e.g. hospital number for a patient that is being admitted for surgery
Field/format/ picture check	To ensure that the information that has been input is in the correct format and combination (if applicable), e.g. the surgery procedure has an assigned code made up of two letters and six numeric digits DH245639
Range check	To ensure that any values entered fall within the boundaries of a certain range, e.g. the surgery code is only valid for a 4-week period (1–4) therefore any number entered over 4 in this field would be rejected
Look-up check	To ensure that data entered is of an acceptable value, e.g. types of surgery can only be accepted from the list orthopaedic, ENT (ears, nose and throat) or minor
Cross-field check	To ensure that information stored in two fields matches up, e.g. if the surgeons initials are DH on the surgery code they cannot represent the surgeon Michael Timbers only Donald Hill
Check digit check	To ensure that any code number entered is valid by adding in an additional digit that has some relationship with the original code
Batch header checks	To ensure that records in a batch, e.g. number of surgeries carried out over a set period match the number stored in the batch header

Analysis tools

A database is of little use if data analysis cannot take place, one function of that can enable this in Microsoft Access™ is that of a crosstab query. A crosstab query and its reporting facility produces a dynaset where the contents of one field are used as row headings. The cells of the query are then calculated on the basis of the fields matching the row and column fields.

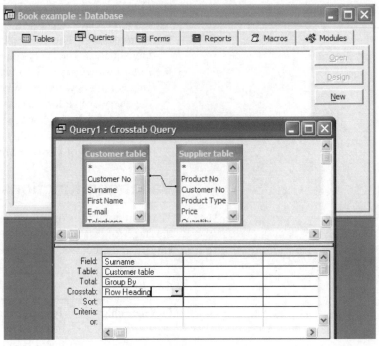

Example of a crosstab query structure

Questions 4.6.1

1. What other analysis tools are available within Microsoft Access™?
2. Provide specific examples of how these analysis tools could be used?

Data mining

Data mining is a generic term that covers a range of technologies. The actual process of 'mining' data refers to the extraction of information through tests, analysis, rules and heuristics. Information is sorted and processed from a data set in the hope of finding new information or data anomalies that may have remained undiscovered.

There are four main operations associated with data mining techniques, these include:

1. predictive modelling
2. segmentation
3. link analysis
4. deviation detection

Predictive modelling can be compared to the actual learning experience of a human. It uses observations to create a model. Predictive modelling can be used to analyse an existing database to determine some of the essential characteristics about the data set. The model that is developed uses a supervised learning approach that has two phases. The first phase, a training set builds a model using a large sample of historical data, tests are then carried out on the old data set whilst modelling the new one.

Segmentation partitions the database into an unknown number of segments or clusters of similar records (records that share a number of properties and are so considered to be homogenous).

Link analysis looks at establishing links called 'associations' between individual and/or sets of records within a database.

Deviation detection uses statistics and visualization techniques to express deviation from some previously known expectation and/or norm. An example of this includes credit card fraud detection.

There is a range of software available that can aid organizations in their quest to mine data, develop predictive models and help with decision making. One of these is 'Clementine'.

Clementine is widely regarded as the 'leading data mining workbench' because it delivers the maximum return on data investment in the minimum amount of time, providing support for the entire data mining process.

Leading organizations that have used Clementine include:

- HSBC
- US government
- West Midlands Police
- Softmap
- Jubii

HSBC Bank USA were able to increase sales by 50% percent and reduce marketing costs by 30% percent through better targeting by using Clementine. Customers were gained by answering questions such as:

> which prospects are most likely to become profitable customers?

The US government intelligence agency used Clementine to focus on most likely security threats. They were able to enhance their infrastructure and public health security by answering questions such as:

> what specific event is most likely to be a security threat?

A federal government agency used Clementine to develop predictive intrusion models, and deployed these into an early warning system that focused personnel on most likely security threats.

West Midland Police were able to match unsolved cases with known perpetrators by using Clementine to answer questions such as:

> is there a pattern between certain crimes and known perpretrators?

The data mining technology used identified key patterns to match up unsolved cases.

Softmap – a leading computer retailer in Japan were able to boost profits by 300%. Customer relationships were strengthened due to questions such as:

> what will this customer want next?

A predictive recommendation engine for its web site was built, and so increased profits by 300%.

Jubii – Denmark's most popular Internet portal used Clementine to predict clickstreams by answering questions such as:

> which clickstream is most likely to lead to a sale?

thus increasing customers with a 30–50% increase in click-through rates thereby increasing media buying by 10–15%.

Questions 4.6.2

1. What are the benefits of 'mining' data?
2. What technologies are associated with data mining? Carry out research to provide a more in depth description of each technology.
3. Compare and contrast the four main data mining techniques.
4. Through research identify two domains that data mining could be of use, e.g. education.
5. How can a data mining tool assist with finding patterns and anomalies within data?

SPSS – Clementine home page and sample tool palette for mining data. (From http://www.spss.com. Reproduced by permission of SPSS Inc.)

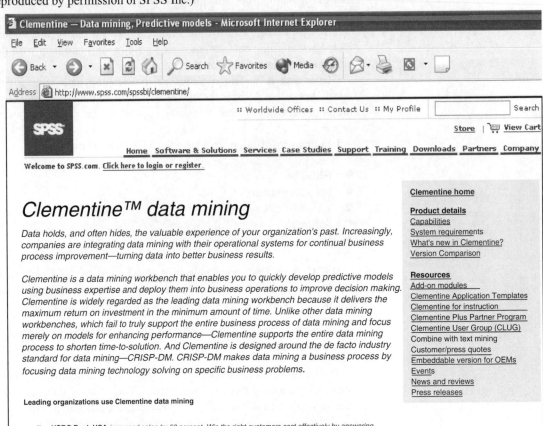

Clementine™ data mining

Data holds, and often hides, the valuable experience of your organization's past. Increasingly, companies are integrating data mining with their operational systems for continual business process improvement—turning data into better business results.

Clementine is a data mining workbench that enables you to quickly develop predictive models using business expertise and deploy them into business operations to improve decision making. Clementine is widely regarded as the leading data mining workbench because it delivers the maximum return on investment in the minimum amount of time. Unlike other data mining workbenches, which fail to truly support the entire business process of data mining and focus merely on models for enhancing performance—Clementine supports the entire data mining process to shorten time-to-solution. And Clementine is designed around the de facto industry standard for data mining—CRISP-DM. CRISP-DM makes data mining a business process by focusing data mining technology solving on specific business problems.

Clementine home

Product details
Capabilities
System requirements
What's new in Clementine?
Version Comparison

Resources
Add-on modules
Clementine Application Templates
Clementine for instruction
Clementine Plus Partner Program
Clementine User Group (CLUG)
Combine with text mining
Customer/press quotes
Embeddable version for OEMs
Events
News and reviews
Press releases

Leading organizations use Clementine data mining

- **HSBC Bank USA** *increased sales by 50 percent. Win the right customers cost effectively by answering questions such as "Which prospects are most likely to become profitable customers?" HSBC Bank USA used Clementine to increase sales by 50 percent and reduce marketing costs by 30 percent through better targeting.*

- **Sofmap boosted profits by 300 percent.** *Grow customer relationships by answering questions such as "What will this customer want next?" Sofmap—a leading computer retailer in Japan—used Clementine to build a predictive recommendation engine for its Web site and increased profits by 300 percent.*

- **Banco Espirito Santo reduced attrition by 15 to 20 percent.** *Keep the right customers longer answering questions such as "What will it take to save this customer?" Banco Espirito Santo used Clementine to reduce attrition by 15 to 20 percent and increase profits by 10 to 20 percent.*

- **U.S. government intelligence agency focused on most likely security threats.** *Enhance infrastructure and public health security by answering questions such as "What specific event is most likely to be a security threat?" A federal government agency used Clementine to develop predictive intrusion models and deployed those models into an early warning system to focus personnel on most likely security threats.*

- **Jubii increased click-through rates by 30 to 50 percent.** *Streamline Web sites to maximize profitability by predicting clickstreams, answering questions such as "Which clickstream is most likely to lead to a sale?" Jubii—Denmark's most popular Internet portal—used Clementine to provide customers with a 30 to 50 percent increase in click-through rates, thereby increasing media buying by 10 to 15 percent.*

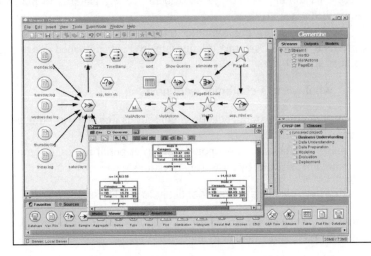

Entity-relationship modelling (ERM)

There are two components to entity-relationship modelling the set of tools used to create an entity-relationship diagram that are illustrated in Section 1.21 form the first component. The joining together of entities with a link 'relationship' forms the entity-relationship diagram.

The second component of ERM is the documentation that supports the entity-relationship diagram. The documentation that is used includes:

1. Entity descriptions
2. Attribute lists

Every entity should have an associated 'entity description' which details items such as:

- Entity name and description
- Attributes
- Relationship types and links

Sample entity description for – supplier

Entity description				
Entity Name: **Supplier**				
Description: An individual or organization that provides stock items to the company				
Attributes: Supplier code Supplier name Supplier address Supplier rating Stock number		Primary key: Yes	Foreign key: Yes	
Must/may be	Either/or	Link phrase	One and only one/One or more	Entity name
Must		deliver	One or more	Stock
Must		place	One or more	Order
Entity volumes: Maximum 150 Minimum 60 Average 100				
User role:		Access rights:		
Stock manager		Read, create, update and delete		
Stock supervisor		Read		
Accounts manager		Read, create, update and delete		
Accounts clerk		Read, create		

Every entity has a set of attributes, if a large system is being investigated a number of entities and their associated attributes will need to be defined therefore an 'attribute list' can be prepared. Attribute lists identify all of the attributes and a description of the attributes. The primary key attribute which is normally made up of numerical data, e.g. supplier number, national insurance number, examination number, is referred to first followed by the remainder of the attribute items.

Producing entity-relationship diagrams

Caddy's Supermarkets

Caddy's Supermarkets is an established chain of supermarkets that are located across the country. Over the past 6 months the Managing Director of the chain Miss Sarah Caddy has discovered that they are losing their proportion of the market to another competitor. Since the beginning of the year their market share has fallen from 16% to 12%.

Caddy's has 15 stores across the region all located in major towns or cities. The structure of the company is very hierarchical with the following lines of command that are generic across all branches:

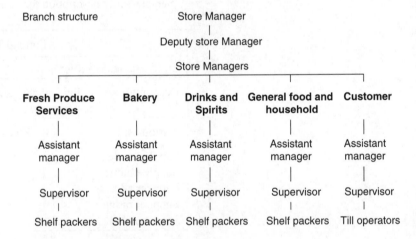

All of the branches communicate on a regular basis. Branches also distribute surplus stock items to other branches if they are running low, to reduce supplier ordering costs.

All of the functional departments are located at the head office, which has the following implications for each branch:

- All recruitment is done through head office for each of the branches which means that all the application forms have to be sent either by post or on-line (if the application was filled in on-line).
- All stock ordering is done through head office who have negotiated local supplier contracts for each of the branches.

- All of the promotions, e.g. 'buy one get one free' and all of the price reductions or special offers are filtered through from sales at head office.
- All salaries are paid via the finance department at head office.
- All deliveries and distribution is made through local suppliers in conjunction with head office instructions.

East Anglia branch

Sarah Caddy has asked for an investigation to take place based at the branch in East Anglia to identify what problems exist with proposals on how they can be addressed. The focus of the investigation is the 'fresh produce' department.

Fact-finding

Using a variety of fact-finding techniques the following information has been gathered:

1. There are 150 employees at the branch
   - Store Manager – Mr Howell
   - Deputy Manger – Miss Jones
   - Five store managers, assistant managers and five supervisors
   - Fifty full-time and part-time check-out staff
   - Forty full-time and part-time shelf stackers
   - Ten stock clerks
   - Ten trolley personnel
   - Three car park attendants
   - Twenty cleaners, gardeners, drivers and other store staff.
2. Each of the store managers control there own areas, with their own shelf-stackers and stock personnel.
3. All stock ordering is batch processed overnight to head office on a daily basis by each of the store managers in consultation with the deputy branch manager.
4. All fresh produce is delivered on a daily basis non-perishable goods are delivered three times a week by local suppliers.
5. All bakery items are baked on-site each morning.

Fresh produce system

Pat and her assistant manager Ken manage the fresh produce department. Within the department their supervisor, John oversees six display/shelf stackers and four stock personnel.

After consultation with a range of employees the following account of day-to-day activities has been given.

Each day Pat holds a staff meeting within the department to provide information about new promotions, special discounts or stock display arrangements.

Any information regarding new promotions comes through from head office. All information received regarding promotions, etc. is filed in the branch promotions file. If any price adjustments need to be made that day the stock personnel are informed to check the daily stock sheets.

After the meeting the stock personnel liase with the shelf/display personnel in regards to new stock that needs to go out onto the shop floor. The information about new stock items and changes to stock items comes from the daily stock sheet. When new items have been put out or stock price adjustments made they are crossed off the daily stock sheet.

Items which have arrived in that day are delivered from the local fresh produce supplier, when the items come in the stock personnel checks the daily stock sheet for quantities and authorizes the delivery. If items have not arrived or there is an error in the order a stock adjustment sheet is filled in, this is kept in the stock office. At the end of the day John will then inform Ken of the stock adjustments. Ken then sends off a top copy of the adjustment sheet to head office and files a copy in the stock cabinet.

Information about stock items running low comes from the daily stock sheet. If an item is low a stock order form is completed. A top copy is sent to head office and a copy is filed in the stock cabinet. Orders should be made 5 days to the actual requirement of the stock, as head office then processes the information and contacts the local supplier. In an emergency local supplier information is held by Pat, who can ring direct to get items delivered. This however costs the company more money because a bulk order has not been placed. Authorization also has to be given by the operations manager at head office. Information also has to be filled in on the computerized stock request form that is e-mailed to head office each day, they then send back confirmation.

Head office dictates that all documents filled in on-line also need to have a manual counterpart, one which is sent off and the other which is filed with the branch.

Items which have arrived in that day are delivered from the local fresh produce supplier, when the items come in the stock personnel checks the daily stock sheet for quantities and authorizes the delivery. If items have not arrived or there is an error in the order a stock adjustment sheet is filled in, this is kept in the stock office. At the end of the day John will then inform Ken of the stock adjustments. Ken then sends off a top copy of the adjustment sheet to head office and files a copy in the stock cabinet.

Information about stock items running low comes from the daily stock sheet. If an item is low a stock order form is completed. A top copy is sent to head office and a copy is filed in the stock cabinet. Orders should be made 5 days to the actual requirement of the stock, as head office then processes the information and contacts the local supplier. In an emergency local supplier information is held by Ken, who can ring direct to get items delivered. This however costs the company more money because a bulk order has not been placed. Authorization also has to be given by the operations manager at head office. Information also has to be filled in on the computerized stock request.

Problems with the system

1. Sometimes the network at head office is down which means that stock items are not received within 5 days.
2. The promotions are not always appropriate because of a lack of certain stock sometimes it works out that the stock for which the branch has a surplus of is wasted because they cannot set their own promotions in-store.
3. The stock cabinet is filled to capacity and because everything is in date order it is difficult to collate information about certain stock items.
4. If there is an error in the stock delivery nothing can be supplied until the paperwork has been sent off to head office or authorization has been given, even if the supplier has the stock requirement on his lorry.

5. Too much paperwork.
6. Little communication with other departments.
7. Targets which are set by head office cannot always be met due to the stock ordering problem.
8. Some stock items that come in are not all bar-coded.

Questions 4.6.3

1. Using the information from the fresh produce department at Caddy's Supermarkets produce an entity-relationship diagram clearly labelling all relationships.
2. Produce a full attribute list for five of the entities.
3. What enhancements would you make to your ERD after examining some of the problems listed.

Structured Query Language

A database language should allow a user to carry out a number of tasks that include the creation of a database and relation structures, perform basic data management tasks and execute both simple and complex queries. The rationale behind a database language is that all of these requirements should be carried out with minimal effort or input from the user. Therefore, the command structure and syntax of the language should be easy to learn and understand.

SQL has two major components:

- DDL that defines the structure.
- DML for retrieving and updating data.

SQL works in two ways, firstly it can be used interactively by entering statements at a terminal and secondly statements can be embedded into a procedural language.

The data manipulation aspect of SQL is derived from four main statements:

SELECT	Queries data in the database
INSERT	Inserts data into a table
UPDATE	Updates data in a table
DELETE	Deletes data from a table

The purpose of the SELECT statement is to retrieve and display data from one or more database tables. The sequence of processing in a SELECT statement is:

FROM	Identifies which table/s is to be used
WHERE	Filters the rows subject to some condition
GROUP BY	Forms groups of rows with the same column value
HAVING	Filters the groups subject to some condition
SELECT	Specifies which columns are to appear in the output
ORDER BY	

Questions 4.6.4

1. What is the purpose of using a database language?
2. What are the key features of SQL?
3. Provide full definitions of:
   - Data definition language (DDL)
   - Data manipulation language (DML)
   what are the differences between the two?
4. Create a simple program using the SELECT, INSERT, UPDATE and DELETE functions of SQL.

4.7 Designing and using databases

Databases

Databases carry out a range of functions to support all types of users. Their primary function is to store volumes of data and specific formats to allow for easy processing and access. Data that is input into a database can then be formatted into meaningful and useful information.

Databases are fundamental to an organization information system and as a result follow a similar application lifecycle as shown in Figure 4.7.1.

Prior to the actual design phases, various preliminary stages take place that enables the developer to ensure that they will be building a database that meets both the system and user requirements. In order to satisfy these requirements an initial systems boundary should be specified outlining what is required, constraints and resources, etc. End users should have some input into how they want the database to look and work as they will be the ones using it once it has been developed.

The design phase is made up of three design elements – conceptual, logical and physical design. The main aims of database design is to:

- identify the data and the relationships between data that is required by application and user areas;
- provide a framework to support any transactions required on the data (a data model);
- specify minimum design that is structured appropriately to achieve the requirements of the system.

The two main approaches to database design are 'bottom-up' and top-down' each lending themselves to the design of either simple or complex databases. Bottom-up design is appropriate for simple database design, starting at a basal level with attributes, entities and associations between entities. In order to acquire the appropriate attributes the process of 'normalizing' data or 'normalization' needs to take place.

For more complex database design a top-down approach is required that starts with the development of data models that contain high-level entities and relationships and then applies successive refinements to the top-level to identify entities at a lower level. The top-down approach is based on the concepts of entity-relationship (E-R) modelling.

The application design focuses on the design of the user interface and the application programs. This phase succeeds the design of the database, although the two can be developed in parallel to ensure functionality.

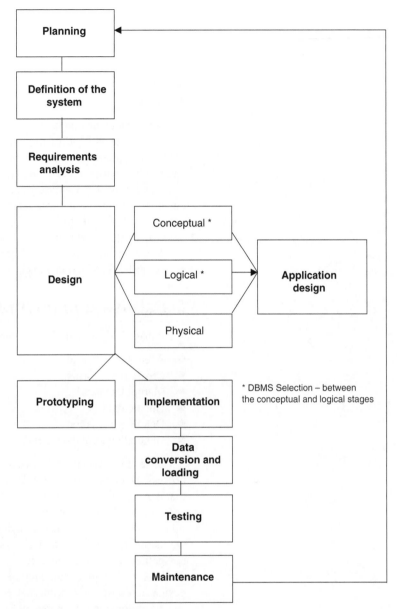

Figure 4.7.1 *Database application cycle*

Prototyping provides an actual working model that has the features of the proposed system. A prototype is used to check the system works to agreed standards.

Implementation, conversion and testing are in some ways integrated phases. Although they are shown as being discrete, the use of data to enforce the security, integrity and validity of the database is inter-linked. Implementation of the database is achieved using the DDL of the selected DBMS. Statements are compiled and used to create database schemas and empty files. Application programs and other components such as the data entry forms or reports are also implemented.

The conversion process concentrates on transferring data between old and new systems, however a utility provision is now quite common on the DBMS to facilitate this.

Testing is carried out to assess the completeness and correctness of a database application. The main testing strategies include:

- Bottom-up
- Top-down
- Thread
- Stress

Each strategy having its own benefits and limitations. Testing does not just happen at the end of the database design process, it is embedded within each phase. The consequence of leaving testing until the very end can result in a total redesign if issues are not resolved as they occur.

Maintaining the database once it is fully operational is essential to ensure that future issues or requirements are addressed. A database is not a static tool it needs to be continually updated to meet the growth and demand of the organization. To support this process personnel can be employed to administrate and manage the system internally, or the responsibility can be outsourced.

Database documentation

A database is of little or no use unless end users know how to:

- Access information
- Create input forms
- Manipulate data
- Update data
- Delete information
- Generate output documents, e.g. reports

Hence documentation is essential and integral to the development process. Documentation for a database can include technical documents that demonstrate the design process, prototyping and testing procedures carried out. Documentation should also include non-technical information for the end users that includes an overview of how the database works, help facilities and step-by-step guides to assist the end user in navigating around the database.

The function of documentation therefore is to justify the database design and describe the internal composition of the database so that it can be maintained by personnel such as administrators and database managers. Another function of documentation is to support end users and facilitate them in using the database.

Activity two – building a relational database

This activity can help students to design a relational database as part of an assessment.

Students will need to use suitable database software such as Microsoft Access™, it is expected that through independent learning students should be capable of using wizard features to create basic tables, forms and reports. With additional tutor support, students should be capable of fulfilling the following criteria:

- generate a fully relational database with at least 20 records;
- use a variety of input screens;

- customize input screens to suit a range of user needs;
- incorporate look up tables, validation procedures, macros, menu systems, search and sort criteria, etc.;
- build at least six working relationships;
- introduce security mechanisms such as passwords, multiuser screen levels, etc.

Each stage of the database design should be fully documented. A user guide could be incorporated into the assessment which students could give to another group member to test the suitability of the database.

To complete these activities a test log should also be produced documenting any faults or problems encountered with the database design.

Normalizing data sets

Normalization is a bottom-up approach to database design that starts with the examination of relationships between attributes. E.F. Codd (1972) first developed the process of normalization. The initial framework was modelled on three stages or tests that were applied to a given 'relation'. These stages extended from:

- First normal form (1NF)
- Second normal (2NF)
- Third normal form (3NF)

An improved version of 3NF was later developed by R. Boyce and E.F. Codd in 1974 and is referred to as Boyce–Codd Normal Form (BCNF). In 1977 and 1979 higher normal forms, fourth (4NF) and fifth (5NF) were introduced by Fagin, however these deal with practical situations that are quite rare.

Example of normalizing data up to third normal form – Unnormalized data set

*Student number	Student name	Module code	Module name	Grade	Lecturer	Room number
CP123/OP	Greene	C122	IS	D	Jenkins	B33
CP938/CP	Jacobs	C123	Hardware	M	Smith	B33
CF489/LP	Browne	C124	Software	M	Osborne	B32
CP311/CP	Peters	C111	Internet	P	Chives	B32
CR399/CP	Porter	C110	Web design	D	Crouch	B33
CD478/JP	Graham	C107	Multimedia	M	Waters	B31
CR678/LP	Denver	C106	Networking	P	Rowan	B31

* Primary key.

The stage of converting an unnormalized data set into first normal form (1NF) involves looking at the structure as all records must be of fixed length. To address this, the data needs to be divided into two:

- Fixed part
- Variable part that contains repetitions

To rejoin the data the variable part must contain a key from the fixed part to make a composite key of Student number/module code as shown.

First normal form (1NF)

Student number	Student name
CP123/OP	Greene
CP938/CP	Jacobs
CF489/LP	Browne
CP311/CP	Peters
CR399/CP	Porter
CD478/JP	Graham
CR678/LP	Denver

Student number	Module code	Module name	Grade	Lecturer	Room number
CP123/OP	C122	IS	D	Jenkins	B33
CP938/CP	C123	Hardware	M	Smith	B33
CF489/LP	C124	Software	M	Osborne	B32
CP311/CP	C111	Internet	P	Chives	B32
CR399/CP	C110	Web design	D	Crouch	B33
CD478/JP	C107	Multimedia	M	Waters	B31
CR678/LP	C106	Networking	P	Rowan	B31

Problems still exist with 1NF that calls for examining any partial dependencies that exist within the data set. Any non-key field that is dependant (can be derived from) only part of the key is said to be partially dependant.

For example: Module name is derived from the module code (it makes no difference which student is taking that module).

However: The grade is not partially dependant because it is the grade for an individual student taking a particular module.

Problems with partial dependence:

1. *Updating* – if for example the name of module C124 (software) changed to (operating systems) every record that contained this old module details would need to be updated.
2. *Insert anomaly* – if a new module needed to be added under the current organization the module details e.g. name are stored with records about individual students taking that module. A new module would have no students enrolled onto it, so where would it be stored?
3. *Deletion anomaly* – if a student decides to drop a module or leave the course all the details of that module will be lost.

Second normal form (2NF)

Student number	Student name
CP123/OP	Greene
CP938/CP	Jacobs
CF489/LP	Browne
CP311/CP	Peters
CR399/CP	Porter
CD478/JP	Graham
CR678/LP	Denver

Student number	Module code	Grade
CP123/OP	C122	D
CP938/CP	C123	M
CF489/LP	C124	M
CP311/CP	C111	P
CR399/CP	C110	D
CD478/JP	C107	M
CR678/LP	C106	P

Module code	Module name	Lecturer	Room number
C122	IS	Jenkins	B33
C123	Hardware	Smith	B33
C124	Software	Osborne	B32
C111	Internet	Chives	B32
C110	Web design	Crouch	B33
C107	Multimedia	Waters	B31
C106	Networking	Rowan	B31

The next step for third normal form (3NF) conversion is to ensure that the data does not show any indirect dependencies. All non-key fields should be defined by the key directly and not by another non-key field.

For example: The room number is defined by the lecturer and not by the module. This creates similar dependency problems of updating and insertion and deletion anomalies.

- If a lecturer moves to another room their room location would also need to be changed.
- A lecturer not allocated to teaching a module cannot have any room details stored.
- If a lecturer stops teaching a module the room details will be lost.

To overcome these problems further divisions in the data structure is required.

Third normal form (3NF)

Student number	Student name
CP123/OP	Greene
CP938/CP	Jacobs
CF489/LP	Browne
CP311/CP	Peters
CR399/CP	Porter
CD478/JP	Graham
CR678/LP	Denver

Student number	Module code	Grade
CP123/OP	C122	D
CP938/CP	C123	M
CF489/LP	C124	M
CP311/CP	C111	P
CR399/CP	C110	D
CD478/JP	C107	M
CR678/LP	C106	P

Module code	Module name	Lecturer
C122	IS	Jenkins
C123	Hardware	Smith
C124	Software	Osborne
C111	Internet	Chives
C110	Web design	Crouch
C107	Multimedia	Waters
C106	Networking	Rowan

Lecturer	Room number
Jenkins	B33
Smith	B33
Osborne	B32
Chives	B32
Crouch	B33
Waters	B31
Rowan	B31

Questions 4.7.1

1. How can normalization impact upon the design of databases?
2. What is meant by a 'bottom-up approach' and how does this differ from the 'top-down approach'?
3. What are the differences between 1NF, 2NF and 3NF?
4. What are the associated problems with partial dependency and how can these be addressed? Give examples to support the overcoming of these problems.
5. Using your own example, normalize a data set to 3NF.

Database issues

Security

Security of data is essential especially with a database system to ensure privacy of sensitive and personal information. Data security is also paramount in complying with legislation that protects users and third parties of data.

A number of organizational security breaches can occur, some of these are amplified by the use of a database because of the integrated approach to data storage and retrieval. Some of these breaches and security issues include:

- Viruses
- Unauthorized access – hacking
- Industrial and/or individual sabotage
- Accidents by users (incompetence)

Table 4.7.1 *Internal and external security measures*

Internal	External
Passwords	Legislation
Encryption	Data Protection Act (1984 and 1988)*
Filtering and monitoring software	Computer Misuse Act (1990)*
Employ a moderator/s	
Virus checkers and protectors	
Internal security policies and generate an awareness of do' and don'ts	
User access levels	
Firewall	

* Will be discussed in detail in Chapter 9.

- Vandalism
- Theft of data

A number of measures can be taken by organizations to ensure that these security breaches do not become a reality. Some of these measures can be enforced internally within an organization, others have been introduced externally through legal controls and legislation – see Table 4.7.1.

The enforcement of legislation can impact upon the procedures of organizations in a number of ways. In order to comply, an organization will have to ensure that they operate within certain legislative boundaries that include informing employees and third parties about how they intend to safeguard systems and any information collected, processed, copied, stored and output on these systems.

Data Protection Act 1984 and 1988

The Data Protection Act applies to the processing of data and information by a computer source. The act is based upon a set of principles which binds a user or an organization into following a set of procedures offering assurances that data is kept secure.

The main principles include:

- Personal data should be processed fairly and lawfully.
- Personal data should be held only for one or more specified and lawful purposes.
- Personal data held should not be disclosed in any way incompatible to the specified and lawful purpose.
- Personal data held should be adequate and relevant, not excessive to the purpose or purposes.
- Personal data kept should be accurate and up-to-date.
- Personal data should not be retained for any longer than necessary.
- Individuals should be informed about personal data stored and should be entitled to have access to it and if appropriate have such data corrected or erased.

- Security measures should ensure that no unauthorized access to, alteration or disclosure or destruction of personal data is permitted and protection against accidental loss or destruction of personal data is given.

The act places obligations on people who collect, process and store personal records and data about consumers or customers.

5   Networking concepts

Summary

The aim of this section of the book is to provide sufficient technical information to enable users to make informed purchasing or specification decisions. The unit requirement to install and manage networks will have to be achieved at each centre as there are so many network architectures in existence. The focus will be on providing sufficient knowledge to communicate with network specialists during network specification and installation.

From the Edexcel unit: '*The importance of networked solutions in the business world grows year on year. The increasingly sophisticated technologies and widening user base means a fundamental understanding of networks is essential for many. The aim of this unit is to provide a rigorous introduction to networks, and practical experience in installing users and software on a network.*

This unit will clarify the issues associated with network use and how this has developed. It will identify the architectural concepts behind networking and help develop the preliminary skills necessary to install and manage networks.'

Introduction

Computing is one of the worst of all subjects when it comes to jargon and networking is the worst part of computing for confusing and often contradictory jargon. Network specialists may refer to a *layer 3 switch* or *cat 5 cabling* and assume that all around understand. The aim of this part of the book is to provide sufficient knowledge to communicate effectively with these specialists.

When specifying a network, the detail is best left to a specialist, it is not an easy task to get all the details correct so the network runs problem free, however, an understanding of what is required is important when agreeing specifications.

5.1 The size of a network

Networks vary in size and complexity and really defy accurate classification. It is the old problem of the difference between a ship and a boat, no-one can really agree where one starts and the other stops. However, it is now accepted that the terms LANs (Local Area Network), WAN (Wide Area Network) and MAN (Metropolitan Area Network) can be used to group networks by size and complexity.

A LAN usually connects machines over distances of 5–10 kilometres. Remember, this is not a definition! The network itself is often owned by one organization and is run in buildings used by them or partners. LANs can be either peer-to-peer or client–server networks and are the most common size of network. Large organizations use LANs as the parts of their other networks. Small LANs are often run without full-time support staff but large LANs frequently do have these people.

A WAN is larger than a LAN, this being the main difference! Often at least some of the network structure is owed by third parties and may even be public such as the phone system. This means WANs can be international. They could also use microwave, satellite, radio, private lines, etc. They require more management than a LAN, have more security requirements and are usually more expensive to run and manage. WANs will always have full-time support staff. A collection of LANs can be networked into a WAN. The largest example of this is the *Internet*. In many respects the Internet does not exist, it is simply a collection of machines and networks that are connected with common protocols, Internet being short for *inter* and *network*.

A MAN is a metropolitan area network, i.e. one that covers one city or similar area. In all important respects, it is just a WAN but one built for a metropolitan or educational organization.

There are also the terms RAN (Rural Area Network) and CAN (Campus Area Network) but as usual with artificial terms, they are not used very often.

Most network technology relates to LANs and WANs.

5.2 Cost–benefit analysis

A *true* cost–benefit analysis cannot really be carried out. Many attempts to show the real cost benefit of a network show a negative result, i.e. they cost more to install and run than the benefit they achieve yet businesses cannot really run in the modern world without them. The reason for this is simple, to calculate a true cost–benefit analysis one would have to compare the same organization with:

- no computers;
- computers not networked;
- computers networked with several separate LANs;
- computers fully networked.

The *costs* of a network come under the headings of:

- Infrastructure, i.e. cabling, routers, bridges, servers, etc. and their installation.
- Application and System Software licensing, especially a comparison with standalone against site-wide or network licences. Such licences may be recurring or involve a one off payment.
- Training costs incurred due to the use of the network (as distinct from other training).
- Extra staff required to administer the network.
- Cost of security, against accidental loss due to fire, etc. and against malicious attack.

The highest cost (or value once you own it) is the organization's information on the network and the staff knowledge. Hardware and software costs are usually lower. If a company lost its network hardware, the same software could be run on other hardware. In the case of banks, etc. often within a few hours of a major loss. If the company lost its staff or all the information on the network, it will probably go bankrupt.

The *benefits* of a network include:

- Improved information flow, more people have access to information.
- The possibility of a 'one version company', i.e. one that uses the network copy of a document as the master copy, not the one in a manager's office filing cabinet. Any changes to the document are immediately visible to all.
- A reduction in the need for paper storage, an idea related to the 'one version company', an employee only needs access to the network.

The main advantage is improved information flow, both quality and speed. Other advantages could be reduction in travel between centres by the use of the network, i.e. meetings and other means of exchanging information being carried out over the network instead of face to face. This advantage has been much lauded but many companies are now bringing back face-to-face meetings. Electronic meetings, video conferencing etc. cannot provide the often vital human interaction. Banks are even bringing back local braches for the same reason!

It is hard to imagine modern businesses of any size that *could* run without any computers. The complexity of business and the need to integrate with suppliers and customers means that computers 'must' be used. Standalone machines are greatly under utilized if the only means of transferring data is by walking from one to the other with a disk! This leads to a 'requirement' in the modern world to have networked machines, even if that only means a simple peer-to-peer network over slow connections.

The main areas of concern regarding costs involve system compatibility. In the past, large organizations, often lead by IT illiterate management, have procured several LANs or related systems, each one in a different part of the organization and each one not compatible with the other. Costs are incurred from these causes:

- transfer of data between systems;
- conversion of data to information suitable each user or department;
- rekeying of data with the inevitable keying errors;
- loss of business owing to loss of faith by customers in such a badly run organization;
- loss of information owing to bad data conversion;
- the time taken to manage the whole poor structure;
- extra staff required to manage the different systems;
- extra staff training costs, the more systems in use, the more training is required;
- distrust of one or more of the systems leading to increased paper based information.

The days of calculating the true cost–benefit analysis are really past. One does not calculate the cost–benefit analysis of the stairs between floors, one accepts that stairs are required. The calculation may however, yield the best network for assumed needs.

5.3 Network architectures

There are many network architectures, all with their own benefits, the descriptions below are the most common. When networks are called 'small' or 'large', remember the old problem: 'what is the difference between a ship and a boat'. There is no *definition*!

● Small networks with a few users normally use Ethernet or token ring networks with one or two servers or no server at all if peer to peer is in operation. See below.
● Medium-sized networks with a few hundred users will have the need to segment the network into logical parts. Client–server is common with medium-sized networks. See below. There may be 10 or more servers and hardware such as routers or switches to provide the segmentation. Ethernet or token ring is still common with this size of network.
● Large networks usually involve many floors or areas in a building and serve a large organization with diverse needs. This results in a network that must be segmented into logical parts for security, to share the load on servers and the need to balance bandwidth for best performance. High speed backbones are used, possibly FDDI, ATM or Gigabit Ethernet.

A critical choice about the specification of a network is the level of traffic, where the traffic is heavy and how can it be reduced. Factors to consider:

● Is the application software on a server or on local PCs?
● Is part of the PC operating system on the server or local PC (particularly the Windows swap file?)
● In the business of the organization, do users need to access large centrally stored databases?
● Is there a requirement for bandwidth hungry applications such as video conferencing?

If software is held locally and the Windows swapfile is held locally, the network traffic is likely to come from transfer of whole files so the total load on the network will vary a fair amount but still be quite light, most of the time only small demands are made on the available bandwidth. The IT Support department now has a larger job as maintenance of the system will require visits to each machine on the site. (One reason for centralizing application software is to reduce this workload.)

If software is held centrally or there is a need to access large central databases, use video, etc. the traffic rises and therefore you must either provide higher bandwidth or take care in the architecture of the network to maximize the available bandwidth.

Small networks

Possible topologies for small networks

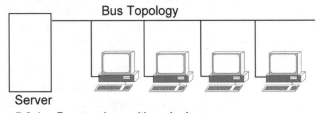

Figure 5.3.1 *Bus topology with a single server*

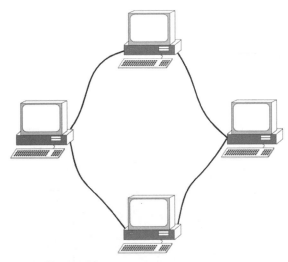

Figure 5.3.2   *Ring topology*

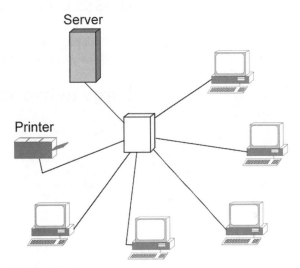

Figure 5.3.3   *Star topology*

The device in the centre of the star topology of Figure 5.3.3 is most likely to be a switch. A switch is a kind of multiport bridge, i.e. it treats each arm of the star as a separate network, sharing the available bandwidth. Typical values are 10 Mbits/sec per PC.

Medium-sized networks

Figure 5.3.4 shows a possible topology for a medium-sized network. The figure shows a router but this could be a switch. The choice depends on how the network is to be segmented.

- Routers allocate segments by use of individual ports, i.e. it is done by the hardware.
- Switches allocate segments by software control, so source and destination addresses can be physically anywhere on the network. This arrangement allows for a VLAN or Virtual LAN. If the segmentation is being done to suit an organization department by department then routers are fine but VLANs allow for greater flexibility either as the organization changes or as accommodation changes.

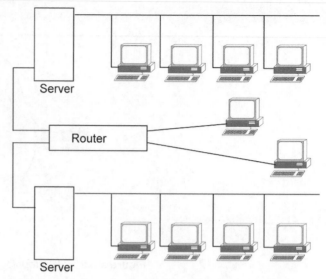

Figure 5.3.4   *Medium-sized network with collapsed backbone*

A collapsed backbone is a strange name, it simply means there is no longer one single backbone.

Large networks

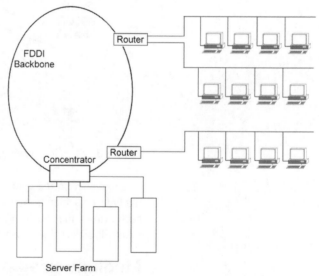

Figure 5.3.5   *Possible topology of a large network using FDDI*

An important difference between medium and large networks is in the management of the bandwidth. It is easy to design a system that has a bottle-neck, a part of the system that slows things down because it is running at full speed but this speed is not sufficient to cope with demand. The solution in existing networks is to use traffic analysis software to determine the exact point of the trouble. In the design of a new network, it is important analyse the bandwidth needs before any design decisions are made. The choice of backbone between FDDI, ATM, Gigabit Ethernet, etc. is not an easy one to make, there are many factors to consider. It is the not the inten-tion of this unit of the HNC Computing to consider all these in detail.

5.4 Layering in networks

Once you have PCs connected together and there is a need for them to communicate, a whole set of new problems arise that must be resolved. The components are designed and made by different manufacturers as is the software both at the operating system level and applications.

In the past single companies have tried to dominate the network market so a user would be 'locked in' to a single supplier. This situation no longer really exists (although some companies still try!). The way that software and hardware is made to work together is by a 'layered' approach.

It is absolutely vital that before continuing with your study of networks you understand this idea of layering. The section below is written as an analogy with human communication because many of the problems of network communication are shared by humans.

As with many ideas in computing, there is a published standard that lays down an ideal specification. In the case of networks, this is called the Open System Interconnection (OSI) seven-layer model. It is an idealized layered architecture, manufacturers generally choose their own often simpler layers, the Internet uses a five-layer model.

The reason a layered approach is so effective in network design is that any layer can be changed without changing the overall aim, to communicate.

The seven layers of the OSI model are:

- Application
- Presentation
- Session
- Transport
- Network
- Data Link
- Physical.

A set of communication rules between humans is called a *protocol*. You would not for instance speak to your family using exactly the same type of language you would use to your friends. People address children differently from the way they speak to old people, etc. Humans have a whole range (of very complex) protocols 'installed' in their brains that are used to communicate.

Computer networks use protocols and because they are layered, the use of the word stack (to refer to layers) has become common, indeed one hears of a 'protocol stack'. The OSI seven-layer model is not always adopted completely, you may find descriptions of say the TCP/IP protocol stack, a five-layer stack used for the Internet. In this sense, a protocol is a set of rules that define aspects of communication. The *Internet Protocol*, IP, is a set of rules.

OSI seven-layer model – an analogy

Set out below is an analogy between the layered approach to network design and communication within a group humans. As with all analogies, you must not take it too far, it is intended as guide only.

Imagine a group of people having a discussion and consider the rules they use to communicate, how they speak, who speaks at any one moment, what language they speak, how loud is their voice, etc. Success or failure to communicate is all that concerns us here. Consider what happens if they break the rules; communication fails to take place.

Layer	Approximate meaning
Application	Speak about the subject you wish to communicate. 'Tell me about the Weather today', 'who will win the election', 'how are you feeling today?'
Presentation	Do you use jargon or plain language. Does everyone communicating know the meaning of the jargon? Speak in French or English or any other human language.
Session	Start or end the conversation, possibly with 'Good Morning' or 'May I speak now'? 'That's all for today, thanks and goodbye'. Not concerned with subject only the establishment of communication.
Transport	If hearer has not heard, how do you know they have not heard? They may send back a message: 'Pardon?' or 'I did quite catch what you said', i.e. message has arrived but not completely received. This is a form of error checking.
Network	Look or point at the person to whom you wish to speak, engage eye contact. Establish a path to someone you wish to speak to.
Data link	Syllables of speech, separate sounds, not speaking if someone else is speaking. (collision detection).
Physical	Sound over the air or over a telephone line, megaphone or radio link.

Consider these points:

1. What happens between the same layers between people, e.g. at the session layer, what happens if you miss these important social points of etiquette. At the network layer, what happens if you do not get a person's attention. The general result is that communication does not take place, at least not effective communication. (Remember, do not take this analogy too far!)
2. What happens vertically, i.e. between say the transport and session layers, it is no use saying 'Good Morning' if the hearer does not hear! Each layer 'talks to' or supports the layer above and below.
3. Can you change the design of one layer without affecting the other layers? Can you for instance replace French with English in the presentation layer without affecting communication? In terms of computers, presentation layer software would be installed (on the PCs). In terms of humans, as long as French is 'installed' (i.e. learnt) by all people communicating, it will have no effect, communication still takes place.

OSI seven-layered network model

Each OSI layer has a particular function and set of behaviours. Each layer provides services to the layers above it, and layers communicate directly only with the same layer on other machines. Each OSI layer provides services that can be ordered and used to describe any arbitrary network implementation. Here is a short synopsis of what each layer is responsible for doing.

Note: Most protocol stacks do not use all seven layers of the OSI model, it is an idealized model and is designed as a guide for future designs. The TCP/IP protocol stack has been included here as a comparison.

OSI/ISO seven-layer model (not every layer is used in every network implementation)	TCP/IP protocol stack
Layer 7: The application layer implements application-specific behaviour, such as the ftp protocol or http (web) session.	TCP/IP Sockets
Layer 6: The presentation layer controls formatting and data exchange behaviour, such as byte-order conversions, data compression, and encryption. It is in charge of how the data is reformatted for presentation to the application layer. Often not used.	Not used in TCP/IP
Layer 5: The session layer encapsulates network transmissions into 'conversations' and controls synchronization and mode switching between the sessions two endpoints. Co-ordinates movement of data from client to server.	Not used in TCP/IP
Layer 4: The transport layer provides data delivery. It can also split data into packets and reassemble those packets on the receiving side.	TCP (Transport Control Protocol) UDP (User Datagram Protocol)
Layer 3: The network layer provides the services we think of as network services: routing, flow control, and so on.	IP (Internet Protocol) ICMP (Internet Control Message Protocol) IGMP (Internet Group Message Protocol)
Layer 2: The data link layer controls transmission and retransmission of data. The data is formatted in accordance with the physical layer's requirements, and higher layer's may reformat or modify it.	ARP (Address Resolution Protocol) RARP (Reverse Address Resolution Protocol)
Layer 1: The physical layer actually moves bits to and from some kind of network medium, whether it is a 10Base-T cable, a satellite link, or a modem connection.	Hardware Interface

Layering in present day networks

Since the OSI seven-layer model has not been implemented fully, it should be noted that a five-layer model that closely fits the TCP/IP model is becoming very common. It may well be the case that no network ever uses the complete seven-layer model. As mentioned elsewhere in the book, 'standards' in the computing business are often defined by first becoming popular then being adopted by official bodies later.

The exact descriptions of the layers are different from the ISO model as are the layer numbers. The key idea to grasp is that of layering itself rather than the details of each layer. Each layer 'talks' to the one above or below in a way that allows hardware or software from different makers to be used but the way the equipment or software works internally can be very different from maker to maker.

The layers in this five-layer model are:

- Application (Layer 5)
- Transport (Layer 4)
- Routing (Layer 3)
- Switching (Layer 2)
- Interface (Layer 1)
- Layer 1, the interface layer, defines the way devices are connected. This is where network standards such as *ATM*, *Token Ring*, *FDDI*, etc. belong, as do the *Ethernet* standards more properly called IEEE 802.3, examples being 10Base-T, etc.
- Layer 2, the switching layer, uses hardware to forward packets of data according to their MAC address. The MAC address is the *Media Access Control*, a number appended to the packet by the NIC, the Network Interface Card fitted in each PC. The MAC address in each NIC is unique across the world.
- Layer 3, the routing layer, allows the network to be partitioned into logical pieces. With the TCP/IP protocol stack, the IP part of the stack is the layer 3 protocol. Each IP packet contains the source and destination address so routing decisions can be made. If a network is split into logical parts, the routing decisions allow packets only into parts of the network where they 'belong' so saving bandwidth. If a network is not split into logical parts, each packet travels to all parts of the network, wasting bandwidth..
- Layer 4, the transport layer, is concerned with the way that user applications are handled on the network. This is the TCP part of the TCP/IP protocol stack and involves things such as the retransmission of packets that were lost in layers 2 or 3 for any reason. Some layer 4 protocols such as *Real Time Protocol* (RTP) are concerned with the sequence of packets and their timing, important when packets must arrive in order and in time to support a real-time multimedia application.
- Layer 5, the application layer, is where applications supply data to layer 4 for transmission. Layer 5 applications are what the users see. Rather than writing the code to communicate directly with layer 4, software such as Microsoft's Winsock is used. A web browser such as Netscape would communicate using Winsock.

5.5 Virtual circuits in local area networks

Packets

The data that travels through networks does so in small groups of bytes called packets. This happens in both Ethernet and Token Ring networks and the whole thing is controlled by a set of rules called protocols. Packets contain transport protocol information depending on the network protocol in use such as Novell's IPX or the Internet protocol stack, TCP/IP. This information is handle by the Network Operating System. A protocol is simply a set of rules that controls communication.

Frames

As the packets must find their way around the network, they must have information attached that gives the address of the destination and of the source of the data together with other information. When packets are wrapped up with this data, the result is called a frame. Frames are made by the Network Interface Card in the PC.

When sending packets over networks the process is called packet switching and differs from older types of network. The old-fashioned POTS used a physical circuit which was maintained without a break throughout the call. If you phoned Edinburgh from London, there would have been a single continuous circuit all the way. In these telephone networks, switching equipment establishes a physical unbroken connection. (Modern telephone systems do not use this technique.)

Networks use a logical connections computer. In order to start a communication session, both sender and user exchange information to establish this logical connection. The user does not need to know the physical path taken by the data.

Below is a table that shows the make-up of two typical frames. You do not need to remember this level of detail, they are shown to illustrate the idea of a packet and of a frame. Different networks have their own frame design. Each frame contains a single packet of data. See the section on Ethernet for more detail.

Ethernet frame

Preamble	Destination address	Source address	Type	Data (packet)	FCS
8 bytes	6 bytes	6 bytes	2 bytes	46–1500 bytes	4 bytes

FCS = Frame Check Sequence

IEEE 802.3 frame

Preamble	SOF	Destination	Source address	Type address	802.2 header	FCS and data
7 bytes	1 bytes	6 bytes	6 bytes	2 bytes	46–1500 byte	4 bytes

SOF = Start Of Frame

Token Ring Data Frame

Start delim	End delim	Frame ctrl	Dest addr	Source addr	Information	Frame check	End delim	Frame status
1 byte	1 byte	1 byte	6 bytes	6 bytes	0–18000 bytes	4 bytes	1 byte	1 byte

The source address and destination address of each frame are often called node addresses but are also called MAC addresses, short for Medium Access Control. Every Ethernet card made has a unique MAC address built into the card.

Segmentation and reassembly of messages

Unlike physical circuits, packets of data (in their frames) do not follow the same path in an unbroken stream.

To send some data, this needs to happen:

- Each message is divided into segments.
- Each segment is turned into a packet by adding transport protocol information.
- Each packet is placed in a frame.
- Each frame is sent over the network.
- On receipt, the packet is extracted from the frame.
- The packet header is read for protocol instructions.
- The data segments are re-assembled into a completed message.
- An acknowledgement is sent back to the sender.

The five-layer protocol stack is closely related to TCP/IP, (Transport Control Protocol/Internet Protocol). In order that data can travel over other network types, frames, packets, etc. are *encapsulated*, i.e. become data for the next lower layer in the stack. To illustrate this, the TCP/IP systems is shown here encapsulated into an Ethernet frame.

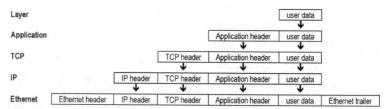

Figure 5.5.1 *TCP/IP frame encapsulated in Ethernet frame*

The maximum distance that data can be sent in a small LAN and the maximum rate at which data can flow is limited by a number of factors. To increase this distance, several different devices are used, *Bridges*, *Routers* and *Switching Hubs*.

Bridging

A Bridge is used to join two LANs together. It works by reading the address information in each frame and only sending those frames that need to be sent, ignoring the others. Overall traffic in the LAN is therefore reduced making better use of the available bandwidth.

Routing

Routers work in a similar manner to bridges except they work on the packet transport protocol information not the MAC address. This means that each packet must have this information, packets that do not have this information come from non-routable protocols such as NetBEUI. In a routable protocol such as TCP/IP the logical address is contained in the packet header. A router is a computer in its own right and builds a table of logical addresses that map to network cards.

Switching hubs

A switching hub is a kind of multiport bridge. The software running in the hub can make 'intelligent' decisions to make bridges between ports so making what is in effect even smaller individual LANs. This reduces the traffic flowing all over the LAN so better use can be made of the bandwidth.

Comparing bridging with routing

Bridging

Good points	Bad points
Simple to install	Limited configuration options
Needs little or no configuration	Lack flexibility
Cheap	Do not work well with routers
Is available from many vendors	Are limited to servicing same type of LANs only

Routers

Good points	Bad points
Can join dissimilar LANs because they process packets not frames	Can be expensive
Can create better data paths dynamically	Do not work with non-routable protocols such as NetBIOS or NetBEUI
	Are often more difficult to configure and administer
	Do not make good routing decisions when used with bridges

5.6 Some fundamental ideas, bandwidth, decibels, etc.

Bandwidth

This term is much used in networking, unfortunately, it is also misused a great deal.

The nature of language is that meanings of words change over time, sometimes developing several meanings. It seems this is happening to the word *bandwidth*. This is a very important concept in networks and data communications so two definitions are presented here.

The informal definition

Some people use the word bandwidth to refer to the speed at which data can be *downloaded*. This is measured in bytes/sec so a 4 Kbyte/sec link would be considered a low bandwidth and 100 Mbytes/sec would be seen as high bandwidth.

The formal definition

The bandwidth of real communication channels is limited by physics. Some channels can transmit high power signals, others cannot and most suffer from *noise*, i.e. random signals caused by outside interference. This interference has many causes such as:

- other electrical devices, e.g. fluorescent lighting, 'dirty' switches as found in refrigerators and central heating systems, electric motors, etc.;
- background radio frequencies from space;
- random activity of the electrons in the wires and electronic components themselves.

In an analogue channel, the bandwidth is the difference between the lowest and highest frequency that can be transmitted.

For example, in the POTS (plain old telephone system) the lowest frequency than could be transmitted was about 300 Hz and the highest was about 3300 Hz so the bandwidth is $3300 - 300 = 3000$ Hz or 3 kHz. You can make experiments with the POTS. If you have an alarm watch that makes a high-pitched alarm, it is quite likely that the frequency is at or above 3300 Hz. If you call a friend and play the alarm down the phone, it is quite likely that your friend will not hear it, i.e. it is not transmitted right through the telephone communication channel. As telephone systems improve, so will the bandwidth, with a modern phone system your friend may be able to hear it! It still makes the point, a channel has a physical limit to the frequencies it will transmit, i.e. it has a limited bandwidth.

If we use the symbols

- P for the power of a signal sent through the communication channel, measured in watts;
- N for the power of the noise coming out of this channel, also is watts;
- W for the bandwidth measured in hertz;
- C for the capacity of the channel in bits/sec.

Then the digital capacity of the channel will be:

$$C = W \log_2(1 + (P/N)) \text{ bits/sec}$$

This is called *Shannon's Law* after Claude Shannon, the first to prove the equation. The ratio P/N is called the *Power to Noise ratio* and is often used as a measure of quality in data and sound transmissions.

Extending the example, with the POTS, the bandwidth is 3 kHz, if we use a signal of 10^{-4} watts and suffer noise of 4×10^{-7} watts then we get a capacity of

$$C = 3000 \times \log_2 (1 + (10^{-4}/4 \times 10^{-7})) = 3000 \times \log_2(251)$$
$$= 25\,000 \text{ bits/sec (approx.)}$$

This is maximum for the channel and is rarely achieved because the equation itself models an ideal channel, real communication channels suffers all sorts of other problems. To increase the bandwidth you can increase the power P or decrease the noise N, unfortunately there is an upper limit to P and noise is very difficult to reduce.

(If your calculator does not have a log_2 key you can find $log_2(x)$ with the formula $log_2(x) = log_{10}(x)/log_{10}(2)$ or more generally for logarithms of any base, $log_{baseN}(x) = log_{10}(x)/log_{10}(N)$)

Here is the language problem. The POTs has a bandwidth of 3 kHz yet can transmit 25 000 bits/sec. These values are not the same but in common language, the POTS has a 'bandwidth' of 25 Kbits/sec.

Modem modems are rated at 56 Kbits/sec but this speed is achieved using data compression, the actual number of 1s and 0s sent using a 56 K modem is lower than the capacity of 25 Kbits/sec because this speed is based on an idealized model.

In some ways it does not matter if the academically correct meaning of the word bandwidth is misused as long as people know what you are speaking about, i.e. you still have effective communication; it does matter when ideas of bandwidth are confused between analogue and digital channels.

When the signal is transmitted through a communication channel, the level drops off at some point due to the physical nature of the channel. You can see from Figure 5.6.1 that bandwidth is not a fixed value, it really depends on how you measure it or at which point on the signal drop-off you choose to measure it.

In Figure 5.6.1, the complete bandwidth is shown as the point when the signal level goes down to zero. At or near this level, the signal to

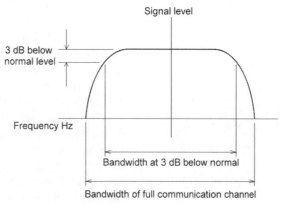

Figure 5.6.1   *Bandwidth at −3 dB*

noise ratio is unacceptably high so a point is taken at some arbitrary point below the maximum level and the bandwidth is taken from there. In this example, this point is taken as 3 dB below normal. This results in a narrower bandwidth but in reality this value is a better guide to bandwidth than if the whole channel width was quoted.

If you see a bandwidth quoted as 100 MHz (3 dB) you will know what it means, the ratio 3 dB is the ratio of the level at which bandwidth is measured against the full signal level.

Baseband and broadband

Baseband it when a cable carries one complete information signal at a time, i.e. the cable is used exclusively for one message at a time and the whole of the physical bandwidth of the cable is used for that signal. Most computer communication is baseband, i.e. PC to printer, PC to modem. Except for the latest designs, most networks use baseband.

Broadband is where two or more signals are present on the cable at the same time so that the bandwidth is shared between them. This requires more complex equipment at both ends of the cable. The TV signal that is in the aerial lead to your television is broadband, it contains all the available TV channels at the same time. Circuits in the TV select or tune into just one, discarding the other signals. Broadband signalling can be achieved using Frequency Division Multiplexing. This is where the digital signal is used to modulate a fixed frequency and this modulated signal is sent down the wire at the same time as other modulated signals of different frequencies. It is often used to mix signals of different types, e.g. voice, data, video, etc.

Decibels

What is a *decibel*? A decibel is 10 times a Bel!

What is a *Bel*? A Bel is simply the log of the ratio of two numbers, log(number1/number2) therefore a decibel is $10 \times$ (log(number1/number2)).

Suppose Fred can throw a javelin 50 metres but Joe can throw one 75 metres. The ratio of their best efforts is 75/50 = 1.5. If we take the log of this we get log(1.5) = 0.176 so we can say that Joe's best efforts are 0.176 Bels better than Fred's.

The reason we use Bels instead of simple ratios, i.e. we use a log scale not a linear scale, is that for very large numbers, a linear scale becomes unusable. The effect of the log scale is to reduce the size of the numbers. Even so, a Bel is not a useful unit because a difference of 1 Bel means that one value is 10 times the other. It is more common to multiply the ratio given in Bels by 10 to give decibels.

In the javelin example, Joe's throw is $0.176 \times 10 = 1.76$ decibels or 1.76 dB better than Fred's.

When you see any measurement given in dB, it is *always* a ratio. If you do not know the 'other number', i.e. the value that is used to calculate the ratio, the measurement is of no use to you. Sound levels are usually quoted in dB, so a sound of 100 dB is high and a sound of 30 dB is very quiet. These sound levels are ratios to a fixed standard sound level that can be found in reference works on acoustics. Decibels are *not* a measurement of sound. In the equation given above, the ratio P/N is the *Signal to Noise Ratio*. This is usually quoted in dB as it is just a ratio of two numbers.

Example 5.6.1

A signal has a power of 2.5 watts and the channel has noise on it with a power of 0.005 watts. What is the signal to ratio, S, expressed as dB?

If the noise could be reduced to 0.00025 watts, what would the signal to noise ratio be then?

Answer

$S = 10 \times \log(P/N) = 10 \times \log(2.5/0.005) = 26.989$ or 27 dB.

For a noise of power 0.00025 watts

$S = 10 \times \log(2.5/0.00025) = 40$ dB.

Example 5.6.2

A communication channel is quoted as having a signal to noise ratio of 97 dB. Is this a good value?

Answer

97 dB means 9.7 Bels. The number that has a log(9.7) is the antilog(9.7) which is 5 011 872 336.273 or approximately 5000 million times. This means the power of the signal is 5×10^9 times higher than the power of the noise. Pretty good!

This shows why it is better to use dB for the ratio of large numbers. It is better to quote 97 dB instead of 5 000 000 000:1!

5.7 Network protocols

This is a term that applies to a wide range of network standards. In the early 1970s, a network was designed by the Xerox Corporation to connect their Altos workstations together. After some time and after joining company with DEC and Intel, the first *Ethernet* specification was published. Since then, the IEEE published a network standard that was based on Ethernet but is not quite the same. This standard is called IEEE 802.3 and in common language is also called Ethernet although it is not an accurate description, another example of where words slowly change their meaning. Ethernet is now used to cover any network that uses CSMA/CD.

Network contention

CSMA/CD

This stands for Collision Sense Multiple Access/Collision Detection. As many network stations are connected to the same wire and this wire uses baseband signalling, only one station must be transmitting at once. When a station wishes to transmit over the network, it waits until the line is quiet. If two stations start to transmit data at exactly the same time, each waits a random amount of time before retransmission, a system that ensures that one will start before the other so avoiding another collision. Humans use this system; imagine you were with a group of people, all having a conversation. Providing you are not arguing, only one person speaks at once, if two start to speak at the same time, both wait for a suitable moment to speak again.

Token passing

On a token ring network, including FDDI, a *token* is sent through the network. The token is used to communicate the busy or free state of the network. If the previous token indicated the network was free, a PC that wishes to transmit sends out a 'busy' token, stopping other machines from sending. The data sent out travels around the ring and arrives back at the sending PC which then responds by sending out a 'not busy' token, allowing access to other machines. Token passing is better than CSMA/CD under heavy traffic conditions.

Table 5.7.1   *Details of some of the Ethernet Physical Layer specifications*

	Original Ethernet	*10Base-5*	*10Base-2*	*10Base-T*	*100BaseT*	*1000Base-LX*	*10Broad-36*
Signalling	baseband	baseband	baseband	baseband	baseband	baseband	broadband
Maximum segment length in metres	500	500	185	100	100	5000	1800
Cable	50 ohm coaxial	50 ohm coaxial	50 ohm coaxial	UTP	UTP	Fibre	75 ohm coaxial

In *Ethernet* networks, the individual standards are known as 10Base-2, 10Base-5, etc. In this coding, the 10 refers to the data rate of 10 Mbits/sec, 'base' refers to baseband and the number is the cable media type and approximates to one-hundredth of the maximum segment length in metres. Using this scheme, 10Base-5 is a 10 Mbits/sec baseband system with a maximum segment length of 500 metres. Some of the specifications are summarized in Table 5.7.1. There are many more. 1000Base-LX is just one from a set of specifications that are called Gigabit Ethernet.

You will see references in the marketplace for 10, 100 and 1000 Mbits/ sec Ethernet. This reflects the enormous rate of progress from the original 10 Mbits/sec Ethernet in 1972. To be more precise, Ethernet and IEEE 802.3 runs at 10 Mbits/sec over coaxial cable, 100 Mbits/sec Ethernet is known as Fast Ethernet and operates at 100 Mbps over UTP and 1000 Mbits/sec Ethernet is known as Gigabit Ethernet that operates at 1000 Mbits/sec using fibre and twisted-pair cables.

You should notice that each type has a maximum cable length for each segment of the network. The length restriction is due to the timing required for the particular Ethernet standard. If you were to fit longer cables, the signal timing would no longer conform to the standard and communication would not be reliable.

References

www.3com.com/technology/tech_net/whitepapers
www.cisco.com/univercd/cc/td/doc/cisintwk/ito_doc/ethernet.htm
www.brother.com/european/networking/

FDDI

This is the *Fibre Distributed Data Interface*, often used to provide a network backbone rather than service to individual PCs.

FDDI is a 100 Mbits/sec network standard that runs over a ring topology. It uses token passing rather than the CSMA/CD used in Ethernet and is designed to run over fibre optic cables. A related standard called CDDI runs over copper cables; it was introduced to avoid the high cost of fibre cabling.

Fibre optic cable are more secure than copper as they do not emit an electromagnetic field that can be picked up by unauthorized users. For related reasons, it does not suffer from electrical interference from outside and has a very high bandwidth. Unfortunately, it is expensive to install.

FDDI uses two rings, the primary ring and the secondary ring. This means that if one fibre is broken, communication can continue over the other. Each FDDI has two ports (called A and B) that attach to the primary and secondary rings. Up to a 1000 stations can be connected but a practical limit of 500 exists because if a fibre breaks, the 500 stations would become 1000 stations. This is due to the way the signals interact in each station.

Some types of network traffic must have data that arrives in time and in sequence. An example of this id real-time video. Other data can arrive without strict timing, such as e-mail or file transport. FDDI supports both kinds of traffic by providing synchronous and asynchronous transport. Time critical applications would use synchronous transport that can use a fixed part of the 100 Mbits/sec bandwidth, other asynchronous traffic takes what is left.

ATM

ATM is *Asynchronous Transfer Mode*, a network standard that specifies data packet format and network switching. It was designed for use by Telephone Companies to provide wide area data transport.

It is characterized by being a high speed packet switching system that uses very short fixed length data packets (48 data bytes + 5 control = 53 bytes). The problem it attempts to solve is the carriage of mixed types of data. The packets for video and other time critical applications must arrive in time, other data such as email does not have this need. ATM can define the quality of service to give constant bit rate (CBR), variable bit rate (VBR) and available bit rate (ABR) depending on the type of traffic to be carried. The speed of ATM varies with the quality of service but values of 155 Mbits/sec over copper and 622 Mbits/sec over fibre are common.

IPX/SPX

This protocol was designed by Novell for their NetWare NoS. Internetwork Packet Exchange (IPX)/Sequenced Packet Exchange (SPX) is a routable protocol so is used to route messages from one network node to another. IPX packets include network addresses so data can be exchanged between different networks. SPX is a protocol that ensures that an entire message arrives intact.

5.8 Synchronous and asynchronous communications

Why synchronization is required

Imagine that someone is talking to you very fast, telling you a great deal of detailed information. If you cannot 'keep up', some of the information is lost, i.e. you do not have all the information they 'transmitted' to you. Computers have a similar requirement. Data are sent as 1s and 0s at a certain speed so the speed of the sender must be matched with the speed of the receiver if the data are not to be lost.

There are two common systems used in computing to provide reliable communication, synchronous and asynchronous communications. In this sense, the 'a' of asynchronous means 'not'. This can cause some confusion. Imagine you agree to meet a friend at 11:30 by the station. To allow this to work, both your watches must run at the same rate and be set to the same time, i.e. they are 'synchronized'; success depends on the assumption that both your watches remain synchronized. If something goes wrong with either watch, you will miss your meeting. In contrast, if you agreed to meet directly after a phone call, this would be 'asynchronous', your watches do not need to be synchronized, you act on a 'signal', a phone call.

Asynchronous communications

Asynchronous communications is more common than synchronous communications. Data are sent as a series of 1s and 0s but if the line is already in a '0' state and the next bit is also a '0', the line stays the same. See Figure 5.8.1. The data byte being sent here is 01101000 (remember a byte is 8 data bits). You can see that the line only changes when the bits go either 0 to 1 or 1 to 0. When no data are being sent, the line is quiet, when a byte is to be sent, a start bit will start the communication.

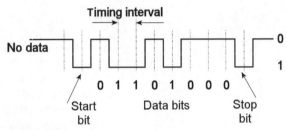

Figure 5.8.1   *Asynchronous transmission*

A problem with asynchronous communication is that each byte has (usually) 2 bits added so $2/8 = 0.25$ or 25% more bits sent than are required by the data alone.

Synchronous communications

In synchronous communications, data are sent as data blocks or frames. The size of these frames varies from about 1000 to 4096 bytes.

Frames are structured with data plus control information. This information is typically as shown in Figure 5.8.2 but will vary in detail from system to system. The parts of the frame are shown in Table 5.8.1.

Table 5.8.1

Flag	8 data bits that indicate the start or end of transmission
Address	is where the frame must be sent
Control	indicates the type of frame
Data	is a varied number of unstructured data bits
CRC	CRC is a Cyclic Redundancy Check. This is where some arithmetic has been performed on the data and the result is stored as the CRC. On receipt of the data, the same arithmetic is carried out; if the result is the same, the assumption is made that the data has arrived un-corrupted. There is only a very small chance of getting the same CRC with corrupted data.

Flag	Address	Control	data	CRC	Flag

Figure 5.8.2   *Data frame for synchronous communication*

In general synchronous communication is more efficient than asynchronous communication because the number of non-data bits is smaller, remember asynchronous communication typically has 25% more bits added for control. If the total for the flags, address, control and CRC was even as high as 20 and the data was 4096 bytes, the proportion of control bytes = 20/4096 = 0.0048 or just a bit less than ½%. The downside is that synchronous communications requires more sophisticated equipment.

For these reasons, synchronous communications are generally used in networks, asynchronous communication is used to connect simple devices.

5.9 Small computer local communication standards

USB

USB stands for *Universal Serial Bus*, a standard being worked on by Compaq, Hewlett-Packard, Intel, Lucent, Microsoft, NEC and Philips.

The idea is that peripherals can be plugged in (or removed) whilst the PC is switched on, they do not need to be initialized during the boot up sequence. When a device is plugged in, the operating system recognizes the event and configures the required device driver software.

Many standard PCs are supplied with two USB ports. Attachment of more than two devices is achieved by USB hubs that allow daisy-chaining, a technique where devices are plugged in one to the next forming a 'chain' thus reducing the amount of cable required. A further reduction in cabling is achieved because USB supplies the power to the devices in the data cable, up to 2.5 watts. Hubs may be cascaded up to five levels deep providing a connection for up to 127 peripheral devices at a transfer rate of either 12 Mb/s (full speed) and 1.5 Mb/s (low speed). The current USB standard, USB 1.1 is about to be superseded by USB 2.0 which will allow a claimed transfer rate of 480 Mb/s.

Firewire

Firewire is the common name for a standard called IEEE 1394. This is a serial connection aimed at very high data transfer speeds, at least, high for a serial link. Speeds between 100 Mbits/sec 800 Mbits/s are possible and a speed of 3200 Mbits/sec is promised. Up to 16 devices can be connected via a single Firewire port. It commonly used to attach digital cameras to PCs, one reason being the very simple cable attachment and set-up that is used.

IrDA

This is an infrared serial communication standard that is intended to dispense with cables and run at a maximum of 4 Mbits/sec. IrDA will also work at standard serial speeds to mimic the old RS-232-C serial standard (see below). Since there is a clear possibility of several devices in one place using IrDA and the infrared signal is 'broadcast' around that place, the standard includes techniques similar to those used in networking, to avoid device conflicts and data being sent to the wrong device. It is common to find IrDA on notebook PCs or smaller devices to allow communication with desktop PCs without cabling.

Serial ports

Serial devices have been around for many years. The earliest machines could be connected to devices such as modems or printers using just three wires, a 'send' wire, a 'receive' wire and a signal return wire. Binary 1s and 0s were sent one after the other, i.e. serially. The maximum speed was quite low. To improve speed, extra wires were introduced to allow 'handshaking', signals that allowed or disallowed the sending of data depending in the readiness to receive. These data and handshake lines and the associated timings, etc. were incorporated into a standard called RS232-C which used a 25-pin 'D'-shaped connector. Since only a few of these pins were actually used, IBM introduced a similar 9-pin 'D'-shaped connector that is now common on modern PCs. Unfortunately, as a standard that has 'evolved' over the years, the 25-pin connectors are still common as are many different arrangements for interconnecting 25 pin, 9-pin old and new devices. Modern PCs with modern serial devices cause little problem but the use of legacy serial devices with any PC can prove to be problematic. The maximum speed of a serial port is currently 115200 bits/sec. With a simple serial link, each 8-bit byte has a 'start' and 'stop' bit added so using 10 bits/byte. 115200 bits/sec would then give 11520 bytes/sec. You may notice that some speeds are given as Mbytes/sec and others as Mbits/sec. This is because the number of extra bits (i.e. not data bits) is variable, depending on the application and the PC industries common practice of quoting the largest number to look attractive in advertisements! Also you should be wary of 'standards'.

Serial ports under Microsoft DOS or Windows have names COM1, COM2, etc. The set-up for these COM ports quote the speed in bits/sec, number of data bits, parity and number of stop bits. A typical set-up may be 9600, 8, none, 1. This means 9600 bits/sec, 8 data bits, no parity and 1 stop bit. Parity is an old error checking system now little used, it is in the set-up to allow connection with legacy devices. You may see 9600 bits/sec quoted as 9600 Baud but the 'Baud rate' is not the same as bits/sec.

Parallel ports

Most PCs have a single port for the attachment of a local printer. This is a parallel port, i.e. it has control lines and 8 data lines, one each for the 8 bits of a byte. Although designed as a single direction port for outputting to printers, some programmers have managed to allow two-way communication. The port is slow by modern standards but as the printers are even slower, no advantage is gained by using a high-speed link.

Under Microsoft DOS or Windows, the parallel port is called LPT1 (for Line Printer 1). It is possible to add more parallel ports by plugging expansion cards into the ISA bus, they would then be called LPT2, etc.

5.10 Network specification

Required bandwidth

Many people suffer from 'upgradeitus', they must have the latest, fastest system because it is available. Some IT specialists are not immune to this. In an era of tight financial budgets and the push for ever-higher savings and productivity, it does not pay to suffer from this unfortunate complaint!

When specifying PCs or networks, a realistic assessment must be made about what performance is required rather than what is available or what someone may 'like'. In the case of networks, the big performance issue is bandwidth.

Providing that application software is on local PCs and that most of the work of the organization use normal office applications such as word-processing, spreadsheets, e-mail of text, etc. the bandwidth requirement will be low. There will be peaks in demand as large files are sent or large print jobs sent to a central printer but most of the time, work is local and does not add to network traffic. The bandwidth demand rises dramatically when applications such as video conferencing (VC) are required. If the network can provide for VC, most other traffic will flow without much trouble. The protocols used must be able to support VC. So how much bandwidth do you need for VC?

A possible 'worst case' bandwidth requirement

Assuming that you plan to use video conferencing, what bandwidth is required? Assuming that you have a 1024 × 768 screen resolution set on a PC, start by deciding what size video image is best. This resolution has a ratio of 1:0.75 so if you choose video images with the same ratio, typical sizes are represented to scale below.

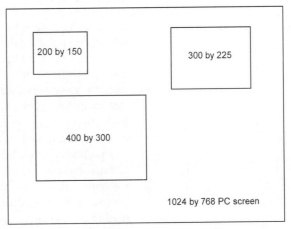

Figure 5.10.1 *Image sizes in proportion 0.75:1*

Problem 5.10.1

If the video has 256 colours and gives say 25 full frames/sec, the same speed as a domestic television, what bandwidth is required?

One answer, without compressing the data

An uncompressed video image size of 400 × 300 has 400 × 300 = 120 000 pixels.
At 256 colours that means 1 byte/pixel or 120 000 bytes/sec.
   At 25 frames a second this gives 120 000 × 25 = 3 000 000 or 3 million bytes/sec.
   As digital bandwidth is quoted in bits/sec, we would need a minimum of 3 × 8 = 24 Mbits/sec, ignoring any control data. A typical 10Base-T network connection to a PC gives 10 Mbits/sec, clearly not enough.
   To fix this, either a higher bandwidth connection to the PC is required (assuming the backbone can supply it), use made of video compression or a compromise made on the picture quality. The frame rate could be reduced, so could the number of colours and the image size.

To take the other extreme, use could be made of the 200 by 150 size image, 16 colours and 10 frames/sec. This would give a very poor, jerky image, a little hard to see but the bandwidth required would be:

$200 \times 150 = 30\,000$ pixels
$30\,000$ pixels at 16 colours $= 15\,000$ bytes (½byte/pixel)
$15\,000$ bytes at 10 frames/sec $= 150\,000$ bytes/sec
$150\,000$ bytes/sec $= 1.2$ Mbits/sec

Clearly a 10 Mbit/sec is now fast enough, but would users want such a poor quality image?

Compression

One possible solution is to use mathematical techniques to compress the image, thus reducing the bandwidth required. There are several standards common in the marketplace but the one that looks like being most common is MPEG (from *Motion Picture Experts Group*). This compression works in a number of ways, one of which is to only transmit frame pixels that are different from the previous frame. If a video scene shows a fixed background with something moving in the foreground, only the moving parts are transmitted.

The problem with MPEG is that either software is used to compress and decompress at each end of the transmission or hardware is used. The software is slower than the hardware, defeating some of the advantage of compression, the hardware is fast but currently not cheap. MPEG is being used in digital television distribution over high bandwidth channels.

The bandwidth required for video therefore depends on the quality of image that is seen as acceptable. Compression helps but a fast PC is required if decompression is done with software. MPEG cards to decompress the image provide a high quality image but are still relatively expensive.

Further information on MPEG can be seen at www.mpeg.org/MPEG/video.html

Video over Ethernet

There is an additional problem with sound and video being sent over a network if it is to be view as it is transmitted, so-called *streaming*. This problem is associated with the nature of the data itself. Taking video as an example, each frame must be ready to view in the correct sequence and at the correct rate. If a frame is 'dropped' or lost because of some transmission problem, there is no time to retransmit it because of the need to show the next frame. If text data is being sent such as an e-mail, and if some part of the data is lost, retransmission of just that part is possible because the delivery of the data is not so time dependant. If the information is sent over a complex network, separate packets could travel different paths in response to local traffic and routing requirements, this means they will arrive at different times. For text-based information this is not a problem, the whole message is reassembled and stored locally but for streamed audio or video this is not acceptable. The ATM protocol was designed to meet the needs of such data and attempts to provide the required *quality of service.*

If the video is sent as a complete file, this problem does not exist, it is simply data that arrives, is re-assembled and stored as a file. Viewing the file then becomes a local problem. This appears to solve the quality of service problem but in fact cause more problems. The files are usually very large requiring storage space and the whole file must be obtained before it can be viewed. There are also copyright issues involved, the copyright owner will often be unwilling to allow local storage as they lose control of further publication.

Streaming video or audio is not simple, it requires relatively high bandwidth. To achieve high quality video, new compression techniques such as MPEG-4 will be required. For 10 and 100 Mbps Ethernet networks, MPEG-2 may be used but users must be satisfied with less than Broadcast quality video. Bandwidth and data compression are related, they both attempt to deliver the maximum amount of data in a given time but the timing of the arrival of data is also important.

5.11 The physical communication media

Cabling

The bandwidth of the cable used to transmit data is limited. Several designs are available but all attempt to obtain the same thing, high bandwidth with low power loss.

Problems to overcome

1. If you operate a simple radio, you may put up an aerial made up of a piece of wire. It may not work as effectively as a well-designed aerial but it will pick up radio signals. The cable connecting parts of a network is no different from your radio aerial, it picks up radio signals as well as electrical interference from common electrical devices. These are known as *Radio Frequency Interference* or RFI and *Electromagnetic Interference* or EMI. RFI comes from various sources such as radio, television, mobile phones, electronic devices such as computers and even space. EMI comes from electrically 'noisy' devices like fridges, electric motors, fluorescent lights, light switches.
2. Cables have a power limitation. The signal-to-noise ratio can be improved by increasing the power, but this cannot be extended too far.
3. Bandwidth. The design of the cable limits the bandwidth. It is no use trying to send a high-frequency signal down a cable with low bandwidth, it will not come out of the other end! For a simple twisted wire pair ('bell wire'), the bandwidth is limited to approximately 1 MHz.

If a cable is made with two or more conductors or wires, the electrical properties are different depending on:

- whether they are laid side by side or are twisted together;
- the distance that separates the wires;
- the diameter of the wire;
- the purity of the copper conductor;
- if they are contained inside a 'screen' of braided copper;
- the length of the wire.

Experiments

1. Turn on a radio and 'tune' it between two stations so that you cannot hear any music or speech. Turn up the volume, the noise you hear is from RFI and EMI. Some of it generated from within the radio itself, most is from external sources.
2. Tune a television between two stations. Providing your television does not give a blue screen in response to 'no station', you will get 'snow', an never ending moving display of black and white dots. If the television were perfect and there was no RFI nor EMI, you would get a black screen. A proportion of the 'snow' is from the microwave background radiation from space.

Common cable types

The two common cable designs to be found are *Unshielded Twisted Pair* (UTP) and *Coaxial.* Coaxial has a single copper conductor surrounded by a braided copper sheath. This sheath is connected to ground so that any unwanted signals picked up are run to earth instead of interfering with the signal being transmitted. If you look at the cable that connects your home television to the aerial, you will find that it is coaxial in design.

UTP is simpler and cheaper to make and being more flexible than coaxial cable, is easier to install. The use of UTP is very attractive but ways must be found to make more use of its effective bandwidth. These ways include special signal processing to reduce the effects of noise in the cable, the bandwidth of UTP is therefore not just a function of the cable itself, it also comes from the devices that connect each end of the cable.

Cabling standards

As is common in the computing industry, cabling is made to conform to standards designed by commercial companies and supported or adopted by official bodies. In the case of networks and cabling in particular, these standards are published by such organizations as the EIA/TIA of the IEEE. The EIA/TIA is the *Electronic Industries Association* and *Telecommunications Industry Association,* a group founded in the USA. The IEEE (known as the I triple E) is the *The Institute of Electrical and Electronics Engineers*, a non-profit, technical professional association of more than 350 000 individual members in 150 countries.

Many Local Area Networks (LANs) are cabled with what is called 'cat 5'. This refers to the EIA/TIA category 5 UTP cables. Various categories are shown in Table 5.11.1. Explanation of the terms will be found in other sections of the book.

Fibre

Fibre optic cables have an enormous bandwidth. They are made from glass of extreme purity drawn down into small diameter fibres. It is said that if a

Table 5.11.1 *EIA/TIA Building cabling standards*

EIA/TIA Category	Uses
1	POTS, the Plain Old Telephone System Analogue Voice Digital Voice
2	ISDN (Data) 1.44 Mbps T1, 1.544 Mbps Digital Voice
3	10Base-T Ethernet 4 Mbps Token Ring ISDN Voice
4	10Base-T Ethernet 16 Mbps Token Ring
5	10Base-T Ethernet 100Base-T Ethernet 160 Mbps Token Ring 100 Mbps Distributed Data Interface 155 Mbps Asynchronous Transfer Mode
150 Ohm STP	16 Mbps Token Ring 100 Mbps Distributed Data Interface Full Motion Video

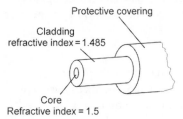

Figure 5.11.1 *Basic construction of fibre optic cable*

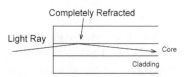

Figure 5.11.2 *Simple light path in a fibre*

block of glass of this purity was made a kilometre thick, it would transmit as much light as a normal window pane. (You should not take such comparisons too literally, they are simply a way of illustrating an idea.)

The fibre is constructed as Figure 5.11.1. The core is made of glass with a typical refractive index of 1.5 and is clad with a layer of glass with a refractive index that is 99% of 1.5 or $1.5 \times 0.99 = 1.485$. If the fibre was always kept perfectly straight, the light would travel right down the centre. Of course the fibre is never straight so the two-layer construction is used to cause the light that enters the core to be totally refracted back into the core as shown in Figure 5.11.2.

It would be a great waste of fibre bandwidth to use baseband signalling unless the signal itself had an enormous bandwidth requirement. Normally this is not the case so broadband techniques are used. This usually involves *Multiplexing*, i.e. sending many signals down the fibre at one time. Fibre cables can carry many simultaneous television channels, data and voice signals all at once.

Fibre is quite expensive to install but the high bandwidth more than offsets this high price. It is generally used to provide the *backbone* of networks where large amounts of data flow.

Radio or wireless

Until recently, wireless LAN connections have been too slow, but he IEEE have now brought out the standard 802.11b (high rate) than defines an 11 Mbit/sec transmission rate which will provide performance equivalent to 'standard' Ethernet.

IEEE 802.11b requires two pieces of equipment, a PC with a wireless NIC and an Access Point. The access point is wired to the main network via its own bridge. Roaming is possible, i.e. just like a mobile phone, the user can take the PC anywhere in range of the set of access points and remain connected to the network. Use of different protocols will also allow peer-to-peer connections.

For more information, see

3Com Corporation at www.3com.com/technology/tech_net/white_papers/503072a.html

Intel at www.intel.com

5.12 Connecting to networks from remote sites

xDSL

A major problem for Internet or networking companies is the cost of providing connections to large numbers of remote users. There exists a huge investment in the local loop, cabling to houses and offices that already carry voice telephone services. ISDN, Cable Modems and the xDSL standards were developed to use this vast investment without the need to recable the world.

The local loop is the name given to the last cable run from the phone company to the buildings supplied with the phone service. It is sometimes referred to as the 'last mile'.

xDSL is the name given to a range of communication standards designed to carry voice and data traffic. The xDSL standard just coming into use in the UK is ADSL.

Data connections are not the only reason that higher bandwidth is required. Better voice telephone services are also required so digital systems are being installed that provide added value services to the user such as caller identification, call waiting, etc.

The xDSL standards are:

- ADSL/ADSL-lite   Asymmetric Digital Subscriber Line
- R-ADSL   Rate-Adaptive Digital Subscriber Line
- HDSL   High Bit-Rate Digital Subscriber Line
- SDSL   Single-Line Digital Subscriber Line
- VDSL   Very High Bit-Rate Digital Subscriber Line

ADSL

ADSL or *Asymmetric Digital Subscriber Line* is a digital standard that provides an 'always on' service to a remote network. There is no concept of making a call, it behaves to the user more like a LAN connection. It is 'asymmetric' because the upload and download speeds are different. ADSL-lite is a slower version intended for the domestic market, it requires less complex equipment at the user end.

R-ADSL or *Rate-Adaptive Digital Subscriber Line* is very similar to ADSL except that the speed can be adjusted to suit cable lengths and conditions.

HDSL

HDSL or *High Bit-Rate Digital Subscriber Line* is symmetric, it has the same bandwidth for uploads and downloads.

SDSL

SDSL or *Single-Line Digital Subscriber Line* is similar to HDSL but will work with single copper wires over restricted distances.

Table 5.12.1 *Speeds of local loop connection standards*

Standard	Upload	Download	Distance (km)
56 kbps analogue modems	28–33 k	56 k	
ISDN	128	128	5.5
Cable modem	128 k–10 M	10–30 M (over shared lines)	50
ADSL-lite	512 k	1 M	5.5
ADSL/R-ADSL	1.544 M	1.5–8 M	5.5
IDSL	144 k	144 k	5.5
HDSL	1.544 M (T1) 2 M (E1)	1.544 M (T1) 2 M (E1)	4.5
SDSL	1.544 M (T1) 2 M (E1)	1.544 M (T1) 2 M (E1)	3
VDSL	1.5 = 2.3 M	13–52 M	0.3–1.3

VDSL

VDSL or *Very High Bit-Rate Digital Subscriber Line* is the fastest of the xDSL standards and can provide sufficient bandwidth to support video but over shorter distances. The standard can be extended by providing a fibre optic link from the telephone provider to a local distribution point but this defeats part of the reason for the xDSL standards, i.e. to use the installed local loop.

Table 5.12.1 shows the speed in either Kbits/sec or Mbits/sec for up and download of data for various standards together with approximate maximum distances in km. The abbreviation T1 refers to a US standard for a 1.55 Mbits/sec telephone connection and E1 is the faster European equivalent.

ADSL modems use a technique that is related to traditional modems but introduce more complexity.

A traditional modem modulates a 'sound' with digital data to make it compatible with the POTS. The POTS was originally designed as a voice only analogue system and as such, will not transmit digital 1s and 0s. There is an exception to this, in the very oldest POTS, opening and closing the lines was used to dial the number, the 'dial' itself was speed controlled to open and close the lines at a set rate to match the speed of the switches in the exchange. This was called 'loop disconnect' dialling. For backwards compatibility, some phones and most modems will still execute loop disconnect dialling. On a phone, you may see a switch marked 'LD' and 'Tone'. LD is Loop disconnect, and 'tone' is the system used now to dial numbers, a set of tones of different frequencies. Because of this history, the POTS could not transmit 1s and 0s so modulated sounds were used instead.

The ADSL modems modulate signals of higher frequency resulting in the ability to provide a higher bandwidth*. As ADSL is asymmetric, one frequency is used for upload and another for download with the higher bandwidth being assigned to download. This is called Frequency Division Multiplexing, It means different signals are carried using different frequencies on the same broadband line. A technique called *echo*

---

* The actual system of modulation used is quite complex but of no interest here.

cancellation allows the frequency bands to overlap so using the available bandwidth more efficiently. A filtering device called a POTS Splitter is used to split off 4 kHz of bandwidth to provide a simultaneous voice channel that works at the same time as data transmission. As is usual with broadband transmissions, the cost and complexity of the equipment at both ends of the line offsets the saving made by using cheap cabling, but the cost of providing high bandwidth cable to support baseband signalling would be prohibitive. This is whole purpose of ADSL.

xDSL can deliver ATM (Asynchronous Transfer Mode) services to the home.

ISDN

ISDN means *Integrated Services Digital Network*. It is a switched service designed originally to provide high quality voice telephone connections to PBXs, Private Branch Exchanges. ISDN 30 provides 30 × 64 K lines to support PBXs but a domestic version is available called ISDN 2 with as the name implies, provides 2 × 64 K lines that can be combined to give a bandwidth of 128 K.

In the UK there has been a slow take up of ISDN lines and the newer ADSL lines seem to offer better bandwidth. ISDN requires a call to be set up in a similar manner to a modem used over a voice line whereas ADSL is an always on service; for this reason, ISDN attracts call charges.

Cable modems

Cable modems do not really belong in this section as they do not use the local loop, they must use the cable provided for cable TV services. They do provide a high bandwidth broadband connection. Once connected, cable modem use a LAN protocol to transport data over the network, so issues of security become more of a concern. One of the first cable modem installations had a fault that allowed each user's C: drive to be visible over the network! Download to the user is via the cable modem but many installations rely on the POTS with a traditional modem to upload data at a much lower bandwidth.

5.13 Network operating systems

A single computer or a number of computers connected together would do nothing at all without an operating system, apart from hum, use electricity and get warm. The operating system does not 'operate' the machine or the network, it *controls* it. In 1903, the Wright brothers were credited with the first human powered flight. Whether or not they were the first, their success is due to their realization that the problem of flight was not how to produce lift, it was how to *control* the aircraft. Taking this analogy a little further, flying can be likened to the layered architecture of a network. The business of flying in a straight line can be thought of part of the operating system of the aircraft. The hardware is working but it is also controlled. What you do with that controlled craft is an *application*, e.g. navigating from London to Coventry. In a PC running say Windows 2000, all you see is the desktop and a few icons. The computer is running (flying) but doing nothing useful until you run an application, like the wordprocessor used to type this.

In a network, the Network Operating System or NOS is responsible for managing and controlling two or more computers and other hardware,

In English, your peer is your equal. In the House of Lords sit the Peers, those in the old days considered equal to each other but high enough to govern. A person being tried in a Crown Court has to face a jury of their peers, their equals. In a peer-to-peer network, each machine is considered to be equal to each other, no one machine is more important than any other.

It is a great shame, but in computing, some words are used that have many different meanings. The word *server* is one of these. You can buy a computer called a server, it is a machine with more RAM, disk space and performance than a desktop PC but it is still only a computer. Its architecture is not all that different from a PC, indeed an PC could be used as a server on a small network.

Another meaning of the word server is for a piece of software such as SQL Server. In this sense, the software is providing a service. To understand which kind of server is being used, you must understand the context in which it is used.

such as hard disks, printers, communication devices. It controls the sharing of network resources including both hardware and software. There are two broad types or *model* of NOS, *peer-to-peer* and *client–server*.

Peer-to-peer NOS runs on every computer in the network. It allows sharing of resources without centralized management. Each computer in the network can access all network resources equally. Examples of peer-to-peer systems include AppleShare and Windows for Workgroups. They are used with a small number of machines, generally in small or very small organizations.

A client–server NOS runs on every computer in the network but not equally; one or more computer becomes the network *server*. A server centralizes and co-ordinates applications and functions, it provides a *service* to the network or users. It is possible to have one NOS running on a server and a different Operating System running on the client. This is quite common, e.g. PCs running Windows 2000 'talking to' a Netware server or Macintosh machines connected to a Unix network.

All network devices other than servers are considered *clients*. Clients send requests to the network server to access resources and services. Client–server networks are more flexible than peer-to-peer designs. It is possible to centralize resources, have better security and is generally more flexible. With every good thing, there is a downside, client–server networks are generally more expensive than peer-to-peer networks, since one or more dedicated servers must be purchased (and not used to run applications). Software suppliers will tell how their system does not need trained professional staff but most users find they need these people to install, configure and run client–server networks. Examples of client–server NOS include Novell NetWare, Windows NT Server and IBM OS/2 Warp Server.

The role of a NOS

A NOS must control at least:

- users, groups and domains;
- printers and other output devices;
- mass storage;
- data security, hacking, virus protection, Firewalls;
- system performance;
- communicating with other network architectures.

Users, groups and domains

To achieve a useful level of security, etc. users who login to a network are assigned certain access privileges, these allow access to only those resources (hardware and software) they are supposed to be able to use.

Using Microsoft Windows NT as an example, user access to the network could be via *workgroups* or *domains*. Even early version of Windows allowed workgroup or peer-to-peer based networks. A workgroup is a group of people allowed to access to each other's computers and the associated resources, printers, etc., with very few restrictions. Workgroups are appropriate in small peer-to-peer networks, e.g. if you have an office with five or six computers, one or two printers and no full-time network administrator. This type of network is simple to set up and administer and because the people working on them usually have similar security requirements, security issues are not generally a significant issue.

In normal English language, the word 'domain' means the area where you live, work, relax, etc. In the context of networks, the word domain means fairly similar things; it means that parts of the network are accessible and others are not. It is similar to the domain and where you live, you are free to occupy that domain but you are not allowed without permission into somebody else's domain.

In larger organizations, the level of security must be greatly improved, that implies that the network is larger and that you have full-time professional network administration. Domain based networks centralize user access control and administration and allow the organization's network to be split into several smaller departmental or divisional units. Even sets of servers can be grouped into domains, e.g. to equate to the departmental structure, allowing the network to suit the organization rather than the organization being changed to suit the network. In contrast, in a workgroup-based system, users log onto a local machine and no user account is created in any centralized database. In a domain-based system, the user account is centralized so that when you log on, access to parts of the network is allowed or not depending on the user's rights rather than their location.

Under NT, user accounts are created by the administrator. Users are assigned a security identification (SID) which is the main reference to the user. The SID is also associated with the user account name, group membership, password, 'home' directory and log-on script. A log-on script is a set of instructions that run when the user logs in to perform repetitive tasks.

When a user logs into a domain, the domain controller authenticates the log-on. Upon success the domain controller provides a list of all the servers in domain (rather than what is on the whole network), the user can see what they're allowed to see. Other servers on the network they are not allowed to access, may be completely invisible to the user, not just 'barred'. In contrast, when the user logs into a workgroup, each server responds to the log-on by reporting its presence, in other words each user can see all the servers.

A network domain is more formally defined as a group for servers controlled by a primary domain controller. The idea is that this group of servers can behave as a single combined unit. The term domain used under Windows NT and is similar to Novell's NetWare Directory Service or NDS in NetWare 4.

It is sometimes appropriate to be allowed to access the resources of another domain. It is possible to set up *trust relationships* so that resources from another domain are accessible. A trust relationship allows access to network resources and user accounts. User accounts include users and user groups, network resources include file servers, print servers, workstations or even data.

Domain-based networks can be built in one of four basic models.

- The first model is called the *Single Domain Model*. As this name implies, there is only one domain and this domain controls all user accounts and all the resources.
- The second model is called the *Master Domain Model* and consists of several domains on the network. Only one of those domains controls user accounts, the other domains control resources. Trust relationships exists with the master domain to control access to resources.
- The third model is known as the *Multiple Master Domain model*. This is where several domains exist and each one contains user accounts and resources. The network is managed by establishing trust relationships between these domains so that users may log on anywhere on the network.
- The last model is known as the *Complete Trust model*. This is a network where there are several domains and each domain is administered as

separate system. No single domain exerts any control over any other domain, trust relationships are set up between individual domains to allow administration of user accounts rights and securities across the other domains. Such a complex network it is vital to have full-time network administrators who are properly trained and experienced. These networks are very far removed from simple workgroup networks!

Printers and other output devices

Networked printers are *logically* detached from desktop PCs. If you login to a client–server network with at least one printer or any other output devices such as a pen-plotter, the task of controlling the operation of the printer is carried out by a *print–server.* Bearing in mind the note earlier in this section about the meaning of the word *server*, in this context it means the process by which the printing task is controlled. With more than one user on the network, the task of printing documents becomes more complex, these documents must be queued, i.e. printed in a controlled order. Whilst it is usual to print on a first-come-first-served basis, it is possible to jump the queue and get your job printed next, assuming the network has given you sufficient network rights to do that. The print–server must also cope with printer failures, the simplest being running out of paper, the user is notified and an operator requested to load more. The idea of separating the printing process is quite old in the computer world, even old simple systems could *spool* jobs to a printer. Spool means Simultaneous Peripheral Operation On-Line which is a fancy name for a system that allows you to get on with your work whilst another part of the system looks after your printing. Even old versions of MS-DOS could queue multiple print jobs to a printer.

To achieve networked printing, the document to be printed is stored as a *print file* under the control of the print–server. A print file is not the text or image that is to be printed but a set of codes understandable by the printer. In the case of a PostScript printer, this code is the language PostScript, a language that was designed by Adobe and had as a predecessor, the language Forth. Other printers uses PCL or Printer Control Language, a system designed by Hewlett-Packard. These are page description languages that are *interpreted* by the printer.

Mass storage

Mass storage refers to hard-drives, tapes, etc. These are often installed in a *file server*, a server whose dedicated task is to store files of different types, e.g. application software, data and system information.

A file server is usually a powerful machine with fast, large capacity mass storage devices as the demands on the machine are often high. If many people use the network and require software or data more or less at the same time, a high performance machine is required to provide that service.

The data on the mass storage device must be organized in such a way that it can be retrieved reliably but also in a way that is secure. Windows NT is able to 'talk to' data stored in different ways but the core system is called NTFS, NT File System.

The key features of NTFS are:

- Volumes up to 16 Eb in size can be supported. An exa byte is 10^{18} bytes. As a Gb is 10^9, an Eb is 10^9 Gb or a giga giga bytes!
- NTFS offers *journaling*, a system related to rollback in databases. A journal in this case is a file that logs system activity; in the event of a system crash, this log can be used to complete or undo recent changes.
- Offers full multiuser security based on Access Control Lists. This system is used to control permissions to file, directories etc. and is more flexible than Unix style permissions.
- Filenames are stored in *Unicode*, allowing multilanguage filenames.
- Files can contain multiple data streams, i.e. one name points to several data areas. As Macintosh files are stored in two pieces (resource and data fork), Mac files are easily stored in NTFS.
- NTFS versions are not all backward compatible, NT ver. 3.x cannot read ver. 4 NTFS file system.
- NTFS can 'talk' to a number of other file systems allowing reading and writing of files to/from systems such as Macintosh HFS or of Sun's Network Filing System (NFS), etc.

NTFS uses a B-tree. Tree data-structures can be searched very much faster than simple arrays or lists.

File servers frequently use one or more RAID systems, a Redundant Array of Independent Disks. This is where multiple hard disks are used to take advantage of better MTBF or Mean Time Between Failure. It is hoped that by decreasing the chance that all the data will be lost if one drive fails, better physical security is achieved. Experience sometimes disappoints!

Physical security of the data can be improved by frequent backups. A backup is where some or all of the data on the file server is copied to a physically separate location. This location is best off-site to avoid data loss in the event of a fire. A *complete backup* copies the entire disk contents and is suitable for use after a complete system failure. An *incremental backup* copies just those files that were created or modified since the last backup. This kind is suitable for use when a few files are lost or corrupted. A complete backup requires some time, especially if tape drives are used. Tapes are slow but cheap. Generally system administrators are reluctant to use a complete backup to retrieve a single lost file so many network users backup their own data files!

> Unicode is a 16-bit character code. The older ASCII uses an 8-bit code allowing $2^8 = 256$ different characters, enough for one language at a time like English but not sufficient for multiple simultaneous languages. As Unicode is a 16-bit code, it allows $2^{16} = 65536$ characters, enough for all languages at once.

5.14 Network administration

A *Network Operating System* (NOS) controls the network. This control entails many different tasks at different layers in the layered architecture. For instance, a major function of a NOS is to provide security but still allow easy access for legitimate users. A NOS such as *Windows NT 4* provides the Network Administrator with a range of tools to manage such tasks. Examples are:

- The *DHCP Administrator* manages the Dynamic Host Control Protocol, a protocol that manages the DCHP servers on the network. DHCP is a TCP/IP protocol that allows client PCs TCP/IP settings to be set up remotely instead of having an IT Support technician visit each machine individually.
- *RAS Administrator*, this is used to Manage Remote Users.
- The *Server Manager* is used to administer the properties of other servers on the network

- *User Profile Editor*. This tool defines user profiles. A profile is a collection of settings that apply to user accounts, these include the running of a script at login time.
- *User Manager.* As the name suggests, manages the user properties of those allowed to use the network.
- *WINS Administrator*. WINS, the Windows Internet Name Service, translates TCP/IP network addresses into human readable names and vice-versa. This software tool is used to administer WINS.

You should have at least some experience of using these or similar network administration tools but as local installations vary so much, it is not intended to include any more practical detail here.

Installation and management tasks should include:

- management of users;
- workgroup management;
- setting up login scripts;
- printing and managing printer queues;
- installation and configuration of applications;
- file server installation and utilities;
- creating large numbers of accounts;
- control and tracing of resource usage;
- installing a piece of network software onto a server to be used by different selected users or groups;
- configure user workstations on the network.

5.15 Network security

Data security, hacking, virus protection and firewalls are very much a 'hot topic' because networks are attacked by morons or criminals.

These people lead such sad lives that they get some kind of pleasure by gaining access to computers, to see what is there but more often to destroy it. Whilst no network can ever be proof against this kind of attack, networks can have good security that prevents damage in from most attacks. Attacks can take the form of:

- Hacking, to gain entry to the system.
- Denial of service attacks that cause a great deal system activity, so much activity that users are denied service.
- Viruses, code that is written to damage data on systems. To be a virus, the code must replicate itself, thereby doing more damage by being carried automatically around different computers and networks.
- Trojans, damaging code that forms part of innocent code so is distributed by well-meaning systems.

Much of the above can be controlled by the use of a firewall but much can be done to avoid damage by good housekeeping.

Hackers attack networks for profit, to be malicious or just 'because it is there'. They do not need any special knowledge because hacking tools are easily obtained from the Internet as is advice on how to attack networks and lists of the latest hacks. Some hackers just do it for kicks but some are very proficient people bent on criminal or at least immoral gain. These people are all a real nuisance.

Why should you protect a network?

You need to keep your intellectual property from the eyes of your competitors. Much of your data is very expensive to generate, loss or damage can put you out of business.

Consider that when a hacker gains access to a network, they may have just had a 'look' at what is there and gone elsewhere. If you cannot be very sure that nothing is modified, your loss is still potentially very large as you must now examine every part of every file to make sure no damage has been done. Even if you have a complete system backup, you must be sure the backed up data was secure before the backup was created. As many hacks are only discovered later on, you may well find that backups several generations old may now be compromised.

The kinds of damage that hackers do are:

- Stealing your data.
- Fraudulent use of your data or funds.
- Denial of Service attacks that stop you using the network.
- Changing your data for any reason including fraud.
- Politically motivated acts.

Firewalls

A *firewall* is a piece of software usually but not always running on a dedicated computer or piece of hardware such as a router. It acts by controlling access to your network from the outside. A firewall defines which parts of the internal system can be seen from the outside and can also act in reverse, it can control what outside services are visible from inside.

Firewalls block incoming hacker attacks; they also use Network Address Translation (NAT) to hide much of the detail in the network traffic so it looks like it all comes from one machine.

The software can be set to screen traffic from:

- a predefined set of addresses;
- a predefined set of users;
- traffic that contains certain kinds of data.

One of the tools used by hackers is the port scanner. This is a piece of software that looks at the structure of a network. Hackers can use this information to target one or more of its parts.

Denial of service attacks are launched by a hacker sending large amounts of data to an address so tying up the machine. To do this the hacker needs the IP address. If a firewall is in place, the IP address is not available as it is hidden. In this case the firewall can react by ignoring the incoming data and even detect to some extent the origin of the attack. Hackers however are aware of this and take steps to hide themselves. Hackers have firewalls of their own.

Firewalls come in different types such as:

- packet filter;
- application-level proxy servers;
- statefull packet inspection.

A *Packet Filter Firewall* works with IP packets in the TCP/IP protocol stack. Packets are examined for their IP address, TCP/IP port number and the type of data. The system administrator can set the controls to many different levels. Although a powerful means to protect data, this method is difficult to set up and small errors can leave a system open to attack. Hackers are adept at what is called 'IP spoofing' that makes the IP address seem as though it has come from a reliable source.

An *Application Level Proxy Server* works on the top-level layers of the protocol stack, i.e. at the application that is using the data. This means that a different proxy server must be set up for each application, e.g. one for the web's http protocol, another for e-mail and a third for ftp, the file transfer protocol.

A firewall that uses *Statefull Packet Inspection* examines every aspect of data packets. Data that was not requested is rejected (because un-requested data may be unreliable). Data that was requested is also checked. This type of firewall is said to be the most reliable.

Some firewalls must work to protect networks where non-requested data packets will arrive. Public servers that provide Internet connections, e-mail servers etc. get non-requested data as part of their normal work. Firewalls that have the rather oddly named feature, the *Demiltarized Zone* allow access to certain parts of the system but lock users, even registered users, out of most of the system. Such firewalls also provide a measure of anti-virus protection and support for encryption.

Virtual private networks

Virtual private networks (VPNs) or VLANs (*Virtual Local Area Networks*) are those networks that use a publicly available system to physically attach to a network but one set of users are kept private from all others by firewalls. System like this are used by people such as employees of one company who can login from anywhere in the world using public telecommunication systems but the network will 'look' like a private one. Clearly the systems are prone to hacker attacks as the physical connection is there. VPNs benefit from the use of data encryption as any hacker to succeed in getting data from the system will not be able to read it. This does not mean that total security has been achieved because you will not be able to tell what has been deleted and encryption will not prevent denial of service attacks.

The other side of the security issue

Legislation

It should be noted that some governments have already made data encryption illegal and other governments are looking to follow their example. Other governments allow encryption provided that a way in for the government is allowed via a *Trusted Third Party*. The reasons given are that police forces need to be able to detect crimes such as illegal drug dealing, sex offenders or terrorists. Whatever the validity of this argument, many people are of the opinion that the chief government concern is their lack of power of taxation over international business transactions. Consider that if you obtain services such as the supply of software from an international source, your home government will not be able to tax you. This has the potential to 'lose' very large amounts of revenue for the home government.

People

Firewalls and related security is administered by one or two individuals in a company, or at the very least, a single department. In most cases this is fine except that these people must be trusted absolutely, they have the security key for the whole business. These people will be a position to do much more damage than a hacker attack, indeed many hackers have been found to have insider information.

The issue of data security will become more and more important as countries move toward the 'information society'. Information is power and those who hold the key to power must be trusted.

There is an often overlooked feature of security, that of the loss of usefulness of the system if it is over protected. It is an unfortunate fact that some humans like locking things away. An IT manager may decide that a given feature on a network is at risk so then decides to set the network operating system security features to prevent some (or all) users from seeing it or using it. This is fine if this manager actually understands the business needs of the organization but can cause real problems when systems are locked or hidden for no good reason.

An example is when networked printers are set for use by a restricted group of people. For example, if person A wishes to print, they are only allowed to print in their own office. This looks fine as it prevents accidental printing in other parts of the building; the 'reason' to lock things away like this is to prevent confidential documents being seen by others accidentally. On the other hand, it may well be that a particular job requires another printer (it may produce colour or print on special paper, etc.). In this case, person A will have to approach some other person to print their work. If the system is locked up, this may be quite inconvenient so person A may well shy away from such efforts and work in a different and less advantageous way, losing some of the benefit of the network. Had the IT manager properly understood the situation, the locking may not be so widespread.

A fact that compounds this situation is the lack of knowledge on the part of many network users about what is or is not possible, they will assume that if a system is not provided, it must not be possible to provide. This is another reason why those in charge of networks must be trusted absolutely, they have an important part to play in the profitability of the organization but equally, may well be preventing better use of the investment put into their care.

6 Personal skills development

Summary

The aim of this chapter is to provide support and guidance to students so that they can develop their practical, interpersonal and transferable skills at a professional level. Personal skills development examines how individuals can critically examine their own knowledge and skill base and develop this with the aid of practical activities: group work, analysis and evaluation.

Industry's perception of 'employability' has shifted over recent years and the requirement for candidates to have good social skills rates highly in the criteria for selection. Technical expertise alone no longer guarantees employment, the balance between theoretical knowledge and practical application has shifted, in many cases to the hands-on approach.

Students will be expected to produce a range of documents, using different data capture, input, processing and output tools and techniques to include: interviewing, report writing, group work and presentations. Students will also be encouraged to appraise certain activities and evaluate their own performance.

Introduction

In today's ever-growing competitive culture, individuals need to be as diverse as possible whilst still retaining their technical skills and knowledge base. The need for diversity can be applied to the way in which an individual projects themselves, verbally and visually. How well can an individual analyse, communicate and evaluate information? How well can an individual function within a team environment and does an individual have the skills and ability to be objective and assess their own performance and development?

This chapter will attempt to address each of these questions by introducing ways to encourage personal skill development. This will be achieved through the application of learning tools and techniques, introduction to set theories on management styles, team building and group dynamics and by encouraging students to reflect on their own personal development.

6.1 Transferable skills

Transferable skills what are they? The boundary around this subject area is quite protean in that there is no definite categorization of what can be included as a transferable skill, but equally any skill that can be transferred could be included.

This chapter attempts to reintroduce students to the basics of communication tools and techniques with the aim of developing their written, visual and oral skills through report writing, production of formal documents, presentations and graphical extracts.

Effective communication

Communication is a way of projecting ideas and thoughts from one person or party to another. To enable effective communication there needs to be three main elements a source, communication tool and a recipient, as shown in Figure 6.1.1.

Figure 6.1.1 *Elements to enable effective communication*

All information will originate from a source of some description. The source generates or initiates the information that is to be sent. Sources of information can include:

- Human resources (people).
- Electronic resources (computer systems, etc.).

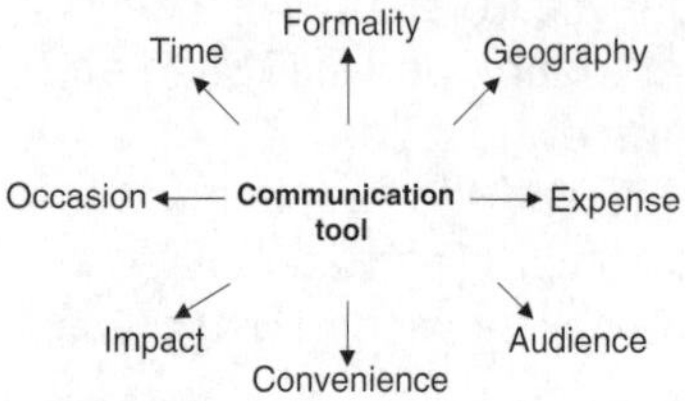

The type of communication tool that is required to transmit the information will vary depending upon a number of factors, some of these factors are identified in Figure 6.1.2. Some communication tools may be more appropriate than others, because of their convenience and or flexibility. For example, the quickest way to get a response to a question from a person sitting next to you is to ask, the communication tool being 'speech'. However, if this person had a hearing impediment the most effective form might then be 'body language', 'sign language' or a form of written communication.

Figure 6.1.2 *Factors determining communication tool use*

Formality: There are instances when a specific communication tool is required to match the formality of the situation. Written communication above other communication tools provides the formality to make certain contracts and transactions legally binding for e.g. birth, marriage and death certificates, employment contracts and the guarantees offered by documents such as receipts.

Geography: The distance over which the communication has to travel will influence the type of tool to be used. It would not be feasible to shout over a distance of 10 miles, it would be more practical to use the telephone, or send an e-mail.

Expense: Different communication tools have different costs. Depending upon the frequency and priority of the communication, costs could range from a few pence (price of a stamp) to hundreds of thousands of pounds (setting up and co-ordinating global teleconferencing facilities).

Audience: The audience or target group will influence the communication tool used to express information. Within an organization you might chat informally to a colleague, e-mail a team leader and send a memorandum to the department.

Convenience: Some communication tools are more convenient to use than others. Sending an e-mail may be more convenient than writing and posting a letter, however to a non-technical individual sending a letter may be more convenient than trying to learn how to send an e-mail.

Impact: An impression that needs to be created can influence the choice of communication tool. It is unlikely that an employer would send an e-mail to a potential employee offering them a contract of employment.

Occasion: This can determine the type of communication tool to be used, for e.g. a birthday might trigger the sending of a card – written format. A meeting with a business colleague might result in the use of physical communication such as a handshake.

Time: A communication tool may be selected based on how long it takes to transmit the information, for e.g. it might be necessary to send a document by fax rather than post because of the urgency of the information.

The final component required to enable effective communication is a recipient. The recipient in conjunction with the sender can be a human or electronic resource. Once information has been received the recipient can respond in a number of different ways:

- firstly, they themselves or the system can pass on this information making them or the system both a receiver and a sender;
- secondly, they or the system can carry out an action as a result of the information received, therefore activating a process;
- finally, on receipt of the information they or the system can do nothing, retaining the information and storing it within their own memory bank as shown in Figure 6.1.3.

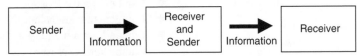

Information is sent to the receiver, who then passes it on to a third party. The recipient thus having a dual role of recipient and sender.

Information is sent to the receiver, who then carries out an action and processes the formation received.

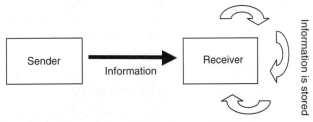

Information is sent to the receiver who stores it within their own memory bank.

Figure 6.1.3 *Actions of a recipient of information*

Ways of communicating

It has been established that for effective communication to take place there needs to be three components, a source, communication tool and a recipient. However, another factor that will influence the effectiveness of communication is the communication format.

Communication can broadly be categorized into four main areas, these are:

- Verbal
- Written
- Visual
- Expressive

Verbal communication

Verbal communication implies that information has been transmitted through speech. Categories of verbal communication can include:

- Enquiring
- Delegating
- Directing
- Advising
- Informing
- Challenging
- Debating
- Persuading

Advantages of verbal communication

Verbal communication has its advantages in that it can be a very open format of communication especially if it is face to face. Other more specific advantages include:

- Can be directed to a specific individual or target audience.
- Can generate an instant response or action.
- Can address a range of audience, single or multiple.
- Can be very expressive.
- Can be quite inexpensive or free (if face to face).

Disadvantages of verbal communication

One of the major disadvantages of verbal communication is the fact that it is all too easy to express emotive issues in the spare of the moment that may not have been expressed if another form of communication had been used. An example of this is, it is easier to demonstrate discontentment over a matter verbally than to write it down in a letter if confronted by the third party. The spontaneity of verbal communication and sometimes the lack of control over emotions can then spill into conversations or disputes.

Interviewing

It is very possible that at some point an individual will be required to attend an interview. An interview may be required for a place into higher education, work placement, training or for a job. Interviews are a standard way of assessing how candidates present themselves, sometimes within a manufactured environment.

Interviews are conducted for a number of reasons, some of these include:

- face-to-face contact to assess how you look and how you present yourself;
- fact-finding exercise to identify what you have done in your academic, social and work life;
- clarify key areas as stipulated on an application form or curriculum vitae;
- assess personality and interpersonal skills.

Interviews are to establish whether you are the right person for the position advertised.

There are a number of ways that interviews are conducted, these can include:

- Telephone interview
- One-to-one interview
- Panel or group interview

Telephone interviews are usually the first stage in the selection process for some candidates, especially if there are a number of applicants. You might be asked a set of questions that require you to draw upon your experiences in order to answer them.

> **Example: Can you give me an example based on your own experiences where you have had to overcome a problem involving other people.**

The telephone interview could also be set up purely to establish your skills and knowledge base in preparation for a second face-to-face interview.

One-to-one interviews are very common, you may be invited in to attend a set appointment with an admissions officer, course tutor, human resource manager or department manager. In a one-to-one interview you are being assessed against a number of criteria as identified in Figure 6.1.4.

Figure 6.1.4 *Interview criteria*

In an interview first impression is very important, therefore you should present yourself appropriately for the occasion, e.g. wearing a suit for a formal interview.

An ability to answer questions put forward clearly and comprehensively when required demonstrates that you have listened and understood a direct verbal action and that you are competent enough either technically, logically or creatively in putting forward a reasoned response. In conjunction your ability to communicate will be assessed against responses given.

In an interview situation a range of interpersonal skills are being assessed. The quality of your written skills may have been demonstrated initially through the submission of an application letter, form and/or curriculum vitae. Verbal skills will be assessed continuously throughout the interview through question and answer and more qualitative statements provided by the candidate. An ability to interact appropriately with the interviewer could demonstrate qualities of being a good team player, manager or independent individual.

Linked to body language, your disposition could reveal traits of being directed, determined, confident and motivated, etc.

Attending an interview can be categorized as a marketing exercise – the product being promoted being yourself. You may only have a short while to sell your skills and qualities and to convince the interviewer that you are the right applicant for the position.

To aid in this process the following eight-step interview points should be acknowledged:

Interview points to remember:

1. *Plan* – you may be competing with a number of other candidates and you may only get one chance to impress, so make sure that you plan in advance what you want to say and how you want to say it, given the opportunity.
2. *Research* – if you can research around the company or education institutes background and find out additional information.

   > Example: If you were applying for a job find out about the organization, its structure, what it does, financial situation, recent coverage, etc.

3. *Present* – dress for the occasion and arrive relaxed and prepared. Ensure that you have another copy of your curriculum vitae, a copy of the job role/specification, evidence of your skills and knowledge, e.g. certificates, record of achievement, letters of commendation, references, etc. If appropriate also bring evidence of your skills which are appropriate to the job role. For example, if you were applying to be a web designer, bring a portfolio of your work and web page designs.
4. *Body language* – always be aware of your body language in an interview situation because some people find themselves tapping fingers, crunching teeth or looking down at the floor without realizing it.
5. *Be alert and attentive* – look enthusiastic and motivated, maintain eye contact (but do not constantly stare as this can be off-putting), feel confident in the situation, respond to questions, do not be afraid to ask for a second to reflect upon an answer if you require it, or to repeat a question if you are not sure.
6. *Sell yourself* – you have reached the interview because you have the skills and knowledge otherwise you would not have applied. You know this but the interviewer may not, all they have is an application form and curriculum vitae. This is your chance to shine, tell your interviewer what you have done and what you are capable of doing, without being too arrogant or lying. Convince them that you are the person they want.
7. *Listen* – listening skills are very important especially in an interview situation. Do not interrupt constantly, wait until you are prompted to give a response. When listening, acknowledge what is being said by smiling or nodding occasionally. As you listen, reflect on what is being said and prepare your response.
8. *Question* – if you can always think of a question to ask at the end, this could be related to the specifics of the job role. For example, I understand that you have six functional areas within the IT department does this mean that the successful applicant will be able to gain experience in working in a range of these areas.

Panel or group interviews are usually set up to provide a range of people access to prospective candidates. The objective of a panel interview is that different skills and information can be recognized from different people on the panel, each panel member possibly assessing different things such as technical knowledge, ability to work in a team, academic skills or interpersonal skills, etc.

Written communication

Written communication is of great importance because of the warranty or assurances that it provides. Filling in an application form for e.g. is identifying and providing assurances of the knowledge and skills of the applicant. Producing a curriculum vitae provides a written confirmation of ability and suitability for a particular task. A receipt is a warranty verifying the sale of an item. Certificates verify an achievement in a particular area such as swimming, qualifications, birth, marriage or death.

Written communication can take on a number of forms and serve a range of purposes and audiences. Written communication can be divided into two categories:

- formal
- informal

Formal written communication relates to official documents that provide guarantees and assurances, these documents can be legally binding. Within an organization formal documents can also include reports, financial summaries and company policies, standards and procedures, e.g. health and safety.

Informal written communication includes more casual documentation such as letters to friends, memos, e-mails and greetings, etc.

Written documents vary in terms of styles and layouts each document type having its own set of criteria that makes it unique. Common documents that have their own unique styling include:

- Letters
- Memorandums
- Reports
- Agendas
- Minutes

Letters

Letters are one of the most common forms of written communication. The style of a letter can vary depending upon the sender, recipient and subject matter, however the overall layout of a letter has four generic qualities that can be broken down into:

1. The identifier/s
2. The introduction
3. The content
4. The closure

The identifiers include items such as the sender and the recipient details such as name and address, the date, any reference codes and identification of who the letter is for.

Identifiers within a letter

Mr James Pearson
46 Crescent Avenue
Little Hampton
Norfolk
NR33 6DL

Mr Graham Green
100 Acres Cottage
Dunnington
Suffolk
IP2 5TL

19 June 2003

Reference: BC112/00P13

Dear Mr Green

The introduction should provide a short overview as to the content and also set the tone for the remainder of the letter.

Letter introduction

Application to join the East Anglia Interactive Computing Group

After reading the advertisement in 'Buzz Computing' I would like to subscribe for a 12-month period to your interactive computing group.

The content of the letter should contain the bulk of the information. The content should be set out clearly and specifically, ensuring that the subject matter is factual and relevant to the audience.

Contents of a letter

Your advertisement in Buzz Computing on 4 June Reference: BC112/ 00P13 invited applications from keen gaming players to subscribe to a new computer interactive group being set up in East Anglia.

My interest in computers and games consoles has increased over the last year with me acquiring a number of rare games consoles and software, which can be considered as 'retro' items. I also enjoy interactive on-line adventure gaming sessions and role-play scenarios.

I feel that I could contribute to your group in a number of ways. Firstly I have an extensive knowledge of hardware and software. I am also a keen programmer and a software enthusiast. I also submit regular on-line reviews of new games to the 'What's New in Computing' magazine.

> I enclose a cheque for £85.00 in respect of 12 months subscription to your computing group, and I hope that you accept my application.
>
> I look forward to hearing from you in the near future.

The closure section focuses on signing off the letter, and informing the recipient of any other documents that are also being sent. The recipient will expect additional documents if Enc. (Enclosure) appears at the end of the letter. In this example, the additional information will be the £85.00 cheque.

Letter closure

> Yours faithfully
>
>
> James Pearson
> Computing Enthusiast
>
>
> Enc.

Complete letter template

> Senders Information
>
> **Mr James Pearson**
> 46 Crescent Avenue
> Little Hampton
> Norfolk
> NR33 6DL
>
> ---
>
> If there is no letterhead the address could go to the right hand margin:
>
> **Mr James Pearson**
> 46 Crescent Avenue
> Little Hampton
> Norfolk
> NR33 6DL
>
> *Recipient Information*
>
> Mr Graham Green
> 100 Acres Cottage
> Dunnington
> Suffolk
> IP2 5TL
>
> Date: 19 June 2003
>
> Reference Number: BC112/00P13 (if applicable)
>
> Salutation: For the attention of Mr Graham Green

Introduction: Application to join East Anglia Interactive Computing Group

Content:

_____

_____

_____

_____

_____

Closure:
Yours faithfully

James Pearson

A letter can be considered as a formal or informal document depending upon the subject matter and audience. A letter could also be classified as being legally binding.

There are a range of other documents that have their own unique styling, some of which are unique to organizations these include memorandums, agendas, minutes and reports.

Memorandums ⟶ Informal document used to communicate general information, not of a confidential nature

Reports ⟶ Used to collate information and provide formal feedback

Agenda ⟶ Used to structure the contents of a meeting in an orderly way

Minutes ⟶ Records the actions taken at a meeting and the people present

Figure 6.1.5   *Documents that can be used within an organization*

Memorandums

Memorandums or memos are used internally within an organization, they are an informal way of communicating and documenting data.

Memorandum template

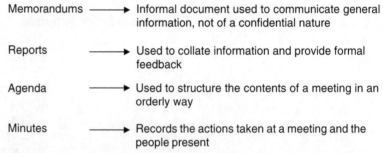

Memorandum

To:
From:
cc:
Date:
Re:

Body of text would be displayed here

Within an organization there are other documents that are used to inform and prepare users, some of these include reports, agendas and minutes.

Reports

Reports are used to collate and present information to a particular audience. A report could be generated as a result of a meeting where actions have to be researched in order to complete a task and feedback to a given audience. Formal written reports should follow a set structure that covers specific areas.

Layout for a formal report

Title page: front sheet identifying the report title, the author, date and who the report is commissioned for.

Staff Restructuring Proposals

Author: Andrew Granger

22 July 2003
Commissioned for Human Resources

Contents page: page referencing the information given on each page, should follow the title page.

Contents

Section layout

1.0 *Introduction*: the introduction should provide a short summary of the overall focus and content of the report.

2.0 *Procedures*: identification of any procedures used to collect, collate, analyse and present information.

3.0 *Main findings*: the main findings section is where the bulk of the report content should be placed. The main findings section should be broken down into task, action or research areas. Each area of the findings section should put forward arguments or statements supported by research and analysis. The main findings section can be broken down further into sub-sections, for example:

3.1　Marketing resources
3.11　Staffing levels
3.12　ICT support
3.13　Staff training

4.0　*Conclusions*: the conclusion section should bring together all of the items discussed within the main findings section and provide a summary of the key areas identified.

5.0　*Recommendations*: this section is solution based, providing the subjects of the report with proposals as to how they can move forward with the report objective. For example, recommendations for staff training could include:

1. Provide residential management training to all supervisors and section managers.
2. Offer in-house ICT training programmes to all data entry clerks within the marketing department.
3. Set up staff training services on a rotary basis of three employees each week for 8 weeks.

6.0　*References*: this section should identify and give credit for all information sources used to include; books, magazines or journals, other documents or reports, and the Internet, etc.

7.0　*Appendices*: this section will provide supporting documentation to give additionality to the report content. Appendices could include lists of facts and figures, leaflets, downloaded information, photocopied material, etc.

Agendas

Agendas are used within an organization to set out a timetable of activities or events in preparation for a meeting, as shown in figure. Agendas provide the structure to a meeting, setting out individual actions to be addressed.

Template for an agenda

AGENDA
Staff Committee Meeting

Tuesday 5 August 2003
Room 7

1. Restructuring programme
2. Appointment of new Section Leader
3. Retirement party for J. Norson
4. New canteen facilities
5. Staff outing proposals
6. Any other issues

Minutes

Minutes are another form of written communication, which are taken during a meeting. The minutes, document items discussed on the agenda and can also be used to provide action planning by nominating people to carry out certain tasks. Minutes also introduce items that were discussed at a previous meeting, and record who is in attendance at the current meeting.

Presentation of written information

The way in which written material is presented can effect the way in which it is interpreted and understood. Factors that can influence apprehension of written materials include:

- Quantity and volume
- Language and style
- Layout

The quantity of pages within a book or other reading source can have an impact on how easily the material is understood. Trying to master a thousand page book on the uses and applications of software could be unproductive if all you need is a couple of pages outlining how to set up a spreadsheet.

In conjunction reading a few pages on surgery would not qualify you to perform surgery.

The way in which a written document is expressed in terms of technical language and formality can also influence the reader. There are certain expectations that some reading materials will be presented in a particular way, examples of these include:

- Exam papers
- Instruction manuals
- Course textbooks
- Letters
- Legal documents

If you picked up a romance novel you would expect the language to be informal and familiar set out within the context of telling a story. A course text book however would be more technical, outlining specific techniques or theories in a more formal way.

The layout of a book can influence how you respond to the text. Layout can refer to a number of aspects including:

1. Size of fonts
2. Font style
3. Pictures, graphics or cartoons

4. Photographic inserts

5. Steps and instructions
   - Fill the kettle
   - Press the switch
   - Pour out boiled water
   - Refill kettle
6. Tasks, case studies and exercises

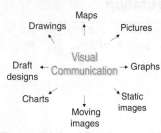

Figure 6.1.9 *Visual communication tools*

Visual communication

Visual communication incorporates a range. Examples of visual communication tools are shown in Figure 6.1.9.

Visual communication tools can be broken down even more specifically, for example – maps:

- underground maps
- ordnance survey maps
- street maps
- mind maps

Maps provide a visual guide aiding direction to a certain point. Maps provide navigational information, which could not be interpreted as easily in a textual format.

Pictures, drawings and static images are used for a number of different purposes which range from providing a general understanding, such as a picture of the human anatomy to humour such as cartoons and comic strips.

Graphs and charts are used to provide visual support to data and tables providing a clear breakdown of key data components.

Different graphs and charts are used to represent different information, some of the more popular ones in use include:

Pie charts

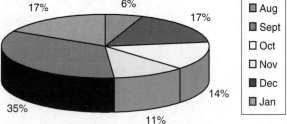

Each segment of the pie chart represents a percentage of games consoles sold for each month from August to January. The smallest segment is 6% for August and the largest is 35% for December.

Bar graphs

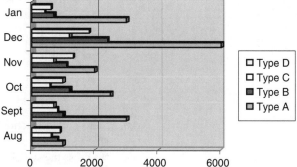

The bars on the graph represent a type of games console ranging from A to D. The bar graph identifies for each month, how many of each console was sold.

Line graphs

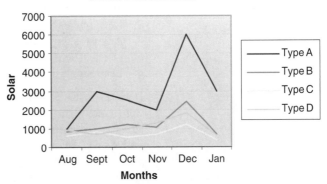

The line graph clearly plots the sales of each console from August to January. It is very evident that Type A console is the best seller and Type C console is the worst seller. From this graph it is also clear that in August, September and January sales were very similar for Types B, C and D.

Scatter graphs

Scatter graphs are best used when there is a lot of numerical data that requires plotting to identify a correlation or pattern in the data. This specific scatter graph is illustrating the pattern of sales for each month 1–6. In August it clearly shows that all four games console types had similar sales figures, however in December these are quite diverse.

Interpreting graphs

Graphs can provide a great deal of information, the one below illustrating the sales of games consoles.

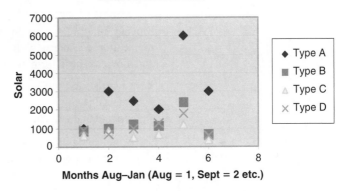

The level of information that can be obtained from the graph includes:

1. Type A console has the greatest sales.
2. Type C console has the smallest sales.
3. December is the best month for sales.
4. August is the worst month for sales.
5. Greatest single console sales is just under 6000 for Type A.
6. Least single console sale is about 300 for Type C.

However, visual communication in itself may not be sufficient. If the titles were removed the graph would make little sense, also the total sales figures have large boundaries extending up in thousands. To provide a more detailed analysis raw data would also need to be included to allow for a more comprehensive understanding and interpretation. With this information more specific calculations such as average sales for example can be made.

Sales of Games Consoles 2001/2002						
	August	*September*	*October*	*November*	*December*	*January*
Type A	1000	3000	2500	2000	6000	3000
Type B	800	1000	1200	1100	2400	700
Type C	600	800	550	700	1200	400
Type D	900	700	1000	1300	1800	600

Moving images have become one of the most important forms of communication especially with the ever increasing popularity of television and movies. These formats of moving images have been used to:

- advertise and sell
- entertain
- instruct and educate

The new medium of communication can be classed as film and television, where actors, actresses, television personalities and soap stars seem to control what we wear, how we live, what we say and do.

Draft designs

Drafts are used for a range of purposes especially in engineering, construction and manufacturing. Draft designs provide the basis for fully implemented plans some examples of drafts and plans include car designs, architectural drawings and housing developments – see Figure 6.1.15.

Visual communication provides a more expressive and colourful alternative to sending and receiving information in a written format.

Expressive communication

Expressive communication is given to the category of communication which includes body signs and language, also within this category falls BSL (British Sign Language) which is a language in its own right.

Expressive communication can include a range of actions such as:

- Smiling
- Frowning
- Waving
- Laughing
- Crying

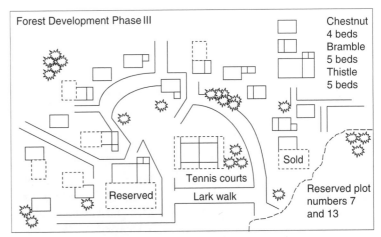

Figure 6.1.15   *Plans for a new housing development*

Each action communicating a specific thought or mood, for e.g. you might frown to express your discontent at a situation or smile to embrace it.

Presentations

Good presentation skills are essential for progression into higher education, training or employment. From the moment that you convey verbal or expressive communication, people will have expectations on your ability to present information clearly, cohesively, relevantly and knowledgeably. These expectations in some cases are so high that your future or career could be dependent upon the way you have presented yourself.

Presentations can be classified as being formal and informal.

Formal presentations can include:

- interview for a job or a place at College or University;
- providing feedback on a project at work;
- representation at a meeting;
- press release;
- awards ceremony speech.

Informal presentations can include:

- presentation given as part of an HND unit;
- feeding back events of a holiday or an event to a friend;
- thank you/congratulations speech to friends or family.

Delivering a presentation

Presentations can be delivered in a number of ways to include:

- Reading from cards and sheets, etc.
- Free style.
- Using presentation software.
- Using aids such as flip charts, Over Head Transparencies (OHTs), whiteboard, etc.

Reading from cards

Some people find it quite difficult to recall large amounts of data and information from memory and therefore would require a prompt to aid in the recall process. Prompts that are normally used in presentations are either small index cards that would contain a few bullet points, or a piece/s of paper. Although these presentation aids do help in the actual reciting of information they can also be quite restrictive in terms of the delivery of the presentation.

If a presentation is going to be delivered using a prompt there are a number of points to remember:

1. The information recorded should be kept to a minimum using bullet points only.
2. Glance at the aids, do not read from them.
3. Ensure that the aids are placed discretely, for e.g. on a desk or podium. If they need to be held ensure that they are not covering the face.
4. Maintain a rapport with the audience by establishing eye contact and acknowledging their responses.
5. Using your voice, be in control of the presentation and captivate the audience, the problem with reading from an aid is that sometimes your tone and expression is lost and pitched at a continuous level.
6. Do not rush trough each bullet point use your own creativity to expand on the point.

Freestyle presentations

Free style presentations are usually given by people who:

a. Know their presentation topic well.
b. Are enthusiastic and motivated by the topic and would therefore rely heavily on body language or another tool to demonstrate the topic.
c. Feel very comfortable with their target audience.
d. Draw heavily upon the participation and interactivity of the audience.

To deliver a free style presentation successfully takes a great deal of planning. You could not stand up and deliver a 15-minute presentation on a subject that you have no or very little knowledge of. When you deliver a free style presentation you should be very aware about what the rest of your body is doing or what signals are being given out when you are speaking. There might be a tendency to look down and admire your shoes, make artistic patterns on the floor with your feet, over excessively use your hands or generally fidget.

Using presentation software

ICT has contributed widely to the way in which presentations are delivered and the overall quality of delivery. The use of applications providing a range of benefits to include:

- Can be easy to use.
- Can be quick to use.
- Provides step-by-step designs.
- Allows for interactivity.
- Integration of sound and images both static and moving.
- Wide availability.
- Ability to customize each presentation.

Presentation software can provide a whole range of features that will enable you to:

- Customize slide background/wallpaper.
- Control the speed of each slide.

- Determine the way in which the slide appears onto the screen (e.g. dissolving in).
- Automatically time the length of each slide.
- Link to other applications or the web.

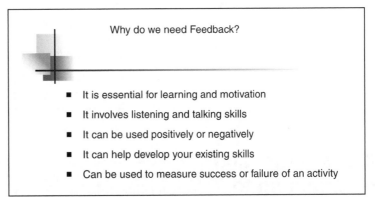

Why do we need Feedback?

- It is essential for learning and motivation
- It involves listening and talking skills
- It can be used positively or negatively
- It can help develop your existing skills
- Can be used to measure success or failure of an activity

Example of presentation software

Using aids

Flip charts, boards or OHTs can assist in the delivery of a presentation. Flip charts are commonly used in the delivery of business presentations to portray sales figures, forecast charts and projection graphs. Flip charts are also useful if you want to encourage audience participation so that thoughts and ideas can be noted and discussed. OHTs are commonly used to display facts and figures and in some case is a preferred substitute to using cards or reading from sheets.

Exercise 6.1.1.

Prepare two 10-minute presentations

Presentation one

You have applied for a job in a large IT company, you have been successful in the first round of interviews and have now been asked to attend a second round that is being assessed on your ability to communicate to a group.

Tasks

Prepare a 10-minute presentation based on one of the following topic areas:

a. The need for team working.
b. The need to communicate at all levels in an organization.
c. The need to delegate.
d. The need to problem solve.

You have half an hour in which to prepare a presentation using any resources available. You must deliver the presentation to your group.

6.2 Working and contributing to groups

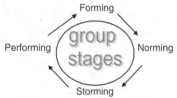

Figure 6.2.1   *Stages of group formation*

There are a number of situations in life that will depend upon individuals working within a group environment. Contributing to a group situation can involve being part of a team at College or University investigating case studies and reporting back the findings. At work, being involved with a project, or assisting colleagues with a particular task or problem. Teamwork can also extend into social environments where individuals might be part of a club or society.

Groups go through various stages of development, Tuckman (1965) identified that the lifecycle of a group evolved around four phases as shown in Figure 6.2.1.

Forming: when individuals try to establish their identity within the group. Can be a strained period as individuals behave differently so as not to upset or offend other group members.

Storming: individuals settle into their normal characters. Personal agendas may start to emerge and challenges for leadership may be made.

Norming: following a period of initial confrontation if the group has survived it will start to become more relaxed and cohesion will set in amongst the group members. Group roles will appear and move towards achieving the group's objectives and will begin to become more established.

Performing: targets will be achieved, individuals will work together to achieve the objectives of the group – a single common goal.

Recognition of a fifth stage is also required. Once the group has achieved its goal/s the stimulus for remaining as a group is removed and so dissolution of the group takes place.

Characteristics of teams

A number of factors can contribute to the effectiveness of a team, some of these include:

● The purpose of the team – what have they been brought together for?
● The environment that the team has to operate in – is it a formal work environment or an informal social environment?
● The constraints imposed upon the team – timescales, budgets, resources, etc.
● The characteristics of the team – who are the individuals, what skills and traits do they bring to the group, etc.

The characteristics of team members, is a very influential factor in how successful or productive a group bonds together. Belbin (1981) suggests that an effective team is made up of people that fulfil a number of roles, these include:

1 **Coordinator**
Characteristics: Mature, confident, good chairperson; clarifies goals; promotes decision making; delegates well; recognises where team's strengths and weaknesses lie and ensures best use is made of each member's potential.
Tolerable Weaknesses: Can be seen as manipulative; offloads personal work.
Suggested Task Allocation: Should be best person to co-ordinate group effort; ensure that everyone has a useful role and team works towards common and agreed goal.

2 **Shaper**
Characteristics: Challenging, dynamic, thrives on pressure; drive and courage to overcome obstacles; shapes way in which team effort is applied, directing attention generally to objectives and priorities; seeks to impose some shape or pattern on group discussion and on outcome of group activities.
Tolerable Weaknesses: Prone to provocation; offends peoples' feelings.
Suggested Task Allocation: Should be person best suited to overcome obstacles and opposition; create a sense of urgency and ensure that talk is turned into worthwhile action.

3 **Plant**
Characteristics: Creative, imaginative, unorthodox; solves difficult problems; redefines problems; advances new ideas and strategies with special attention to major issues and possible breaks in approach to group problem.
Tolerable Weaknesses: Ignores incidentals; too preoccupied to communicate effectively.
Suggested Task Allocation: Should do most problem solving or be responsible for generating new strategies or ideas and proposing solutions to rest of team.

4 **Monitor Evaluator**
Characteristics: Sober, strategic, discerning; sees all options; judges accurately; analyses problems; evaluates ideas and suggestions so team is better placed to take balanced decisions.
Tolerable Weaknesses: Lacks drive and ability to inspire others.
Suggested Task Allocation: Should be responsible for ensuring all worthwhile options are considered; needs a key role in planning; an arbiter in event of controversy.

5 **Resource Investigator**
Characteristics: Extrovert, enthusiastic, communicative; explores opportunities, develops contacts; explores and reports on ideas, developments and resources outside group; creates external contacts that may be useful to team; conducts negotiations.
Tolerable Weaknesses: Over-optimistic; loses enthusiasm once initial enthusiasm has passed.
Suggested Task Allocation: Should be responsible for developing outside contacts and exploring new opportunities; needs a chance to conduct negotiations but must report back to group.

6 **Team Worker**
Characteristics: Supports members in their strengths; e.g. building on suggestions, underpinning members in their shortcomings, improving communications between members and fostering team spirit generally.
Tolerable Weaknesses: Indecisive in crunch situations.
Suggested Task Allocation: Should play a floating role, using versatile qualities to help with features of work that others cannot manage. Should use diplomatic skills to overcome conflict.

7 **Implementer**
Characteristics: Turns concepts and ideas into practical working procedures; carries out agreed plans systematically and efficiently.
Tolerable Weaknesses: Somewhat inflexible. Slow to respond to new possibilities.
Suggested Task Allocation: Should be appointed organiser, responsible for procedures and practical steps to be taken once team reaches significant decisions.

8 **Completer Finisher**
Characteristics: Ensures team is protected as far as possible from mistakes of both commission and omission; actively searches for aspects of work that need a more than usual degree of attention; maintains sense of urgency within team.
Tolerable Weaknesses: Inclined to worry unduly. Slow to respond to new possibilities.
Suggested Task Allocation: Should ensure team's work meets necessary deadlines and conforms to highest standards. Responsible for ensuring no inaccuracies or errors.

9 **Specialist**
Characteristics: Feeds technical information into group; translates from general into technical terms. Contributes professional viewpoint on subject under discussion.
Tolerable Weaknesses: Contributes on only a narrow front; dwells on technicalities.
Suggested Task Allocation: Should provide focus on technical issues confronting team; should provide knowledge and techniques in short supply.

Larson and LaFasto (1989) have also identified effective teamwork attributes, by identifying eight characteristics that could help ensure the success of a group project, these include:

1. a clear, evaluating goal – a sense of mission being created through the development of an objective which is understood, important, worthwhile and challenging;
2. a results-driven structure – the structure and composition of the team should commensurate with the task being undertaken;
3. competent team members – balance of personal and technical competence;
4. unified commitment – creating an environment of 'doing what has to be done to succeed';
5. foster a collaborative climate – encourage reliance on others within the team;
6. standards of excellence – through individual standards, team pressure, knowledge of the consequences of failure;
7. external support and recognition – where good work is performed, recognize it;
8. institute principled leadership.

In order to get the most from team working the following points should be considered:

T talk and communicate with other group members continuously
E enjoy the experience and relax into any given role
A ask questions to ensure that you understand what is expected of you
M motivate yourself and others
W welcome thoughts and ideas from other team members
O offer your skills and knowledge willingly for the benefit of the group
R review and reflect on what you have done and how you could have improved on your contribution
K keep within the framework of any timescales and deadlines
I include others in any decision-making process
N notify the team of any problems sooner rather than later
G Give 100% at all times

6.3 Problem solving

What is a problem – an obstacle, something that you have to overcome or something that requires the application of a solution. Whatever the definition, problems occur on a regular basis, at home, at college or in the workplace.

In order to address a problem some form of reasoning needs to take place. The application of reason being based on a rational or logical decision-making process as shown in Figure 6.3.1.

Within organizations, decisions are made on a frequent basis, these could include:

- the need to reorder stock;
- decisions to down-size, de-layer or make redundancies;
- diversification into new markets or product ranges;
- training staff;
- upgrade the computers/network;
- enforce a more rigorous health and safety policy.

All of these decisions being triggered by underlying problems such as:

- stock shortage and infrequency of deliveries;
- fall in company profits;

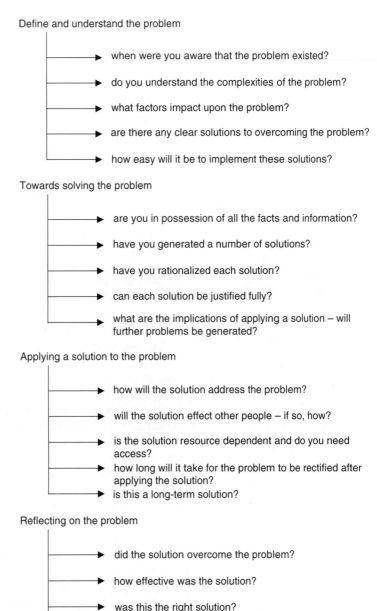

Define and understand the problem

- when were you aware that the problem existed?
- do you understand the complexities of the problem?
- what factors impact upon the problem?
- are there any clear solutions to overcoming the problem?
- how easy will it be to implement these solutions?

Towards solving the problem

- are you in possession of all the facts and information?
- have you generated a number of solutions?
- have you rationalized each solution?
- can each solution be justified fully?
- what are the implications of applying a solution – will further problems be generated?

Applying a solution to the problem

- how will the solution address the problem?
- will the solution effect other people – if so, how?
- is the solution resource dependent and do you need access?
- how long will it take for the problem to be rectified after applying the solution?
- is this a long-term solution?

Reflecting on the problem

- did the solution overcome the problem?
- how effective was the solution?
- was this the right solution?
- are there any repercussions from the application of the solution?
- has the problem gone?

Figure 6.3.1   *Problem solving factors*

- need to remain competitive within the market;
- unskilled workforce with little specialism;
- obsolete system that is inefficient and unreliable;
- lack of knowledge about health and safety procedures amongst employees.

Within organizations decisions are made at a number of different levels. These levels determine the complexity of the problem and the overall impact upon existing resources such as staff, hardware, software, products or premises, etc.

Within a typical organization three levels of management exist, each level representing a different decision type, see Figure 6.3.2.

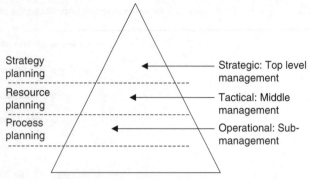

Figure 6.3.2 *Levels and types of decision*

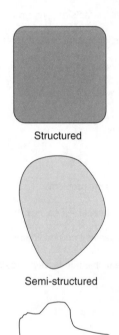

Structured

Semi-structured

Unstructured

Figure 6.3.3 *Three types of decision types*

The strategic level represents the highest levels of management, i.e. managing director, chief executive and senior managers. Decisions at this level encompass planning for the future, strategy decisions such as mergers and take-overs, forecasting markets and trends.

The tactical level represents middle management levels to include heads of departments and assistant directors. The decisions focus on project plans, resource issues and financing.

The operational level focuses on day-to-day decision-making tasks, the mechanics of the organization. This level which is positioned at the base of the organizational structure includes the majority of the work-force at sub-management levels.

Decisions that are made within an organization are not only confined to different levels but conform to various strata running through each level. These decisions can be identified in accordance to the nature of the decision to be made. For example is the decision to do with routine processing and daily tasks, or is the decision more high level focusing on issues of recruitment or company expansion. These three types of decision strata can be referred to as 'structured', 'semi-structured' and 'unstructured' as shown in Figure 6.3.3.

Structured decisions tend to be based on low level or repetitive decisions, for this type of decision there may be a limited number of outcomes.

Semi-structured decisions can be made at all levels of an organization. They strike the balance between everyday routine decisions that require quite a limiting thought process and more unstructured decisions that are more thought provoking and less frequent.

Unstructured decisions tend to be based on higher level decisions, where there could be a wide range of outcomes based upon a complex problem. Unstructured decisions are usually made at a management level, calling upon the expertise and knowledge of the decision-maker. Decisions in this category are made more infrequently and on a much larger scale. An example of an unstructured decision could be whether or not to diversify and launch a new product-line.

Each of the three decision types are not confined to a single organizational level, they will apportion themselves between each level. The bulk of a structured decision however will fall within the operational level, and the bulk of an unstructured decision will appear within the strategic and tactical levels as identified in Figure 6.3.4.

The decision-making process evolves around the selection of a response or action to a particular problem, process or activity. Within an organization decisions at all levels are made and problems are solved on a day-to-day basis.

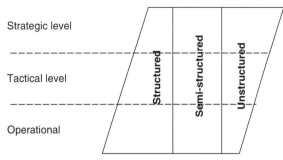

Figure 6.3.4 *Distribution of structured and unstructured decisions within an organization*

Everyday problems can arise that will trigger the decision-making process of rationalizing thoughts and generating solutions, examples of this include:

● how to tackle an assignment;
● where to begin a piece of research;
● which course or pathway to take;
● whether to take a gap year;
● whether to do a sandwich year and get commercial or industrial work experience;
● whether to go to college/university or go straight into the workplace.

Each problem that arises will automatically yield decisions. The thought process in terms of finding a feasible solution taking a second, days or weeks of consideration.

6.4 The learning experience

Individuals learn and develop at different rates. The way in which we learn has been cited as being a cyclical experience by Kolb et al. (1984).

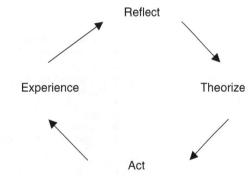

Figure 6.4.1 *Kolb – learning cycle*

Where we do something – enrol onto an HND programme, live the experience, reflect on what has been achieved academically/vocationally and the progress made and then hypothesize about the experience was it positive or negative? What changes could be made to enhance the learning experience next time.

There are a number of underlying skills that can be developed and enhanced to enable individuals to be more effective learners. Some of these skills cover areas of research, reading, writing, language and interpretation skills.

Research skills

To be an effective communicator includes listening, reading and writing skills, arguably another skill that is required to complete the package is that of research skills.

The ability to research a topic will provide greater depth and understanding of the subject matter which can then feed into a conversation or written piece of work.

To be an effective researcher you should follow a set plan as shown in Figure 6.4.2 to ensure that you have a good balance of resources and time.

Start and completion dates: Every research plan will have a start and completion date. These dates are important because it allows you to focus your research on a specific time period, for e.g. a week, 1 month, 6 months.

Objectives of the research: The objectives of any research can be taken from the set tasks of the project or assignment, these could be quite broad, for e.g. 'identify universities in the North of England and Scotland' or quite specific get a UCAS form.

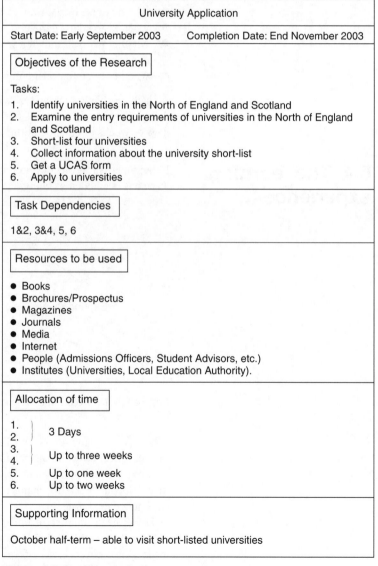

Figure 6.4.2   *Research plan*

Task dependencies: Some of the tasks will have dependencies on another task, these should be identified so that the research can be planned more effectively – why use a particular resource for only one task when it could be used to gather information on two or three tasks.

Resources: Identifying appropriate resources prior to the research will save time and also provide a structure to the research.

Allocation of time: Allocating time to each task is essential because it identifies how and when certain tasks need to be undertaken and if they all fall within the scope of the allocated time.

Additional information: Any additional information will also aid the research plan, in the example used, the October half-term will provide the opportunity to research the short-listed universities by visiting the campuses, after which tasks five and six need to be complete before the end of November which is feasible.

When carrying out a piece of research it is important to record:

- what you have researched;
- where the information has come from;
- when it was collected;
- comments about the research tool.

One way of doing this is to use research templates such as the ones provided in Figures 6.4.3 and 6.4.4.

By using standard templates it is easier to collate the research information together and present the resources more professionally.

Book Title	Author
Date of Publication:	Publisher:
Edition:	ISBN:
Page/s viewed:	
Information Summary:	

Figure 6.4.3   *Book research template*

Search Engine: (if applicable)	Web page address:
Web site category: (academic, commercial, industrial)	Links used:
Summary of site information:	

Figure 6.4.4   *Internet research template*

Research tools

There are a number of research resources that can be used to assist in coursework, personal skills development and work. The range of resources available can be broken down into two categories:

- paper based
- electronic

Paper-based resources include books, magazines and journals, etc. Electronic resources include material accessed via a computer – CD-ROM, the Internet, microfiche, teletext, etc.

The Dewey decimal system

In order to locate reading material in a library a system has been set up to provide easy identification and access to books. This system originates from Melvil Dewey (1851–1931). This systems of categorizing information is based on 10 broad categories, each category identified by a three digit code number which comes before the decimal point:

000.   General books
100.   Philosophy
200.   Religion
300.   Social sciences
400.   Language
500.   Science
600.   Technology
700.   Literature
800.   Geography, history
900.   Biography, autobiography

Each category is further sub-divided into specialist categories:

600.   Technology
610.   Medicine
620.   Engineering
630.   Agriculture

and again into discrete sections which focus on specialist subject areas within that category. For example medicine can be further divided into sections such as surgery, anaesthetics, paediatrics, etc.

The Internet

The Internet is one of the most dynamic research tools available, it provides a bank of information on a multitude of topics, however obscure or diverse. One of the major advantages of using the Internet to carry out research is the fact that everything can be accessed from a single computer, there is no need to physically visit different places to gather information, although this is what the Internet is doing on your behalf.

There are many advantages of using the Internet as a research tool, these include:

- Diversity of topics and interests can be found.
- Concentrated source of research – no need to physically collect information from different places.
- Relatively quick.

- Can be a cheaper method of data collection than some other research tools.
- Can be easy to use and to source information.
- On-line help provided to assist in the gathering of research.
- Do not need to depend on a third party for the physical delivery of the information.
- Information can be presented in a variety of formats to aid understanding and learning.
- Can receive up to the minute information.
- Information and ideas can easily be shared on-line through user groups.

Problems of using the Internet as a research tool can occur if users are not familiar with its use and how to search for information. It can be frustrating to use a search engine for information on a broad topic such as 'universities' because anything with 'universities' in the title will be displayed from all over the world, bringing up maybe 10 000 or more sites.

A certain familiarity with the way in which search engines work, advanced features, Boolean operators, links and the basics of typing in a web address are also essential to get the most out of Internet research.

Punctuation, spelling and grammar

Throughout your life you will need to communicate through the writing of letters, memos, e-mails, reports and even completing business or education documents. To do this effectively you need to ensure that what you are writing is correct in terms of grammar, spelling and punctuation.

It is all too easy to rely on tools such as 'spell check' or 'grammar check' to correct our language mistakes, however, without these tools how well do we actually communicate in a written format.

Exercise 6.4.1

Read the following advertisement for a job and complete the tasks

IT Solutions

Systems Administrator
£19K plus benefits

We are looking to recruit a dynamic young graduate that has successfully completed a relevant computing qualification such as an HND or degree.

Must have experience of working within a team and have good interpersonal skills. Should also have technical experience of computer hardware, software and networks. Web based or programming skills are also desirable.

Please send in a covering letter with your CV to:
Mr Steven James, IT Manager
IT Solutions, 11-13 Langston Road, Norwich,
NR34 7DD

Closing date: 2 November 2003

1. Hand-write a covering letter in response to the advertisement for the job.
2. Once you have completed the letter write down a list of things which you were unsure of, e.g. spelling, punctuation, grammar, formality, etc.
3. Type the letter into a word processing package to check the concerns on your list.
4. Were the mistakes the same? Were there more mistakes than expected?

This exercise can demonstrate that even the most proficient communicator can sometimes have difficulties with written communication. However, there are ways to overcome this and that is to create a better awareness and appreciation of the English language, especially if the last time that punctuation, grammar and spelling was addressed was in school – how many years ago was that?

Punctuation

Punctuation provides the clarity, breaks and context to a sentence. Punctuation allows you to break down written extracts into manageable chunks through the use of:

Syntax	Descriptor	Some examples of use
'	Apostrophe	Can state possession if used with the letter 's', e.g. the student's work
:	Colon	Indicates stops or breaks in clauses, usually used to introduce examples
,	Comma	Used to indicate breaks in a sentence between groups of words or a list of items
–	Dash	Denotes additionality to a sentence
" " ' '	Direct speech marks or Inverted commas	Specifies what was spoken and by whom, also identifies a quotation or title
!	Exclamation mark	Denotes the feeling of surprise or other emotive expressions
.	Full stop	Represents the end of a sentence or an abbreviated word for example, e.g. or etc.
-	Hyphen	Link between words or parts of words
( )	Parentheses	Separate primary and secondary ideas
?	Question mark	Represents the ending of a direct question
;	Semicolon	A pause which is longer than a comma but shorter than a full stop, a dramatic pause

Spelling

Spelling corrections has been made easier through the use of applications software and tools to provide facilities such as 'spell check'.

However, spelling does not necessarily improve because of this. Some may argue that the level of literacy skills has declined because less of an effort has been made to practice and learn how to spell, the dependency falling on software.

There are a number of guidelines that can help improve the general level of spelling, these include:

- Rules of thumb
- Plurals
- Prefixes and Suffixes
- Homophones

Rules of thumb

These are general guidelines on what should happen under certain conditions with certain words and spelling.

1. 'q' is nearly always followed by a 'u'
2. 'i' before 'e' accept after 'c'
3. If a word ends in a single 'l' and the letter before was a vowel, the 'l' will need to be doubled before anything else (suffix) can be added

e.g.	*usual*	$\longrightarrow$	*usually*
	casual	$\longrightarrow$	*casually*

Plurals

Plurals can be achieved by adding an 's'

e.g.	*work*	$\longrightarrow$	*works*
	show	$\longrightarrow$	*shows*
	eat	$\longrightarrow$	*eats*

For some words adding 's' is not enough and 'es' is required

e.g.	*tomato*	$\longrightarrow$	*tomatoes*

Some words ending in 'y' the plural becomes 'ies'

e.g.	*personality*	$\longrightarrow$	*personalities*
	hospitality	$\longrightarrow$	*hospitalities*
	lorry	$\longrightarrow$	*lorries*

Words ending in a 'y' which are preceded by a vowel add 's' to plural

e.g.	*boy*	$\longrightarrow$	*boys*
	bay	$\longrightarrow$	*bays*
	tray	$\longrightarrow$	*trays*

Words ending in 'f' in the singular become 'ves' in the plural

e.g.	*hoof*	$\longrightarrow$	*hooves*
	calf	$\longrightarrow$	*calves*
	shelf	$\longrightarrow$	*shelves*

Words ending in: 's' 'x' 'z' 'ch' 'sh' and 'ss' in the singular become 'es' in the plural

e.g.	*fizz*	$\longrightarrow$	*fizzes*
	lunch	$\longrightarrow$	*lunches*
	push	$\longrightarrow$	*pushes*

Some plurals are quite different to the original singular word

$$e.g. \quad die \quad \longrightarrow \quad dice$$
$$stimulus \quad \longrightarrow \quad stimuli$$

Prefixes and suffixes

Adding a prefix or a suffix to a word does not necessarily alter the original word, it gives additonality.

$$e.g. \quad disappear \quad \longleftarrow \quad appear \quad \longrightarrow \quad disappearing$$
$$\text{prefix} \qquad\qquad \text{suffix}$$

In some cases the word does change and a letter is dropped, in this case the 'e'

$$e.g. \quad misbehave \quad \longleftarrow \quad behave \quad \longrightarrow \quad misbehaving$$
$$\text{prefix} \qquad\qquad \text{suffix}$$

Homophones

These are words that sound the same but are spelt differently, examples of these include:

fair	fare
their	there
horse	hoarse
flee	flea
compliment	complement
past	passed
claws	clause

Grammar

Using correct grammar formats will aid in the process of improving written communication skills. There are certain grammar formats that are used to convey different aspects of a sentence, these can include nouns and pronouns, verbs and adverbs, adjectives, articles, conjunctions, prepositions and interjections.

Each sentence that is spoken or written will contain a variety of these grammar formats, each format providing their own distinct contribution as shown in Table 6.4.1.

Table 6.4.1   *Grammar table*

Identifier	Description	Example
Adjective	Describing word	large, pretty, heavy, cold
Adverb	Extension to adjectives or verbs, how, where, when	slowly, friendly, happily, cautiously
Article	Definite and indefinite	*the* assignment *a* job
Conjunction	Linking words	and, next, when, if, after
Interjection	Feeling or emotion	ouch, yippee, oh, wow
Noun	Naming word	cat, car, computer, book
Preposition	Locators	under, across, over, up
Pronoun	Naming or identifying words	refers to people or things *Who* did you invite?
Verb	Doing word	writes, plays, jumps, shouts

Reading and note taking techniques

People read in different ways, some people skim read through chapters picking out key words and phrases, others might examine a piece of text from cover to cover. Some people read slowly, constantly referring back to text in order to reflect on the information, others take notes to assist in their understanding.

The ability to improve the speed at which you read and the ability to increase the level of understanding from what you have read can be increased by setting yourself targets and measuring progress made. There are recognized ways and practice exercises that can help improve your reading skills, as developed by Tony Buzan, some of these include:

- *Rapid page turning* – skim down a page and then turn it over after 3 seconds, after 10 attempts decrease the time to 2 seconds.
- *Muscle exercises* – fixate between the top left-hand and right-hand corners of a page moving your eyes between them as quickly as possible. Progress to top and bottom and diagonally across the page – speed up after each attempt.
- *Speed reading* – read as fast as you can for 1 minute, marking the start and finish points, read for another minute, aiming more at comprehension of significant points, note the end point. Count and record how many words per minute – increase the density of the materials each time.
- *Reducing fixations* – point at every third word or second if this is too difficult and move your marker every 1.5 seconds between words. Try to increase the speed at which the marker is moved and the distance between words moved.
- *Progressive acceleration* – start with light to medium material and read with comprehension. Aim for 100 words per minute, read for a minute and then try to increase your speed for a further minute until after 4 minutes you can read approximately 500 words per minute faster than the initial starting speed. Practice this exercise again and hopefully the speed and comprehension should be higher than the original.
- *Scanning* – using light reading material, set a marker for your start and end points. Scan read to the marker taking a few seconds per page. Go back and read the section again, aiming for comprehension. Practice this exercise using similar marker guidance to increase the speed and comprehension of reading material.

Note taking techniques

Another vital skill, which is always useful to improve upon, is that of note taking. People take notes everyday to jot down facts, summarize information such as a lesson, record data such as times and activities. Whatever method you use to take notes, it will probably fall into one of the categories shown in Figure 6.4.5.

Bullets and key points: taking notes using these methods is very quick, specific and easy to apply, especially with built in bullet and numbering features of application software packages. Information in this format can be condensed in a single key word or short sentences, an example of this can

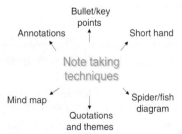

Figure 6.4.5 *Methods of note taking*

be seen in the following extract:

Issues to consider when setting up a web site

1. Costs
   - Hardware
   - Software
   - Connection
   - ISP charges
   - Maintenance and service charges
   - Security
   - Design

Shorthand: unique styles of scribing complete words into short symbols, to enable faster note taking as shown in Figure 6.4.6.

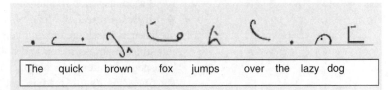

Figure 6.4.6 *Short-hand extract*

Spider/fish diagram: a method of taking notes visually using keywords and word or subject associations.

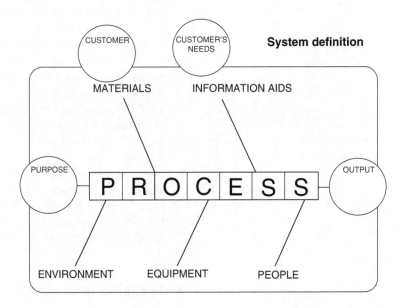

Quotations: it is sometimes appropriate to jot down specific phrases or quotations from particular authors that can be used as references for future research.

Mind maps: Tony Buzan (1989) developed a style of transferring notes into a diagrammatic format known as a 'mind map' or 'brain pattern'. The core of which starts with a word or phrase in the centre of a page that represents the main theme, from this branches extend outwards incorporating links to that theme, and again into sub-themes.

Annotations: used to provide an expansion to thoughts or ideas. Annotations can be textual or graphical.

Read and respond to written material

The ability to read and absorb information can vary to a degree depending upon a number of factors. This can include:

- Subject matter
- Objectives of reading
- Level of material
- Presentation of material

Subject matter

Reading material such as a book or magazines that is of interest to you will increase the level of understanding and the will to absorb information. For example, reading through a book which is telling a story or portraying an event will usually stimulate the reader to continue through to the end of the chapter or book. 'Who dunnits' make an interesting read because the stimulus to identify the culprit is sustained throughout, the level of mystery and suspense encouraging the reader to continue.

The more interesting the text, the higher the chances of understanding the theme which will improve the chances of completing it through to the end.

Objectives of reading

People read for different reasons, the objectives for reading fall into several categories:

- To investigate facts.
- To understand and allow comprehension.
- To consolidate prior learning.
- To improve learning.
- For enjoyment.

Reading objectives fit together to form a cycle of continuous acquisition and improvement of learning skills through reading as shown in Figure 6.4.7.

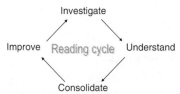

Figure 6.4.7 *Cycle of reading objectives*

Investigate

The need to investigate facts and information could be self-directed or imposed. Self-directed investigation implies that the individual seeks out appropriate reading material for their own personal gain.

Imposed investigation could be a stipulated requirement from a third party such as a lecturer at college.

Understand

Although the objective of reading six pages by a certain deadline through self-directed or imposed requirements is the same, the way in which you understand and respond to the reading can be very different.

Being told to do something can be seen as restrictive and the enjoyment factor could be reduced, thus hindering the process of understanding. Taking the initiative to read six pages for yourself can change the focus making it more positive, therefore the level of understanding can be greater.

The objective of reading purely to understand facts can be seen in the following examples:

- Car manuals
- Test logs
- Computer guides
- Maps

You would not necessarily read a map book from cover to cover, to allow for easier and quicker understanding, you would identify the desired region or destination and source the appropriate page or pages.

Consolidate

Reading to consolidate information again uses different reading skill techniques. You might be revisiting a piece of text that has been previously read in preparation for a test. Revision reading is one way to consolidate the reading and understanding process. Using this technique a chapter of a book that may have been reviewed at the beginning of a course is examined again at the end to consolidate any additional information collected, or to serve as a refresher for new ideas.

If between the time of first reading the book at the investigation stage and the return to the book in the consolidation stage new information has been sourced, the revisiting will act as a consolidation of both existing and new information sourced.

This theory can be contextualized using an example of a car manual:

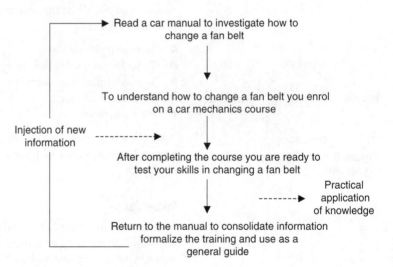

The consolidation stage is cyclical within itself because as learners we constantly refer back to resources and revisit materials to aid with the transition into the final stage of 'improving' our own knowledge and skill base.

Improve

Improving knowledge and skills through reading is an expectation on a majority of vocational and academic courses. Although we learn by 'doing' from a practical aspect, to aid us in this learning process we constantly refer to reading materials.

Level of the material

The level at which you read can have an impact on how you read and understand the material, this is because everybody has certain boundaries when it comes to interpreting and comprehending written information.

Reading a computing degree level text book on an intermediate computing course will probably be too difficult for some because of the expectations of existing knowledge of a typical degree student compared to those of intermediate status.

Trying to read a book beyond your level of understanding can create a negative reaction to reading and stifle the learning experience. In conjunction, you would not necessarily read an intermediate text on the basics of programming if you had reached an advanced practitioners level, because there would be very little stimulus in regards to learning new and exciting information.

Identifying the level of reading ability is not necessarily a science. Although reading ability is tested at school to determine a particular level, this may not be a true reflection of an individual's overall reading ability skills. Reading in a controlled environment to meet a specific objective or requirement can put pressure on an individual creating a knowledge vacuum. To overcome this, a variety of texts and styles of writing need to be read whenever possible from journalistic, instructional, biographical technical even fictional to ensure that the mind and stimulus to absorb information in these formats remains incessant.

Presentation of material

The presentation of material can have a profound effect on how individuals read and respond to written materials. Reading materials are nearly always presented in a specific format, for e.g. newspaper articles in column format and textbooks in subject/material specific format for e.g. 'report writing skills' in a personal skills development chapter.

A familiar layout can help the reader familiarize themselves with the overall style and adapt to that style of reading.

Tools and techniques for personal skills development

The acquisition of new skills and knowledge is an on-going learning experience that contributes to an individual's personal skills development.

There are a number of issues to consider when exploring these opportunities for personal skills development. These can include:

- The stimulus for undertaking a development task.
- The time frame.
- Outcome measurability.

Why improve yourself, why take the time to update and develop knowledge and skills? The stimulus for doing this varies between individuals. For some there is an imposed need to update or reskill because of market demand and competition for jobs or higher education placements. For others meeting personal targets and goals provides the stimulus of striving to achieve more.

Objective and target setting can help individuals to focus on what they plan to do, and the timescales for doing them. The rationale for setting objectives being modelled on CSMART:

- Challenging
- Specific
- Measurable
- Achievable
- Realistic
- Time framed

where each objective set should address the indicated areas. In terms of personal development these can provide the stimulus, time frame and outcome measurability.

The achievement or outcome measurability is an important factor in the updating of skills and knowledge. Defining and quantifying what you have learnt represents how far you have had to travel to reach your personal goal. Recognition of this can be in the form of a certificate, verbal acknowledgement, or a new or improved aptitude in a certain skill.

There are a number of tools and techniques that can be used to support individuals at all levels to facilitate the process of planning, updating and developing new and existing skills and knowledge. Some of these tools include:

- SWOT analysis
- Gantt Charts
- Impact analysis

SWOT analysis

A SWOT analysis examines the strengths, weaknesses, opportunities and threats of a given issue. In conjunction with personal skills development the strengths and weaknesses are examined from an internal (individual's) point of view and the opportunities and threats are examined from an external point of view – how influences outside can impact upon your personal development.

For example, SWOT analysis for doing a part-time day release-computing course.

Strengths	Weaknesses
• Learn more specific hardware and software skills • Certificate issued on completion • Recognized industry standard course	• Need to give up one day and one evening a week to attend • Requirement to do weekly on-line assessments
Opportunities	Threats
• Progression onto more advanced courses • Ability to apply for a wider range of jobs	• Course not being offered due to low enrolment figures

In order to assess whether or not an activity would be viable the strengths should outweigh the weaknesses and the opportunities should exceed the threats.

Gantt chart

Gantt charts provide a diagrammatic overview of the sequence and timing of activities for a particular task-based project. It illustrates what will take place by stating the predicting start and end time of activities and also examines the ordering of particular tasks as illustrated.

Gantt chart to show assessment timescales:

May					June				July	
Week no.	1	2	3	4	5	6	7	8	9	10
Activity:										
Do research	▓	▓								
Examine task requirements		▓	▓							
Generate proposals			▓							
Present proposals				▓						
Plan designs				▓						
Implement designs					▓	▓	▓	▓		
Test designs							▓	▓	▓	
Evaluation										▓

Impact analysis

An impact analysis examines the impact of a proposed idea or activity. The degree of the impact is quantified in terms of being positive or negative. The aim of carrying out an impact analysis is to assess how achievable and realistic a proposal is. It would be unrealistic to have a proposal that involved learning a new skill with no negative impacts because of the constraints imposed, for e.g. possible costs, limited time requirement to have prerequisite knowledge.

To carry out an impact analysis a number of issues should be identified from which a table can then be drawn up to identify whether the impact is positive or negative.

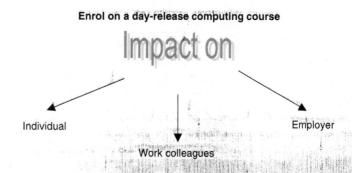

Enrol on a day-release computing course

Impact on

Individual   Work colleagues   Employer

Example of an impact analysis table

Enrolling on a day-release computing course

Areas examined	Impact +ve or −ve	Rationale
Individual	+ve	Learn new skills
	−ve	Heavier workload at work due to day release, tasks completed over four and not 5 days
Employer	+ve	Knowledge and skills can be used within the workplace
	−ve	Cost of the course and release from work
Work colleagues	+ve	Opportunity to share information and course material
	−ve	May feel resentment due to day-release from work to do the course

The importance of updating practical, personal and interpersonal skills is paramount in today's society. The requirement to be a more rounded individual is the message that is being relayed by industry and also education. The integration and expectation of students at all levels to undertake Key Skills and the emphasis on future employees to have good communication skills has created a demand for students with these qualities. The Personal Skills Development unit being possibly the first step for individuals to stop and assess their own skill and knowledge base, reflect, and be pro-active in addressing any skill shortfalls for the future.

7 Quality systems

Summary

This unit will enable students to learn about the concepts of quality assurance through the process of analysing and designing computer systems. It will deal with the quality assurance and professional issues related to the management and implementation of computer systems. It also covers the project management aspects needed within the development of software products and introduces the legal requirements currently affecting the computer practitioner. It will enable students to learn about the quality process as applied to information technology related systems development and the establishment of standards by which projects are measured.

Introduction

The need for a 'quality product' cannot be overstated. This is especially important within the world of computing and software development. We have often heard of the product that is not produced on time and launched within a number of problems (bugs). This is why the combined techniques of project management and quality assurance need to be developed and applied over the whole lifecycle of the software product.

This chapter further develops the concepts developed in the systems analysis unit. It looks at the analysis and design tools used within the software development process and applies CASE tools to produce graphical and text-based models. The syntax and semantics of the model will be tested to ensure the quality of the product conforms to the stated requirements.

You will further develop the techniques of traditional lifecycle models and object-oriented models, and how they are developed, documented and quality assured for a simulated customer specification.

The concepts of project management are developed within the chapter to ensure the development process is planned and implemented within prescribed deadlines and checked at various milestones to ensure the verification and validation processes.

All completed systems require some maintenance to be carried out to handle any problems that may occur or update certain aspects of the software. The concept of a software maintenance contract is introduced.

You will be introduced to the basic concepts of 'quality assurance' and how it interacts across a software development project. Estimating and costing factors need to be considered along with the timing and testing issues for a software product under development. You will need to hold reviews, walkthroughs and inspections and be able to produce recognized quality assurance documents.

Legal implications surrounding the development of a product and its associated staff are addressed. For example, the Software Project Manager needs to approach health and safety in a strictly systematic way by assessing *the risks and hazards in the workplace* and taking steps to ensure that their house is in order. Also the manager needs to be aware of the issues involving storage of 'Data', i.e. recorded information.

Professionalism and standards are key issues developed by any successful manager. Students need to understand the importance of these issues and how they are implemented within a quality development programme. The concept of professionalism implies taking responsibility, accounting for one's work and performing work to the highest standards. Factors like ISO, British Standards, training (CPD), etc. need to be considered in the quest for producing 'quality professional software development personnel'. These issues are especially important if a professional body like the British Computer Society validates your course.

7.1 Quality assurance

Software quality assurance

Introduction

Software Quality Assurance (SQA) is an activity that is applied throughout the whole development lifecycle of the product. One of the main aims of SQA is to produce a product that meets the customer's requirements. Some software quality assurance definitions are shown:

> A planned and systematic pattern of all the actions necessary to provide adequate confidence that the software conforms to established technical requirements.
>
> *ANSI/IEEE*

> Conformance to explicitly stated functional and performance requirements, explicitly documented development standards, and implicit characteristics that are expected of all professionally developed software.
>
> *Pressman*

> Quality consists of those product features which meet the needs of the customer and thereby provide product satisfaction.
>
> *Juran's Quality Control Handbook*

Above all a product must be fit for the purpose that it developed for, it must be free of any deficiencies. SQA is a term used to describe those activities that ensure a contractually acceptable product is delivered to the customer or end users. It includes good practices like: holding reviews, producing quality and project plans, precise documentation and thorough verification and validation practices.

Oakland in his book *Total Quality Management* (TQM) identifies two major causes of quality problems:

- acceptance of failure;
- misunderstanding of quality.

These problems were picked up from the perspective of the customer or end user. A view that has been very strong in Japan, where customer satisfaction has been placed higher than immediate profit. This leads to the concept of TQM where it is claimed that 'quality is free'. Adding TQM procedures to a project will add initial costs, but these will be overcome with:

- *Keeping customers*: The company may make a larger profit 1 day, but this is no good if the customers do not come back. Extra effort is made with supplying a quality product, even if this initially means reduced profit margins which will be recuperated at a later date.
- *Making concern for quality visible*: This makes the associated processes and development procedures with assuring quality also visible and a new source of expenditure is not seen.

Therefore, *Quality Management* involves taking the customers view of quality. While TQM involves the process of quality management being passed down the whole chain, i.e. all staff are involved in the quality process.

Software Quality Management (SQM) has to successfully balance the requirements of time, budgets and software quality using a variety of tested methods to satisfy their business plans and the needs of the end user of the product.

Within a software development company an independent quality assurance team that reports directly to the line manager above project management level should carry out quality assurance procedures. The team should be independent of any development group but should be responsible for quality assurance across the whole organization. A typical company layout is shown in Figure 7.1.1.

This is a general layout and there are many interpretations of this structure within modern software houses, the main point to note is that the Quality Manager and Development Manager are not too strongly associated with a specific project. It is the role of the quality assurance team to ensure quality within the software process by:

- defining process quality standards;
- monitoring the development process to ensure quality standards are being maintained;
- providing reports to product management and the customer.

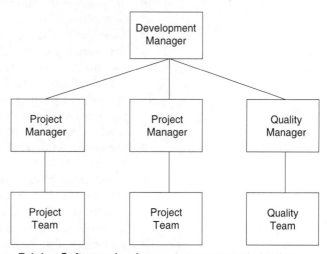

Figure 7.1.1   *Software development management structure*

SQM involves the developer balancing various aspects of the production process. Such aspects could include production schedules and their prescribed milestones (the timing of events), production costs and their allocated budgets and the quality of the product under development.

SQM = budget versus quality versus time

An old saying within product development states:

better, faster, cheaper: pick two because you cannot have all three

Professional Quality Assurance Agencies try to overcome this problem by measuring the quality aspects against the specified schedules and associated budgets and make any necessary improvements to ensure the quality of a product given the constrains of time and cost factors.

Quality assurance factors

The factors that effect software quality can be divided into two categories: those that can be directly measured and those that can only be measured indirectly (e.g. usability and maintainability). High quality software can be characterized by the following attributes:

- *Efficiency*: This refers to how a system operates within its given environment. Execution speed and data storage are two factors that an end user requires for efficient software.
- *Reliability*: We can see from the previous section that one aspect of software maintenance was to remove errors within software. Any error may effect the reliability of software although some may be acceptable to the customer if the product still meets its original requirements. Reliability is therefore the measure of the number of times a system fails to perform correctly.
- *Testability*: This relates to how easily a software system can be tested. We shall see later in this section that code can be structured to aid the testing process and hence aid the elimination of errors to produce an acceptable product.
- *Maintainability*: This refers to the concept a change and how it can be implemented within a system under development.
- *Usability*: This relates to how easy a piece of software is to use. We have seen a greater push towards graphical user interfaces (GUI's) over the past few years that have improved the way systems can be used. Usability also effects the way in which the application can be controlled, e.g. a user may require a quick response from the system (the keyboard input would be to slow), so some other input like a touch screen may be more appropriate.
- *Portability*: How easy is it to transfer the application to a new environment.
- *Reusability*: The concept of reuse of code is an important attribute in the development of modern software systems, especially those developed using object-oriented concepts. Therefore reusability relates to how easy it is to reuse code sections from one system into another system. Remember this code may already be thoroughly tried and tested and so improve the quality of the new product.

Software quality assurance factors should focus on the following three aspects of a software product under development:

- its operational characteristics;
- the ability of the product to undergo change;
- how it can be adapted into a new environment.

Software quality assurance must therefore be involved with the whole software development process. It needs to monitor each phase of development and carry out required improvements, ensuring that all the agreed standards and procedures, set in the quality manual, are implemented and any resulting problems dealt with.

Verification and validation

Verification and validation (V&V) is concerned with checking the software under development to ensure it meets the needs of the original requirements. It has two main objectives:

- to test for any faults in the system;
- to find out if the system is fully operational in its working environment.

Verification checks that a product in the software development process agrees with the product of the previous activity. The product of the system analysis phase is the system analysis document and the process of checking that it reflects the negotiated statement of requirements document is classified as verification.

Validation is the process that checks to see if a component of the software product correctly reflects the original requirements. Certain testing procedures come under this heading, e.g. system testing and acceptance testing.

Barry Boehm defines V&V as:

- *Verification*: To establish the truth of correspondence between a software product and its specification.
- *Validation*: To establish the fitness of worth of a software product for its operational mission.

or summarized as:

- *Verification*: Are we building the product right?
- *Validation*: Are we building the right product?

Software quality systems

We have seen within this book that sound engineering practices have been applied to the development of software. This broadly comes under the heading of 'Software Engineering' and the transition of standards from one discipline to another has caused some concern within the software industry. To ensure that software systems do meet the same standards that have been inherent in a number of other industries for many years, the software industry needs to conform to its own standards. Outlined below are definitions for four internationally standardized terms that are basic to any quality assurance system:

- *Quality*: The totality of features and characteristics of a product or service that bear on its ability to satisfy stated or implied needs.

Question 7.1.1

1. What is the difference between verification and validation?
2. Why is usability a characteristic of high quality software?

- *Quality policy*: The overall quality intentions and direction of an organization as regards quality, as formally expressed by top management.
- *Quality management*: That aspect of overall management function that determines and implements quality policy.
- *Quality system*: The organizational structure, responsibilities, procedures, processes and resources for implementing quality management.

(BS 4778/ISO 8402)

Although these standards are carefully defined they are still a little hard to follow and implement. The quality system definition is perhaps a little less ambiguous and in many cases provides a starting point for planning the quality assurance procedures for a new project. It is management's responsibility to produce a quality policy for a proposed quality system. The original standard outlined for this is:

> The supplier's management shall define and document its policy and objectives for, and commitment to, quality. The supplier shall ensure that the policy is understood, implemented and maintained at all levels in the organization.
>
> (BS 5750/ISO 9001)

The *International Standards Organisation* (*ISO*) is a non-governmental organization that was established in 1947. The main organization is based in Geneva and is the head organization for standardization's from approximately 100 countries. Its work results in international agreements that are published as international standards, over 10 000 to date (i.e. ISO 9000 series). Examples of some national standards are shown below:

AFNOR – Association Francaise de Normalisation (France)
ANSI – American National Standard Institute (USA)
BSI – British Standards Institute (UK)
DIN – Deutsches Institute fuer Normung (Germany)

Currently a set of standards make up the ISO 9000 family. These standards are constantly being reviewed and updated and need to be checked for implementing them within a quality framework. The standards have earned a global reputation for establishing QMS and form a basis for continual improvement and business excellence. Generally standards are documented agreements containing precise criteria and technical specifications that aim to ensure that the end product is 'fit for its purpose'.

ISO Quality Standards from the ISO 9000 family are outlined below:

Standard	Purpose
ISO 9000:2000, *Quality Management Systems – Fundamentals and vocabulary*	Establishes a starting point for understanding the standards and defines the fundamental terms and definitions used in the ISO 9000 family which you need to avoid misunderstandings in their use.
ISO 9001:2000, *Quality Management Systems – Requirements*	This is the requirement standard you use to assess your ability to meet customer and applicable regulatory requirements and thereby address customer satisfaction.

Standard	Purpose
	It is now the only standard in the ISO 9000 family against which third-party certification can be carried.
ISO 9004:2000, *Quality Management Systems – Guidelines for performance improvements*	This guideline standard provides guidance for continual improvement of your quality management system to benefit all parties through sustained customer satisfaction.
ISO 19011, *Guidelines on Quality and/or Environmental Management Systems Auditing* (currently under development)	Provides you with guidelines for verifying the system's ability to achieve defined quality objectives. You can use this standard internally or for auditing your suppliers.
ISO 10005:1995, *Quality Management – Guidelines for Quality Plans*	Provides guidelines to assist in the preparation, review, acceptance and revision of quality plans.
ISO 10006:1997, *Quality Management – Guidelines to Quality in Project Management*	Guidelines to help you ensure the quality of both the project processes and the project products.
ISO 10007:1995, *Quality Management – Guidelines for Configuration Management*	Gives you guidelines to ensure that a complex product continues to function when components are changed individually.
ISO 10013:1995, *Guidelines for developing Quality Manuals*	Provides guidelines for the development, and maintenance of quality manuals, tailored to your specific needs.
ISO/TR 10014:1998, *Guidelines for managing the economics of quality*	Provides guidance on how to achieve economic benefits from the application of quality management.
ISO 10015:1999, *Quality Management – Guidelines for Training*	Provides guidance on the development, implementation, maintenance and improvement of strategies and systems for training that affects the quality of products.

Source: International Standards Organisation

As you can see this is a comprehensive list and to give an example of what each heading contains details of the ISO-9001: 1994/ISO 9000-3: 1997 4.1 standard are outlined below:

ISO 9000-3: 4.1 Management responsibilities

- Define a quality policy. This should include the objectives for quality and your organizations towards quality. This should be understood, implemented and maintained at all levels within the organization.
- Define the organizational structure that is required to manage your quality system.
- Define quality system responsibilities and authority. Ensure the interactions between staff are clearly specified. Make sure all these are well documented.
- Identify and provide the resources that people will need to manage, perform and verify quality system work.

- Appoint a senior manager with executive responsibilities to:
  - establish an ISO 9001 compliant quality management system (QMS), implement and maintain it.
  - provide a link, and report to, senior management on the development and production of the QMS.
- Define procedures for use by senior managers to review the effectiveness of your QMS. This could involve interaction with the customer to:
  - obtain feedback about the system;
  - ensure the software meets the customers requirements;
  - verify and accept any test results.

Above all the need to conduct and document periodic reviews of the QMS.

This one area outlines some of the important requirements that should be inherent in a quality system. Standards and procedures require a lot of paperwork that has to be carefully prepared and maintained. As with a lot of software engineering concepts there cannot be too much emphasis put onto the production of quality, ordered and accurate documentation. The quality system for an organization should be documented in a quality manual that contains the following guidelines:

- Specifying the responsibilities (both internal and external to the organization) regarding the achievement of quality.
- The meetings or formal reviews to be carried out along with their composition requirements.
- The format for a corresponding quality plan that details how the developer intends to ensure the software product meets its stated quality objectives.

Standards are forever changing and the ISO has just updated its 9001 series by updating the ISO:9001, ISO:9002 and ISO:9003 1994 standards into one new standard the ISO:9001 2000 set. The 20-clause structure outlined in the 1994/1997 standards will be replaced with a new format containing five sections. ISO states that this produces a more logical structure and to make it more compatible with the ISO 14001 Environmental Management standard. The ISO:9004 2000 standard also deals with QMS but lays down guidance for performance improvements, that go beyond the basic requirements specified in ISO:9001 2000. It is intended as a guide for organizations that wants to further expand and improve the QMS after implementing ISO:9001 2000.

For companies wishing to implement the ISO 9001-2000 standards there are five activities that need to be addressed. These are:

- Product realization
- Quality management system
- Management responsibility
- Resource management and measurement
- Analysis and improvement.

There are eight quality management principles listed in the documents ISO 9000:2000 and ISO 9004:2000 and provide the basis for the performance improvement outlined in ISO 9004:2000. The eight quality management principles are:

- Customer focus
- Leadership

- Involvement of people
- Process approach
- System approach to management
- Continual improvement
- Factual approach to decision making
- Mutual beneficial supplier relationships.

ISO Standards in action

Below are two examples that have used ISO standards to improve their quality provision:

> A computer software developer serving a niche market recognized that as their user base expanded they would be faced with issues concerning product management and configuration control. Changes to base products, user hardware and regulatory requirements were compounding customer service issues. ISO 9004:2000 provided the guidance they needed to establish documented procedures to control process change and improvement. ISO 10006:1997 and ISO 10007:1995 provided additional assistance as they managed the project and prepared procedures for configuration management. They later acquired another software developer and were able to use their quality management system to integrate the acquisition into their own structure very quickly with a minimum of disruption to customers.
>
> A bank decided to implement a quality management system for its on-line Internet banking services. They ensured that their quality manual made clear that their other conventional banking services were not included in their quality management system. While adopting the requirements of ISO 9001:2000, the bank obtained guidance from ISO 9000:2000 to interpret words and phrases used in the standard for their application. They applied all the requirements of Clause 7, recognizing that design and development is an important part of creating new service processes. The bank used ISO 10013:1995 to prepare their documentation, which they posted on their internal computer network to ensure current procedures are available to their staff.
>
> (*Source*: International Standards Organisation)

The ISO 14000 standards deal with environmental issues. Such issues include: Prioritising Environmental Issues (ISO 14040), Integration of Environmental Aspects in Design and Development (ISO 14062), Communicating Environmental Performance (ISO 14020 and ISO 14063), Monitoring Environmental Performance (ISO 14030) and Monitoring System performance (ISO 19011).

As we have seen within this section a quality system needs to adhere to certain standards in order for it to meet its classification. We have mentioned the influence of ISO standards, but other standards also effect the quality of software system. These include the IEEE (Institute of Electrical and Electronic Engineers), BSI (British Standards Institute) and others, some dependent on the country of origin of the product. For example, the IEEE 1008 standard for Software Unit Testing or the BSI BS-7738 Specification for Information Systems Products using SSADM are alternative stands that effect the production of quality system. There are also further ISO standards that are relevant to software development, e.g. ISO 5218 Representation of Human Sexes (i.e. 0 = not known, 1 = male, 2 = female and 9 = not specified to represent it as a 1 character numerical code). And so it goes on. But the application of standards to a software quality system has many advantages to the developer of the product, e.g.:

- customer satisfaction;
- effectiveness of budget and time requirements;
- improved management structure;
- trust in the product;
- legal compliance;
- improved product development;
- international standards help export the product.

Above all a quality product employing standards is efficient, commercially viable, credible and from both the development and customer point of view 'safe'. Customers and end users of a system value the aspects of safety and quality that such standards install within the product. Standards install trust in a product that improve marketability and product satisfaction.

Question 7.1.2
1. What is ANSI an abbreviation for?
2. What is ISO and how does it influence the development of software systems?
3. What are the eight Quality Management Principles that are inherent in the 9000:2000 and 9004:2000 ISO standards? What do you think are the key benefits of principle 1 (Customer Focus)?
4. What are the advantages of implementing international standards within the software development process?
5. What standard's institution is inherent within the UK?
6. What is a Quality Management System (QMS)?

Exercise 7.1.1

This is a research exercise. At the time of writing this section the ISO 9001 2000 standards are now being implemented by companies seeking certification. The aim of this exercise is to investigate the latest progress of ISO standards and how they effect the development of software systems. Give a further example of where such standards have been implemented.

Costs and benefits of software quality systems

From certain perspectives it looks like developing a quality system involves a lot of extra work and costs a lot of money. On the other side software failures cost a lot of money and in some cases involve injury or loss of life. There have been several examples of severe software failure that are expensive to fix and take up valuable time.

Exercise 7.1.2

Another research exercise. Investigate a software system that has failed with severe consequences. Find out what type software system it was? what caused the problem, how it effected the users and how it was corrected. As a guide the

London Ambulance Service installed a new system in 1992, after a short period it suffered severe failure which resulted with problems dispatching ambulances to emergency situations. It was said that this resulted in a number of unnecessary deaths. Two major problems were identified:

1. A small piece of test code was left in the system which took up available memory every time a call was made until the storage area was full.
2. A backup system was recommended during development but was never implemented.

Research a similar case.

Software failures cost money and take up valuable time to put right. This process can be made harder if the software was not developed using sound quality standards. As we have already seen, working to improve quality can cost money in the short term, but is beneficial in the long term. Often a contract is produced without fully considering the costs of maintenance activities. Figure 7.1.2 outlines the costs over the whole lifecycle of a project.

It can be seen that there are high costs during the maintenance phase for a system developed without using sound quality system principles. If a little extra capital is spent on activities prior to the hand-over date then the quality of the system should be significantly improved. A careful balance needs to be maintained by the project manager to ensure saving during maintenance are significantly larger than the extra costs occurred prior to the hand-over date. If this is not the case the law of diminishing returns will arise and the profits will vanish.

It may be in certain cases that a developer may enter into a 'lost leader' situation for one product, but hope to regain the initiative by selling the product to other clients. This is OK if there is a ready market for the product, especially a quality system that has undergone severe quality standard procedures prior to its release. But care needs to be taken if the product is for an individual client with unique requirements, as any financial loss may not be acceptable to the business.

Software problems become business problems

Despite the availability of international standards the software quality problem is still growing at a high rate. The world of business has seen a

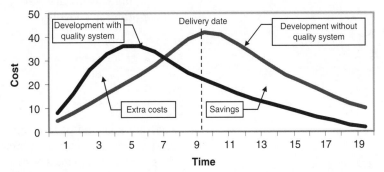

Figure 7.1.2 *Cost comparisons for software projects*

rapid increase in the use of software; two main reasons are behind this trend. First we have the Internet explosion where businesses develop transactions electronically and the progress of microprocessor technology that enables the running of complex software into many products and processes.

A term often quoted: 'for businesses to succeed, their software must work'. If not the following business problems could arise:

● Loss of revenue
● The Reputation of the goods may suffer
● The Company could face legal/liability costs
● A loss of production.

A report issued by the National Institute of Standards and Technology (NIST) in June 2002 states:

> Defective software costs the US economy an estimated $59.5 billion each year. Of that total, software users incurred 64% of the costs and software developers 36%. NIST suggests that improvements in testing could reduce this cost by about a third – or $22.5 billion – but that testing improvements would not eliminate all software errors.
> (from the NIST planning report June 2002, US Department of Commerce)

A quote by Gary McGraw in the Software Quality Management Magazine states:

> Business risk management models have traditionally ignored software, largely because software's impact on business operations was considered minor. In the digital age, however, software failure can lead directly to business failure.

Risk hierarchy

We can look at the concept of risk in two ways. First when applying it to the completed project, i.e. is the software safe and second how risky is it building a product in order to complete it on time and within budget?

From the British Standards RISK is specified as:

> Risk may be specified as a quantified probability or a combination of quantified probabilities but it is not possible to specify the software safety integrity in the same manner. Software safety integrity is specified as on or more of five levels:
>
> 1. Very high
> 2. High
> 3. Medium
> 4. Low
> 5. Normal

The very high end of the range deals with safety critical systems that carry a high risk in terms of 'time and budget' constraints for the developer. Such a system must be made 'faultless' as any problems may cause injury or loss of life to people in depending on it.

A definition of *risk* from Webster's:

Risk is the possibility of suffering loss

In general the risk (i.e. the risk of completing the project on time and within budget) can be specified under three broad heading. This is outlined in the table below:

Risk hierarchy	Example systems
High risk	Real time or safety critical systems, e.g. fly-by-wire aircraft systems, weapons guidance systems, patient-monitoring systems, etc.
Medium risk	Commercial Data Processing, Banking and Insurance systems, etc.
Low risk	Mathematical and Statistical Applications, etc.

From his book on Risk Analysis and Management, Charette outlines three underpinning concepts that are always present during the development of a software system:

1. risk concerns future happens;
2. risk involves change;
3. risk involves choice.

From a developers point of view risk is an everyday occurrence. We have already looked at the concepts of change, so 'risk' it needs to be carefully considered at the start of every new project. Risk analysis is a software engineering discipline that combines four separate activities:

- risk identification;
- risk projection;
- risk assessment;
- risk management.

Risk analysis can take a lot of planning and once in place will need to be monitored. But if you can foresee problems then any areas that may present a risk to the developers time and budget predictions can be planned for.

Risk management

Risk management is a software engineering activity involved with the managing of risks within a project under development. Basically it provides an organized approach involving:

- check thoroughly what may go wrong (potential risks);
- ascertain if the risks are important and may effect the project development;
- employ methods to remove the risks that are important.

Risk management needs to interact with the customer in order to analyse the software requirements and identify where any problems, flaws, etc. may impact on their business. For example, is there a 'risk' that a certain design component cannot be completed on time or are adequate staff available to implement the coding requirements. Risk management needs to active over the whole lifecycle of the project, it involves the following steps:

- Search and find any areas of risk before they become problems.
- Analyse the risks as to their impact and prioritize them accordingly.
- Plan and implement actions to remove the risk element.

- Monitor the actions to ensure they are removing the risk element as required.
- Control any change requirements that may need to be introduced.
- Communicate on the progress of the employed activities.

It is often said that risk and opportunity are linked closely together. When a new process is embarked upon often an element of risk is involved. Without this, the achievement to advance current capabilities would not have taken place and older, sometimes less efficient methods, would still be used.

Roger Van Scoy: *Software Development and Risk: Opportunity, Not Problem*, states:

> Risk in itself is not bad; risk is essential to progress, and failure is often a key part of learning. But we must learn to balance the possible negative consequences of risk against the potential benefits of its associated opportunity.

Professional standards

We have seen over the last two decades a revolution in the use if IT within a number of organizations and home use. The UK government has committed to 100% electronic delivery of its services by 2008. A recent survey showed that over 95% of ISO 9000 registered companies have access to the Internet. As more and more data is now stored electronically some control must be put into place to ensure the data is correct, safe and easily assessable for the user. Establishing and managing a secure, controlled and LEGAL environment is a challenge facing many organizations in the new millennium. The risks are always increasing as more undesirable practices are uncovered, such as hacking or planting viruses. There are also a number of risks that can arise internally from within organizations such as deliberate or accidental misuse of systems by employees.

As part of risk management in an organization there should be a variety of distinct business functions involved in IT legal compliance. These should include:

- *Personnel department* – recruiting the right staff and applying the appropriate work practices.
- *IT department* – set up Internet and Email policies.
- *Management board* – set up appropriate management structures to ensure all legal risks are covered.

There are independent standards that enable companies to undertake a legal risk assessment of their IT provision. Companies need to hold risk assessment reviews that investigate the legal, financial and managerial implications of risks associated with the IT provision. Many organizations have to pay fines and legal costs because they do not meet the legal requirements set by the government. Independent surveys have shown that up to 29% of UK business may be using illegal software that increases to 50% in smaller businesses. The ideal solution is for every UK organization to review its IT strategy on a regular basis and ensure the correct management policies are in place to ensure any bad practices or misuses are resolved quickly and efficiently. The following UK laws governing IT use and potential penalties are outlined below:

- Data Protection Acts (1984 and 1998)
- Copyright, Designs and Patents Act (1988)

Question 7.1.3

1. What are the main risks facing the use of IT within organizations?
2. What analysis has been obtained about organizations within the UK reference planning for major IT business risk?
3. Is 'risk' always a problem? Justify your answer.

- Computer Misuse Act (1990)
- Companies Act (1985)
- Electronic Communication Bill (2000)

In order to ensure staff within a software development team reach a required *professional standard* during their employment, the company needs to ensure they develop certain inherent skills. Such skills will not only improve the performance of the staff, but enhance the status of the team by having a more professional and competent workforce. Such skills should include:

- inter-personal skills;
- written communication skills;
- verbal communication skills;
- presentation skills;
- project leadership skills;
- management skills;
- budgeting and control techniques;
- legal legislation requirements.

These skills can be developed in a number of ways, through line management, training programs, in-house seminars, college/university courses, etc. Whatever method is adopted the progress of developing staff needs to be carefully monitored to ensure the skills have been obtained. This could be checked by the line manager carrying out a yearly review that is designed to aid the development of the staff member, as well as checking their progress.

Professional bodies

1. British Computer Society

The BCS is a professional institution for everyone who is concerned with Information System Engineering. It offers IT professionals the opportunity to participate in the development of their profession. The aim of the society is to provide a structure to support you in developing and maintaining professional skills through your entire career. Member services include:

- professional qualifications;
- professional information;
- professional network;
- BCS examinations;
- accreditation of university courses;
- professional development;
- industry skills model;
- other benefits.

The BCS stresses the importance of *professionalism* that implies taking responsibility and accounting for one's work and performing the work to the highest possible standards. In order to achieve this it is important that the individual is trained to the highest possible standards and is thoroughly up-to-date with the latest techniques, theories and standards.

Two important issues are specified by the BCS for HE courses that require accreditation:

- Project Standards are maintained;
- Professional elements are embedded within the course.

Obtaining skills does not finish with a college of university qualification. New skills need to be developed to meet the ever-changing requirements of the computer industry. This can be achieved through *Continued Professional Development* (*CPD*) with the aim of creating an environment that enables you to remain professionally competent throughout your working life. The BCS provides an excellent guidance outline of how to carry out a continued professional development program, which includes how it can be measured, use of log books, mentoring, the behavioural skills, etc.

The benefits of CPD are basically:

For individuals

- improved job performance and satisfaction;
- enhanced career development;
- potentially more earning power.

For Employers

- more capable, motivated staff;
- improved business performance;
- better recruitment, retention and deployment of staff.

Continued Professional Development (CPD) may be achieved by attending or undertaking:

- short courses;
- conferences or exhibitions;
- symposia and society meetings;
- private study/self directed learning;
- distance learning;
- further education studies;
- higher education studies;
- post qualification studies;
- imparting knowledge;
- committee work;
- official meeting or reviews;
- relevant voluntary work;
- on the job training.

All activities should be recorded in an official CPD logbook which is specially designed to include all continuing education, on/off the job training courses, etc. and should be presented at the next professional review.

2. Engineering council

The mission of the Engineering council is to enhance the standing and contribution of the UK engineering profession in the national interest and to the benefit of society. The Council, together with its partner Institutions work together to maintain a world-class engineering profession for the benefit of the nation. The organization of the Council is made up of a Senate that comprises of elected members for the supporting institutions and Privy Council nominees. It is supported by two Executive Boards, the Board for Engineering Profession (BEP) and the Board for Engineers' Regulation (BER). As an example the British Computer Society is a supporting institution.

The Engineering Council sets the standard for registration as a professional engineer or technician as:

- Chartered Engineer (CEng)
- Incorporated Engineer (IEng)
- Engineering Technician (EngTech)

Details of the requirements for membership of the above classifications are contained in SARTOR (Standard and Routes to Registration). The proposals for the fourth edition (SARTOR 4) have just been released (April 2003). Most of the provisions under SARTOR 3 are being phased in over a period of several years. The main impact at the moment is within higher education where universities are now offering courses that have been accredited under SARTOR 3, like 4-year MEng or 3-year BEng courses for potential Chartered Engineers. There will be changes to this as the new SARTOR 4 becomes fully implemented once the proposals have been accepted.

An educational base requirement for an Incorporated Engineer (IEng) is:

- a three-year programme comprising either an engineering, technology or science bachelor degree (not necessarily honours), which has been accredited for IEng registration under the criteria given in SARTOR 3 Part 2 Section 4.1.2 *or*
- 'HND' – a programme accredited for IENG plus an accredited or approved matching section *or*
- 'HNC/HND' – a programme accredited for IENG plus an accredited or approved matching section.

The requirements of *Matching Sections* could be met through:

- Edexcel-BTEC Professional Development Qualification programmes (full time, part time or modular), particularly those which integrate technology and engineering business management, or which lead to a specialist sub-discipline.
- Programmes designed by a university or college as a bridge between its accredited HND and its own degree programmes which are accredited for IEng. Ideally, the total package of such provisions should be accredited together.
- Edexcel-BTEC programmes which provide for progression from the 10 unit HNC to the 16 unit HND, as the first stage of this process for those progressing from an HNC base.
- Equivalent schemes appropriate to SQA-SCOTVEC Higher National and Professional Development Awards.
- Education, training and development programmes operated by private and public sector employers such as consultants, industrial companies, the civil service and armed forces. These schemes often include the equivalent of an academic year of 'educational development' in technology, management, personal skills, etc. in addition to 'training and experience'.
- Integrated Development Schemes and College-Business Partnerships (Teaching Company Schemes for FE).
- Distance learning packages aimed at particular graduate employment opportunities in specialist fields or at those in remote locations or mobile jobs.
- Employment-based or institution-based schemes leading to a particular form of employment. Whilst statutory or NVQ/SVQ certification

of competent performance may be involved, it is the development of the knowledge, understanding and transferable skills which is a key to matching sections. An NVQ/SVQ used for this purpose would have been recognized by the institution concerned, in accordance with the Engineering Council's 'Guidance to Institutions and Awarding Bodies on Occupational Standards, N/SVQs and Registration'.

Educational base for Incorporated Engineer, full details are contained in SARTOR 3 and the following section are included:

- standard and expectations;
- educational preparation for Incorporated Engineers (IEng);
- admission guidelines;
- personal and professional development;
- route to IEng from Cognate Courses.

Figure 7.1.3 outlines the routes for Incorporated Engineers:

There are other professional institutions that carry the status required by SARTOR, these include the: Institute of Electrical Engineers (IEE) and the Institute of Incorporated Engineers (IIE). But they all carry the same code of ethics reference the professional issues that surround the development and progression of people within the computer profession.

Question 7.1.4

1. What is CPD and who should undertake it?
2. What are the aims of the BCS Professional Development Scheme (PDS)?
3. What are the three main grades of membership for engineers and engineering technicians specified by the Engineering Council?
4. What does SARTOR stand for and what are its main objectives?

Exercise 7.1.4

1. If you are not already a member of the British Computer Society, find out what the requirements are for joining as a 'student member' and if possible, join! Write a report on their approach to professional development for their members.
2. Carry out research to establish if there are other registered institutions within the UK that may be of benefit to the computer professional. Who exactly are they aimed at and what is their mission statement.

Service level agreements

Service level agreements (SLAs) are legal documents that define the rules, requirements and terms of engagement between a company and

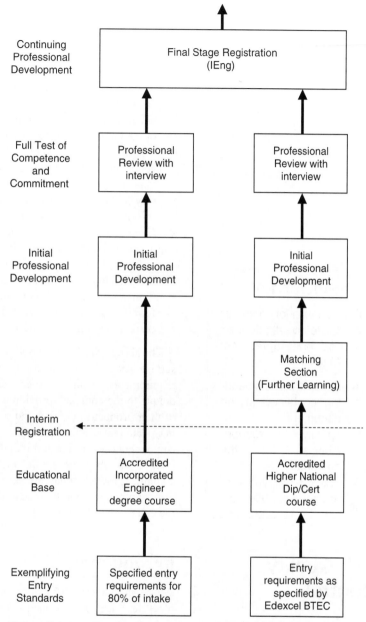

Figure 7.1.3 *Benchmark routes for incorporated engineers*

the user/buyer of their product. SLA's specify the relationship properties between the two parties involved, an example of some main areas are listed below:

● *Products covered under the agreement* – this will normally outline the goods supplied (these may be new or reconditioned), what is not covered and where the customer can find details of the goods (e.g. this may be specified on the invoice).

● *Service outline* – overall explanation of what services are to be included. The company may offer different level of services (e.g. 2 hour callout, next day exchange, return to base, etc.). A special help line may be available or queries may be handled by e-mail, etc.

- *Limit of services* – for example, the duration of the agreement, the service contract may be broken if the item has had an unauthorized repair or has undergone accident, misuse or abuse, etc. When and where the company can be contacted.
- *Customer duties* – the company must receive payment for the SLA within a specified period of sending out an invoice. Customers should have all relevant information ready when contacting the company under the agreement (e.g. their service number, make/ serial number of the goods, operating system used, etc.)
- *Guarantees or Warranties* – what the main manufacture terms are to the goods supplied, i.e. length of initial warranties. The agreement does not remove your legal rights under the Sale of Goods Act. The company may state that they guarantee that their services will carried out in a professional way that is consistent with industrial standards, etc.
- *General Terms* – this may include the 'term and renewal' dates associated with the agreement. It may provide an option for the customer to 'upgrade' the service prior to the end of a contract. Other factors included may include the 'cancellation' rights for both parties.
- Transfer of the agreement – this states if the agreement can be transferred to a new customer. If it can be transferred it will outline the correct method to achieve this.

The above list is only an outline of some of the heading contained in a service level agreement. Many will contain other sections, e.g. legal requirements, security issues, management issues, etc. Each SLA is unique to the company providing it, in that it will define precise details of their product(s) defined under the agreement. For example, the SLA may state that it will supply new or reconditioned items for a particular component (i.e. hard disk drive) that has found to be faulty.

SLA have become a fundamental requirement for many buyers of computer products today. We see them in use for both hardware and software components and their cost often forms a large budgetary outlay for the end users of the product.

Question 7.1.5

For a supplier of computer hardware investigate their service level agreement (SLA) to:

1. outline the main heading contained in the document;
2. specify the responsibilities of the customer;
3. specify the limits of the services offered.

7.2 Quality control

Introduction

We saw in Chapter 2 that *maintenance* forms an activity within the software lifecycle. It has to be planned from the earliest stages and any design decisions that are made need to consider how they will effect the maintenance of the produce. A good system requires a product that is easily maintained so that its future is ensured. Remember that if a software product that is not maintained it dies. If we take a word processor application the manufacture will keep maintaining the product and bring out new versions or updates in order to keep up with market requirements. If this process of maintenance does not take place the product will not be marketable and sales will fall.

Professional programmers spend a lot of time on maintenance activities. The results of a survey by Lientz and Swanson are shown below:

Activity	Time (%)
Maintenance	48
New development	46.1
Other development	5.9

Further surveys indicate that changeability is the second most important attribute after reliability for the development of large software systems. The cost of maintenance is often over 50% and sometimes reaching 75% of the total software lifecycle costs for the development of a product.

In order for Lientz and Swanson to establish the importance of maintenance versus new software within the software development industry they surveyed several companies. Their results are shown in the table below:

Importance	%
Maintenance is very much more important than new development	33.3
Maintenance is more important than new development	21.7
Maintenance is equal to new development	34.8
Maintenance is less important than new development	5.8
Maintenance is very much less important than new development	4.3

It can be seen from the table that 55% of the responses thought that maintenance was more important than new development. Some companies are only responsible for one major product and their existence relies on its continued success. For them new development is not a major issue because they need to ensure the existing system is thoroughly maintained. If their system does encounters problems the company needs to ensure all available effort is put into any required changes/updates, etc. The company needs to ensure that the product fully meets the requirements of the end user at all times and hence provide continued success for them as a viable software producer.

Maintenance is not always easy and encounters the same problems as those seen with an original project. But it has additional problems as often the people carrying out the maintenance activities are not the same as those producing the original software. Poor documentation can present problems, we saw a major example of this when systems underwent changes to avoid the so-called 'millennium bug' problem. Systems that had been in operation for several years required modifications, but this took time due to the lack of documentation especially in the area of internal coding and associated structures.

Lientz and Swanson surveyed nearly 500 companies to establish the distribution of effort in software maintenance. Their results are shown in the table below:

Activity	Participation (%)
Emergency debugging	12.4
Routine debugging	9.3
Data environment adaptation	17.3
Changes to hardware or operating system	6.2
Enhancements for users	41.8
Improve documentation	5.5
Improve code efficiency	4.0
Other	3.4

Unlike hardware, software products do not wear out. But they will die if they are not maintained. Dead products do not need maintenance. Therefore systems must be maintained if they are to remain a viable product in their specified environment.

The table shows that only a small percentage is assigned to emergency debugging (12.4%) and the largest maintenance activity is for enhancements to be made for the users. This would include any changes, modifications, updates, etc. that enhance the product to improve its capabilities and provide a better tool for the customer or end user.

Another survey by Lientz and Swanson looked into the types of maintenance that was carried out within software organizations. The types established are listed in the table below:

Type of maintenance	Employed (%)
Adaptive: changing a system to work in a new operating environment	18
Corrective: changing a system to correct deficiencies, i.e.	17.4

- it will not run
- incorrect results are obtained
- does not perform as expected
  in order to meet the specified requirements

Perfective: changing a system to add new functionality, i.e. making it	60

- better
- faster
- more compact
- better documented
- easier to use
- modern

Others: including *preventive* maintenance which changes software to improve future maintainability or reliability or to provide a better basis for future enhancements	4.6

The important issue resulting from these studies is that maintenance can be managed. The requirements of the adaptive and perfective types can be anticipated by the development team and measures for scheduling, monitoring and estimation can be managed in the same way as a new project. Some corrective maintenance can also be managed leaving about 10% that require special, immediate handling.

Maintenance requests

A software product that delivers large systems may take months or even years to complete. During the development process the original specification, that the system must be designed to, may become out of date so that when it is complete its lacks important functions or at worst, it may not be usable. Systems need to be developed flexibly so that modifications can be made easily through program units that have been selected to cope with anticipated changes. Such changes can be implemented during the lifecycle of the project through maintenance procedures. The following steps

---

Question 7.2.1

1. What are the main goals of software maintenance?
2. Why is it important to keep on 'updating' software?
3. From the surveys conducted by Lientz and Swanson which type of maintenance activity has the most time spent on it, and why?

outline the stages taken during the maintenance process:

- A *change request* from the customer or market requirements triggers the maintenance process;
- Often changes are implemented into a new version of the system;
- If changes are made to an installed application the corresponding documentation needs to be updated to reflect the modified structure.

The maintenance request may be activated somebody issuing a 'change request form' which specifies all the new requirements that are to be implemented along who issued the modification. An example of a 'change request form' is shown below.

The *change request* is submitted and evaluated by the project manager and senior staff to ascertain its technical merit, potential problem areas,

Change request form	**Reference Number** ....
I request that this change request form be submitted to the next scheduled maintenance control meeting for discussion.	
Name:	Date:
Position:	Internal Extension:
Department:	E-mail:
Project Title:	
Implementation Version:	
Proposed Change:	
Affected Modules/Units:	
Reasons for Change:	
Improvement Plan:	
Fallback Plan:	
Other Information:	

impact on other units within the project and the potential cost. The output of the evaluation process is a *change report* that is presented to the change control authority who make the final decisions about the proposed changes to the system.

The improvement plan is structured into project, group and corporate elements. The project level is concerned with the need for improved software tools that are essential for maintaining existing poor quality code. The group level issues specify the need for improved communications and roles for the maintenance team. The corporate issues focus on the creation of an environment in which the maintenance activities are seen as an integral part of the overall software development field and quality assurance issues. The main headings to be included in the improvement plan are outlined below:

- Introduction.
- Improvement process – to include overall quality issues and required needs for the proposed change. Reviews the overall process and specifies problem areas and how they can be overcome.
- Project level plan – to include required tools and training requirements for their use.
- Group level plan – ensuring who is to receive information and their status within the maintenance process.
- Corporate level plan – communication channels and sub-contract requirements. Design requirements, customer links and quality standards.
- Scheduling of the plan and progress checks.
- Summary.

Maintenance activities

The activities required to complete the maintenance work can be classified under two headings:

- Unstructured maintenance
- Structured maintenance

Unstructured maintenance takes place when the only element to work on is the source code. Documentation is often poor and the resulting maintenance process has to evaluate code sections that are difficult to ascertain and interpret.

Structured maintenance occurs if the complete software engineering documentation for the project exists. Here the activity begins with the evaluation of the design document, followed by assessing the impact of the required modification and planning a method of implementation. Finally the design is modified, reviewed, coded and tested. Figure 7.2.1 shows the layout of structured versus unstructured maintenance.

Configuration management

The main aim of configuration management is to establish and maintain the viability of software system products throughout their development lifecycle. It involves identifying the configuration of the software at given time intervals, controlling any changes to the configuration, maintaining

---

Question 7.2.2

1. What is the purpose of completing a change request form and how should it be processed with an organization?

2. What are the two maintenance activities that are used when implementing 'change' on a software system. Which method is the lost efficient?

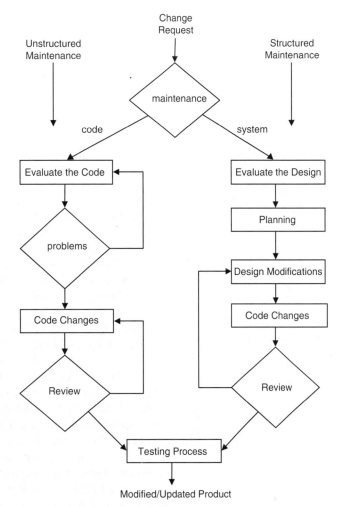

Figure 7.2.1 *Maintenance structures*

traceability and integrity of the configuration throughout the development lifecycle of the project. Configuration management is about implementing and controlling change of a software system product.

The components placed under software configuration management include software products that are delivered to the customer including the requirements documents, code and any other items that have been identified to create the software product (e.g. software tools, compiler, etc.). The main goals of configuration management are:

- all configuration management activities are carefully planned;
- any affected teams or individuals are informed of the status and content of any changes to be implemented;
- the products placed under configuration management need to be identified and available to the team;
- any changes are made to the software work products need to be controlled by the configuration management team.

The table below shows some of the normal activities carried out by configuration management during the lifecycle of a product.

Lifecycle activity	Configuration management
Requirements analysis	Expand configuration management practices from the system project plan
Systems analysis and design	Control versions of documentation produced
Implementation	Control versions of code and documentation produced

Software configuration management can mean many things to different people within the software development industry. For example, people see it as version control, configuration identification, status accounting, configuration control boards and modification request tracking. But the one main factor that is agreed between people working in the field is that it is seen a crucial element in the support of software development and maintenance. As we have already stated for software to remain successful it needs to undergo maintenance and this maintenance strategy needs to be carefully planned and implemented. A coherent maintenance strategy therefore represents one of the main aims of successful configuration management.

The responsibilities of the staff involved with configuration management will alter as the project develops over its lifecycle. For example, during the system design phase more and more documents will be produced by staff responsible for the software system. These documents will need to be checked and controlled against the project's documentation standards. Changes to the negotiated statement of requirements and the system specification must also be monitored and acted on accordingly. This volume of work will increase as the project develops, the changes in many documents may rebound on earlier phases of development. Hence there are many changes to many documents that have to be controlled.

Configuration is therefore the discipline of co-ordinating software development and controlling the change and evolution of software products and their associated components.

Version control

During the maintenance phase or when an iterative activity occurs within the software lifecycle different versions of the documentation is produced. The documents that comprise all information produced as part of the software engineering process is collectively termed a *configuration*. Version control is a method used to keep track and manage changes that are carried out on a software system. For any software system to be successful a process must be put into place to ensure the development team are working on the latest version of the product. If an earlier version was to be used then the developer could be faced with repeating work that had already been carried out, or working on something that is no longer required. Either way, problems like this can hinder the development process and effect the efficiency of the product being produced.

Lets look at some issues that may occur during the lifecycle of a product:

- Customers want to modify the requirements. The Project Manager as part of an innovation process wants to modify the approach taken to develop the product. How are these changes going to be controlled?
- When developing part of a system the programmer notices that the listing does not match what the program is doing. The question raised is, what version of the program is this?

- Bailey the programmer is asked to modify part of a program, whilst Bess is asked to reduce its complexity. How are we going to make sure that each of them is not interfering with each others work?

The solution is to employ the following techniques:

- Configuration Management (CM) – see the last section.
- Version Control (VC) – is part of configuration management which organizes the storage of different versions of documents and controls changes to documents when new versions are produced.

Version control tools provide a means for helping multiple users to make simultaneous changes to a collection of documents or files without damaging each other's work. Most version control systems carry out the following sequence of events:

- *Connect operation* – a database is created somewhere on the system.
- *Add operation* – files need to be added to it, both existing and any new ones.
- *Checkout operation* – you are required to tell the database which files you are working on and some tools allow files that can be modified at will and submitted when the developer has finished making the changes.
- *Undo checkout command* – if required you can revert to the last version of the file.
- *Checkin operation* – when the changes have been made and tested they need to be put back into the database for permanent storage. This allows other members of the development team to see the files if required. The person saving the modified files will be asked to add a description and details of where the new version is.
- *Label operation* – once all the changes have been completed and the system is ready the files can be labelled to state the version number for future reference.
- *Get operation* – the developer can go back and look at earlier versions, or at latest versions that have been added by someone in the development team.
- *Rename operation* – this allows files to be renamed if required.
- *Delete operation* – this allows files to be deleted if they become obsolete.
- *Report operation* – provides reports about the files that are stored in the database.

One of the most important facilities provided with some version control systems is the ability to automatically backup copies of your work on a storage device other than your own development disk system. If changes are made by mistake on the developer's version then the checkout operation will allow you do deliberate about what changes are made and save overwriting some important work.

A document is said to be a *baseline document* when it reaches a certain stage in the development process. The project manager at the outset of the project usually determines when this will be. For example, a design document is baselined for approval or a code module is baselined once it has successfully undergone testing requirements. *Baselining* is therefore a common technique used for controlling change of documents, i.e.

- Before a document is baselined, changes can be made by a member of the development team quickly and informally.
- After a document is baselined changes can still be made, but they need to follow formal guidelines to evaluate and verify the change.

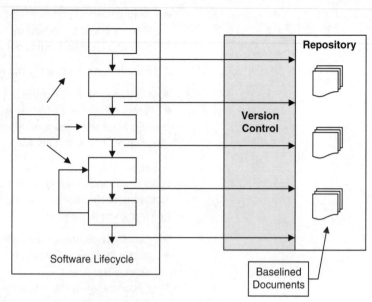

Figure 7.2.2   *Version control using a repository*

The changes need to be formally controlled by version control activities that track and modify the status of the document from its baseline date until the end of the project

Version control tools

In order to implement the 'Add Operation' most tools provide a *repository* which holds the baseline documents. When a document is baselined within a repository it becomes subject to version control. This process is outlined in Figure 7.2.2.

Each team member is allocated an area known as a workspace that prevents project members from accessing the work of others. Generally the use of a workspace contains the following actions:

- in order to carry out a change on a document it is first transferred from the repository to the project members workspace;
- changes can then be made to the document without effecting the repository;
- once any changes to the document have been accepted it is copied back to the repository.

The revision control system

This is a version control system that stores all the updates of a single document in a special file called a *revision group* contained in an revision control system (RCS) directory. When a file is baselined a revision group for it is set up and the initial version of the document is numbered 1.1. When a new version of the document is checked then a new number is allocated to it, before added to the revision group. The numbering system is based on a hierarchical tree structure that allows branching for:

- corrections to released documents;
- development modifications;
- processing conflicting changes.

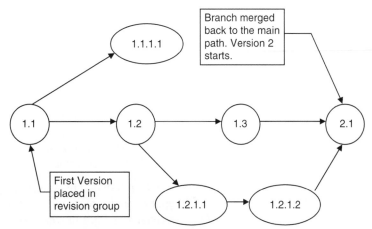

Figure 7.2.3 *RCS branching within revision groups*

A typical tree structure is outlined in Figure 7.2.3.

The RCS system controls the changes that can be made to files by providing locks. A lock for a revision group must be obtained before a new version can be checked in. Only one user can hold a lock at a time thus allowing only one user the access to make changes to a specified version at a time. The RCS system has facilities for group use where each team member has a link to the central repository within their workspace.

Within the RCS environment the name and version number identifies documents. This could take the form of MYSYSTEM-1.0 allowing different versions to be grouped together in a configuration.

Specified below is an example of RCS system:

ComponentSoftware Revision Control System (CS-RCS)

This is a revision control system that allows you to manage multiple versions of your documentation in an efficient manner. It is a powerful and robust document RCS that monitors changes made to files that are accessed by standalone or networked terminals. The system allows you to see how and when a file was changed or easily returned to an earlier version.

CS-RCS provides the following version control facilities:

- Retrieve and revision by any criteria anytime.
- See what has changed between two revisions.
- Avoid any loss of work by backtracking.
- Save disk space.
- You know how does what and when.
- Avoids two users modifying the same document at the same time.
- Specifies when there is a modified version of a shared document.
- Operate on a variety of server applications.
- UNIX and Windows users can share common files.
- Conversion facilities UNIX to DOS and DOS to UNIX.

CS-RCS is based on the GNU RCS Revision 5.7 standard that is currently used by lots of users in the UNIX field. It is based on the original command line interface, but CS-RSC has provided a modern graphical user interface application that can fully integrate with the Windows environment.

CS-RCS can be found via Component Software at:

http://www.componentsoftware.com/csrcs/swintro.htm

Other Version Controls Systems and information can be found at:

http://www.greymatter.co.uk/gmWEB/nodes/NODE0865.htm
http://www.thefreecountry.com/developercity/version.html
http://www.cvshome.org/docs/blandy.html
http://www.systemanage.com/cff/versioncontrol/
http://www.qumasoft.com/feactures.htm
http://www.download.cyclic.com/pub/

Other systems are available, e.g. *shapeTools* that provides tighter integration with other configuration management requirements as well as version control. But whatever system is used the overall principle is the same, that of controlling the storage of baselined documents to ensure it they come under strict version control rules. We have often heard terms like; 'I did not mean to change that file', 'Are we working on the latest version?' or 'Am I working on the same document as another project member?' which effect the productivity of the development process. The aim of version control is to improve productivity by providing a system that keeps track, and manages changes, to the documents that are produced during the development lifecycle.

Question 7.2.3

1. Under what management activity does version control fit into?
2. What do you need to do in order to carry out the 'checkout' procedure for a version control system?
3. What does the term 'baselined' mean?
4. What is a repository?
5. What multi-platform characterizes are specified for the CS-RSC system?

Exercise 7.2.1

Download or install a RCS version control system (if one is not already available) and:

1. Check-in: create a simple text file and add it to the repository.
2. Check when the file was last changed.
3. Check-out the latest revision of the file.
4. Check-in a new revision.
5. View the revision history of the file.
6. Produce a detailed report for the file.

Quality assurance tools

Quality plan

The quality plan is specified in the project plan and gives details of how the quality measures are to be implemented. It provides information on how the software developer is to implement the standards and measures outlined in the company quality policy. The main aim of the quality plan is to show to the customer or the end user how the developer will ensure the requirements of the system are met. Below is an extract from the ISO 9001 standards on quality system requirements:

ISO 9000-3 4.2 Quality System Requirements

- Establish a quality system and document it in a quality manual.
- Develop and implement quality system procedures that are consistent with the quality policy.

- Define and document quality plans that show how the quality system requirements are to be implemented. Quality plans should be developed for products, processes, projects and customer contracts.
    - Develop quality plans to control software development projects.
    - Develop a quality plan whenever there is a need to control the quality of a specific project, product or contract.
        - The quality plan should explain how the company intends to tailor the quality system so that it applies to a specific project, product or contract.
        - Develop detailed quality plans and procedures to control configuration management, product verification, non-conforming products and corrective actions.

There is also an earlier ANSI/IEEE standard that outlines a series of headings on how to structure a project plan. It includes areas like management, supplier control, documentation, reviews and audits, standards, etc. The project manager should document the intentions of the software development process within the quality plan. Like every other public domain standard they should be adopted critically and customized to meet the needs of the company business plan.

Outlined below is an example extract for a quality plan:

2.1 Requirements analysis

A number of reviews are to held during this phase. Two basic types are to be conducted. Internal Reviews and External Reviews.

Internal reviews: To check a component part of the customers requirement document to ensure it is clear, concise and unambiguous. The reviews will be held for each partitioned section of the system and will contain the following personnel:

- Chair: The Project Manager.
- Software Engineer involved with developing the component part of the system.
- Software Engineer with experience in the field that is under development.
- Quality Assurance representative.

The meeting will be formally minuted and any unresolved matters need to be documented as actions. The unresolved matters will be resolved before the next scheduled meeting. The minutes will be available for team members to see and if required the customer.

External reviews: This review will involve the customer (or customer's representative) who will check that the resulting specification meets the needs of the original requirements. The following people will be present at the review:

- Chair: The Project Manager
- The Customer (or representative)
- Software Engineer involved with the sub-system under development
- The team leader (or line manager).

This review will normally be 1.5 hours long and arrangements for any unresolved matters will be the same as for the internal reviews. Further details will be found in the Project Plan (Section 2, Paragraph 2.4.3).

Another example of information contained in the project plan involving testing issues:

Integration Test Requirements

Once unit testing has been completed and the partitioned units are brought together and series of integration tests will be implemented. The integration tests will check the units link together and they are brought together. Each test will be carefully documented and contain the following headings:

- Test name
- Explanation of the test
- System units to be integrated
- Where the system units are stored
- Test data to be used (or its location)
- Expected output from the tests
- Actual test results
- Location of the integrated system
- Additional information.

At this level the tests are carried out internally with the development team under control of the team leader. Information about the results of the tests must be made available to the customer (or representative).

Question 7.2.4

1. What is the quality plan?
2. How should a quality plan be structured?
3. Why is early acceptance of the quality plan by the customer important?

The quality plan needs to be understandable to all parties concerned with the project. This must include the customer who will view the document and ascertain whether the developer is going to conduct techniques that will produce a product to fully meet the requirements. It correctly documented the quality plan can inspire confidence in the customer who will be able to see the quality measures that will be adopted. For the developer they need to carefully assess the plan to ensure it defines clearly the methods to be adopted for achieving the desired quality objectives. All development activities including validation and verification requirements need to be included in the quality plan. Producing a high quality software system relies on planning and monitoring techniques to ensure its success. The quality plan is one of the techniques that aids the development process and inspires confidence in the customer.

Quality manual

A quality manual should meet the ISO 9001:2000 requirements. In the past these have been expensive to produce, but the electronic age has seen an increase in companies that provide the resources for businesses to complete the manual on standard templates using directed techniques. The key points for creating a successful manual are:

- they should be well organized;
- the content should be clear, concise and unambiguous;

- it should be well presented and easy to use;
- the language should be at a high level specifically aimed at the end users.

People do not like manuals if they are not precise, or contain too much detail, or are poorly presented. It is essential that all manuals follow the guidelines above to ensure they are properly presented, well organized full definitions included.

In some cases it may be necessary to seek legal advice about the document before it is published. This will ensure that it complies with national and local legislation and other legal issues that may be present.

The quality manual will state in a clear and concise way the policies and objectives of the company and how the desired level of quality are to be achieved.

Below is a list of heading that may appear in a typical quality manual:

1. General information
2. Background to the company
3. Conventions and definitions
4. Quality management system
5. Responsibility of management
6. Resources
7. Product realization
8. Analysis, measurement and improvement.

Quality manuals should be dynamic in structure. This is because changes within an organization can occur from time to time and they need to be reflected within the manual. When changes are made they need to be consistent with the original format as they may impact on other policies. Finally ensure that there is a clear record of revisions made by staff involved and that current information is circulated at regular intervals to all relevant employees.

> **Question 7.2.5**
>
> 1. What items do you think should be included in the General section of a Quality Manual?
> 2. How would you note down the revision history as the Quality Manual undergoes many changes?

Test plan

Testing is a validation activity and if carried out correctly provides valuable evidence that the system (or sub-system) performs as it should. A test plan provides a basis for specifying tests that are to be carried out during the development of the project.

We have already seen that a number of tests are carried out over the lifecycle of a project. Each test will require a different set of criteria, e.g. a unit test will need to conform to its detailed design structure, while an integration test will need to ensure the interfacing between units is correct. Below is an extract from a negotiated statement of requirements:

> When the school administrator types in an STUDENT_ID command the system will respond with the student name, course and registration details. The STUDENT_ID must be unique and made up of alphanumeric characters (two letters representing the students initials and a six number code), e.g. SM123214. If the student is new the administrator adds the details to the file.

On implementing this section the developer would assume that data validation was important for the end user. This could result in the following tests being applied:

STUDENT_ID command

Test 1
The system should show that if an incorrect identifier was entered by the user, a suitable error message is displayed and the system does not crash.

Test 2
The system should demonstrate that if a correct identifier is entered and the student has withdrawn a suitable message should be displayed.

Test 3
The system should demonstrate that if a correct identifier for a student is entered and the student is currently active the name course and registration details should be displayed.

Test 4
If an identifier was accepted but no matching file is found a suitable message should be displayed. For example, the ID may not yet be allocated.

Test 4
The system needs to ensure that all identifiers are unique. If a new identifier is added and the same one already exists a suitable error message should be displayed.

Test 5
The system should accept three fields for each new student. IF the operator forgets to fill in one field then a suitable warning message should be displayed. This is not an error, as a student may not be allocated a course yet.

The test plan is part of the quality plan and relates directly to the testing activities being carried out. Separate sets of tests are to be specified for each test activity outlined in the original plan. Testing is about demonstrating the correctness of a system or sub-system. It is about finding errors and correcting them to produce a quality piece of software. A extract from Myers outlines this concept:

Testing is the process of executing a program with the intent of finding errors

Question 7.2.6

1. What is the test plan
2. What overall plan is it part of?

When to stop testing is difficult, this again comes down to time and money. You can never assume that all errors have been detected. A thorough approach to testing procedures and documentation will improve the run-time capability of the product providing an efficient and sound application that is marketable in the real world.

Reviews

A review is a managerial activity that is used in both verification and validation processes. It involves a meeting of a number of team members and other interested parties with the view of analysing part of a document or code section produced within the system. A review will determine the correctness of a product with respect to the original requirements. They are used continually throughout the development process and are conducted under strict guidelines. They are formal meeting that are scheduled at regular intervals throughout the lifecycle and need to run to a pre-set agenda, be formally minuted and resulting actions carefully documented. As we have seen the quality of a product depends on whether the final product meets the customer's requirements. A review provides a simple, but effective method for checking the process of development and providing feedback to interested parties. There are many types of review ranging from informal meetings through to a formal technical review (FTR). The guidelines for a formal technical review are outlined below:

- the meeting should contain between 3 and 5 people and contain a chairperson;
- it should be prepared in advance and an agenda produced and distributed;
- the meeting should not be too long, a maximum of two hours is sufficient;
- minutes should be taken and distributed;
- any suggested actions should be carried out before the next meeting.

It has got to be remembered that it is the product that is under review and any noted faults need to be pointed out to the developer carefully. Any comments should be constructive to ensure the moral of the development team and help provided where possible. A review is an essential tool in the development of modern software products, but there success is dependent on how they are conducted and how resulting actions are implemented.

Exercise 7.2.2

1. Set up a test plan for a practical application that you have previously developed.
2. Carry out a review that is carefully documented to analysis the test plan developed in exercise 1 and its resulting implementation results.

7.3 Project management

Introduction

One of the main aims of software project management is to complete a quality product 'on time and within budget'. The end result must be a product that is fit for the purpose that was outlined in the original specifications. The product must be completed without exceeding predetermined costs that were set at the beginning of the work. Time deadlines need to be ensured in order for the completed application to be delivered to the customer or end user when they expect it to be ready.

Problems with time and budget can lead to a poor market reputation and may effect continuing projects that the organization has planned for. The aim of good software project management is to avoid these problems and ensure success in all areas of the project. The project manager needs to plan a project around the concepts of:

- Quality
- Cost
- Budget

These three characteristics are known as the 'triangle of primary objectives' and determine the priority each should play in the software development process. Project planning consists of estimating effort, scheduling tasks and monitoring their progress. The effort required to complete various activities is estimated in terms of recourses needed to implement them. Scheduling involves allocating tasks to individuals and determining the start and finish times for the associated activities. Monitoring checks the progress of a developing project against its original aims.

A *software project manager* may face the problem of directing a large development team consisting of analysts, software engineers, programmers, hardware technicians, quality assurance specialists and other related staff, where the end application will contain several thousand (or even millions) of lines or code. Research has shown that the best software products are achieved when a good manager motivates the team and they feel part of the overall plan for producing the application. It is down to the project manager to get the most from his staff in order to provide a finely tuned professional workforce that is capable of ensuring success for any given product application.

Roles of a project manager

There are no set guidelines for the tasks that a project manager has to carry out. There are many varied tasks, some of which are outlined below:

- *Controlling* – is the process of ensuring a project meets its stated objectives. The project manager will be involved in reallocating resources when a problem occurs and providing leadership by directing staff every day as to what is required and helping as necessary.
- *Planning* – this is the process of deciding what to do and will involve specifying events, cost estimates, meeting stated objectives, risk assessment and sub-dividing tasks.
- *Monitoring* – this involves the project manager checking the progress of a project ensuring that both internal and external milestones are met. The external milestones will be carried out with agents of the customer so they are aware of the development progress. The main objective here is to check the project is on time to meet its specified delivery date. Progress problems identified in this area may lead to new measures being put into place that come under other task headings specified in this list.
- *Organizing* – this involves the organization of staff and resources and outlining the duties and responsibilities of the people within the team. The project manager will need to ensure clear lines of communication that is set up within the team in order to provide a coherent framework for information to be distributed.
- *Representing* – the project manager will need to represent the company and especially the application under development with people outside the organization. This could involve liasing with the customer, or associated agents, for which the project is being developed. The project manager will need to meet with the customer in order to report on the progress (or lack of progress) of the project under development.
- *Staffing* – here the project manager will ascertain the required staff needed to successfully complete the project. Identifying any training requirements that may be required and encouraging staff by providing promotion opportunities. This category sees the project manager playing the role of a personnel officer with the responsibility to assign staff positions from senior management down to junior and trainee appointments.
- *Innovating* – this involves the project manager developing new ideas that will improve the work being carried out on the project. An example

could be a new CASE (Computer Aided Software Engineering) application that has just come onto the market which may improve the analysis and design techniques that are already in place.

Information requirements of a project manager

It is important that the project manager has information that is relevant to applications under current development. Some sources of information that should be readily available are outlined below:

- For any planning to be carried out data on earlier projects is required. This historical information is useful for estimating and costing a current project that has similar characteristics to previous projects. The project manager will be able to ascertain the possible resources required and provide a time analysis breakdown leading to a possible completion date.
- For developing any software system initial documentation is created before it starts production. Such documentation would include project plans, quality plans, cost estimates, risk estimates, etc. and should be readily available to the project manager. Documentation that is created during the software development lifecycle also needs to be available and will include the following: requirements analysis, specification (both functional and non-functional), system design, implementation and maintenance, etc. The project manager needs to ensure that a system of 'version control' is in place in order for the information held to be the latest available.
- Data is required which helps the project manager make changes that will improve the efficiency of a project under construction. Such data would come from a number of sources, both internal and external. Within an organization any information on innovation strategies needs to be available and how the modifications can be compared across activities to ascertain their overall effectiveness. External sources may include information on existing or new tools that are available and can be implemented within the development process to improve efficiency. Above all the project manager needs to ensure that any changes made will have an economic benefit for the company.
- In order to successfully monitor the progress of a project, information including graphical data, needs to be available to the project manager. Graphical data would include Gantt charts and associated critical path networks. These would clearly show the required deadlines, stage completion dates, delivery date and any associated milestones that are required during the development lifecycle.
- If during the monitoring process it was found that the project was slipping behind schedule the project manager will need to make changes to improve the progress. This will involve rescheduling activities and documentation needs to be available that shows how any changes made in one part of the project impacts on other areas of the project.

Software project planning

All projects need to be carefully planned, failure to do so will result in an application that is difficult to manage. Large projects are generally planned in outline before development commences where the main elements are specified. These include an estimation of the project cost, required resources and how the project lines up with the company's business plan. Once the customer has accepted the project a full planning document needs to be produced. This document is called the *project plan*, an example outline of what should be included is shown below:

Company project plan

Chapter 1 – Project outline
1.1   overview of the project
1.2   overview of the development stages
1.3   customer contacts and integration
1.4   work description and product delivery

Chapter 2 – Project planning
2.1   task lists with associated dates and people responsible
2.2   significant event points
2.3   responsibilities of the project team

Chapter 3 – Software and hardware requirements
3.1   software and hardware facilities required
3.2   analysis and design tools
3.3   additional support requirements
3.4   specified development strategies
3.5   required software development standards

Chapter 4 – Configuration management
4.1   strategies for handling change during development
4.2   version control requirements

Chapter 5 – Documentation requirements
5.1   documentation format
5.2   documentation standards
5.3   publishing and validating responsibilities

Appendices
A   test strategies to be adopted
B   quality plan

Question 7.3.1

1. List the main roles of a project manager.
2. What does monitoring involve for a project manager?
3. Within a project plan as outlined in the previous table, explain what should be included for the following Section: 3.2 analysis and design tools?

When any application has been completed the project manager should have learned something from it. Most projects involve a steep learning curve because tasks differ in complexity and new development tools come onto the market all the time. Software is increasing in complexity as the power of the hardware increases adding more challenges for the project manager. But any experience gained will be beneficial to any subsequent projects that have to be developed by the project manager.

Milestones

A milestone is a significant event point that occurs during the lifecycle of a project. It is normally based on the planned production of a piece of the project and is used to track the progress made during development. Milestones often occur at highly visible points in the development process, e.g. at the end of the requirements analysis phase. When adding milestones to project management tools they are classified as tasks with zero duration.

Milestones can be classified as:

- *Internal Milestones* – The developer will be interested in both major events and minor events and is mainly used by the project manager to monitor progress of the system under development. There are usually many of these and will include external milestones and other significant event points that happen in between the external milestones. An example could be the completion of a test system for a particular component of the project.
- *External Milestones* – These are mainly used by the customer and the project's senior staff. Here the milestones correspond to the significant events that can be measured. An example would be the acceptance testing for a completed project.
- *Informal Milestones* – Individuals in the development team use these to monitor their progress against the overall development of the project. These can be very informal, e.g. set by an individual programmer, or more details, as set by a senior programmer.

The project manager will use reports on the completion of each milestone to measure the progress of the project.

Question 7.3.2

From any example of a software development project give an example of an:

1. external milestone
2. internal milestone
3. informal milestone

Tools used in project planning

Planning provides a technique for the project manager to ascertain the requirements of what is to be done and how best to initiate a course of action. Some of the main planning tools are outlined below:

- *Estimating* – this will find out how long the proposed work will take to complete and the total cost of the work to be completed. Estimating will also involve the project manager seeking to establish what resources (both human and equipment) that will be required.
- *Network diagrams* – these help to establish the relationship between tasks, the time taken for each task to be completed, the links between each task and any parallel interaction.
- *Critical path analysis* – this takes the components of network diagrams a little further to establish the minimum time taken for a project to be completed. If anything should go wrong throughout this path it could have severe time (as possibly cost) repercussions that would need to be addressed.
- *Bar charts* – these normally form the starting graphical display based on having time on the x axis and the tasks on the y axis.

Project planning is an essential phase for the project manager and his/her team. It must be set at the correct level for the task to be completed. There is no one fixed method of planning a project, it will differ on the task at hand, the number of people involved, customer requirements, financial constraints, etc. Good planning is an essential ingredient as a foundation for success of a project and cannot be understated or under-developed in any way.

Project management tools

Gantt charts

Gantt charts were developed by Henry Gantt (1861–1919) an industrial engineer and have been in widespread use as planning aids within project development since. Gantt charts show various activities as blocks on the diagram that are plotted against a time base (or 'x' axis). It gives an overall outline of the scheduling of tasks throughout a given project and will be used by developers to specify the start and end dates for their associated activities. A Gantt chart is therefore a form of bar chart where activities are listed down in the diagram and plotted against a horizontal time base. An example of Gantt chart is shown in Figure 7.3.1.

Within any project some activities cannot be started until other activities have finished. This means that some activities are dependent on others and this fact needs to be specified in a table before the Gantt chart is completed.

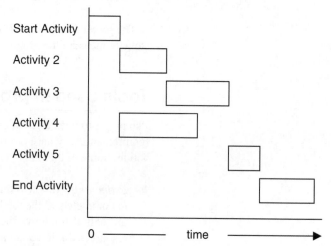

Figure 7.3.1   *Outline Gantt Chart*

Example 7.3.1

From the following table create a corresponding Gantt chart.

Activity	Estimated duration of the activity (in days)	Dependant
A1	12	–
A2	27	A1
A3	10	A2
A4	29	A1
A5	21	A3, A4
A6	12	A2
A7	10	A5, A6

Suggested solution:

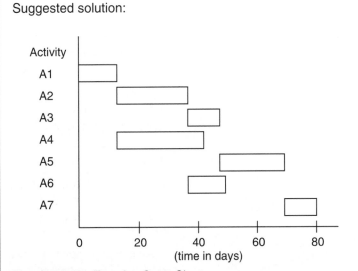

Figure 7.3.2 *Exercise Gantt Chart*

Note that the time taken to the end of the project is ascertained from the activities and their associated dependencies. The final time shown in the chart will represent the end of the project and when it is ready for delivery to the customer.

The levels expressed in a Gantt chart can act as a schedule by which the progress of a project can be ascertained. If any problems occur the following actions should be employed:

- find the critical areas of the project where any delay can effect the date the project is due to be completed;
- check the progress of the project to ensure it is still on target to reach its planned completion date;
- if any activities need to be rescheduled ascertain what effect the changes will have on the rest of the project.

To achieve these goals the best tool available to the project manager is that of critical path analysis through network diagrams. This technique will provide a means of determining the effect changes have on the time periods allocated to each activity for a specified project. Critical path methods employ network diagrams that show the relationships between activities and their estimated durations.

Network diagrams

Network diagrams come in a variety of forms:

- CPM – critical path method
- CPA – critical path analysis
- ADM – arrow diagrams
- PERT – project review and evaluation technique
- PDM – precedence diagrams

They provide analysis of results of project progress reports and allow decisions to be made by the project manager. An outline of the objectives of a network diagram are stated below:

- identify any possible problem areas before they are encountered;
- provides a focus for critical activities;
- provides a means of evaluating the relocation of resources;
- provide a tool for monitoring the progress of a project.

In order to produce a network diagram the activities need to be stated with their estimated duration times. An example table for an engine oil change is shown below:

Activity	Description	Estimated duration
1–2	Empty old engine oil	10 minutes
2–3	Fill with new oil	5 minutes
3–4	Run engine and check level	12 minutes

An important point to remember here is that the duration time for each activity is kept in the same units, i.e. minutes, hours, days or months. A simple network structure to represent this table is shown in Figure 7.3.3.

The network figure contains information about the duration of each activity and the corresponding cumulative time taken over the whole project. For more sophisticated diagrams additional information may be required which includes the following terms:

- The earliest start time or the earliest expected time (EET) which represents the earliest time that a particular activity can start to be developed within a project.
- Earliest finish which specifies the finish time for an activity that started its development at the early start time.
- Latest start or latest allowable time (LAT) which specifies the latest time an activity may start in order for it to be completed on time.
- Latest finish specifies the latest time an activity may finish in order to keep the overall project on schedule.
- Maximum span is the maximum time period that an activity has to be completed in. It is calculated by subtracting the earliest start time (EET) specified at the start of an activity from the latest finish time (LAT) specified at the end of the activity, i.e. LAT (end of the activity) – EET (start of the activity) = maximum span
- Total float is thus calculated as the maximum span minus the estimated duration. This is very important when ascertaining the critical points within a project as activities that have a total float of zero are said to be on the critical path.

One way of showing this amount of data is to use a precedence diagram that provides a clear representation of the activities and their start and finish times relative to their immediate predecessors and successors. Most modern project management tools (Microsoft Project, CS Project

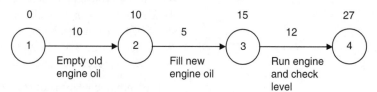

Figure 7.3.3 *Network diagram using arrow notation*

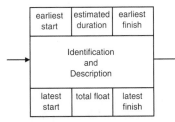

earliest start	estimated duration	earliest finish
Identification and Description		
latest start	total float	latest finish

Figure 7.3.4 *Activity using a 'precedence' structure*

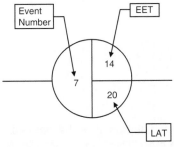

Figure 7.3.5 *Network diagram event*

Professional, Project Commander, etc.) support the precedence notation or a similar structure. An example of the notation used for an activity is shown in Figure 7.3.4

Program evaluation and review technique

This technique was originally developed by the US Navy in the late 1950s and has been widely used ever since as a project management tool within education, industry and government circles. The steps taken to develop this process require the identification of all the activities and placing them in sequence. Then the timing of each activity needs to be estimated along with their associated dependencies. Once this has been established it is documented in a table from which the network diagram can be constructed and the critical path established. From then on the project manager can use the diagram for monitoring purposes. It can then be modified, if required, to take into account any rescheduling requirements and changes to the critical path.

Figure 7.3.5 shows the notation that we are going to use to develop this procedure. The figure shows an event which is used at the start or the finish of an activity and from which the estimated duration and total float can be ascertained.

When creating network diagrams it may be necessary to include 'dummy activities'. These are shown as dashed lines and are used to specify the dependence between activities on the diagram. They do not constitute any real work and have no time allocation associated with them. They just act as a logical link to ensure the network diagram correctly represents the stated dependencies.

The following example takes you through the stages of using PERT to develop a network structure, ascertaining its critical path and tabulating the resulting information.

Example 7.3.2

This example is based on the table used in Exercise 5.1.3.1 and assumes the activities have already been established in their correct order for development. For your information the table is repeated below:

Activity	Estimated duration of the activity (in days)	Dependant
A1	12	–
A2	27	A1
A3	10	A2
A4	29	A1
A5	21	A3, A4
A6	12	A2
A7	10	A5,A6

Question

From the table:

1. construct a network diagram.
2. construct a table to show the maximum span and total float.

3. specify the critical path and emphasize it on the network diagram.

Suggested solution:

1. First layout the diagram to show the activities and the event numbers. This should be achieved by looking at the activities and who they are dependent on.

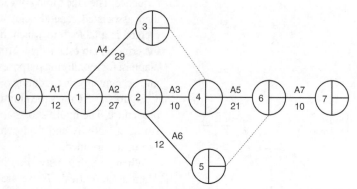

Figure 7.3.6   *Outline network diagram*

Next add the EET to each event which specifies the earliest time that a particular activity can start. This can be achieved from the table or better still the Gantt chart.

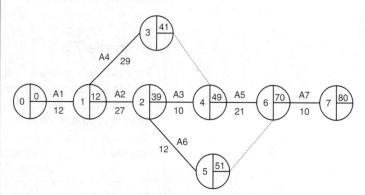

Figure 7.3.7   *Network diagram showing earliest start times*

Next add the LAT times which relate to the latest time an activity may start in order to still complete it on time. This is a little more tricky, remember that the LAT for the final event must be the same as the EET. Work back from there by subtracting the estimated duration from the final LAT (i.e. 80 − 10 = 70 and 70 − 21 = 49, etc.). Note the LATs shown for the start of the dummy activities are the same as the LATs at the end of the activity. This is because dummy activities do not have any time period associated with them.

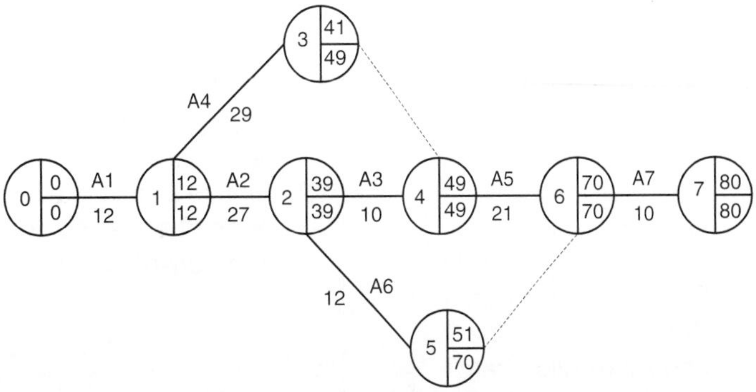

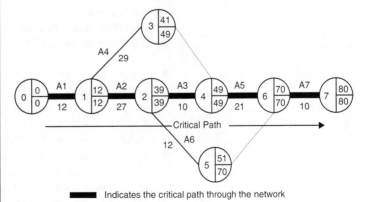

Figure 7.3.8 *Network diagram showing latest allowable times*

2. The table is shown below, remember that the total float is calculated from subtracting the estimated duration from the maximum span.

Activity	Estimated duration	Maximum span	Total float
A1	12	12	0
A2	27	27	0
A3	10	10	0
A4	27	37	10
A5	21	21	0
A6	12	19	19
A7	10	10	0

3. The *critical path* lies on a line where the activities have a total float of zero. In this case the critical path lies along the line containing activities:

A1 – A2 – A3 – A5 – A7

This is been emphasized in Figure 7.3.9 (using bold lines):

■■■ Indicates the critical path through the network

Figure 7.3.9 *Network diagram showing the critical path*

Question 7.3.3

1. What is a Gantt chart used for?
2. What does PERT stand for and what is its main function?
3. What do the terms EET and LAT mean?
4. What is important about the critical path?
5. How is the total float calculated and what is important about its value?

Exercise 7.3.1

An partly complete network diagram is shown below:
1. Complete the network diagram to fill in the missing EETs and LATs.
2. Set up a table that shows the maximum span and total float.
3. From the results obtained in (2) show the critical path on the network diagram.

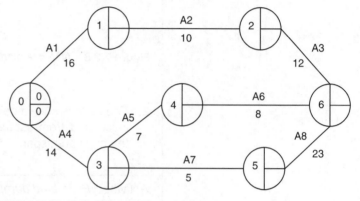

Figure 7.3.10   *Outline network diagram*

Project management tools in action

We have seen that project management consists of planning, organizing, monitoring, staffing, innovating, representing and controlling. In order to help document these requirements a number of professional 'project management' tools are available to assist the project manager plan a software project. The tools will allow the project manager to co-ordinate a variety of specified tasks that need to be set against a specific timeframe and an allocated budget. The advantage of a computerized model is that change requirements can easily be implemented, critical paths viewed and checked and analyses the resource issues inherent in the project. It sets out a plan of action that provides a tracking tool for monitoring progress, assesses the quality issues and cost requirements and prepares a flexible publication framework for use by the project management team and other interested parties.

Some basic terms that are associated with a number of project management tools are outlined below:

● *Tasks* – these represent the main areas of work that are to be completed during project development. For example, the 'requirements analysis' phase of a software project could be considered as a task. Tasks represent the division of the work that has to be completed in order to carry out all the specified project goals.
● *Task type* – these provide a means of recalculating variables when resources are allocated to a particular task. Such types include *fixed units, fixed work* and *fixed duration*.
● *Duration* – the allocated time for each task. Note that a *milestone* is a task with a zero duration.
● *Links* – these provide a 'link' between tasks. For example, if task 'B' is dependent on the completion of task 'A' then a *finish to start* link

needs to be created between tasks 'A' and 'B'. The former is called a *predecessor* link and the latter is termed its *successor*.

● *Constraints* – these allow for the possibility that intermediate deadlines may need to be set. Constraints can be classified as *flexible* or *inflexible*.

● *Resources* – these specify what resources are to be included with the project. They are classified as *work resources* which are usually the people requirements or the equipment needs and *material resources* which defines the stocks and supplies that are required to complete the project.

● *Assignments* – these provide a means of assigning a resource to a task.

● *Costs* – here the number of hours that a resource is operational is calculated against the hourly cost to give the *resource cost rate*.

The basic requirements for using any project management tool are outlined below:

● establish the tasks that make up the entire project;
● determine the dependencies that establish the predecessor relationships;
● set the start date and duration for each task;
● define when the project is to start.

Exercise 7.3.1 outlines a simple project implementation created in Microsoft Project 2000.

Example 7.3.3

Below is a copy of the table used in Example 7.3.2

Activity (task)	Estimated duration of the activity (in days)	Dependant
A1	12	–
A2	27	A1
A3	10	A1
A4	29	A1
A5	21	A3, A4
A6	12	A2
A7	10	A5, A6

This table is to be documented within a project management software tool.

1. Open up the software tool and create a new project.
2. Enter the tasks above to form a corresponding Gantt chart.
3. Display the corresponding network diagram.
4. Add the following two milestones (Milestone 1 after task A3 and Milestone 2 after task A5).
5. Set up in the resources sheet the following; Team A and Team B both classified a 'work resources'. Do not worry at the stage about costs etc. Team A is to be responsible for task A2 and Team B is responsible for task A6. Show these on your Gantt chart.

Suggested Solution

1. Open a project management tool, set the required start date, schedule, status, calendar, etc. then name and save the project. Ensure that the correct working and non-working

days are allocated (i.e. to include weekends and bank holidays, etc.). Also you may need to set the correct working times for each day.

2. Gantt chart.

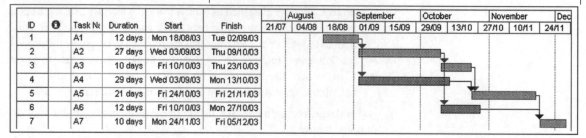

ID	❶	Task Nε	Duration	Start	Finish
1		A1	12 days	Mon 18/08/03	Tue 02/09/03
2		A2	27 days	Wed 03/09/03	Thu 09/10/03
3		A3	10 days	Fri 10/10/03	Thu 23/10/03
4		A4	29 days	Wed 03/09/03	Mon 13/10/03
5		A5	21 days	Fri 24/10/03	Fri 21/11/03
6		A6	12 days	Fri 10/10/03	Mon 27/10/03
7		A7	10 days	Mon 24/11/03	Fri 05/12/03

Figure 7.3.11   *Gantt chart layout*

3. Network diagram.

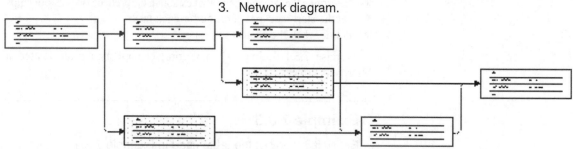

Figure 7.3.12   *Network diagram layout*

4. Modified diagrams (Gantt and network) with milestones added.

ID	Task Nε	Duration	Start	Finish	Predε
1	A1	12 days	Mon 18/08/03	Tue 02/09/03	
2	A2	27 days	Wed 03/09/03	Thu 09/10/03	1
3	A3	10 days	Fri 10/10/03	Thu 23/10/03	2
4	M1	0 days	Thu 23/10/03	Thu 23/10/03	3
5	A4	29 days	Wed 03/09/03	Mon 13/10/03	1
6	A5	21 days	Fri 24/10/03	Fri 21/11/03	5,3,4
7	M2	0 days	Mon 13/10/03	Mon 13/10/03	5
8	A6	12 days	Tue 14/10/03	Wed 29/10/03	2,7
9	A7	10 days	Mon 24/11/03	Fri 05/12/03	6,8

Figure 7.3.13   *Gantt chart layout with associated milestones*

5. Resources – please see the diagram below

ID	Start	Finish	Predε	Resource Names
1	Mon 18/08/03	Tue 02/09/03		
2	Wed 03/09/03	Thu 09/10/03	1	
3	Fri 10/10/03	Thu 23/10/03	2	Team A
4	Thu 23/10/03	Thu 23/10/03	3	
5	Wed 03/09/03	Mon 13/10/03	1	
6	Fri 24/10/03	Fri 21/11/03	5,3,4	
7	Mon 13/10/03	Mon 13/10/03	5	
8	Tue 14/10/03	Wed 29/10/03	2,7	Team B
9	Mon 24/11/03	Fri 05/12/03	6,8	

Figure 7.3.14   *Gantt chart layout with associated milestones and work resources*

Question 7.3.4

Below is a table containing a number of tasks for a specified project:

Activity (task)	Estimated duration of the activity (in days)	Dependant
A1	11	–
A2	9	A1
A3	12	A2, A5
A4	8	–
A5	13	A4, A6
A6	10	–
A7	17	A6
A8	5	A7

Use a suitable project management software tool to implement the table:

1. Open up the software tool and create a new project.
2. Enter the tasks above to form a corresponding Gantt chart.
3. Display the corresponding network diagram.
4. Add the following milestone (Mile 1 after task A6 and before the next task on the critical path).
5. Add suitable team resources for each task. A team is to be allocated to each task and the diagram should show the minimum number of teams required in order to complete the entire project.

Project assurance teams

When taking a management approach to the development of a product, project tasks are divided between independent development teams and quality assurance teams. This model allows testing and quality assessment to be carried out along side each other as the projects develops. This often results in shorter development phases and a greater emphasis on quality at each phase of the lifecycle.

As we have seen a number of projects run into trouble with problems accumulating over time and gradually eroding the business application under development. Problems like handling unanticipated risks, coping with change and funding issues are all to evident. In order to overcome problems the company may set up a project assurance team, headed by a Project Assurance Manager. The main aim of the team is to establish if the project is being organized, controlled and implemented in the correct manner and that no unforeseen risks are being taken.

The project assurance team would be involved with the monitoring and control of the development process and assess the quality of progress against the initial plan. The team would use techniques like an Earned Value Analysis technique to evaluate the development phases and to check that no serious deviation is occurring as the project proceeds.

Each organization will set its own quality standards and at the onset of a project its own quality requirements will be set out in the quality manual. The quality team will check how closely the development team are meeting the quality criteria set for the project and how well the quality processes and procedures are being implemented. The team will also document areas of 'good practice' that can be used for future projects which can then be disseminated to project managers and other interested parties.

Some of the main responsibilities of a Quality Assurance Project Manager are to manage the:

- quality assurance testing program
- software configuration management
- quality assurance team
- project improvement program
- production control program
- quality requirements as specified in the original plan
- meetings and walkthroughs for each application area.

The Quality Assurance Project Manager will need to have the following attributes:

- leadership
- quality management
- business knowledge
- communication skills
- software testing skills
- customer focus.

Quality review meetings

In carrying out their work the project assurance team may hold reviews/meetings to check application areas under development to ensure all standards are being adhered to and provided a comprehensive testing method. Recommendations from the meetings would be fedback to the appropriate development personnel and the project manager and any resulting action implemented accordingly.

A software review is a basic tool for software quality assurance. There is a lot of controversy as to what type of review provides the most efficient and effective method for the quality assurance program. One method often used is the 'inspection', but recent research has called into question its value. Whatever method is used the meeting must be well organized with the correct staff present. The findings of the meeting must be correctly documented and distributed to the appropriate staff for any resulting action to be taken. We have heard phases like 'meetings: can't live with them, can't live without them' and in many organizations meeting take up a significant proportion of the working time. So to avoid terms like 'too long' and 'boring, I nearly fell asleep' the meeting must be well structured, have a sound agenda, not get stuck on one point, not go over old ground and avoid getting stuck with people who have hidden agendas.

The quality review meeting must follow these guidelines. It is a powerful forum where the team can confront quality issues, make decisions and avoid a status quo situation where all people passively accept the outcomes obtained.

Risk assessments

An important task when planning a project is identifying and documenting any factors that may cause the project to be delayed or over budget.

This is termed a *risk assessment* and it specifies the 'risky' areas that may be present in any application area.

When estimating the risk probabilities of any application area the following should be considered:

- How experienced are the staff involved with developing the application area?
- Is this a completely new application area or can it be modelled on a previous development used in a previous project?
- Does the application have to link with another application that carries a high element of risk?
- Is it a large application? It may involve large staff and computer resources where communication may be a problem. Are all the computer resources able to cope with the demands of the application and is the software compatible across systems?

Generally, there is a hierarchy of risk associated with project development. For *real time* software the risks are great and may require large budgets to ensure the quality of the end product is ensured. An example is the US space shuttle where they may spend a hundred times more per line of code than a standard commercial software application.

Some of the heading that should be included in a risk assessment are outlined below:

- *Staff factors* – this will list all the staff associated with the project, their experience and qualifications, their availability, training needs and their job description associated with the project.
- *Hardware and software factors* – what hardware and software is to be involved during the development of the project. Is the software going to operate correctly with the hardware, is the hardware compatible with the customers system, is both the hardware and software up to date and are there any restrictions that may affect the availability of the system?
- *External factors* – are sub-contractors to be involved? Will the system need to go live over the Internet (i.e. are broadband lines in place). Are representatives of the end used to be involved in any way?
- *Customer factors* – what personnel and systems does the customer have in place. How experienced are the staff (will customer staff training be required?), what interaction is to take place during the development of the project and what feedback is required. If this is a new customer then more interaction (involving staff from both organizations) may need to planned, this may depend on how knowledgeable the end users are and the complexity of the application area under development.

Cost estimate

We have seen that many software projects not only end up being delivered late but also over budget. It is important during the planning of a project to set up a cost estimate that is realistic and suits the companies business plan and is competitive in the market that it is aimed at.

Metzger in his book *Managing a Software Project* outlines a number of potential cost items that are present in any software project. The main cost headings are outlined below:

- *Staff costs* – this must include all staff involved both technical and non-technical.
- *Computer time costs* – this not only needs to include the direct development costs and testing activities, but also any indirect costs like using support programs (like project management tools, version control documentation tools, etc.).
- *Data entering costs* – this would include non-technical staff entering the system documentation and any other associated data.
- *Physical facilities costs* – this would include the fixtures and fittings like office furniture, storage areas, space, etc.
- *Consumable costs* – this would include items like laser ink, paper, disks, CD's, DVD's, requirements for the final documentation, etc.
- *External costs* – this could include sub-contractor costs, external equipment (hardware and/or software), using an external agency for specialized work, etc.
- *Travel and subsistence costs* – many projects will involve staff travelling (sometimes overseas) to visit and end user to ascertain their requirements. The company may also require sales staff to visit potential customers in order to market the product.

Once all the factors have been considered it is necessary to check the estimates to ensure that they are realistic. This will involve checking that a figure for an application area matches a previously completed similar application, that similar sections of the project have estimates that match, the resource estimate matches similar resource figures for previous projects and that the differences between simple and complex parts of the project adequately reflect the estimates.

When the cost estimate has been checked a profit figure needs to be added. This figure will be inherent in the companies business plan and the current financial policy of the company board of directors.

A number of mathematical models have been developed over the years to aid the estimating process. One example was outlined by Norden in his paper '*Project lifecycle modelling: background and application of lifecycle curves*' where he set out an equation devoted to each phase of the lifecycle. The result of the equation is a graph based on a time base against resources, where the area under the curve represents the number of person months used in a phase up to time t. See the mathematics in action table.

Organizations may use a combination of both mathematical and pragmatic methods. Research in mathematical models is still on-going and modern computer software applications are available to assist the cost estimator to produce a realistic figure that both suits the needs of the organization and the end user of the product.

Mathematics in action

$$y = 2kate^{-att}$$

where y is the number of staff working on a project at time t; k is the total number of person months in the phase; a is the factor which indicates how short a phase is; t is the number of months from the start of the phase

Estimating quality factor

Deriving from the work of DeMarco the *Estimation Quality Factor (EQF)* sets out to provide a graphical and numerical measure on how successful the estimating process has been over the life of the project. The quality of an estimate is a function of how the estimating value over certain stages of a project converges to the actual cost. The result is a unitless number between zero and infinity. From the studies carried out by DeMarco, the cost estimating process over the life of a project can be deemed to be successful if the resulting numerical value is a high number. He states that given a standard error of 25% or less an EQF of 4 or higher in 68% of projects can obtain a better than average estimating process. Note that the time can be in days, weeks or months as long as it is kept standard throughout the analysis. The following essential rule outlines the estimator's motivation expectations:

> Success for an estimator must be defined as a function of convergence of the estimate to the actual cost of the project and of nothing else

Mathematics in action

To obtain the EQF you need to first complete a graph of the estimating costs plotted against the time taken during which the estimate is relevant. The Actual Cost line is inserted first and is represented by a horizontal line across the graph. The other estimates, starting from the original one, are then added as blocks to represent time period that they are active.

$$EQF = \frac{\text{total area under the actual cost line}}{\text{sum of the areas calculated from the top of the bars to the actual cost line}}$$

if: EQF $>=$ 4 and applying the criteria laid down by DeMarco the quality of the estimating process of the life of a project can deemed to be successful.
Example 7.3.4 outlines this process.

Example 7.3.4

From the table below:

a. Complete a graph that represents this data contained in the table
b. Form the graph calculate the EQF
c. Comment on the results (i.e. are they acceptable or not)

Estimate	Date	Cost (£m)
1	1-1-2000	1.3
2	1-3-2000	1.8
3	15-6-2000	2.5
4	15-8-2000	2.2
Actual	1-12-2000	2.1

Suggested Solution:

a.

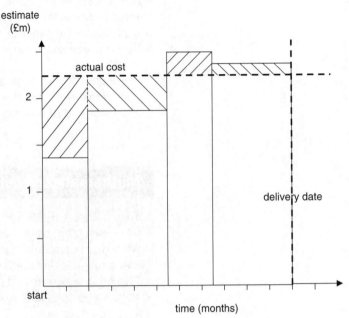

Figure 7.3.15   *EQF graph*

b. First we need to calculate the sum of the areas that are shown hatched on the graph. For example if we take the first estimate, the cost difference between it and the actual cost is 2.1 − 1.3 = 0.8 and the time period is from 1-1-98 to 1-3-98 a total of 2 months, therefore the area for this shaded section is 2 × 0.8 = **1.6**. For the second hatched section we have, time = 3.5 and the cost difference = 2.1 − 1.8 = 0.3, therefore the area = 3.5 × 0.3 = **1.05**. Third hatched section = 2 (months) × 0.4 (£m) = **0.8** and the fourth hatched section = 3.5 (months) × 0.1 (£m) = **0.35**.

Total shaded area = 1.6 + 1.05 + 0.8 + 0.35 = **3.8**
Area under the actual cost line = 2.1 (actual cost) × 11 (total time) = **23.1**

Therefore the EQF = 23.1/3.8 = 6.079

c. For the criteria specified by DeMarco an EQF of 6.079 can be accepted as a good estimating process (because 6.079 > 4 which is the minimum figure specified by DeMarco as an acceptable quality factor).

Question 7.3.5

1. Discuss the cost issues of developing a quality system as opposed to a system that is built not using quality methods.

2. Below is a table which includes the estimating costs for a completed project:

Estimate	Date	Cost (£m)
1	1-3-97	2.7
2	1-6-97	2.9
3	15-10-97	3.8
4	15-1-98	3.6
Actual cost	1-5-98	3.5

    a. Complete a graph that represents this data contained in the table.
    b. Form the graph calculate the EQF.
    c. Comment on the results (i.e. are they acceptable or not)
3. What does a developer need to carry out risk analysis during the early stages of project development?

7.4 Systems development review

Conventional analysis and design techniques

The aim of this section is to build on the techniques covered in Chapter 2 by expanding basic concepts and developing additional techniques that need to be established to fully represent a required system. All people involved with the development of software systems need to be aware of all the possible documentation sources that can be created during the project lifecycle. This becomes more important when aspects like quality assurance and maintenance are to be fully implemented to ensure professional standards are upheld and change requirements installed.

> My experience has shown that many people find it hard to make their design ideas precise. They are willing to express their ideas in loose, general terms, but are unwilling to express them with the precision needed to make them into patterns. Above all, they are unwilling to express them as abstract spatial relations among well-defined spatial parts. I have also found that people aren't always very good at it; it is hard to do ... If you can't draw a diagram of it, it isn't a pattern. If you think you have a pattern, you must be able to draw a diagram of it. This is a crude, but vital rule. A pattern defines a field of spatial relations, and it must always be possible to draw a diagram for every pattern. In the diagram, each part will appear as a labelled or coloured zone, and the layout of the parts expresses the relation which the pattern specifies. If you can't draw it, it isn't a pattern.
>
> Christopher Alexander (1979) in
> *The Timeless Way of Building.*

The above quote from Christopher Alexander sums up the need to express graphically the requirements of a given system. This is especially true for systems analysis and design, in Chapter 2 we saw a number of graphical techniques used; Yourdon, SSADM, UML and Data Modelling, all with similar structures and syntactical correctness. Whatever method was used by a completed system all aspects should be thoroughly understood in order for the development team to modify the requirements so the software product remains a viable product for existing and potential customers.

Mini-specifications

A *mini-specification* is a document that contains a specification of a primitive data process (a process that has not been refined). These range in the level detail which they contain, from a simple high level description, through to a structured table layout. There is no standard layout structure for a mini-specification and often they contain a mix of formal and informal notations. A example layout for a mini-specification is shown below.

Process Name:	
Input Data Flows:	
Name:	Type:
Input Flows from Stores:	
Name of Store:	Component:
Output Data Flows:	
Name:	Type:
Output Flows to Stores:	
Name of Store:	Component:
Process Description:	
This could be a high level English description, a basic program design language or a formal description using pre- and post-condition syntax.	

The table contains the process name, details of the flows passing in and out of the process within a data flow diagram. It highlights the data that is passed to and from storage devices and finally a description of what the process is to do.

Question 7.4.1

The following diagram represents part of a security system which checks the input codes to ascertain if they are correct. The codes are checked against a set of stored values and a suitable output message is displayed. For example if the code is acceptable the output message will state 'valid code' and if it is not in the database list, a message saying 'code not recognised' is produced.

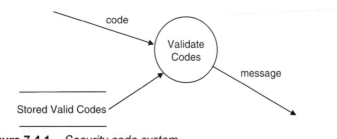

Figure 7.4.1   *Security code system*

Complete a mini-specification of the system.

Data dictionaries

This is a central repository for information flowing through a system and modelled via a data flow diagram. The information must have:

- *Structure* – ascertained by looking at the converging and diverging flows and the data components held in associated stores.
- *Meaning* – implied through meaningful names and documentation evidence from the negotiated statement of requirements.

A data dictionary will contain more detailed information than a mini-specification and formal notations like the BNF (Backus–Naur Format) syntax definitions can be employed. Data dictionaries vary in the way they are presented, but generally they will contain the following:

- Details of all data flows and stores for a specified set of diagrams.
- Abbreviated terms or aliases are specified. These derive on large diagrams where the developer has used an abbreviation instead of a full-length word. For example SPR could have been used instead of System Pressure Result. Technically they should be avoided, but this is not always possible as long names can sometimes over clutter the diagram.
- Extra information about the data is recorded in order to provide clarification and ensure correctness.

Data dictionaries are designed so they can be easily modified and expanded throughout the system development and maintenance processes can thus allowing additional information to be included when or if it becomes available.

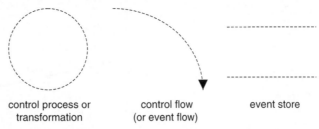

| control process or transformation | control flow (or event flow) | event store |

Figure 7.4.2   *Control symbols used within a data flow diagram*

Control aspects

Data flow diagrams give an overall picture of the system requirements but they do not convey any dynamic or time-related aspects to the developer. If the developer is to produce a complete model for a system specification then the dynamic components of the required system must be analysed and documented. The dynamic aspects can be represented by control components that are first outlined in a data flow diagram and refined as state transition diagrams.

Within the Yourdon Essential Model the main components used to represent control components in a data flow diagram are outlined in Figure 7.4.2.

A *control process* represents the interface between the data flow diagram and the control specification. The name of the control process indicates the type of control activity carried out within the control specification. A control process acts on the input control flows to produce output control flows. The exact nature of the control process is documented in the control specification. The child of a control process is either a control specification or a state transition diagram (STD).

The main difference between a *control flow* and a discrete flow is that the latter has both an occurrence (at some point in time) and content, i.e. some data is sent down the flow line. A control flow just has occurrence and NO content, a signal is sent down the flow line to activate and deactivate a receiving process. You will find that terms like: enable, disable, trigger, on, off and activator are used as control flow names. A typical control flow will be discrete-valued as opposed to continuous, it is a pipeline through which control information is sent. Its name should consist of nouns and adjectives only and may consist of a single element or a group of elements.

To enable a process means that it is activated by a corresponding data flow and will stay 'activated' until a disable signal is sent to it. When a process is not active all data flowing to it is ignored and not queued for later use. To trigger a process is to activate it so that it carries out its task and it is automatically deactivated as soon as it is finished. The processes enable, disable, trigger, etc. are called prompts and they can only originate from control transformations. Events and other control activities can originate from data transformations. Some examples of correct and incorrect syntax are shown in Figure 7.4.3.

Figure 7.4.3 shows (a) syntactically correct as control flows are allowed as activators for control processes to produce prompts as output flows, (b) is not syntactically correct because data flows are not allowed as input flows to control processes and (c) again is not syntactically correct because prompts are not allowed as input flows to control processes.

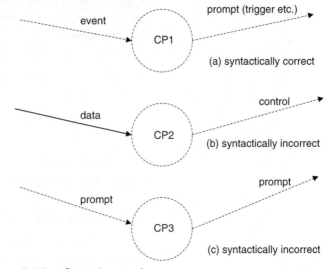

Figure 7.4.3   *Control examples*

An *event* or *control store* represents control information that has been frozen in time. The information stored may be used any time after it has been stored and used in any order. The main difference between a control (event) store and an ordinary store is that the former stores control information only. A control (event) store should be named with a noun that describes its contents.

Example 7.4.1

The following is an extract from a negotiated statement of requirements:

> The Carabaz Chemical Plant Company requires a plant control system that closes down the plant if critical temperatures are reached. The control system is initially manually activated and automatically shuts down the chemical plant when a certain (critical) temperature has been reached. The temperature is continuously read into the system via a transducer mechanism and regular readings are stored in a database. If a critical temperature reading is reached an appropriate signal is sent to the 'control plant' system and this then triggers the plant to close down. If the plant is shut down an appropriate message is displayed on the operator's console. When the chemical plant is closed down the control system is switched off. An operator can type in commands to view the latest stored temperature readings for the plant or print out a report of a series of stored temperature readings. An appropriate error message is displayed if the operator enters an incorrect command.

Use an appropriate CASE tool to complete:

1. a CONTEXT diagram to represent the system;
2. a CHILD of the context diagram to display the main components including control aspects;
3. produce a SYNTAX CHECK to ensure the correctness of the diagrams and their link with each other.

Suggested solutions:

1.

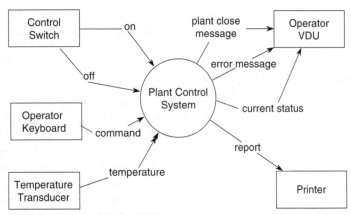

Figure 7.4.4 *Context: Chemical plant company*

2.

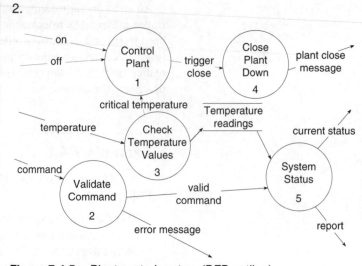

Figure 7.4.5   *Plant control system (DFD outline)*

3. A check is shown below:

Project: C:\MYDOCU~1\SELECT\SYSTEM\CONTROL\
Title: Plant Control System
Date: 13-Sep-2000 Time: 12:0

Report: Diagram Consistency checking

This report contains a consistency check of all the diagrams in the project.

Checking **CONTROL1.DAT**   (CONTEXT DIAGRAM)

No Errors detected, No Warnings given.

Checking **CONTROL2.DAT**   (CHILD DIAGRAM)

No Errors detected, No Warnings given.

Note: The above example would need further decomposition in order to provide a full solution to the specification. At this Stage I am more interested in introducing the concepts of control (the dynamics aspects of the system) and not refining data flow diagrams that were covered in Chapter 2.

Control specifications

This document follows along the lines of a process specification (and to some extent mini-specification) and is created as a child of a control process.

A control specification is a decomposition of a control process and is used to document the time dependent, or event-response, nature of the system. The control specification describes the relationship between control inputs and control outputs on the parent control process, either textually, using Structured English, or State Transition Diagrams, or using state tables.

The table below highlights a typical control specification that was created from the previous example (7.4.1) using the Select Yourdon case tool application.

```
@IN = critical temperature
@IN = off
@IN = on
@OUT = trigger close

@CSPEC 0.1 Control Plant

The system is activated by an 'on' signal from the Control Switch
        When 'on' the Control Plant System waits for a critical
        temperature signal.
        On receiving the critical temperature signal the Control
        Plant System outputs a trigger close signal to shut down
        the plant.
The system is de-activated by an 'off' signal and no further
monitoring takes place.

@
```

Like the process specification the input and output flows are specified and the body must contain the associated flow names in order for it to be syntactically correct.

State transition diagrams

Control processes can be refined to produce a model called a *state transition diagram (STD)*. An STD specifies how a control process is to respond to its input and output flows by specifying the states involved and their corresponding conditions and actions. An example of how a state transition diagram is structured is shown in Figure 7.4.6.

State Transition Diagrams consist of the following objects:

- State
- Start-up state
- Transitions
- Conditions
- Actions.

Diagrams normally start with a *start up state* that has an incoming arrow above it and may contain a single action such as initialize or trigger start. The final state is signified by the fact that there is no transition line leaving it. A state can be considered as a stable condition for a system. Once in a state you have sufficient information on the systems past history to determine the next state according to input events. A states name should be meaningful in that it should represent the real condition held by the system. States are represented by rectangles.

Transition lines are normally drawn straight either horizontally or vertically and are labelled by conditions and corresponding actions. They indicate the movement of one state to another. Transitions between states are event driven. In other words, something happens which causes the system to change from one state to another. However, it should be noted that not all events will necessarily cause a transition from a particular state and that a given event does not always cause a transition into the same state.

A condition is an event, or events, that cause a transition to occur and are displayed above the vertical line. An action is an operation that takes

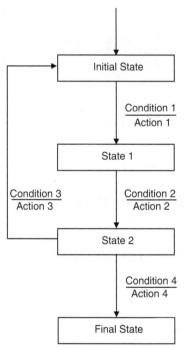

Figure 7.4.6 *Example state transition diagram*

place as a transition occurs. The input control flows to a control process must appear as conditions on state transition diagrams. The output flows from a control process must appear as actions within a state transition diagram.

Example 7.4.2

From the data flow diagram created in Example 7.4.1

1. Create a state transition diagram (STD) from the specified control process.
2. Test the resulting diagram to ensure it is syntactically correct.

Suggested solutions

1.

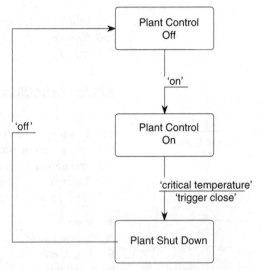

Figure 7.4.7   *State transition diagram (plant control system)*

2. Test check shown below:

Project: C:\MYDOCU~1\SELECT\SYSTEM\CONTROL\
Title: Plant Control System
Date: 15-Sep-2000 Time: 12:2

Checking STDCONT1.DAT

No Errors detected, No Warnings given.

----- End of report -----

Exercise 7.4.1

The Bailey Comfortable Room Company requires a computer system to control its air conditioning systems when installed on customers' premises. The system needs to operate three main components; a heater, a cooler and an air vent. The components can each be in one of two states:

- Heater can be on or off
- Cooler can be on and off
- Vent can be open or closed.

The system will compare temperature reading at regular intervals with the requirements for operating the components. Normally this will be within 2 degrees of the target values, any change outside this figure will instigate a change of state. To cool a room that is too warm the system goes through various stages:

1. The heater is turned off
2. The vent is opened
3. The cooler is switched on

To warm a room the reverse is required:

1. The cooler is switched off
2. The vent is closed
3. The heater is switched on.

If a temperature is correct for a required component then it is left in its current state and only one change can be made at a time.

When given a problem you need to ascertain the exact number of possible states. The maximum number of states that this system can have is eight (three components each with two states). But not all are acceptable, for example it is not practical to have the heater 'on' at the same time as the cooler or the vent open with the heater 'on', etc. This can be set up as a truth table:

Components			Possible state
heater on	vent closed	cooler off	✔
heater on	vent closed	cooler on	✘
heater on	vent open	cooler off	✘
heater on	vent open	cooler on	✘
heater off	vent closed	cooler off	✔
heater off	vent closed	cooler on	✘
heater off	vent open	cooler off	✔
heater off	vent open	cooler on	✔

This leaves four possible states (those with a tick). Complete a STD to represent these states for the Bailey Comfortable Room Company. Test your diagram to ensure it is syntactically correct.

Question 7.4.2

1. What are the main components of a data dictionary?
2. What is the main difference between a mini-specification and a data dictionary?
3. What children can be created from a control process?
4. What is a Transition within a STD? and how is it labelled?
5. What data should be contained within the body of a control specification?

System design

System design takes the functional specification from within the system specification document and provides a base for a solution of the problem. Design takes the developer from the process of defining what the system should do, to how it is going to be structured. Most designs will initially use graphical techniques to specify the problem in a modular structure with communication links between them, which provides the passage of data around the system. Two important characteristics need to be inherent within any good design process, they are:

● It must match the specification and be correctly structured by successfully undergoing both verification and validation testing procedures.
● It must be easy to maintain – a design that can reduce the amount of maintenance will result in a larger reduction in project costs.

A typical design process is shown in Figure 7.4.8.

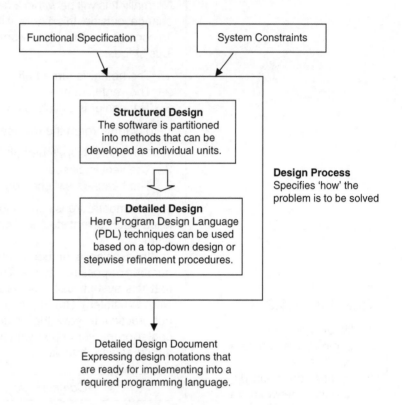

Figure 7.4.8   *System design layout*

Research has shown that systems that have been designed using a structured method are easier to understand, develop, document and modify. One of the people who originally researched this work was Larry Constantine who initially spend some ten years studying various systems before producing his diagrammatic methods to represent structured design.

Structure charts

A structure chart is a graphical representation that depicts a control hierarchy of units or modules. It is used as a tool to carry out structured design and specifies an interface between modules that have been determined from the functional requirements. The symbols used within a Constantine Structure Chart are shown in Figure 5.4.9.
Explanation of the symbols shown in Figure 5.4.9:

a. Modules are used to represent processing that is local to the Constantine diagram. A module is identified by a name, by which it can be referenced.

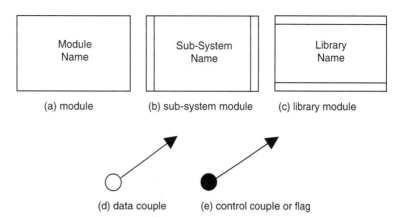

(a) module   (b) sub-system module   (c) library module

(d) data couple   (e) control couple or flag

Figure 7.4.9 *Constantine structure chart symbols*

b. Sub-systems are pre-defined modules that are detailed through decomposition on further diagrams. Sub-system modules can be used many times by many diagrams. Here the developer uses decomposition to produce a sub-system that is made up of a structure chart in its own right.

c. A library is a pre-defined module in a Constantine diagram that can be used by many different systems. The designer can take its operation for granted as its content has already be constructed and tested.

d. Data couples are flows of data between modules. They are placed on the module-calling flows. The arrowhead indicates the direction of data flow. When implementing the structure chart they could be considered as a parameters passing between code functions or procedures.

e. Flags show control-information passing between modules on a Constantine diagram. You place flags on the module-calling flow. Examples of flags are *End of Data*, *Loop End*, *Command Entered* or *Received OK* that represent a control signal being sent between modules. The arrowhead indicates the direction in which the flag is being passed.

A structure chart describes three important areas of information:

● Shows the partitioning of information into modules.
● It shows the hierarchical relationship between modules.
● Describes the interface between modules.

Structure charts are designed to show three distinct areas of data on a diagram. These are specified as input (sometimes called afferent) control, transform control and output (sometimes called efferent) control. Basically the afferent modules handle the input of data flowing into the main controlling module (i.e. the main part of the program), the transform control area *transforms* the data flowing into it and the efferent modules handle the output of data. A basic layout is shown in Figure 7.4.10.

Note how the data flows from the input module through the central module and into the transform module where it is acted on or transformed. Likewise the *newValue* data couple flows through the central module and on the output module. This is important as the central module only controls the flow of data through the system and any processing is carried out by the subordinate modules. Note also that the subordinate modules are shown on the same level within the diagram. This is normal practice when completing structure charts, because the hierarchical layout specifies to the developer the level of module processing involved with respect to the main module and the delegation of processing tasks to subordinate modules.

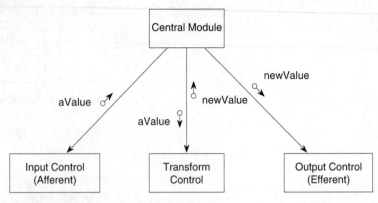

Figure 7.4.10   *Basic structure chart layout*

One of the main problems with structure charts is ascertaining which modules fit into the required categories. There is often overlap and developers need to specify a line across each boundary. This may be achieved on the original data flow diagram that outlines the main components that need to be included in the structure chart.

Example 7.4.3

A system takes a customer order number that is input from an operator's keyboard and produces a goods reference number which is transformed into a goods list. The goods list is then used to produce an invoice that is printed off and sent to the customer.

Carry out the following steps:

1. create a data flow diagram to represent the system;
2. split the data flow diagram into three separate components (input, central transform, output) and pick out the modules required for the structure chart;
3. complete the structure chart;
4. produce a valid test procedure on the final diagram to show it is syntactically correct.

Suggested solution:

1.

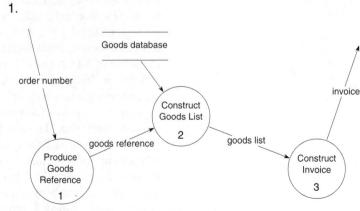

Figure 7.4.11   *DFD customer invoice system*

2.

Components	Module
Input	Get order number
	Transform order number into goods reference
	Get goods reference
Central transform	Transform goods reference into goods list
Output	Put goods list
	Transform goods list into invoice
	Put invoice

3.

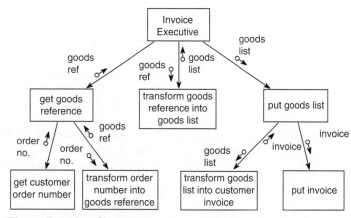

Figure 7.4.12   *Customer invoice system structure chart*

4.   A syntax check is shown below:

Project: C:\MYDOCU~1\SELECT\SYSTEM\INVOICE\
Title: Customer Invoice System
Date: 17-Sep-2000 Time: 12:5

Report: Diagram Consistency checking

This report contains a consistency check of all the diagrams in the project.

Checking INVOICE1.DAT   (DFD CONTEXT
                                                       DIAGRAM)
No Errors detected, No Warnings given.
Checking INVOICE2.DAT   (DFD DIAGRAM
                                                       Fig. 5.1.1.11)
No Errors detected, No Warnings given.
Checking INVOICE3.DAT   (STRUCTURE
                                                       CHART)
No Errors detected, No Warnings given.

----- End of report -----

Object-oriented analysis and design

In Chapter 2 we built up the three basic concepts of object-oriented analysis that aid the way we develop models that represent class structures. The concepts covered were:

- *Class* – describes the behaviour of a set of objects of a particular kind.
- *Associations* – the relationships between objects. Where an object is an instance of a class.
- *Responsibilities* – which describes the behaviour of a class. Responsibilities take two forms: responsibilities for recording information and responsibilities for carrying out some action.

We need to add a further component to this list in order to provide a full analysis and design specification which is ready for implementing into an object-based programming language. The fourth concept is that of collaboration:

- *Collaboration* – An object may carry out its responsibilities by collaborating with other objects. This means that an object can send a message to another object (the receiver) to obtain some behaviour characteristic(s) that are inherent within it.

Object-centred viewpoint

One method of developing an object-oriented system is to use the 'object-centred view' which gains an understanding of the system from the perspective of the individual objects that make up the application. The object-centred view leads to the analysis and design concept of CRC (classes-responsibilities-collaborations). CRC design focuses on:

- Classes (or abstractions)
- Responsibilities (or behaviours)
- Collaborations (the other classes that an object needs to effectively carry out its responsibilities).

An objects collaborators are those other objects that it explicitly needs access to, in order for it to carry out its task. For example, if object X requires object Y to perform its function then Y is X's collaborator. The collaborators of a class generally consist of the superclass and subclasses that it has direct knowledge of and occasionally other global classes it may need to reference. Some texts use alternative terminology for collaborations, for example colleagues or helpers.

Object-community viewpoint

Here the developer gains an understanding of the interactions between the individual objects that make up an application. This approach will focus on the relationships between classes and their appropriate responsibilities. The two main tools used in this area are:

- Use-cases (example uses of the application that illustrates inter-object behaviour).
- Class Hierarchy Integration (taking classes from an existing library and determining if they are identified in the CRC design).

Walk-through

A walk-through take some coherent piece of behaviour that the system must exhibit – like recording the enrolment of a student onto a course – and investigates how this behaviour can be constructed with the object model. The main steps taken in a walk through are:

- Stage 1 – Understanding in Application Area terms (or understanding in problem domain terms)
  - what information is the system provided with?
  - what must the system do with that information?
- Stage 2 – Understanding in Terms of Instances of Classes and Associations. Take the action that the system must carry out and deciding for each action what classes and associations are involved. This leads to the first structural layout for classes, i.e.
  Class: Dog
  Responsibilities:
  Maintains the dogs name and age.
  Determines the group a breed of dog comes under.
- Stage 3 – Understanding in terms of Responsibilities and Collaborations. The collaborators are often determined by reading the description of the responsibilities. The structure in Stage 2 is refined as:
  Class: Dog
  Responsibilities:
  Maintains the dogs name and age.
  Determines the group a breed of dog comes under.
  Collaborators: Breed

(this can be read as 'Breed' is a collaborator for 'Dog')

The object that makes a request for the service of another object is termed a *client* and the object that receives the request (and responds by providing a service) is termed a *server*.

Question 7.4.4

1. What two viewpoints are often used during object analysis and design?
2. What is a 'collaboration' between classes?
3. What is the function of a walk-through?
4. For the example shown in Stage 3, identify the client and the server.

Example 7.4.4

The following is an extract from a specification for the Bernese University:

> The Canine faculty of the Bernese University contains several lecture rooms that are uniquely named. The seating and equipment for each room allows for a maximum of 28 students to be present. The faculty administration system has the responsibility for recording information about their allocated lecture rooms, the tutors who staff them and the students that are allocated to them. The administration system will also be responsible for recording new student details and their entry to a given lecture room group. A single tutor is responsible for each lecture room group and their names and study room numbers need to be recorded by the system. Information about the pupils needs to include their name, address and emergency contact telephone number.

(i) Analyse the extract using the process of textual analysis to ascertain the classes to be developed within the system. Try to avoid any classes that are not directly relevant to the specified problem.
Suggested classes are: FacultyAdmin, LectureRoom, Student and Tutor

(ii) Complete a class-association diagram to represent the system

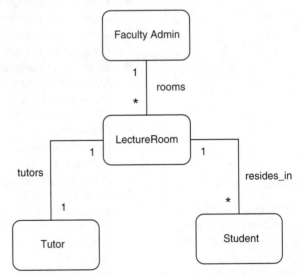

Figure 7.4.13 *Class-Association for the Canine Faculty*

(iii) Layout the class text structure that represents the diagram outlined in Part (ii)

Class: FacultyAdmin
"There is only one instance of this class and it is the orchestrating instance"

Class: LectureRoom
Responsibilities:
Records the name of the lecture room

Class: Student
Responsibilities:
Records the student's name, address and emergency contact number

Class: Tutor
Responsibilities:
Records the tutors name and study room number

Note that there is a restriction on the system that needs to be specified as an invariant.

Invariant
Any given instance of LectureRoom is associated with instances of Student via the resides_in association. The maximum number of Student instances that may be associated with any one instance of LectureRoom are 28.

This technically means that students can not be in two lecture room groups at the same time and each lecture room has a maximum capacity of 28 students.

(iv) More detail needs to be added to the class layouts in order to provide a full analysis model. This can be achieved by carrying out a 'walk-through' to ascertain the full responsibilities and collaborations.

Walk-through
Stage 1: **Understanding in application area terms**

What information is the system provided with?
1. New student details (name, address and emergency telephone number)
2. The lecture room group the student has joined

What must the system do with that information?
1. Record the new student information
2. Record that a student belongs to an individual lecture room group

Stage 2: **Understanding in terms of instances of classes and associations**

Processing the admission of a new student requires the following actions:
1. Create a new instance of Student with an associated name, address and emergency telephone number
2. Locate the LectureRoom instance corresponding to the named lecture room
3. Create a new instance of the resides_in association type

Stage 3: **Understanding in terms of responsibilities and collaborations**

Class: FacultyAdmin
'There is only one instance of this class and it is the orchestrating instance'
Responsibilities:
Records admissions of new students into the faculty
Keeps track of LectureRoom instances corresponding to named rooms within the faculty
Collaborators:
Student
LectureRoom

Note: In order for one class to collaborate with another class, a message needs to be sent to an instance of the collaborating class. For example within C++ we could have:

LectureRoom newLectureRoom; //create an instance of class LectureRoom
cout ≪ "Enter lecture room name:;
cin ≫ newLectureRoom.name; //send name message

Class: LectureRoom
Responsibilities:
Records the name of the lecture room
Keeps track of the Student instances corresponding to the students within the lecture room
Keeps track of the Tutor instance corresponding to the assigned tutor

Class: Student
Responsibilities:
Records the student's name, address and emergency contact number

Class: Tutor
Responsibilities:
Records the tutors name and study room number

Invariant
Any given instance of LectureRoom is associated with instances of Student via the resides_in association. The maximum number of Student instances that may be associated with any one instance of LectureRoom is 28.

(v) So far we have not considered any aspects of inheritance. When we investigate the responsibilities, both the Tutor and Student have to record their respective names. This is a common factor between classes and could be represented in a parent class called FacultyMember. Technically this would be abstract as no instances would need to be directly initiated form it. Redraw the class-association diagram to represent this design modification

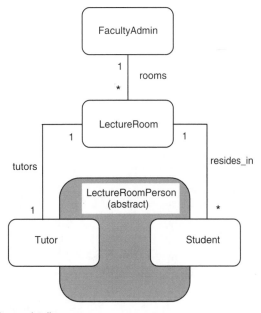

Inheritance details:

Class: FacultyMember
Responsibilities:
Maintaining the names of the faculty members (students and tutors)
Class: Tutor
is-a-subclass-of: FacultyMember
Responsibilities:
Recording the staff room number
Class: Student
is-a-subclass-of: FacultyMember
Responsibilities:
Recording the student address and emergency telephone number

Figure 7.4.14 *Modified Class-Association diagram for the Canine Faculty*

At this stage the grounds for formal design are implied. The class structures have been specified but their individual components (variables and methods) need to be brought out. This would be carried out in the design stage (full details are contained the object-oriented development unit). As an example for the Student class two private variables are required (one for the address and one for the emergency telephone number) with corresponding 'getter' and 'setter' methods. Remember nothing is required within the Student class for *name* as this is will be implemented within the superclass (FacultyMember).

(vi) Use an appropriate CASE tool to design the class structures to incorporate the attributes and operations that would be required to implement the faculty model into an appropriate high level object-oriented programming. Remember the attributes will represent the required variables (private or public) that a class will contain and the operations represent the methods that can access the variables or carry out other required functions (see Figure 7.4.15).

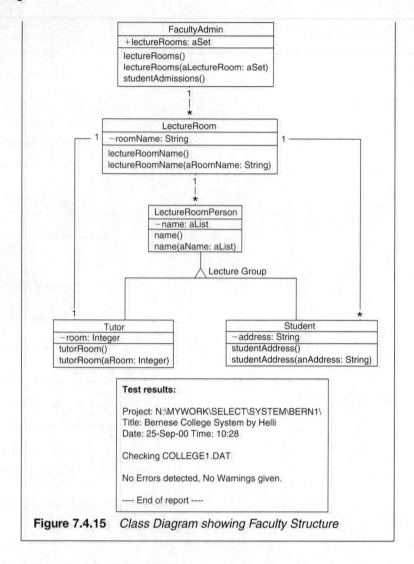

Figure 7.4.15　*Class Diagram showing Faculty Structure*

Case tool applications

Select CASE tools have been used to develop some of the applications within this section. The main tools used are:

Select Enterprise® for completing:

- Class diagrams
- Collaboration diagrams
- General graphics
- Interface class diagram
- Process hierarchy
- Process Thread
- Sequence diagram
- State diagram
- Storage class
- Text document
- Use case diagrams

Select Enterprise® is an advanced interactive tool set for modelling, designing and building next-generation enterprise applications. It is ideally suited for developing object-oriented models by offering a component-based development with 'reuse' of designs as well as code.

Select Yourdon® for completing:

- Constantine diagrams
- Control specifications
- Data flow diagrams
- Data flow (Hartley) diagrams
- Entity-relationship diagrams
- General graphics
- Jackson diagrams
- Process specifications
- State transition diagrams
- Text documents

Select Yourdon® is designed for real time software development projects using the Yourdon Method. It incorporates full support for Yourdon methods including Jackson, Constantine techniques and both the Hatley and Ward-Mellor real-time extensions.

Other products include:

- Select SSADM® which is designed for application development projects using the Structured Systems Analysis and Design Method (SSADM). It provides support for the full range of SSADM techniques, helping development organizations realize all the benefits of adopting SSADM.
- Select SE® is a model-driven application development tool set, supporting data modelling and data management.
- Select CASE tools that are produced by the Princeton Softech company and can be found at: www.princetonsoftech.com

---

Question 7.4.5

1. What does the abbreviation CRC stand for?
2. When designing class structures what is meant by:
   - attribute
   - operation
3. Two new classes are to be added to an Agility Dog Club system. They are CommitteeMember and OrdinaryMember. Their outlines are shown below:

   Class: CommitteeMember
   Responsibilities:
   Record the committee member name, number and role
   Class: OrdinaryMember
   Responsibilities:
   Record the ordinary member name, number and classification (classification relates to the classes that the members are eligible to compete in)
   Note that both classes share common responsibilities i.e. member name and member number and therefore need to be designed as subclasses of a common superclass. Construct part of a class diagram to represent this inheritance structure, include any attributes and operations needed to implement the design.

The testing process

During the development of a software project a number of tests are required to ensure the product conforms to its original requirements. All large software products are developed using partitioning where the product is developed using small workable units. These units will require testing in their own right before they can proceed any further. Such testing is called 'unit testing' which uses white box techniques to focus on issues like internal data structures, boundary conditions and its error handling characteristics.

When all the units are complete they need to be brought together to form a complete system. The testing carried out during this phase of bringing the units together is called 'integration testing'. Integration testing involves constructing the program structure, from unit-tested units, and checking for errors associated with the interfacing of the units. If for example, you were constructing a program in C++, you would need to ensure the formal parameters from one unit matched the actual parameters to another unit. Integration testing is conducted by bringing the units together gradually and testing their interaction, as opposed to bringing them together first then testing (a technique known as the 'big bang approach'). When the program is complete, a series of 'system tests' are carried out in order to validate the requirements of the system. Such tests are carried out in-house with the development team to fully test the system as if was working in its operational environment. Finally the full system will be taken to the customer and run under its proposed operational environment. This process is called 'acceptance testing' which checks the system with the customer. Acceptance testing may form the final phase before the product is handed over and finalizes the contractual agreement between parties. The testing process over the lifecycle of a product is outlined in Figure 7.4.16.

Testing methods include:

- *Black box testing*: Does not test the internal components of a code module but checks its operational capabilities for the input and output of data.
- *White box testing*: This closely checks the internal code structures of a module. The logical data paths through the code are examined, i.e. the conditional and iterative structures, to ensure the results obtained by the variables and data structures correspond to predicted status. We shall be looking at the work of McCabe later in this chapter which looks at methods of deriving a complexity measure by examining code sequences.

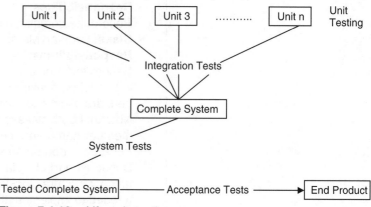

Figure 7.4.16   *Lifecycle testing processes*

- *Alpha testing*: Testing which is carried out with a customer for a specific product. Acceptance testing is an example of this method.
- *Beta testing:* A product is produced for a large market. Certain customers are sent (or they can download it from the Internet) an early version of the product to use and check. This is often called a 'beta version' which can be used free of charge during the testing phase and any problem encountered are reported back to the manufacturer. The manufacturer will then make any necessary modification to the product before releasing the final system.

Tests associated with verification and validation (V&V):

- *Statistical testing*: This provides an estimate of the run-time reliability of the system in relation to the number of user inputs.
- *Defect testing*: this provides a means of checking for faults (bugs) in the system during execution.

Software metrics

Software metrics provide numerical methods for measuring quality issues associated with the development of software system. Numerical measures give the project manager a clear and concise indication of how a project is progressing. Numerical measures deal with facts that are accurate as opposed to people's opinions which might not be so precise. There are two main categories of software metrics, they are:

- *Results metric*: This measure is normally implemented at the end of a project or at the end of a particular stage of the project.
- *Predictor metric*: These are applied during various stages of the project and provide numerical feedback as to the structure and complexity of code sections. They may be used to ascertain the program size (number of lines of code) which is useful for estimating the final resources needed when the program goes live.

The following models have been developed over the years to put into practice the measurement techniques for the quantitative assessment of software quality. They are all indirect techniques that do not directly measure quality but some aspects are associated with it.

- Software Quality Indices
- Halstead's Software Science
- McCabe's Cyclomatic Complexity Metric

Cyclomatic complexity (McCabe)

In order to test the relationship between the control structures inherent in a section of program and the amount of testing required, Thomas McCabe developed his cyclomatic complexity measure. Although a little dated by modern standards it does make the developer think about the code structures under development. Complex sections of code are difficult to test and can effect the runtime efficiency of the program if they are unnecessarily complex. His method uses a graphical technique to represent the code structure and a resulting formula to ascertain the complexity.

We shall start this process by looking at the diagram structures used to represent the flow of the program code. The diagram, or directed graph as it is sometimes called, is constructed using arcs and nodes. A node

Question 7.4.6

1. What testing strategies take place over the lifecycle of a product?
2. What is 'white box' testing?

Question 7.4.7

1. What is a software metric?
2. What are their main categories?

represents the start or end point of some processing activity (normally a line of code, or code structure) i.e. a point where a decision is made, and is represented by a small circle. An arc represents the processing that occurs within a program or code section and is represented by an arrowed line (or arc) indicating the direction of the data flow. The three main structures used within a directed graph are outlined in Figure 7.4.17.

Within a directed graph the arcs are labelled with numbers and the nodes with lower case letters. Figure 7.4.17 shows the three main components of a directed graph that are accompanied by program code. In this case C++ has been used, but the method could easily be applied to a program design language (PDL) in the detailed design stage of development. Note how each line of code matches an arc containing the direction of the flow. The conditional statement always assumes an 'else' option even it is not used with both arcs moving down the diagram. The iteration statement provides two structures, Figure 7.4.17 shows the post-conditioned loop example with an arc that moves back up the graph

McCabe's Cyclomatic Complexity

1. Linear Sequence:

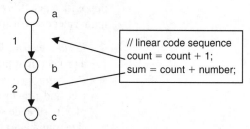

2. Conditional Structure

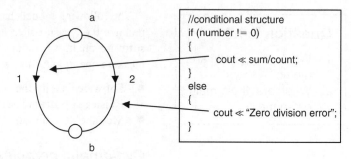

3. Iterative Structure (post-conditioned loop only)

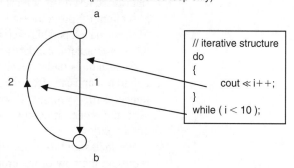

Figure 7.4.17 *Directed graph components*

every time iteration occurs. Figure 7.4.18 shows the sequence for a pre-conditioned loop.

Remember, with a pre-conditioned loop it is possible that the condition is false when the loop is encountered, this would mean that the loop was never entered into and the flow of the program moves on to the data below the loop. This is shown in Figure 7.4.18 where the outer arc (1) jumps from node 'a' to node 'd' and the loop is never executed. If the condition is true the loop is entered, the sequence of code lines executed and the flow returns ('c' to 'a') to check the loop condition again. Please note that in some texts a directed graph is known as a *flow graph* or a *program graph*. Example 7.4.5 outlines an example of directed graph for a C++ code section.

McCabe's Cyclomatic Complexity

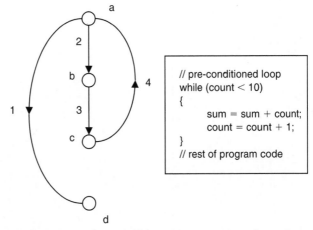

Figure 7.4.18 *Pre-conditioned loop structure for a directed graph*

Example 7.4.5

From the following section of C++ code complete a directed graph to represent the logical control of the data components.

```
// code fragment
float sum = 1;
int index = 1;
do
{
    sum = sum / index;
    if ( sum < 0.5 )
    {
        cout << sum + 1;
    }
    else
    {
        cout << sum - 1;
    }
    index++ ;
}
while ( index < 10 );
sum = sum + index;
```

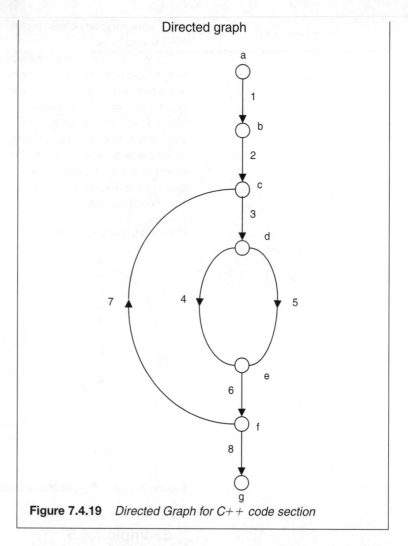

Figure 7.4.19   *Directed Graph for C++ code section*

So what has a directed graph got to do about complexity measures? Directed graphs has been used for many years by mathematicians within engineering circles and provide a sound base for measuring data. McCabe's cyclomatic complexity measure is based on the following equation:

Mathematics in action

Cyclomatic Complexity Measure

$$v = a - n + 2$$

where v = cyclomatic complexity of the graph; a = number of arcs present in the graph (numbers); n = number of nodes present in the graph (letters)

if v < 10 then this is an acceptable measure (see following text).

Research by McCabe established that the higher cyclomatic complexity of a directed graph representing the PDL or code the more difficult the program is to read, understand, implement and test. In a paper containing his work McCabe suggested that a cyclomatic complexity of a value greater than 10 was not acceptable and the code should be redesigned. This is a reasonable hypothesis because to obtain a figure like this the code needs to be extremely complex containing a large amount of nested structures which effect the efficiency of design.

Example 7.4.6

Question:

From the directed graph obtained in Example 7.4.5 (and shown in Figure 7.4.19)

1. calculate the cyclomatic complexity;
2. comment on the resulting value (is it acceptable or not?).

Answer:

1. We can see there are 8 arcs and 7 nodes

    therefore $v = a - n + 2$
    $$v = 8 - 7 + 2$$
    $$v = 3$$

2. From the research of McCabe we can see that the cyclomatic complexity is smaller than 10 (i.e. $3 < 10$) so the code can be accepted as not being to complex and hence does not need to be re-designed.

Question 7.4.8

From the following code section:

1. complete a directed graph;
2. calculate the cyclomatic complexity;
3. comment on the results.

```
//C++ code extract
int space = 0, index = 0, question = 0, count = 0;
strcpy(line , "Is Bailey a dog? is he large? where does he
live? please check");
do
{
        count = count + 1;
        while (line[index] == ' ')
        {
                space = space + 1;
                index = index + 1;
        }
        if (line[index] == '?')
        {
                question = question + 1;
        }
        index = index + 1;
}
while (line[index] != '\0' );
cout << "The % of question marks to characters
is" << question/count*100;
```

Dynamic analysis

The cyclomatic complexity method used for testing code is said to be a static analysis method. Dynamic analysis occurs during the execution of a program where the number of structural elements is monitored to produce summary information. The information obtained will normally be stored in a database call an execution history. Some examples of the type of information stored is outlined below:

- values of variables at certain point in the program;
- minimum and maximum value of variables;
- the most executed statements;
- information on statements that are not used at all;
- information on branching;
- paths taken by the test data.

One way of collecting this information is to insert special code sections either manually or automatically using a dynamic analyser. Entering test data into a program is not new, in fact is has almost been around as long as computer programs themselves. We have often inserted printout lines inside code sections to find out the value of variables, to see if an array goes out of range, to see what is happening inside a loop etc. Dynamic analysis does this in a more efficient way on larger code sections. Once the execution history data has been stored during dynamic analysis it needs to be analysed. The tools used for this analysis can be independent of the program code. This means that programs written in different languages can be analysed by the same tool as long as they write the same information to the database. Full use of dynamic analysis is beyond the scope of this chapter, but the end result of dynamic analysis will be compared with the end result of static analysis to obtain a measure of the extent to which the program has been tested. This is known as the percentage coverage that is used as a measure to quantify test effectiveness.

Patches and fixes

Within the software development lifecycle a *patch*, *fix* or *quick fix engineering (QFE)* are specialized cases of another version of the product. They are classified as small upgrades or modifications that are distributed to the users of the software product so they can be installed within the application. They provide an efficient method of updating software between prior to releasing a new product.

Debugging

It is often the case that a finished piece of software contains errors. Even the most careful programmers sometimes have problems with their finished code which prevents the application from running as expected. Finding these errors is part of the testing process and many programming environments contain application tools that are there to help locate possible faults. The errors that may occur within your program code are listed below:

- *Syntax errors* – these are errors that violate the rule of 'language syntax'. The code will not compile and errors must be detected before execution can continue. Such errors include typographical mistakes, poor punctuation, type mismatch faults, undeclared variables etc.
- *Semantic errors* – these are also classified as runtime errors. The code contains valid statements, but the statements cause errors when

they are executed. For example you may try and open a file which does not exist or cannot be found.

● *Logical errors* – again the code contains valid statements, but the execution of the program does not give the expected results. For example, logic errors occur when incorrect variable values are entered into a mathematical equation giving the incorrect result.

One tool that can help with the second two error problems is a system debugger. This tool will help you find out what is happening within the program code by checking variable values as you trace through the program. A typical debugger enables the programmer to:

● check the value of the variables as the program proceeds;
● change and update variable values during the debugging process;
● control the execution of the program.

In order to make the best use of a debugging tool a typical programming environment will allow you to set 'breakpoints' at certain points within the program code to halt execution. This allows you to check the value of variables or data structures by viewing inspection or 'watch' facilities when the program breaks. If the results are not expected at this point then the fault can be traced back and corrected as required.

Question 7.4.9

The following is a piece of code (written in C++) that allows you to enter a number of integers into a loop structure, adds the values and finds their average value. The loop is controlled by a sentinel value (-1) which provides the exit criteria when all the required values have been entered (in order to exit the loop).

```
int number, count, sum;
float average;
cout ≪ "Average calculator" < endl;
count = 0;
sum = 0;
do
{
    cout ≪ "Enter a number (end with − 1):;
    cin ≫ number;
    sum = sum + number;
    count++ ;
}
while ( number ! = −1 );
average = sum/count;
cout ≪ "The average is: " ≫ average;
```

The code does not give the correct result. Enter the code as outlined above within any C++ code editor.

1. What types of error are present?
2. Debug the code to analyse the values of the variables as the program is 'traced' through by using appropriate 'watch' or 'inspection' facilities.
3. Correct the faults to ensure the program runs as expected.
4. Check the modifications are correct by analysing the modified code structure (i.e. repeat the checks made above).

Appendix A
Hexadecimal and other number bases

If you remember back to arithmetic lessons in your primary school days, you were shown hundreds, tens and units, often written as h t u. The sum $137 + 15$ would be set out like this:

```
h    t    u
1    3    7
+    1    5
_____
1    5    2
```

The meaning here is that 3 refers to 3 tens or 30, the 1 refers to 1 hundred because we use numbers by position, you know the 3 refers to 30 and not 3 because it is in the tens column, i.e. its position tells you more that just the digit.

As $1 = 10^0$, $10 = 10^1$, $100 = 10^2$, $1000 = 10^3$ and so on we could head the columns like this instead of using h t u, it all means exactly the same.

```
10²   10¹   10⁰
1     3     7
+     1     5
_____
1     5     2
```

The fact that we use 10 as a number base is due only to the fact that humans were born with 10 fingers, there is nothing 'natural' about numbers to the base 10. If we were born with 8 fingers, we would use numbers to the base 8 (called *octal* numbers) and think that numbers to the base 10 very odd indeed! We can use any number we please as a base, 10 is the 'everyday' value but bases of 2, 8 and 16 are common in computers.

Hexadecimal means 16, hex for 6, decimal for 10 and we can use 16 as the number base in just the same way as we use 10. Numbers to base 10 use 10 symbols, i.e. 0–9, so hex numbers must have 16 symbols. The problem is that we run out of symbols past 9 so the letters A to F are used in addition. This means that numbers in hex run 0–F, equivalent to 0–15 in decimal numbers but of course 15 uses 2 symbols, 1 and 5. Counting in both looks like this:

Dec	Hex	Dec	Hex	Dec	Hex
0	0	16	10	32	20
1	1	17	11	33	21
2	2	18	12	34	22
3	3	19	13	35	23
4	4	20	14	36	24
5	5	21	15	37	25
6	6	22	16	38	26
7	7	23	17	39	27
8	8	24	18	1000	3E8
9	9	25	19	1024	400
10	A	26	1A	1025	401
11	B	27	1B	1026	402
12	C	28	1C	2048	800
13	D	29	1D	4096	1000
14	E	30	1E	65536	10000
15	F	31	1F	1048576	100000

The columns in a hex sum would be headed 16^2, 16^1, 16^0 using the same system as above, each column uses the next greater integer as a power.

16^2	16^1	16^0
1	3	7
+	1	A
1	5	1

The mechanics of the sum are just the same.

Note that hex $19 + 1 = 1A$ not 20! Hex 19 converted to decimal equals $(1 \times 16) + 9 = 25$ because the 1 is in the 16^1 column, the 9 is in the 16^0 column, i.e. numbers by position.

Examples

Hex 1B $= (1 \times 16^1) + (B \times 16^0) = 27$
Hex 5D $= (5 \times 16^1) + (D \times 16^0) = 93$
Hex 2A7 $= (2 \times 16^2) + (A \times 16^1) + (7 \times 16^0)$
$= 512 + 160 + 7 = 679$

Working the other way

Decimal 68 $= (6 \times 10^1) + (8 \times 10^0)$, converting this to hex, $68 = 64 + 4$ and $64 = 16 \times 4$ so decimal $68 = 44$ hex

A simple way to convert decimal to hex is to:

divide the number by 16 and write down the remainder,

679 DIV 16 = 42 remainder 7

divide the quotient 42 by 16 and write down the remainder,

42 DIV16 = 2 remainder 10

divide the quotient 2 by 16 and write down the remainder,

2 DIV16 = 0 remainder 2

and repeat until the quotient is zero.

The number in hex is now in the set of remainders 2, 10 and 7 but of course 10 is written as A so 679 decimal = 2A7 hex.

Set out in a table it looks like this:

Dec	Base	Quotient	Rem base 10	Rem base 16
679	16	42	7	7
42	16	2	10	A
2	16	0	2	2
			so 679 decimal	= 2A7 hex

Here are some more examples.

Dec	Base	Quotient	Rem base 10	Rem base 16
1329	16	83	1	1
83	16	5	3	3
5	16	0	5	5
			so 1329 decimal	= 531 hex
397	16	24	13	D
24	16	1	8	8
1	16	0	1	1
			so 397 decimal	= 18D hex

Binary

The same rules apply to using numbers to the base 2 or binary numbers. Numbers to base 10 need 10 symbols so binary numbers only need 2 symbols, 0 and 1. We still use numbers by position so all the normal arithmetic operations apply.

In decimal $1 = 10^0$, $10 = 10^1$, $100 = 10^2$, $1000 = 10^3$ and so on and these form the column headings in our numbers by position system. In binary, the same rule applies but the column headings will be $2^0, 2^1, 2^2, 2^3$, etc. translating to 1, 2, 4, 8, etc., i.e. each column is double the previous one.

If we write the decimal number 9 it is made up of 8 + 1. The binary number 1001 equates to 9 decimal because we have 1 in the 2^3 (or 8s) column, none in the 2^2 or 2^1 columns and 1 in the 2^0 (or 1s)column as shown below:

2^7	2^6	2^5	2^4	2^3	2^2	2^1	2^0
				1	0	0	1

By the same system, the decimal value 65 = 64 + 1 or 1000001 in binary as below:

2^7	2^6	2^5	2^4	2^3	2^2	2^1	2^0
	1	0	0	0	0	0	1

Any leading zeros are ignored.

The same system as used above can be used to convert decimal to another base, in this case the base 2. In the example below, the decimal number 38 is divided by the new base, 2, and the remainder placed in the remainder column. The quotient is copied to the next line down and the process repeated until the quotient is zero. The binary number is then read off the remainder column from the bottom, i.e. 100110.

Decimal	Base	Quotient	Remainder
38	2	19	0
19	2	9	1
9	2	4	1
4	2	2	0
2	2	1	0
1	2	0	1
			so 38 decimal = 100110 binary

Another example, decimal 297:

Decimal	Base	Quotient	Remainder
297	2	148	1
148	2	74	0
74	2	37	0
37	2	18	1
18	2	9	0
9	2	4	1
4	2	2	0
2	2	1	0
1	2	0	1
			so decimal 297 = 100101001

Converting binary to decimal is easy. The number $100110 = 32 + 4 + 2 = 38$

	2^7	2^6	2^5	2^4	2^3	2^2	2^1	2^0
Decimal equivalent	128	64	32	16	8	4	2	1
			1	0	0	1	1	0

Hex to binary and binary to hex

You may be wondering why we use hex numbers at all. One reason is that converting hex to binary and binary to hex is very easy. The trick is to realize that each hex digit can be encoded by 4 binary digits, so hex A = 1001. If you split a binary number like 101100100100010 into groups of 4 digits starting from the right like this:

101 1001 0010 0010

you can encode each group of 4 into a hex digit directly so

101 1001 0010 0010 = 5922,

similarly, 10 1010 = 2A. This is shown in the table below.

101	1001	0010	0010
5	9	2	2

and

10	1010
2	A

The process is just as easy to reverse, the hex number 41 = 0100 0001 in binary, each digit is written as a 4-bit binary number and the results joined together.

Questions
App A.1

Practise conversion to and from binary. Fill in the blanks in this table. Answers on page 411.

Decimal	Hex	Binary
69	–	1000101
193	–	11000001
200	–	11001000
255	–	11111111
254	–	11111110
–	2DC	1011011100
–	200	1000000000
–	377	1101110111
–	8D	10001101
–	31E	1100011110
410	–	–
416	–	–
685	–	–
153	–	–
350	–	–
–	–	1000101111
–	–	1001101001
–	–	1011100111
–	–	1000110011
–	–	11000110

Appendix B
ASCII character set

Before the days of computing, communication systems required each character to be sent as a code. Simple systems used 1s and 0s for transmission just like today so binary numbers were used to encode characters. You could not send an 'A' character directly but you could send binary 1000001 in its place. This eventually lead to a 'standard' set of characters that were used to control printing devices before the widespread use of VDUs. ASCII stands for American Standard Code for Information Interchange but there are other character encoding systems around like Extended Binary Coded Decimal Interchange Code (EBCDIC) and Lotus International Character Set (LICS) and they work in a similar way but ASCII is the most widespread.

In ASCII, the codes from 0 to 31 were called 'control characters'. These were used to control the movement of the old mechanical printers so we have terms like 'Carriage Return' (now known as Enter or just Return) that actually caused the carriage that held the paper to return to the left-hand side. Understanding this historical basis of the control characters help you to understand the names they are given which now seem a little odd. If a control character (written as CTRL A, etc.) is sent to a printer or screen, it usually results in an action rather than a printable character. Because some of the codes only have real meaning for mechanical printers, some modern uses do not always make sense of the original name.

Before the widespread use of Microsoft Windows, most machines responded directly to these control characters. As an experiment, try opening a DOS window and type a command. Instead of pressing the Enter key, press CTRL M instead, you should find it does the same thing as pressing Enter. The Enter key is just a CTRL M key in DOS. If you try this using Microsoft Word, CTRL M has a different effect. If you are using Unix or Linux, try using CTRL H in place of the backspace key, it should work unless it has been remapped on your machine.

The ASCII control characters

Dec	Hex	Keyboard		Binary		Description
0	0	CTRL @	00000	NUL		Null Character
1	1	CTRL A	00001	SOH		Start of Heading
2	2	CTRL B	00010	STX		Start of Text
3	3	CTRL C	00011	ETX		End of Text
4	4	CTRL D	00100	EOT		End of Transmission
5	5	CTRL E	00101	ENQ		Enquiry
6	6	CTRL F	00110	ACK		Acknowledge
7	7	CTRL G	00111	BEL		Bell or beep
8	8	CTRL H	01000	BS		Back Space
9	9	CTRL I	01001	HT		Horizontal Tab
10	A	CTRL J	01010	LF		Line Feed
11	B	CTRL K	01011	VT		Vertical Tab
12	C	CTRL L	01100	FF		Form Feed
13	D	CTRL M	01101	CR		Carriage Return
14	E	CTRL N	01110	SO		Shift Out
15	F	CTRL O	01111	SI		Shift In
16	10	CTRL P	10000	DLE		Date Link Escape
17	11	CTRL Q	10001	DC1		Device Control 1
18	12	CTRL R	10010	DC2		Device Control 2
19	13	CTRL S	10011	DC3		Device Control 3
20	14	CTRL T	10100	DC4		Device Control 4
21	15	CTRL U	10101	NAK		Negative Acknowledge
22	16	CTRL V	10110	SYN		Synchronous Idle
23	17	CTRL W	10111	ETB		End of Transmission Block
24	18	CTRL X	11000	CAN		Cancel
25	19	CTRL Y	11001	EM		End Medium
26	1A	CTRL Z	11010	SUB		Substitute or EOF End Of File
27	1B		11011	ESC		Escape
28	1C		11100	FS		File Separator
29	1D		11101	GS		Group Separator
30	1E		11110	RS		Record Separator
31	1F		11111	US		Unit Separator

Characters in ASCII are easy to remember, they run from A = 65 to Z = 90. This may look like an odd choice of numbers until you convert the 65 into binary and get 1000001, i.e. 64 + 1. This means that any letter is easy to calculate, it is 64 plus the position in the alphabet. M is the 13th letter in the alphabet so in ASCII, M = 64 + 13 = 77. To make it lower case, just add 32. This is a good choice as 32 encodes as a single binary digit. Lower case m is then 64 + 32 + 13 = 109. Of course it would be better to use hex, so A = 41, M = 4D, a = 61, m = 6D etc. Numerals are just as easy, '0' encodes as 48, '1' encodes as 48 + 1 = 49, etc.

The full set of 7-bit printable ASCII characters is shown here.

Char	Dec	Hex	Binary	Char	Dec	Hex	Binary	Char	Dec	Hex	Binary
Space	32	20	100000								
!	33	21	100001	A	65	41	1000001	a	97	61	1100001
"	34	22	100010	B	66	42	1000010	b	98	62	1100010
#	35	23	100011	C	67	43	1000011	c	99	63	1100011
$	36	24	100100	D	68	44	1000100	d	100	64	1100100
%	37	25	100101	E	69	45	1000101	e	101	65	1100101
&	38	26	100110	F	70	46	1000110	f	102	66	1100110
'	39	27	100111	G	71	47	1000111	g	103	67	1100111
(	40	28	101000	H	72	48	1001000	h	104	68	1101000
)	41	29	101001	I	73	49	1001001	i	105	69	1101001
*	42	2A	101010	J	74	4A	1001010	j	106	6A	1101010
+	43	2B	101011	K	75	4B	1001011	k	107	6B	1101011
,	44	2C	101100	L	76	4C	1001100	l	108	6C	1101100
–	45	2D	101101	M	77	4D	1001101	m	109	6D	1101101
.	46	2E	101110	N	78	4E	1001110	n	110	6E	1101110
/	47	2F	101111	O	79	4F	1001111	o	111	6F	1101111
0	48	30	110000	P	80	50	1010000	p	112	70	1110000
1	49	31	110001	Q	81	51	1010001	q	113	71	1110001
2	50	32	110010	R	82	52	1010010	r	114	72	1110010
3	51	33	110011	S	83	53	1010011	s	115	73	1110011
4	52	34	110100	T	84	54	1010100	t	116	74	1110100
5	53	35	110101	U	85	55	1010101	u	117	75	1110101
6	54	36	110110	V	86	56	1010110	v	118	76	1110110
7	55	37	110111	W	87	57	1010111	w	119	77	1110111
8	56	38	111000	X	88	58	1011000	x	120	78	1111000
9	57	39	111001	Y	89	59	1011001	y	121	79	1111001
:	58	3A	111010	Z	90	5A	1011010	z	122	7A	1111010
;	59	3B	111011	[	91	5B	1011011	{	123	7B	1111011
<	60	3C	111100	\	92	5C	1011100	|	124	7C	1111100
=	61	3D	111101	]	93	5D	1011101	}	125	7D	1111101
>	62	3E	111110	^	94	5E	1011110	~	126	7E	1111110
?	63	3F	111111	_	95	5F	1011111	del	127	7F	1111111
@	64	40	1000000	`	96	60	1100000				

You will notice that the codes only extend to 127. This is because the original ASCII only used 7 binary digits and was referred to as a 7-bit code. Whilst there is some standardization of the codes 128 to 255, some machines will give different characters for codes 128 to 255, for instance, older machines will give an é for code 130 whilst more modern machines will give an é for code 233.

Whilst it is not important to remember ASCII codes, it is often useful, especially when writing text or string handling parts of programs. If you remember that 'A' = 64 + alphabet position (40 in hex) and that 'a' = 'A' + 32 ('A' + 20 in hex) you can work out all of the alphabet. The '0' character is 48 and the digits are 48 + their value. If you also remember that a Carriage Return is 13 (0D hex) and that Line Feed is 10 (0A hex) you will be able to remember about half of the codes and be able to interpret some hex-dumped files.

Question AppB.1

Write down the ASCII values in decimal and hex for the string 'HNC Computing 2000'. Try to work it out so you should not look at the code table. Don't forget the spaces are ASCII characters as well. Answers on page 411.

Text	H	N	C		C	o	m	p	u	t	i	n	g		2	0	0	0
Decimal																		
Hex																		

Unicode

ASCII characters, although universally accepted, present one serious problem, there are not sufficient characters to cover all symbols and characters from different languages. The solution adopted until the introduction of *Unicode* was to set up each computer to have its own character set according to country or language. This makes it harder to communicate files between computers set up for different countries; try finding the pound sign on an American keyboard! Unicode uses 16-bit characters so there are $2^{16} = 65\,536$ possible characters, more than enough to cover all the world's main languages. The ASCII character set has been incorporated so character 65 is still an 'A' but the 65 is a 16-bit value. The Unicode standard is developing all the time, the latest situation is presented on their web page at www.unicode.org/unicode/standard/standard.html. This describes the current version 3 which defines 49 194 different characters and the work in progress to add more.

Conversion of ASCII to Unicode is very easy as the codes are simply changed 8 bit into 16 bit. Conversion from Unicode to ASCII may result in the loss of data as ASCII cannot support more than 256 different characters. Some operating systems will work with both character sets; the more modern ones will use Unicode as the native code.

Unicode is developing all the time with new characters being added, etc. See the latest information on the website www.unicode.org.

Appendix C
Colour

The amazing human ability to perceive colour comes from a complex interaction between the eyes and the brain. What we 'see' is not always exactly what is in front of us! An example of this is the 'white' area of a monitor. If you look with a magnifier, you will see only red, green and blue dots, nothing 'white'.

Light is part of the electromagnetic spectrum. The wavelength of visible light is between approximately 400 and 700 nanometres, the shorter wavelength being perceived as violet, followed by blue, green, yellow and finally as red at the longer wavelength. Light is detected in the human eye by two sorts of cell in the retina, these are known as rods and cones. The rods are not colour sensitive but can detect low-level light. There are three kinds of cone cell, one each that detects red, green and blue. This explains why at night, colours seem much less intense, the rods are more active and the cones less so. In very dark conditions, colour disappears altogether. It is not that the colour is not there, it is the way we 'see' it.

For an ordinary object, the colour we see depends on the light that is used to illuminate it and the object itself. As sunlight contains 'all the colours of the rainbow', a blue object will appear blue in sunlight because it absorbs the other colours and reflects blue light. If the light did not contain blue, the same object would appear to be black.

Additive colour system

Blue is one of the primary colours of light, the others are red and green; if areas of equal intensity of these colours are made to overlap, the result is white light. Different colours are made by changing the 'amount' of each in different combinations.

Red and blue combine to make magenta
Green and blue combine to make cyan
Yellow is made by combining red and green

The colours, cyan, magenta and yellow are the 'complementary' colours of red, green and blue respectively. Blue is complementary to yellow, i.e. if sunlight had all the blue filtered out, it would look yellow. It is this effect that makes sunsets change colour, some of the colours in the sunlight no longer reach your eyes (due to refraction in the atmosphere) so you no longer 'see' white light. The way that coloured light can be combined in this way is called the additive colour system and applies when you consider colour RGB (Red Green Blue) monitors.

Subtractive colour system

Providing that a printed page is illuminated with white light, the colour of dyes or pigments you see depends on the amount of each colour absorbed by the ink. Cyan is complementary to red, it looks cyan because it absorbs all the red light and reflects the other colours. Cyan, magenta and yellow (known as the secondary colours) are used in combination to make different colour inks. This is called the subtractive colour system.

In theory, cyan, magenta and yellow inks will combine to make black ink. In practice, you get a muddy brown colour. To counteract this effect, printers use a black ink when black is needed, leading to the minimum requirement of four ink colours. This is known as CMYK for *Cyan, Magenta, Yellow and blacK* (B is already used for Blue).

Dithering

If you use opaque inks applied unmixed to make colour combinations, the colour achieved is the colour of the last ink applied. Clearly this does not give the required result. The solution is to use patterns of coloured dots where the combination of the colours gives the impression of a new colour. These combinations of different colour dots are called 'dither patterns'. Dithering is the technique used on lasers, thermal wax and inkjet printers because the inks are opaque. Dye sublimation printers use transparent inks so the photographic quality is better, i.e. dot free.

Experiment

Use a magnifier to examine the colour printed images in a magazine or the coloured images on the front cover of this book. Most use dithering techniques and the patterns of dots are very clear. When viewed from normal reading distance, the dots appear to blend into each other to form 'solid' colour. As was stated at the top, what we 'see' is not always exactly what is in front of us!

Appendix D
A brief network glossary

Mnemonic	Meaning	Comment
API	Application Program Interface, e.g. Windows API	
ARP	Address Resolution Protocol	Part of TCP/IP
DLC	Data Link Control	
FTP	File Transfer Protocol	Internet layer 7 protocol
HTTP	HyperText Transport Protocol	Internet layer 7 protocol
ICMP	Internet Control Message Protocol	Part of TCP/IP
IEEE	Institute of Electrical and Electronic Engineers	For the setting of standards, e.g. IEEE 302
IGMP	Internet Group Message Protocol	Part of TCP/IP
IP	Internet Protocol	Part of TCP/IP
IPX	Internetwork Packet Exchange	IPX/SPX is Novell's routable datagram protocol
ISO	International Standards Organization	
LLC	Link Layer Control	
LSL	Link Support Layer	
NBT	NetBEUI over TCP	Microsoft
NCP	Netware Core Protocol	Novell
NDIS	Network Device Interface Specification	Microsoft's answer to ODI
NetBEUI	NetBIOS Extended User Interface	Microsoft native transport protocol, not routable
NetBIOS	Network Basic Input Output System	From old Microsoft LAN systems, not routable
NIC	Network Interface Card	The actual Network card

(continued)

Mnemonic	Meaning	Comment
ODI	Open Data Link Interface	Novell
OSI	Open Systems Interconnect	7-layered model from the ISO
RARP	Reverse Address Resolution Protocol	Part of TCP/IP
RIP	Routing Information Protocol	
RPC	Remote Procedure Calls	Novell
SMB	Server Message Blocks	Used in all Microsoft networks for file and print service
SMTP	Simple Mail Transport Protocol	Internet layer 7 protocol
SNMP	Simple Network Management Protocol	Part of TCP/IP
SPX	Sequenced Packet Exchange	IPX/SPX is Novell's routable datagram protocol
TCP	Transport Control Protocol	Part of TCP/IP
TLI	Transport Layer Interface	
UDP	User Datagram Protocol	Part of TCP/IP

There are many glossaries available free on the Internet.

For networks, a 'standard' version can be found in a file called a 'request for comments', an odd sounding name for what amounts to an Internet standard. The network glossary is called rfc1983 and it can be found all over the Internet. The main link page to find it is at

www.rfc-editor.org/rfc.html

and a typical site where it can be found is

ftp://ftp.isi.edu/in-notes/rfc1983.txt

or you can search for the word glossary at

www.rfc-editor.org/rfcsearch.html

which will point to sources of rfc1983 and other standard network glossaries.

Mapping of learning outcomes

Chapter 1

Outcomes	Assessment criteria	
1. Investigate computer systems	● Select machine components or sub-systems appropriate to given tasks	1.6–1.10
	● Evaluate the performance of the selected system	1.12
2. Investigate operating systems	● Contrast the functions and features of different types of operating systems	5.14 and College specific
	● Understand how to customize operating systems	College specific
3. Design a computer system	● Investigate and identify the key components for a computer system for a particular user	1.1, 1.3, 1.13
	● Specify a complete computer system to suit a given task	1.13
4. Test a computer system	● Produce a plan that checks the main hardware and software components, using standard techniques	1.6–1.13
	● Produce user documentation of your system	1.6–1.13
	● Produce a security policy for your system	5.16
	● Demonstrate that the system meets health and safety requirements	College specific

Chapter 2

Outcomes	Assessment criteria	
1. Understand the **systems analysis lifecycle**	● Identify the functions and purpose of each stage of a systems lifecycle	2.1 (page 65)
	● Provide evidence to support an understanding of the lifecycle	2.1 (college specific)
	● Compare different lifecycle models	2.1 (page 74)
2. Understand **systems analysis tools and techniques**	● Use data modelling techniques	2.2 (from page 74)
	● Use entity-relationship diagrams	2.2 and 2.4
	● Use modelling documentation	2.2 (inherent) and 2.3
3. Perform a **system investigation**	● Investigate a given problem domain	2.3 (page 124)
	● Identify system requirements	2.3 (page 116–121)
	● Document an investigated system	2.3 (page 122)
4. Perform **functional and data modelling**	● Identify system processes and functions	2.4 (page 124–126)
	● Produce a functional model	2.4 (page 126)
	● Perform data modelling	2.4 (page 127–143)

Chapter 3

Outcomes	Assessment criteria	
1. Design and develop code using structured programming methods	● Identify and select appropriate predefined data types	3.3
	● Use simple input/output and appropriate operators with the above	3.3
	● Identify and use appropriate selection structures and loop structures for the given task	3.5
	● Produce programs to desired standards	3.10, 3.13
2. Use modularization appropriate to the chosen programming language	● Construct a program from a design and use appropriate functions/procedures	3.10, 3.7
	● Demonstrate the effect of scope and life-time of variables	3.7
	● Pass data effectively between modules	3.7
3. Produce appropriate documentation for a given program application	● Produce user documentation for a completed programming application including the user interface design	3.10, 3.13
	● Develop technical documentation for a predescribed program application	3.13
4. Create and apply appropriate test schedules	● Demonstrate discrimination between semantic and syntax errors	All unit 3
	● Produce test documentation	3.13
	● Successfully construct and use test data and schedules to detect logic errors	3.11, 3.12
	● Use appropriate techniques for detecting errors	3.11, 3.12

Chapter 4

Learning outcome	Content	Chapter section	Page reference
Understand database environments	● Database environment ● DBMS ● Database uses	1.1, 1.2, 1.21, 1.22, 1.23, 1.3, 1.4 1.5, 1.51–1.54	
Use and manipulate appropriate database software	● Database software ● Tools and techniques	1.6, 1.61–1.63 1.6, 1.61	
Design a database	● Normalization ● Methodology ● Documentation	1.72 1.7 1.71	
Demonstrate the database	● Format ● Documentation	1.7 1.71	

Chapter 5

Outcomes	Assessment criteria	
1. Evaluate the benefit of networks	● Produce a coherent argument as to the advantages and disadvantages of using networks within an organization	5.3
	● Enumerate the various cost, performance, security and utility values associated with the installation of a network	5.3
	● Provide an overview of a network operating system and how it works	5.4–5.9
2. Apply architectural concepts to the design/ evaluation of networks	● Design a LAN for a specific purpose or assess an existing network for fitness of purpose	All unit 5
	● Identify the various parts (software and hardware) of a network system and relate it to the 7-layered model	5.5
	● Differentiate between different kinds of network, network topologies and network operating systems	5.4
3. Install network software	● Set up a software network environment, for example departments in an organization	College specific
	● Install a piece of network software onto a server to be used by different selected users in a group	College specific
	● Configure user workstations on the network	College specific
4. Perform network management responsibilities	● Write a report on the rights and responsibilities of the network manager and the network user	5.14–5.16
	● Apply control mechanisms in a typical network for managing users	College specific
	● Control printer queues and other forms of resource usage	College specific

Chapter 6

Learning outcome	Content	Chapter section	Page reference
Demonstrate and deliver a range of transferable skills	● Transferable skills ● Delivery formats	2.1, 2.11–2.14 2.14	
Working and contributing to a group situation	● Contributing ● Group dynamics ● Team role	2.2 2.2 2.2	
Identify a problem and provide feasible solutions	● Stages ● Methodology ● Decision making ● Techniques	2.3 2.4 2.3 2.3	
Monitor and review own learning experience	● Critique ● Documentation ● Evaluation	2.4 2.41, 2.42 2.43–2.46	

Chapter 7

Outcomes	Assessment criteria	
1. Understand the need for **quality assurance** during all stages of the development of an IT system	● select appropriate standards for a system ● assess the risks associated with the development of a system ● examine the level of service requirements of a system	7.1 (page 312) 7.1 (page 318) 7.1 (page 324)
2. Employ standard documentation in the **quality control** of development and maintenance	● produce a quality plan for selected system ● identify the contents of a quality manual for a system ● recommend a referencing facility for system documentation	7.2 (page 336) 7.2 (page 338) 7.2 (page 332)
3. Employ **project management** tools	● Define timescales and milestones of system development ● Apply project planning and management tools ● Evaluate system documentation using suitable tools	7.3 (page 344) 7.3 (page 345) 7.3 (page 352)
4. Contribute to the **review** of stages of **system development**	● Justify the selection of a development methodology ● Specify appropriate quality procedures and documentation ● Verify conformance of development to quality procedures ● evaluate testing strategy of system development	7.4 (page 361) 7.4 (college specific) 7.4 (page 365 and college specific) 7.4 (page 382)

Answers

1.3 What is a microprocessor?

Question 1.3.1

$2^{20} = 1048576$ addresses or 1 Mb can be addressed by 20 address lines.

Question 1.3.2

Reference to the table will show that at least 26 addresses are required to address 64 Mb of memory.

Power of 2	Bytes	Mbyte
2^{20}	1 048 576	1 Mbytes
2^{21}	2 097 152	2 Mbytes
2^{22}	4 194 304	4 Mbytes
2^{23}	8 388 608	8 Mbytes
2^{24}	16 777 216	16 Mbytes
2^{25}	33 554 432	32 Mbytes
2^{26}	67 108 864	64 Mbytes

1.7 Memory: RAM and ROM

Question 1.7.1

Reference to page 7 will show that Moore's law assumes a doubling every 18–24 months. If we assume a doubling in 24 months (2 years) then the average size of a disc drive in the year 2012 is shown in the table below. Is it 72 times bigger.

Year	Size
2000	10 Gb
2002	20 Gb
2004	40 Gb
2006	80 Gb
2008	180 Gb
2010	360 Gb
2012	720 Gb

If we take a doubling every 18 months (1½ years) we get a staggering result, a size more than 2500 times the size. This is not a prediction that this will happen but similar explosive growth in speed and capacity has happened in the past. What do you predict?

Year	Size
2000.0	10 Gb
2001.5	20 Gb
2003.0	40 Gb
2004.5	80 Gb
2006.0	160 Gb
2007.5	320 Gb
2009.0	640 Gb
2010.5	1280 Gb
2012.0	2560 Gb

1.8 Video graphics

Question 1.8.1

One pixel needs 3 bytes and there will be $1280 \times 1024 = 1\,310\,720$ pixels so the storage required will be $1\,310\,720 \times 3 = 3\,932\,160$ bytes or just a little less than 4 Mb. If your machine only has 2 Mb of video RAM but will support a 1280×1024 resolution you will not be able to set 24 bit or Trucolor at the same time as 1280×1024.

Question 1.8.2

Reference to the table below will show that a resolution of 1920 by 1340 is possible. (It is possible either the graphics card or the monitor may not support this resolution.)

Video RAM required against resolution and colour depth

Resolution	1 byte/pixel (256 colours)	2 bytes/pixel (65536 colours Hicolor)	3 bytes/pixel (16 777 216 colours Truecolor)
640×480	307 200	614 400	921 600
800×600	480 000	960 000	1 440 000
1024×768	786 432	1 572 864	2 359 296
1152×864	995 328	1 990 656	2 985 984
1280×1024	1 310 720	2 621 440	3 932 160
1600×1200	1 920 000	3 840 000	5 760 000
1920×1340	2 572 800	5 145 600	7 718 400
2048×1536	3 145 728	6 291 456	9 437 184

1.9 Printers

Question 1.9.1

A4 = 210×297 mm

$(210 - 20) \times (297 - 20) = 52630$ square mm.

600 dpi = $600/25.4 = 23.6$ dots per mm so there are $23.6 \times 23.6 = 558$ dots per square mm.

$558 \times 52630 = 29\,367\,599$ dots

$29\,367\,599/8 = 3\,670\,950$ bytes or 3.5 Mb

Question 1.9.2

In readable ASCII	ESC, '@', ESC, '5', ESC, '–', 1, 'H', 'N', 'C', ESC, '–', 0
In decimal	27, 64, 27, 53, 27, 45, 1, 72, 78, 67, 27, 45, 0
In Hex	1B, 40, 1B, 35, 1B, 2D, 1, 48, 4E, 43, 1B, 2D

Of course the actual data is sent in binary, these are only human readable forms of the same data. To understand better the meaning of the numbers, see the list of ASCII codes.

Note: The actual codes used in an escape sequence depend on the particular printer in use. One of the tasks of a Printer Driver is to translate a call for underlining into these particular codes.

Question App A.1

Decimal	Hex	Binary
69	45	1000101
193	C1	11000001
200	C8	11001000
255	FF	11111111
254	FE	11111110
732	2DC	1011011100
512	200	1000000000
887	377	1101110111
141	8D	10001101
798	31E	1100011110
410	19A	110011010
416	1A0	110100000
685	2AD	1010101101
153	99	10011001
350	15E	101011110
559	22F	1000101111
617	269	1001101001
743	2E7	1011100111
563	233	1000110011
198	C6	11000110

Question App B.1

Text	H	N	C		C	o	m	p	u	t	i	n	g		2	0	0	0
Decimal	72	78	67	32	67	111	109	112	117	116	105	110	103	32	50	48	48	48
Hex	48	4E	43	20	43	6F	6D	70	75	74	69	6E	67	20	32	30	30	30

2.1 Systems analysis lifecycle

Question 2.1.1

1. The main activities are:
   - Requirements analysis
   - Specification
   - Design
   - Implementation
   - Maintenance
   - Verification and validation
2. The resulting documents are:
   - Negotiated statement of requirements
   - System specification document
   - Design document
   - Programs
   - Modified programs
3. Verification and validation provides the quality assurance activity that acts over the whole lifecycle of the project and ensures the end product reaches an acceptable level of quality. Validation ensures

that the output from each activity meets the user requirements. Verification ensures the project is being built in the correct way and the output of each activity is a correct conversion as an input to the next stage.

From DeMarco:

Validation – Are we building the right product?

Verification – Are we building the product right?

4. It is sometimes called a 'waterfall model' because the way data flows down the activities is analogous to water flowing down a waterfall. You start at on end of the model and progress through to the end.

Question 2.1.2

1. A software prototype is a tool to demonstrate how a system or a component of a computer system will function in its environment. A prototype will visualize to the user what a proposed system will do for them.

2. The basic stages are:
   - Establish prototype objectives
   - Select functions for including in the prototype
   - Develop a prototype
   - Evaluate a prototype system.

3. (a) *Exploratory Programming* – Develop an initial prototype and refine it until it meets the user requirements.

   (b) *Throwaway prototyping* – The prototype is developed from an outline specification once evaluated it is 'thrownaway' and a complete new system developed.

   (c) *Reverse Engineering* – Start with existing code written for some other application and restructure it to meet the requirements of the new system.

4. Possible problems:
   - Important system features may be left out to simplify rapid prototyping
   - Inadequate bases for a contract between a client and a developer
   - Non-functional requirements are not stressed
   - A prototype may not provide a true picture to the user about its operational capability.

5 Some suggested benefits are:
   - Misunderstandings between software developers and users may be identified as the system functions are demonstrated.
   - Missing user services may be detected.
   - Difficult to use or confusing user services may be identified and refined.
   - Software development staff may find incomplete and/or inconsistent requirements as the prototype is developed.
   - A working, albeit limited, system is available quickly to demonstrate the feasibility and usefulness of the application to management.
   - The prototype serves as a basis for writing the specification for a production quality system.

Question 2.1.3

1. Objects model real world or fake world entities. Anything we can see, interact with or quantify in some way can be classified as an

object. Objects are therefore real things with unique properties and each has its own set of characteristics. They provide an ideal structure for the re-use of developed code sections (or class structures).

2. (a) *Encapsulation* allows for certain data types and methods to be hidden from the user. This provides for a binding of data structures and methods into a class of objects. The result of this is a more efficient programming structure with a reduction in the possibility of data becoming corrupted.

    (b) *Inheritance* allows for one class to inherent the characteristics of another class. Developers can exploit the property of inheritance by creating an 'ancestor' class that has attributes and behaviours that are appropriate for its own execution and reusing the ancestor class to describe new ones.

    (c) *Polymorphism* is the ability for a number of classes to share names of methods. The methods, that are named the same, behave appropriately to the particular class for which they were designed.

3. Objects are defined as 'instances of a class'. A class provides the code structure for an object-oriented language, therefore an instance is a member of a class i.e. an object.

4. The main aim of object-oriented analysis is to establish the classes inherent in a specification document and establish the associations that may exist between classes. From this a class-association can be constructed.

5. All objects react to receiving messages and they respond with an answer. The object that is sent a message is called a receiver.

Question 2.1.4

Like all analysis models the method adopted depends on a number of factors like, what systems are we currently using, what development tools are available, what is the current application running in, what implementation method are we going to use, etc. For the college management information system it would be appropriate to use a object-oriented approach because each real world entity within the organization can be modelled by a class structure. Instances of the classes than then be created to represent components of the entities. For example, Fred Smith could be an instance of the Student class.

2.2 Systems analysis tools and techniques

Question 2.2.1

1. A context diagram can have ONE process only.
2. A process must have at least one input flow and one output flow.
3. Terminators are either SOURCES or SINKS.
4. A discrete flow represents data that is present at certain discrete time intervals. A continuous flow represents data that is present at all times.
5. They should be named with a nouns (and possibly adjectives but not verbs).

Question 2.2.2

1. The outputs should be considered as alternatives. This can be treated as an 'or' condition to the developer with the output coming from one or another of the flows.

2. A process acts on, or transforms, data form a given input flow. It produces output flow(s) according to the action implied on the process name.
3. Process specification
4. A store represents data that has been frozen in time. The data stored may be used any time after it has been stored and in any order. It should be named with a noun that describes its contents.
5. Discrete flow.

Question 2.2.3

When developing a data flow diagram for a proposed system it is often necessary to introduce stores that hold data for permanent storage. If a number of stores are introduced to the system they could have some link between them. These links can be further refined by the creation of an entity-relationship (E-R) diagram. For example, a college administration system could have two stores: Student and Lecturer. A relationship could exist between the stores as the Lecturer may tutor certain Students. The *tutors* relationship could then be defined as a one-to-many association between Student and Lecturer and shown graphically in an E-R diagram.

Question 2.2.4

1. *Stage 0* – Feasibility
   Stage 1 – Investigation of current requirements
   Stage 2 – Business systems options
   Stage 3 – Definition of requirements
   Stage 4 – Technical systems options
   Stage 5 – Logical design
   Stage 6 – Physical design
2. To establish whether it is feasible to progress with a given project given the constraints placed upon it. A systems house needs to ascertain if it has the resources (manual and physical) to provide a competitive bid that meets the company business plan or to comply with current legislation. They need to carry out a through strategic plan before they spend too much time and effort on projects that can not be cost justified or are just technically unworkable.
3. *Step 210* – This step offers a set of guidelines and suggested procedures and not precise techniques. The stated steps are:
   a. *Task 10* – establish minimum requirements for the proposed system.
   b. *Task 20* – produce outlines for a number of BSO normally about 6.
   c. *Task 30* – discuss the outlines with the users to produce a shortlist.
   d. *Task 40* – carry out a cost benefit and impact analysis for each short listed BSO.
4. To produce a detailed and rigorous specification of system requirements. By the end of Stage 3 the developer will have moved into the area of system design. The main objective of this step is to provide sufficient detail for the logical design of internal processing requirements of the new system to take place.
5. This specifies the non-functional requirements of the system. It will outline the main hardware and software needs for the system and how they are to be implemented.

Question 2.2.5

1. Processes represent the activities to be carried out and are trigged by data being passed to them. They represent a high level abstraction in user terms and not a equate directly with computer code. A process refers to the business activity that it supports.
2. These are the final processes that have been refined as far as possible to produce a complete diagram of what the system is to do. They are designated with an asterisk and each elementary process is accompanied with a process description.
3. You cannot connect an external entity directly to a data store and you cannot connect two store together with a data flow.
4. External entity.
5. A LDM consists of two parts:
    - Logical Data Structure (LDS)
    - Set of Associated Textual Descriptions
      a. Entity descriptions
      b. Relationship descriptions
      c. Attribute descriptions
      d   Grouped Domain descriptions.

Question 2.2.6

1. Objects are classified as instances of a class and can be associated to other objects. This is termed as an *association* between the classes for which the objects are instances. For example, Fred Smith is an instance (object) of a Person class.
2. *Student* – This comes under a *Role* class structure
    Library – This is a physical entity and therefore is classified as Tangible.

Question 2.2.7

1. Suggested example of a 1:1 association:

There is one Principal in charge of the college and he appoints a single Vice Principal. The Vice Principal is responsible to one Principal only.
2. Suggested example of a *m:n* association:

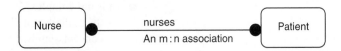

A Nurse is responsible for many Patients and each Patient can be trearted by by many Nurses.

Question 2.2.8

1. Textual analysis is carried out to ascertain from a specification likely class candidates.

2. Suggested example of inheritance:

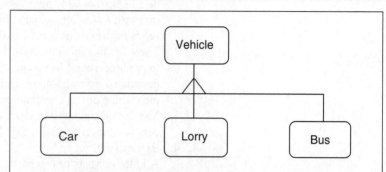

Vehicle provides some basic characteristics that can be inherited by the sub-classes car, lorry and bus. The sub-classes can then incorporate additional requirements suitable for their individual needs.

3. An invariant is a rule that places a constraint on the allowable instances of classes and associations.
4. Use of a class-association matrix.
5. This relates to a class that is extra to the needs of the diagram. It can be expressed through other classes and therefore is 'redundant' to the model being developed.

Question 2.2.9

1. UML was created at Rational Software by methodologists Grady Booch, Ivar Jacobson and Jim Rumbaugh with input from other leading methodologists, many software vendors, as well as end users.
2. UML – some stated advantages:
    ● is sufficiently expressive to represent and connect the concepts of abstraction within software development across a number of domains which include:
        – information systems
        – real time systems
        – web systems.
    ● it can handle the modelling of business processes
        – their logical and physical software models
        – provide references to their implementation.
    ● it is not complex
        – the unified modelling language is built from a small number of concepts applied consistently across a number of modelling problems.
    ● it provides an excellent base for object-oriented analysis and design.

Question 2.2.10

1. Use case diagrams have the following advantages (any two will do):
    ● capture requirements from users' perspective – it provides a diagrammatic base for user involvement and validation;
    ● helps manage delivery – prioritize use cases to define processes for delivery and help estimate requirements;

- progresses the development – can identify objects and provides a base for user manuals and test plans;
- improve quality – aids tracing of requirements and identifies faults earlier.

2. Use Case diagram for Hospital System

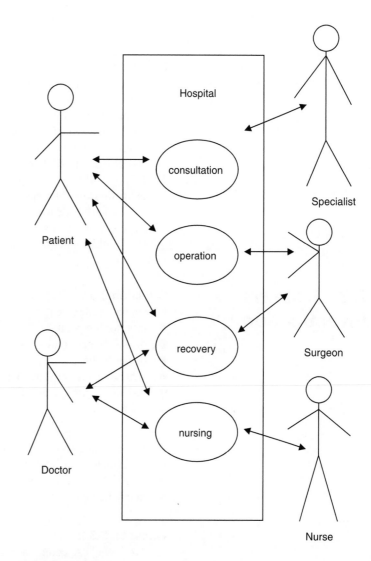

Question 2.2.11

1. An object diagram is a variation of the class diagram and uses similar notation. It differs in the fact that it shows a number of object instances of a class instead of just classes.
2. Visibility specifies the *private* and *public* members specified in the attribute compartment of a class.
3. Operations are used to manipulate the attributes to perform certain actions.
4. Association – Generalization – Dependency and Refinement.
5. An association defines the routes for sending messages between classes and relates to the operations that objects must meet in order to carry out their responsibilities. An association name must be expressed so that it describes its exact relationship between classes.

Question 2.2.12

Class diagram for Lecturer/Tutorial Group

Question 2.2.13

1. *Composite aggregation* – A composition (composite aggregation) indicates that any parts of an object 'live' inside a unique whole. That is, the part will live or die together with the whole. Diagrammatically this is represented by a black diamond and is shown in Figure 2.2.44 where a Statement 'lives' inside the Transaction and if the Transaction is destroyed the Statement will die along with in.
2. *Responsibilities* – A responsibility is normally expressed in terms of obligations to other elements. It is normally expressed as a string and attached to a class in its own name compartment.
3. *Aggregation versus inheritance* – Aggregation operates at object level, unlike inheritance that operates at class level.

2.3 Systems investigation

Question 2.3.1

Functional requirements:
- monitor temperatures
- display temperatures
- detect faults
- write temperature data to a database
- provide engineers check
- archive data.

Non-functional requirements:
- implemented on the company computer system
- 1 Mb memory available
- VAX/VMS operating system
- magnetic tape storage.

Question 2.3.2

1. *Platitude* – A common place statement that is no direct meaning within the context that it is used.
2. *Omission* – Something that is left out of a requirements document. An example could be: 'what happens if an operator enters a wrong command?'
3. *Ambiguous statement* – This could cause a doubtful or double meaning within a document. Any ambiguity needs to be cleared up to ensure the requirements document is correctly understood by all parties and is clear in its intent.
4. *Extraneous detail* – This relates to unnecessary information that does not help the analysis process. Sometimes several words can be omitted where the meaning may be inferred from a simple word.
5. The negotiated statement of requirements should contain, in an unambiguous way, what the proposed system is to do, its functions and what the limitations on the developer are. It is a description of

'what' a system is to do in application terms. It is the key document on which all subsequent activities in the software project depend. In legal terms it may provide a basis for a contract between the customer and the developer.

Question 2.3.3
1. Main objectives of an interview:
    *   Ascertain the customer needs and desires
    *   Clarify the priorities for the proposed project
    *   Find out about the current system and associated personnel
    *   Determine the environment to which the system must be interfaced to
    *   How staff will accept change when implementing the new system
    *   Support requirements for installing and using the new application
    *   Staff responsibilities within the organization.
2. A questionnaire contains a list of questions which are designed to produce a formal response from the person completing it and allow for additional information to be inserted if required.
3. During an investigation of a current system it is possible for the analyst to move into the area of how the new system is to be developed as opposed to what it should do. This may not provide a true picture for specifying the functional requirements of the new system, i.e. an accurate base for developing the new system.
4. A suggested agenda should contain a list or the items to be covered in the meeting. A typical layout is shown below:
    *   Apologies for absence
    *   Minutes of the last meeting
    *   Matters arising from the minutes
    *   Agenda items specific to the meeting
    *   ,,
    *   ,,
    *   ,,
    *   ,,
    *   Any other business
    *   Date of the next meeting.

2.4 Functional and data modelling

Question 2.4.1
(Delphi Code for fiddle VAT holiday company)

```
procedure TForm1.Button3Click(Sender: TObject);
begin
   Close;
end;

procedure TForm1.Button1Click(Sender: TObject);
var country : String;
   weeks : integer;

begin
   country := ComboBox1.Items[ComboBox1.ItemIndex];
   weeks := strToInt(ComboBox2.Items[ComboBox2.ItemIndex]);
   if (country = 'France') then
    totalCost := weeks * 250.75
else
   if (country = 'Germany') then
   totalCost := weeks * 225.25
```

```
                                else
                                   if (country = 'Greece') then
                                   totalCost := weeks * 282.55
                                 else
                                   if (country = 'Italy') then
                                   totalCost := weeks * 371.5
                                else
                                   if (country = 'Portugal') then
                                   totalCost := weeks * 325.6
                                else
                                   if (country = 'Spain') then
                                   totalCost := weeks * 199.99
                                else
                                   if (country = 'Switzerland') then
                                   totalCost := weeks * 465.5
                                else
                                   if (country = 'Turkey') then
                                   totalCost := weeks * 345.77;
                                Edit1.Text := '£' 1 FloatToStr(totalCost);
                                end;

                                procedure TForm1.Button2Click(Sender: TObject);
                                var
                                   change : real;
                                   amountTendered : real;
                                   tenPounds, fivePounds, twoPounds, onePound, fiftyPence :
                                integer;
                                   twentyPence, tenPence, fivePence, twoPence, onePence :
                                integer;
                                   penceChange : longInt;

                                begin
                                   tenPounds := 0;
                                   fivePounds := 0;
                                   twoPounds := 0;
                                   onePound := 0;
                                   fiftyPence := 0;
                                   twentyPence :5 0;
                                   tenPence := 0;
                                   fivePence := 0;
                                   twoPence := 0;
                                   onePence := 0;
                                   amountTendered := strToFloat(Edit2.Text);
                                   if (amountTendered < totalCost ) then
                                     ShowMessage ('You need to tender more CASH! ')
                                   else
                                     begin
                                      change := amountTendered-totalCost;
                                      Edit3.Text := FloatToStrf(change,ffCurrency,7,2);
                                      penceChange : = Round(change * 100);
                                      while (penceChange div 1000 > 0) do
                                       begin
                                       tenPounds := tenPounds + 1;
                                       penceChange : = penceChange - 1000;
                                       end;
                                       while (penceChange div 500 > 0 ) do
                                       begin
                                       fivePounds := fivePounds + 1;
                                       penceChange := penceChange - 500;
                                       end;
                                       while (penceChange div 200 > 0) do
                                       begin
                                       twoPounds := twoPounds + 1;
```

```
                    penceChange := penceChange - 200;
                    end;
                  while (penceChange div 100 > 0) do
                    begin
                    onePound := onePound + 1;
                    penceChange := penceChange - 100;
                    end;
                  while (penceChange div 50 > 0) do
                    begin
                    fiftyPence : = fiftyPence + 1;
                    penceChange : = penceChange - 50;
                    end;
                  while (penceChange div 20 > 0) do
                    begin
                    twentyPence := twentyPence + 1;
                    penceChange := penceChange - 20;
                    end;
                  while (penceChange div 10 > 0) do
                    begin
                    tenPence := tenPence + 1;
                    penceChange := penceChange - 10;
                    end;
                  while (penceChange div 5 > 0) do
                    begin
                    fivePence := fivePence + 1;
                    penceChange : = penceChange - 5;
                    end;
                  while (penceChange div 2 > 0) do
                    begin
                    twoPence := twoPence + 1;
                    penceChange := penceChange - 2;
                    end;
                  while (penceChange div 1 > 0) do
                    begin
                    onePence := onePence + 1;
                    penceChange := penceChange - 1;
                    end;
                Edit4.Text := IntToStr(tenPounds);
                Edit5.Text := IntToStr(fivePounds);
                Edit6.Text := IntToStr(twoPounds);
                Edit7.Text := IntToStr(onePound);
                Edit8.Text := IntToStr(fiftyPence);
                Edit9.Text := IntToStr(twentyPence);
                Edit10.Text := IntToStr(tenPence);
                Edit11.Text := IntToStr(fivePence);
                Edit12.Text := IntToStr(twoPence);
                Edit13.Text := IntToStr(onePence);
              end;
end;

initialization
totalCost := 0.0;
end. {end of program}
```

Question 2.4.2

Relationships from diagram 51
Bailey *Studies* Intro. to programming Bailey *Studies* Computer Architecture
Morgan *Studies* Networks

Bruce *Studies* Networks Bruce Studies Web Site Management
Simons *Studies* Visual Programming
Peters *Studies* Networks Peters Studies End User Support
Hill *Studies* Web Site Management
Patel *Studies* Visual Programming
Gardner *Studies* Web Site Management
Khan *Studies* End User Support Khan *Studies* Systems Software
Wilson *Studies* Web Site Management Wilson *Studies* Systems Software

Question 2.4.3

1. 1:n – Several students can study in the library and there is only one library in the college.
2. 1:1 – One head teacher supervises the school and each school is only allocated one head teacher.
3. m:n – A number of passengers can travel on a bus and a number of buses are provided for people to travel on.

Question 2.4.4

1. The main components are:
    *   Entities (which represent 'things' from the real world). A entity represents independent data that is always present in the system. It may or may not be related to other entities in the system.
    *   Relationships (which represent the way things are related). An unrestricted relationship will always exist as long as the corresponding entities exist.
2. A relationship is a link between entities and can contain the following degrees:
    > 1:1 (one to one)
    > 1:n (one to many)
    > m:n (many to many)

    A degree specifies the number of instances that a entity is involved within a relationship.
3. Some suitable attributes are:
    Student (StudentID, StudentName, StudentAddress, StudentContact Number, StudentAge, Course, Qualifications)

Question 2.4.5

1. In Access you can go to **View** then **Design View** and the following information is displayed in the diagram below. The **Data Type** for each field can be set according to the domains specified in the attribute diagram. For example if you select number the **Field Size** in the general section below can then select the required Number type, i.e. Integer, Single, Double, Long Integer, etc.

Selecting Field Data Types

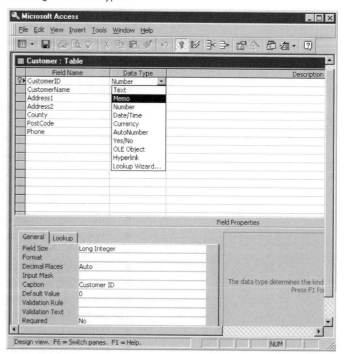

2. Forms are used to help you input and manipulate data that includes:
   - Data-entry form to enter data into a table.
   - Switchboard form to open other forms or reports.
   - Custom dialogue box to accept user input and carry out an associated action.
3. You use queries to view, change, and analyse data in different ways. You can also use them as the source of records for forms and reports.
4. They can be used for similar activities, but a report differs in the way it is presented. Reports are designed for displaying printed data with a professional appearance of the table contents.
5. A database wizard provides a template for developing database tables for a specified application. You can use a Database Wizard to create in one operation the required tables, forms, and reports for the type of database you choose, this is the easiest way to start creating your database and steps are provided to aid this process.

7.1 Quality assurance

Question 7.1.1

1. *Verification & Validation* (V&V) is an activity that acts over the whole lifecycle of a product. Verification involves checking that a program conforms to the original negotiated requirements, validation involves checking that the system meets the expectations of the customer of end user of the product.

   Boehm summarized the activities:
   - Validation: Are we building the right product?
   - Verification: Are we building the product right?
2. *Usability* From the users point of view this relates to how easy a piece of software is to use. We have seen a greater push towards graphical

user interfaces (GUI's) over the past few years that have improved the way systems can be used. Usability also effects the way in which the application can be controlled, for example, a user may require a quick response from the system (the keyboard input would be to slow), so some other input like a touch screen may be more appropriate.

Question 7.1.2

1. *ANSI* – American National Standards Institute.
2. *ISO* – International Standards Organisation. Together with the IEC (International Eletrotechnical Commission) they concentrate on harmonizing national standards all over the world. Using standards for the development of software products can produce the following benefits for the business:
   - customer satisfaction;
   - effectiveness of budget and time requirements;
   - improved management structure;
   - trust in the product;
   - legal compliance;
   - improved product development;
   - international standards help export the product.
3. The basic Management Responsibilities are:
   - Define a Quality Policy.
   - Define an Organizational Structure.
   - Define Quality System Responsibilities and Authorities.
   - Identify and Provide Resources.
   - Appoint a Senior Executive.
   - Review the Effectiveness of the QMS.
4. Advantages are:
   The aim of international standardization is to facilitate trade, exchange and technology transfer through:
   - enhanced product quality and reliability at the correct price;
   - improved health, safety and environmental protection;
   - greater compatibility;
   - improved usability;
   - reduced costs with the reduction of models;
   - increased distribution efficiency;
   - ease of maintenance.
5. Within the UK the institution is the British Standards Institute (BSI). It has nearly a century of standards experience and will celebrate its century year in 2001. The BSI ensures the views of British industry are represented in Europe and worldwide.
6. A quality management system (QMS) is a set of policies, procedures and working methods collated in such a way that they will form and understandable, structured quality system. When a QMS is operating effectively these processes are used as a management tool for operating the project, determining the outputs and constantly modifying the processes contained within it.

Question 7.1.3

1. Main risks can come from hacking or viruses corrupting data. Also most of the elements of risk lie with company users who deliberately or accidentally misuse systems.
2. Nearly 70% of UK companies fail to plan for major business risk (survey by SGS) and only one in three companies is taking steps to prepare against unplanned events.

Question 7.1.4

1. *CPD* – Continued Professional Development. Computer professionals, who want to remain professionally competent over their working lives, should undertake it. It provides a base for planning your learning needs, updating skills and recording activities (for example in a special log book). By undertaking CPU you will:
    *   demonstrate your continuing commitment to your profession;
    *   develop good practice of regularly reviewing needs and selecting relevant learning activities.

    A statement from the BCS:

    'If you think education is expensive, just try ignorance'

2. The BCS Professional Development Scheme aims to regulate and monitor the training of young professionals and keep established personal up-to-date.
3. The three main grades of membership are:
    *   Charted Engineer (CEng)
    *   Incorporated Engineer (IEng)
    *   Engineering Technician (EngTech)
4. *SARTOR* – Standards and Routes to Registration. It main objective is to lay down the educational and professional criteria for becoming a registered engineer.

Question 7.1.5

1. Products, Service outline, Limit of services, Customer duties, Guarantees or Warranties, General terms and Transfer terms.
2. *Customer duties* – the company must receive the payment for SLA within a specified period of sending out an invoice. Customers should have all relevant information ready when contacting the company under the agreement (e.g. their service number, make/serial number of the goods, operating system used etc.).
3. *Limit of services* – e.g. the duration of the agreement, the service contract may be broken if the item has had an unauthorized repair or has undergone accident, misuse or abuse etc. When and where the company can be contacted.

7.2 Quality control

Question 7.2.1

1. This basically falls into the following main categories:
    *   *Debugging* – removal of errors that were not uncovered during the initial development phase;
    *   *Modification* – as specifications change to reflect what is required in the real world, so the software needs to be updated to include these changes.
2. Maintenance is required in order for the product to remain useful in its working environment. As software becomes older and the expectations of the end users increase the product starts to become dated and not always useful. In order for a product to keep-to-date with the needs of the users and more complex hardware systems, it will need to be updated or maintained. Remember if a product is not maintained it dies.
3. *Perfective maintenance* – this activity occurs if a software product is successful. As the software product is used recommendations for new capabilities, modifications to existing methods and other requirements

are requested from the end users. This activity accounts for some 60% of the total effort spent on software maintenance.

Question 7.2.2

1. It is a document that is initiated by a customer of market requirements that triggers the maintenance process. The document contains information about the proposed change, who is effected and how it is to be implemented. Once submitted the form will be discussed at the next scheduled maintenance meeting that could include the project manager, the configuration manager, members of the maintenance team other development personnel as required. If the change involves the customer then he/she should also be present.
2. The two maintenance activities are:
   - structured maintenance;
   - unstructured maintenance.

   The most efficient would be structured maintenance and it builds on previous good software engineering foundations. This is due to the existence of software configuration that reduces the amount of wasted effort and improves the overall quality of a modification or a change.

Question 7.2.3

1. *Version Control (VC)* – It is part of configuration management which organizes the storage of different versions of documents and controls changes to documents when new versions are produced.
2. *Checkout* – You are required to tell the database which files you are working on and some tools allow files can be modified at will and submitted when the developer has finished making the changes.
3. *Baselined* – A document is baselined when it reaches a certain stage within the development process. Once a document is baselined it becomes available for others to use and so becomes subject to change. Once baselined any changes need to come under a formal procedure, i.e. a baselined document becomes subject to Version Control.
4. *Repository* – This is storage area for baselined documents. It keeps track of various revisions of files by ensuring all data stored here is subject to version control. The process for adding a file to a repository is called 'checking-in'.
5. It targets both Unix and Windows users so they can share common files. Provides a text file conversion from Unix to DOS and vice versa.

Question 7.2.4

1. *Quality Plan* – It is part of the project plan that specifies how the software developer intends to ensure that the quality of the system meets the standards defined in the company quality policy. It should reference the following items:
   - quality objectives;
   - identification of test activities;
   - identification of verification and validation activities;
   - plans and test specifications;
   - methods and tools to be employed;
   - entry and exit data for each phase of development;
   - planning to include: schedules, resources and approval authorities;
   - specific responsibilities for reviews and tests, configuration management, defect control and corrective action.

2. This depends on the company carrying out the work. Many companies will use international standards (ISO, IEEE, BSI, etc.) as a guide and tailor them to suit their individual requirements.

3. It should be accepted early by the customer because it determines the conduct of many of the activities to be carried out. It provides reassurance that the project is going to be carried out using documented quality procedures and meets the stated requirements. It also acts as an agreement between the developer and the customer to ensure the development of the product produces what is required.

Question 7.2.5

1. Below is a list of heading that may appear in a typical quality manual:
    a. General information;
    b. Background to the company;
    c. Conventions and definitions;
    d. Quality management system;
    e. Responsibility of management;
    f. Resources;
    g. Product realization;
    h. Analysis, measurement and improvement.

2. Here you would need to incorporate a version control system. A good numbering system that denotes the latest edition needs to be incorporated. It is essential that all staff are working to the latest version so the latest version needs to be circulated to all concerned parties.

Question 7.2.6

1. *Test Plan* – This will fully document all the testing procedures that are to be carried out over the whole lifecycle of the project. It will contain all information relevant to testing and will normally be divided into sections to cover the various testing activities that are to be carried out.

2. The test plan is part of the quality plan.

7.3 Project management

Question 7.3.1

1. The main roles are:
    - Organizing
    - Planning
    - Staffing
    - Monitoring
    - Controlling
    - Innovating
    - Representing

2. This involves the project manager checking on the progress of the project, ensuring that any milestones are kept and that the project is on time to meet its delivery date.

3. For analysis and design tools the document needs to specify:
    - What tools are to be employed.
    - Where they are going to used within the project.
    - Who is trained to use the tools.
    - Who needs training to use the tools.
    - Who is responsible for their maintenance.
    - What peripheral devices are required for the tools.
    - Documentation sources associated with the tools.
    - Benefits to the customer.

Question 7.3.2

1. The completion of a system design document is a good example of an external milestone. The completion of the acceptance test process with the customer is an other example.
2. The design phase for a particular section of an application is a good example of an internal milestone. Preparation of a test data for a particular system application is another.
3. Completion of a code section that forms part of a larger application is a good example of an informal milestone. Intermediate tests on a particular application assigned to a particular systems analyst is another.

Question 7.3.3

1. Gantt charts show various activities as blocks on the diagram that are plotted against a time base (or '*x*' axis). It gives an overall outline of the scheduling of tasks throughout a given project and will be used by developers to specify the start and end dates for their associated activities. A Gantt chart is therefore a form of bar chart where activities are listed down the diagram and plotted against a horizontal time base.
2. *PERT* – Program Evaluation and Review Technique
    This technique requires the identification of all the activities and placing them in sequence. Then the timing of each activity needs to be estimated along with their associated dependencies. Once this has been established it is documented in a table from which the network diagram can be constructed and the critical path established. From then on the project manager can use the diagram for monitoring purposes. It can then be modified, if required, to take into account any rescheduling requirements and changes to the critical path. Three time estimates are required for each activity, these are:
    *   most optimistic time
    *   most likely time
    *   most pessimistic time.

$$\text{estimated duration} = \frac{\text{most optimistic time} + 4 \text{ most likely time} + \text{most pessimistic time}}{6}$$

The estimated duration is then calculated using the following equation:
    This figure is repeated for all activities and the results used to check if the project can be completed within the specified deadline.
3. EET is the earliest estimated time that a particular activity with a project may start. LAT is the latest allowable time that an activity may start in order to complete it within the estimated time.
4. It highlights the path within a project that shows where any slippage in time deadlines would cause the problems in keeping to the scheduled completion date.
5. Total float = maximum span – estimated duration. Activities having a total float of zero are said to be on the critical path.

Question 7.3.4

1. Open a project management tool, set the required start date, schedule, status, calendar, etc. then name and save the project. Ensure that the correct working and non-working days are allocated (i.e. to include

weekends and bank holidays, etc.). Also you may need to set the correct working times for each day.

2. See Gantt Chart below:

ID	❶	Task Name	Duration	Start	Finish	Prede
1		A1	11 days	Mon 18/08/03	Mon 01/09/03	
2		A2	9 days	Tue 02/09/03	Fri 12/09/03	1
3		A3	12 days	Thu 18/09/03	Fri 03/10/03	2,5
4		A4	8 days	Mon 18/08/03	Wed 27/08/03	
5		A5	13 days	Mon 01/09/03	Wed 17/09/03	4,6
6		A6	10 days	Mon 18/08/03	Fri 29/08/03	
7		A7	17 days	Mon 01/09/03	Tue 23/09/03	6
8		A8	5 days	Wed 24/09/03	Tue 30/09/03	7

3. See Network Diagram below:

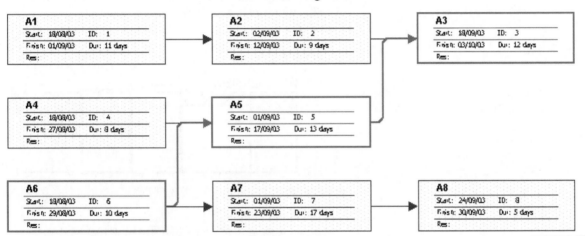

4. With additional milestones added:

ID	❶	Task Name	Duration	Start	Finish	Prede
1		A1	11 days	Mon 18/08/03	Mon 01/09/03	
2		A2	9 days	Tue 02/09/03	Fri 12/09/03	1
3	▦	A3	12 days	Mon 13/10/03	Tue 28/10/03	2,5
4		A4	8 days	Mon 18/08/03	Wed 27/08/03	
5		A5	13 days	Wed 24/09/03	Fri 10/10/03	4,6,7
6		A6	10 days	Mon 18/08/03	Fri 29/08/03	
7	▦	Mile 1	0 days	Tue 23/09/03	Tue 23/09/03	6
8		A7	17 days	Mon 01/09/03	Tue 23/09/03	6
9		A8	5 days	Wed 24/09/03	Tue 30/09/03	8

5. Resource Teams added:

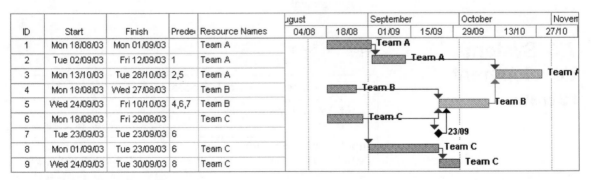

ID	Start	Finish	Prede	Resource Names
1	Mon 18/08/03	Mon 01/09/03		Team A
2	Tue 02/09/03	Fri 12/09/03	1	Team A
3	Mon 13/10/03	Tue 28/10/03	2,5	Team A
4	Mon 18/08/03	Wed 27/08/03		Team B
5	Wed 24/09/03	Fri 10/10/03	4,6,7	Team B
6	Mon 18/08/03	Fri 29/08/03		Team C
7	Tue 23/09/03	Tue 23/09/03	6	
8	Mon 01/09/03	Tue 23/09/03	6	Team C
9	Wed 24/09/03	Tue 30/09/03	8	Team C

Question 7.3.5

1. To build software that undergoes quality methods costs additional money in the first place. But this is more than offset by producing a reliable quality product that works without problems when it is delivered. Maintenance costs are reduced, confidence in the product is increased and the company along with its system gain in stature within the computing industry. Care must be taken though to ensure the money spent during the early stages of the lifecycle is matched by reduced costs during and after delivery. If we look at the software produced for the American Space Shuttle, then large amount of money was spent during the development phase (up to 100 times per line of code compared to other systems). The software for the shuttle is a safety critical system, without it the craft cannot be controlled (it uses a fly-by-wire system). Failure may therefore involve injury of loss of life, so initial high-cost 'quality activities' must be ensured for the reliability of the product in its working environment.

2. a. EQF graph

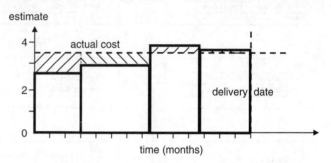

b. Calculation.
   Hatched Area $= (0.8 \times 3) + (0.6 \times 4.5) + (0.3 \times 3) +$
   $(0.1 \times 3.5) = 6.35$
   Total area under the actual cost line $= 3.5 \times 14 = 49$
   Therefore the EQF $= 49/6.35 = 7.72$

   c. From the criteria specified by DeMarco an EQF of 7.72 can be accepted as a satisfactory estimating quality measure (as $7.72 > 4$ which is the minimum acceptable value).

3. Risk analysis is concerned with planning for potential problems that may hinder the development of the project, i.e. what risks may cause the project to go wrong? How will changes affect the time constraints placed on the project? What are the best tools to use? If we are implementing new procedures do they pose a risk? Basically is the project going to be delivered on time and within budget? Risk analysis is divided into four areas, identification, projection, assessment and management.

7.4 Systems development review

Question 7.4.1

Process Name:	Validate Codes
Input Data Flows: Name: code	Type: discrete
Input Flows from Stores: Name of Store: Stored Valid Codes	Component: N/A

Output Data Flows:	
Name: message	Type: discrete

Output Flows to Stores:	
Name of Store: N/A	Component: N/A

Process Description:
Look up the database code list to see if the code is present or not.
If the code is present then answer = 'valid code'
Else answer = 'code not recognized'

Question 7.4.2

1. A data dictionary will contain:
   - data flow details;
   - abbreviations used;
   - notes to ensure clarifications and correctness.
2. A data dictionary will contain more detailed information than a mini-specification and formal notations like the BNF (Backus–Naur Format) syntax definitions can be employed.
3. Two children can be created from a control process:
   - A control specification
   - A state transition diagram (STD)
4. A transition indicates a movement from one state to another state, shown as a line with a solid arrow at the end. The transition name represents an event that is the reason for the transition and consists of a single and multiple conditions. A transition can define a number of actions that occur as the transaction takes place.
5. A control specification will contain details of the flows flowing into and out of the process. It will also contain a body that specifies in a high-level way what the process is to do. The flows must be included in the body specification.

Question 7.4.3

1. Data couples are flows of data between modules on a structure chart diagram. They are placed on the module-calling flows. The arrow-head indicates the direction of data flow.
2. The three main areas are:
   - Input (or afferent control)
   - Transform control
   - Output (or efferent control)
3. The three types of module are:
   - *Modules* – these are used to represent processing that is local to the structure chart diagram. When implementing the design the code will need to be constructed to directly suit the module requirements.
   - *Library* – a library is a predefined module in a structure chart diagram that can be used by many different systems. A library module contains data that is already written and can be reused inside the new design.
   - *Subsystems* – Subsystems are predefined modules in a structure chart diagram that are detailed through decomposition on further diagrams. Subsystem modules can be used many times by many diagrams. The developer will need to look at child diagram(s) to ascertain to exact requirements of the module.
4. A module is identified by a name, which should specify what the module is to do. Names like 'Validate Receipt' should be used, as

opposed to 'Process Command' that is meaningless for the developer of the product.

5. The main verification activities are:
   - Each process in the data flow diagram is represented as a module within the structure chart.
   - All the data flows present in the data flow diagram are represented in the structure chart where each input and output become a module.
   - For more detailed diagrams pre and post-assertions can be specified which outline the conditions in which the input and output parameters should satisfy.

Question 7.4.4

1. Object-centred viewpoint and Object-community viewpoint.
2. *Collaboration* – An object may carry out its responsibilities by collaborating with other objects. This means that an object can send a message to another object (the receiver) to obtain some behaviour characteristic(s) that are inherent within it.
3. A walk-through take some coherent piece of behaviour that the system must exhibit – like recording the enrolment of a student onto a course – and investigates how this behaviour can be constructed with the object model. The main steps taken in a walk through are:
   - Understanding in Application Area terms.
   - Understanding in Terms of Instances of Classes and Associations.
   - Understanding in terms of Responsibilities and Collaborations.
4. Client is Dog and the Server is Breed. We can say that Breed is a collaborator for Dog.

Question 7.4.5

1. *CRC* – Stands for Classes, Responsibilities and Collaborations.
2. Attributes represent the variables that are required to implement the class. They can be expressed as public ($+$) or private ($-$) which specifies the visibility of class variables with reference to other variables.

   Operations can be used to manipulate the attributes. Typical operations would be 'accessor methods' which provide the access route to the private variables. In C++ the operations would be implemented as methods within the given class structure.
3. Inheritance structue required for modifying the Agility Dog Club System

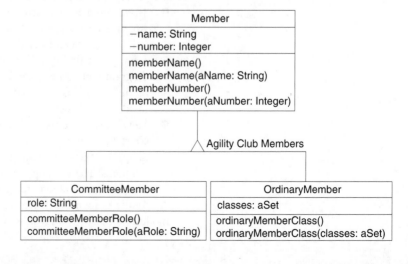

Question 7.4.6

1. *The main testing activities during the software development lifecycle are* – Unit Testing, Integration Testing, System Testing and Acceptance Testing.
2. *White box testing* – a method of testing which shows how a software component produces its results. This is achieved by looking at the internal structure of the module to ascertain whether the code executes its computations correctly.

Question 7.4.7

1. The aim of software metrics is to produce precise measurements for software quality. They represent indirect measures, quality is not measured directly but some manifestation of it. Metrics are used to measure certain characteristics of software and provide a standard of quality for a system to be explicitly stated.
2. The two categories of software metrics are:
    -   *Results metric* – this measure is normally implemented at the end of a project or at the end of a particular stage of the project.
    -   *Predictor metric* – these are applied during various stages of the project and provide numerical feedback as to the structure and complexity of code sections. They may be used to ascertain the program size (number of lines of code) which is a useful for estimating the final resources needed when the program goes live.

Question 7.4.8

1.

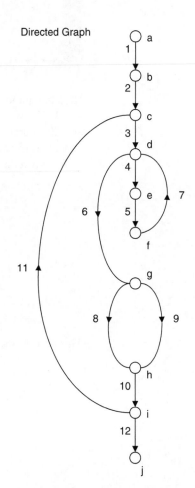

2. Cyclomatic complexity (v)

$$v = a - n + 2$$
$$v = 12 - 10 + 2$$
$$v = 4$$

3. Based on the research by McCabe the cyclomatic complexity of the code section is acceptable and does not need to be redesigned. The cyclomatic complexity result is smaller than 10 (i.e. $4 < 10$) which confirms the hypothesis.

Question 7.4.9

(Testing Tools or Debugging?)

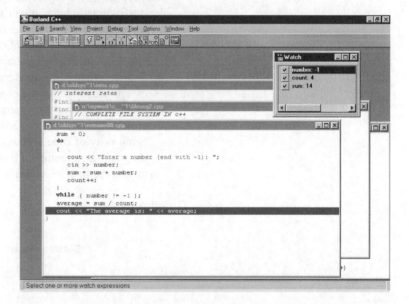

Here the numbers 4, 5 and 6 were entered and the loop terminated with a -1. The watch shows that the -1 has been subtracted from the total and the counter has incremented once too many time. The variable sum should be 15 and the variable count should be 3.

To correct this an inner 'if statement' should be added inside the loop, i.e.

```
do
{
        cout<<"Enter a number (end with -1): ";
        cin>>number;
        if (number != -1)
        {
                sum = sum + number;
                count++;
        } // end if statement
}
while (number !5 21);
```

This ensures the correct variable values as you exit the loop.

Index